BORN
IN
BLACKNESS

ALSO BY HOWARD W. FRENCH

Everything Under the Heavens: How the Past Helps
Shape China's Push for Global Power

China's Second Continent: How a Million Migrants
Are Building a New Empire in Africa

Disappearing Shanghai: Photographs and Poems
of an Intimate Way of Life (with Qiu Xiaolong)

A Continent for the Taking:
The Tragedy and Hope of Africa

BORN
IN
BLACKNESS

*Africa, Africans, and the
Making of the Modern World,
1471 to the Second World War*

Howard W. French

LIVERIGHT PUBLISHING CORPORATION
A Division of W. W. Norton & Company
Independent Publishers Since 1923

Maps on pages 14, 84, 144, 230, and 330 by Wang Boxia

For information about permission to reproduce selections from this book,
write to Permissions, Liveright Publishing Corporation,
a division of W. W. Norton & Company, Inc., 500 Fifth Avenue, New York, NY 10110

For information about special discounts for bulk purchases, please contact
W. W. Norton Special Sales at specialsales@wwnorton.com or 800-233-4830

Manufacturing by Lakeside Book Company
Production manager: Devon Zahn

Library of Congress Cataloging-in-Publication Data

Names: French, Howard W., author.
Title: Born in Blackness : Africa, Africans, and the making of the modern world,
1471 to the Second World War / Howard W. French.
Description: First edition. | New York : Liveright Publishing Company, 2021. |
Includes bibliographical references and index.
Identifiers: LCCN 2021025763 | ISBN 9781631495823 (hardcover) |
ISBN 9781631495830 (epub)
Subjects: LCSH: Slave trade—Africa, West—History. | African Diaspora—History. |
History, Modern. | Africa—Relations—Europe—History. | Europe—Relations—
Africa—History. | Africa—History.
Classification: LCC DT31 .F86 2021 | DDC 960.22—dc23
LC record available at https://lccn.loc.gov/2021025763

ISBN 978-1-324-09240-7 pbk.

Liveright Publishing Corporation, 500 Fifth Avenue, New York, N.Y. 10110
www.wwnorton.com

W. W. Norton & Company Ltd., 15 Carlisle Street, London W1D 3BS

1 2 3 4 5 6 7 8 9 0

For my sisters and brothers.
And for Tania, too.

All these words from the seller, but not one word
from the sold. The Kings and Captains whose words
moved ships. But not one word from the cargo.

—ZORA NEALE HURSTON,
Barracoon

Not knowing it was hard; knowing it was harder.

—TONI MORRISON,
Beloved

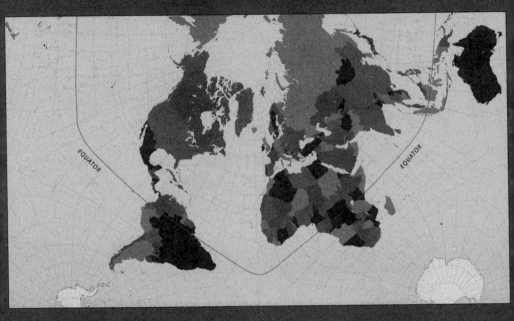

NARUKAWA MAP
(Hajime Narukawa)

CONTENTS

BORN
IN
BLACKNESS

INTRODUCTION

I T WOULD BE UNUSUAL for a story that begins in the wrong place to arrive at the right conclusions. And so it is with the history of how what we routinely think of as the modern world was made.

Traditional accounts have accorded a primacy of place to Europe's fifteenth-century Age of Discovery, and to the long-yearned-for maritime connection it established between West and East. Paired with this historic feat sits the momentous, if accidental find of what came to be known as the New World.

Other explanations for the emergence of the modern reside in the ethics and temperament that some associate with Judeo-Christian beliefs, with the development and spread of the scientific method, or, more chauvinistically still, with Europeans' often professed belief in their unique ingenuity and inventiveness. Ideas like these have become associated in the popular imagination with the Protestant Reformation and with the strong work ethic, individualism, and entrepreneurial drive that supposedly flowed from it in places like England and Holland.

There is no gainsaying the significance of the voyages of Iberians like Vasco da Gama, who reached Calicut via the Indian Ocean in 1498, Ferdinand Magellan, who traveled west to Asia, skirting the southern tip of South America, and other famous mariners of their era. This is all the more so for Christopher Columbus, even though he mistook the islands of the Caribbean for Japan and India, errors he went to his death still clinging to. As one writer has elegantly said of Columbus, when he sailed west "he had been a medieval man from a medieval world, surrounded by medieval notions about Cyclops, pygmies, Amazons, dog-faced natives, antipodeans who walk on their heads and think with their feet—about dark-skinned, giant-eared races who inhabit the lands where gold and precious gems grow. When he stepped onto American soil, however, he did more than enter a new world: he stepped into a new age."

But however common in the popular imagination, the commencement of modern history with these most famous of feats of discovery, presented as if to be viewed on a trapeze in the center ring of a three-ring circus, obscures the true beginnings of the story of how the globe became permanently stitched together and thus became "modern." It also so dramatically miscasts the role of Africa that it becomes a profound mis-telling.

The first impetus for the Age of Discovery was not Europe's yearning for ties with Asia, as so many of us have been taught in grade school, but rather its centuries-old desire to forge trading ties with legendarily rich Black societies hidden away somewhere in the heart of "darkest" West Africa. Iberia's most famous sailors cut their teeth not seeking routes to Asia, but rather plying the coastline of West Africa. This is where they perfected techniques of mapmaking, and navigation, where Spain and Portugal experimented with improved ship designs, and where Columbus came to understand the functioning of Atlantic Ocean winds and currents well enough so that he would later be able to reach the western limits of the sea with a confidence that no European had previously had before him, of being able to return home.

Well before he mounted his expeditions on behalf of Spain, Columbus, an Italian from Genoa, had sailed to provision Europe's first large, fortified overseas outpost in the tropics at Elmina, in modern-day Ghana. Europe's expeditions to West Africa of the mid-fifteenth century were bound up in a search for the sources of that region's prodigious wealth in gold. Indeed, it was the huge trade in this precious metal, discovered by the Portuguese in 1471, and secured by the building of the fort at Elmina in 1482, that helped fund da Gama's later mission of discovery to Asia. This helped make it possible for Lisbon, until then the seat of a small and impecunious European crown, to steal a march on its neighbors and radically alter the course of world history.

Bartolomeu Dias, another habitué of Elmina, rounded Africa's Cape of Good Hope in 1488, proving the existence of a sea route to what would become known as the Indian Ocean. But no onward voyage to Asia would even be attempted for nearly a decade after that, when da Gama finally sailed to Calicut. The teaching of history about this era of iconic discoveries is confoundingly silent not only on that decade, but on the nearly three decades from the Portuguese arrival at Elmina until their landing in India. It was this moment, when Europe and what is nowadays styled sub-Saharan Africa came into permanent deep contact, that laid the foundations of the modern age.

Although fundamental to understanding how today's world was built, this elision is merely one of numerous examples in a centuries-long process of diminishment, trivialization, and erasure of Africans and of people of African descent from the story of the modern world. A central aim of *Born in Blackness* is to restore key chapters like these to their proper place of prominence in our common narrative of modernity. Although often obscure, most of what is written here does not consist of freshly discovered information. In reality, history seldom works that way. Rather, siloed and piecemeal, the facts that I relate have been silenced or repeatedly swept into dark corners. Of central concern in the following pages is the deeply twinned and tragic history of Africa and Europe that began with geopolitical collisions in the fifteenth century. Events and activities that flowed from Afro-European encounters set the most Atlantic-oriented Europeans onto a path that would eventually propel their continent past the great civilizational centers of Asia and the Islamic world in both wealth and power. This ascension was not founded upon any innate or permanent European characteristics that produced superiority. To a degree that remains unrecognized, it was built on the foundation of Europe's economic and political relations with Africa. The heart of the matter here, of course, was the massive, centuries-long transatlantic trade in slaves who were put to work by the millions growing sugar, tobacco, cotton, and other cash crops on the plantations of the New World.

The long thread that leads us to the present began precisely in the elided decades mentioned above, when commercial linkages blossomed between Portugal and Africa, sending a newfound prosperity washing over what had previously been a marginal European country, a prosperity that would become the very mother's milk of modernity. It drove urbanization there on an unprecedented scale, and created new, modern identities that were gradually freed from previously unbreakable feudal ties to the land. Indeed, one of these novel identities was nationhood, as we understand it in the contemporary sense of the word, and the dawning of this kind of consciousness was bound up in questing for wealth in faraway lands and soon thereafter, in emigration and in colonization in the tropics.

As Portugal ventured out into the world in the early fifteenth century—and for nearly a century this meant almost exclusively the world of Africa—its people were among the first to make another conceptual leap. They began to think of discovery not merely as the simple act of stumbling upon assorted novelties or arriving wide-eyed in never-before-visited places, but rather as something new and more abstract. Discovery became a mind-set and this would become another cornerstone of modernism; it meant understanding that the world was infinite in its social complexity, and this required a broadening of consciousness, even amid the colossal violence and horror that accompanied this process, and an ever more systematic unmooring from provincialism.

Modernity, to be sure, remains a deeply contested term, one given to many, often contradictory interpretations. In a book that will make strong claims about Africa's unheralded role in its emergence, therefore, it is perhaps appropriate to weigh in right here with a kind of functional definition. In writing about modernity, the Canadian philosopher Charles Taylor has postulated two very different notions of what people mean by this term, one cultural and the other acultural. We will eventually employ both of these usages, but here, it is the cultural vision of modernity that concerns us most. "In [that] take," he writes, "we can look at the difference between present-day Western society and, say, that of medieval Europe as analogous to the difference between medieval Europe and medieval China or India. In other words, we can think of the difference as one between civilizations, each with their own culture." Drawing on Taylor's notion, *Born in Blackness* will show that the fateful engagement between Europe and sub-Saharan Africa, which began in the early fifteenth century, and then rapidly accelerated and deepened toward that century's end and beyond, produced civilizational transformations in both of these regions as well as in the wider world; ones that, looking back today, produced like few other things ever have a crisp division between "before" and "after."

BACK THEN, EUROPEANS were themselves mindful of this reality. As late as the 1530s, which is to say well after the commencement of Portugal's more famous spice trade with Asia, Lisbon still recognized Africa as the leading driver of all that was new. João de Barros, a counselor to that country's crown, for example, wrote: "I do not know in this Kingdom a yoke of land, toll, tithe, excise or any other Royal tax more reliable . . . than the profits of commerce in Guinea."

But as remarkable as Barros's acknowledgment of African vitality was, his omission of slavery as a pillar of the relationship may have been the first time that the centrality of Black bondage to epochal social and economic change was denied or simply passed over in an informed account of the experience of modernity in the West. It would not be the last. When Barros wrote, Portugal overwhelmingly dominated Europe's trade in Africans and slavery was beginning to rival gold as Portugal's most lucrative source of African bounty. By then, it was already on its way to becoming the foundation of a new economic system based on plantation agriculture that over time would generate far more wealth for Europe than African gold or, for that matter, Asia's famously coveted silks and spices.

Sounding like an updated Barros, Malachy Postlethwayt, a leading eighteenth-century British expert on commerce, called the rents and revenues of plantation slave labor "the fundamental prop and support" of his country's prosperity and social effervescence. The British Empire, then in full flower, he described as "a magnificent superstructure of American commerce and naval power [built] on an African foundation." Around the same time, an equally prominent French thinker, Guillaume-Thomas-François de Raynal, described Europe's plantations worked by African slaves "the principal cause of the rapid motion which now agitates the universe." Daniel Defoe, the English author of *Robinson Crusoe*, but also a trader, pamphleteer, and spy, bested them both when he wrote: "No African trade, no negroes; no negroes, no sugars, gingers, indicoes etc.; no sugar etc no islands no continent, no continent, no trade."

Postlethwayt, Raynal, and Defoe were surely right, even if they were far from comprehending all of the reasons why. As this book will make clear, more than any other part of the world, Africa has been the linchpin of the machine of modernity. Without African peoples trafficked from its shores, the Americas would have counted for little in the ascendance of the West. African labor, in the form of slaves, became the providential factor that made the very *mise en valeur* or development of the Americas possible. Without it, Europe's colonial projects in the New World, such as we know them, are simply unimaginable.

Through the development of plantation agriculture, and a succession of history-altering commercial crops—tobacco, coffee, cacao, indigo, rice, and, above all, sugar—Europe's deep and often brutal ties with Africa drove the birth of a truly global capitalist economy. Slave-grown sugar hastened the coming together of the processes we call industrialization. It radically transformed diets, making possible much higher worker productivity. And in doing so, sugar completely revolutionized European society. As readers will discover, this includes playing a critical but largely uncredited role in the anchoring of democracy on that continent.

In sugar's wake, cotton grown by slaves in the American South helped launch formal industrialization, along with an immense second wave of consumerism. After plentiful calories, abundant and varied clothing for the masses became a reality for the first time in human history. As revealed here, the scale and the scope of the American antebellum cotton boom, which made this possible, were nothing short of astonishing. This made the value derived from the trade and ownership of slaves in America alone, as distinct from the cotton and other products they produced, greater than that of all of the country's factories, railroads, and canals combined.

Born in Blackness is, in part, an account of forgotten European contests over control of the African bounty that built the modern world. Spain and Portugal waged fierce naval battles in West Africa over access to gold. Holland and Portugal, then unified with Spain, fought something little short of a world war in the seventeenth century, with control of trade in the richest sources of slaves in Africa, present-day Congo and Angola, flipping back and forth between them. On the far side of the Atlantic, Brazil, the biggest producer of slave-grown sugar in the early seventeenth century, was caught up in this same struggle, and repeatedly changed hands. Later in that same century, England fought Spain over control of the Caribbean. Why did faraway powers contend so fiercely over such things? Tiny Barbados provides an answer. By the mid-1660s, just three decades or so after England initiated an African slave-labor model for its plantations there—one that was first implemented in the Portuguese colony of São Tomé little more than a century earlier— sugar from Barbados was worth more than the metal exports of all of Spanish America.

As much as this book is a story of classical military struggle for control of the richest plantation lands and the most prolific sources of slaves, and of the economic miracles they produced at different stages of this history, it is also an account of another kind of conflict altogether, both unconventional and ceaseless: a war on Blacks themselves. It is one that very conservatively speaking continued at least until the end of Jim Crow in America, where this book concludes. This involved the consistent pursuit of strategies to beat Africans into submission, enslave one another, to recruit Blacks as proxies and auxiliaries, whether to secure territories from native populations of the New World or joust with European rivals in the Americas. To say this is not to deprive Africans of agency, a question that will be taken up at length in these pages. The impact of this warfare on Africa's subsequent development, another wage of modernity, however, has been immeasurable. Nowadays, the consensus estimate on the numbers of Africans brought to the Americas hovers around 12 million. Lost in this atrocious but far too neat accounting is the likelihood that another 6 million Africans were killed in or near their homelands during the hunt for slaves, before they could be placed in chains. Estimates vary, but between 5 and 40 percent perished during brutal overland treks to the coast, or while being held, often for months, in barracoons, or holding pens, as they awaited embarkation on slave ships. And another 10 percent of those who were taken aboard died at sea during an Atlantic transit that constituted an extreme mental and physical test for all those who were subjected to it. When one considers that Africa's total population in the mid-nineteenth century was probably around 100 million, one begins to gauge the enormity of the demographic assault that the slave trade represented.

This war on Black people raged just as fiercely on the western shores of the Atlantic, as did the resistance, and these, too, we must reckon with here. In most of the New World plantation societies the average remaining life span of trafficked Blacks was reckoned at seven years or less. In 1751, an English planter on Antigua summed up the prevailing slaveowner sentiment this way: "It was cheaper to work slaves to the utmost, and by the little fare and hard usage, to wear them out before they become useless, and unable to do service; and then to buy new ones to fill up their places."

Born in Blackness takes us all the way to the penultimate stages of this war, with the story of how Big Cotton burst forth in late-eighteenth-century America, creating a unique fusion of book-keeping and brutality. In 1808, a typical picker in South Carolina, then still the heart of America's cotton-growing region, averaged 28 pounds per day of harvest. By 1846, the average Mississippi cotton picker delivered up 341 pounds to his masters, a rate of increase fully in step with the growth of factory productivity in Manchester.

IN CREATING THIS ACCOUNT, it was important for me to be able to locate as many of the physical traces of the history covered herein as possible, and to breathe the air and tread the ground where many of the events and processes described transpired. I was aided in this by the remarkable degree of coincidence, here and there, between the places written about and with my own life, meaning both biographical details bound up in family history, and in my four-decade-long career as a journalist and writer. Almost everyone who reads this book is somehow a product of the histories explored here. But as the child of two African American parents of mixed and diverse heritage, I am especially conscious of this.

I am fortunate to know quite a bit about my family, especially on my late mother's side, which has old and clearly traceable roots in slavery in Virginia, including the kind of involuntary racial mixing made most famous by Thomas Jefferson, and indeed in the case of my ancestors, involving a friend of America's third president, who designed his home. This account will close with a meditation on what that has meant to me and how it shaped this narrative.

I was lucky to be introduced to Africa while still a university student, first as an enthralled visitor during college breaks, and later living there for six years following graduation. I cut my teeth as a journalist writing about Africa and traveling widely, and I married a woman who had grown up in Côte d'Ivoire, but whose family hails from a nearby part of Ghana. I wasn't at all aware of it at the time, but it was within a few miles of her ancestral village that Europeans first stumbled upon the abundant sources of West African gold that they had been searching for feverishly for several decades in the fifteenth century. It was a discovery that changed the world.

I left West Africa to join the staff of *The New York Times* in 1986. Some three years later, my first assignment as a foreign correspondent for the paper was to cover the Caribbean basin. Here were gathered some of the most important staging areas for subsequent global transformations of the first order. Specialists aside, few imagine that islands like Barbados and Jamaica were far more important in their day than were the English colonies that would become the United States. The nation now known as Haiti, even more so. In the eighteenth century it became the richest colony in history, and in the nineteenth, by dint of its slave population's successful revolution, Haiti rivaled the United States in terms of its influence on the world, notably in helping fulfill the most fundamental Enlightenment value of all, ending slavery. Now and then during my time in the Caribbean, I could see glimmers of this region's extraordinary meta-narrative. These came when I stood knee deep in the heavily silted seawater witnessing an archaeological dig in the Dominican Republic that sought to identify a wreck from Columbus's first voyage, or when I hiked a verdant peak in northern Haiti. There, Henri Christophe, that country's early Black leader, built the formidable Citadelle Laferrière, the largest fortress in the Western Hemisphere, arming it with 365 cannons to defend the country's hard-won independence from France. Other hints came when I wandered into the mountains and rain forests of Jamaica and Suriname, respectively, and was thrilled to be able to make myself understood speaking bits of Twi, the lingua franca of Ghana learned while courting my wife, as I spoke with the descendants of proud runaway slave communities known as maroons. But back then, I still had no big picture in mind; like most correspondents, I was too busy following the news to pursue sweeping historical connections very far.

Later, I was sent back to West Africa by the *Times*. In a handful of years there in the late 1990s, I spent large amounts of time in the Sahel, the site of the medieval African empire building discussed herein, and in the coastal bloodlands that fed the slave trade most heavily.

I went into this project already well aware of the silence and enforced ignorance that surround the central contribution of Africa and of Africans in the making of the modern world that we all inhabit today. But I was not prepared for how difficult it can be in place after place to access some of the physical traces of this history, or to find local forms of remembrance and commemoration that raise this African role to its proper dimension.

I have seen this in a great many places that have profoundly marked our common history, in countries like Nigeria and the Democratic Republic of the Congo, where the publicly established sites of Atlantic memory are few. I saw it in São Tomé, the island where the slave-plantation-complex model that would dominate history in the Western Hemisphere, and drive wealth creation in the North Atlantic for four centuries, was perfected, a fact for which there is nary a plaque or commemoration.

In Salvador, the capital of Bahia, the blackest and most slavery-marked area of the rich Portuguese colony's entire history, I hired a Black Brazilian guide who had come highly recommended. But when we met face-to-face and I specified that I wanted to tour plantation ruins and visit rural communities that descended from runaway slaves, she was nonetheless taken aback. "I never imagined that people could be interested in sugar plantations," she said, explaining that in years of business, she had never received such a request.

My biggest surprise, though, came in Barbados, whose slave-produced sugar, arguably more than any other place on earth, helped seal England's ascension in the seventeenth century. I disembarked on the island in March 2019 determined to find as many traces of this legacy as possible, only to discover how thoroughly they had been hidden or effaced. Among my top priorities was to visit one of the largest slave cemeteries anywhere in the hemisphere, including the excavated remains of nearly six hundred people. It took me several efforts spread over three days, though, to even locate

the cemetery, which had no signage from any public road. Conversations with residents of the area whom I repeatedly importuned
made clear that very few were aware of its historical importance or
even of its existence.

All I discovered when I drove down a bumpy dirt road, proceed-
ing as far as I could until instinct told me to get out and walk, was a
modest clearing alongside an active plantation whose cane had grown
as high as I am, at six foot four. There stood a faded sign attached to a
rusty iron post. It announced the site to be part of something called
"The Slave Route," but it provided no further information. With
the sun racing downward in the western sky, I paced about briefly,
snapped a few photographs, and then finally collected myself as the
wind whistled through the cane. I tried mightily to conjure some
sense of the horrors that had transpired nearby, and of the abundant
wealth and pleasure that the sweat of the dead had procured for others. In the moment, there was little else I could do to render proper
homage to the countless lives that had been mercilessly ground up
in the production of sweetness and cheap calories for faraway markets. This book constitutes my effort to carry this reflection as far as
I can extend it.

I would be remiss if I didn't make clear that the most egregious
forms of historical erasure do not involve an assortment of mostly
small, former slave-trading or plantation societies scattered around
the Atlantic Rim. The most important site of forgetting, by far, has
been the minds of people in the rich world. As I write these words,
the United States and some other North Atlantic societies, from
Richmond, Virginia, to Bristol, England, have recently experienced
extraordinary moments of iconoclasm. Here and there, statues have
been pulled down of people who were long perceived to be heroes
of imperial and economic orders that were constructed on the basis
of the violent exploitation of people extracted from Africa. But for
these gestures to have deeper and more lasting meaning, an even bigger and more challenging task remains for us. It requires of us that
we transform the way that we understand the history of the last six
centuries and, specifically, of Africa's central, yet largely invisible

role in making nearly everything that is today familiar to us possible. This will necessarily involve rewriting grade-school lessons about history just as much as it will require reinvention of university curricula. It will challenge journalists to rethink the way we describe and explain the world we all inhabit. It will require all of us to reexamine what we know or think we know about how the present-day world was built, and to begin incorporating this new understanding in our everyday discussions. One book alone cannot possibly hope to achieve all of that, but the present volume should be read against that challenge, and with this spirit and goal in mind.

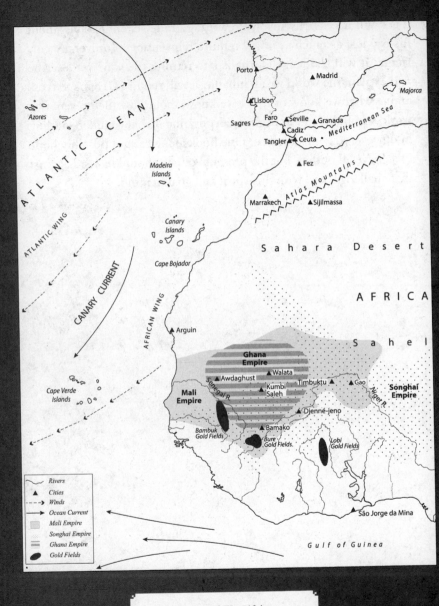

Iberia and West Africa,
with ocean winds and currents

PART I

THE "DISCOVERY" OF AFRICA

Gold was not only the engine
of the economy, but beyond all social
activities, of civilization itself.

FERNAND BRAUDEL,
"Monnaies et Civilisations"

THE CRACKLING SURFACE

BY 1995, VISITING DJENNÉ, a small and seemingly time-forgotten city in the southwest of Mali, had nearly become a pilgrimage for me. I'd first gone there fifteen years earlier, as a backpacking college student, with my younger brother in tow, to see the city's great, spired mosque, famous for being the largest adobe building in the world.

When I had returned this time, as a correspondent for *The New York Times*, what had drawn me was excavation work then under way on what was still reputed to be the oldest known city in Africa outside of Egypt.* It was also, and indeed remains, the most recently discovered example anywhere in the world of a major ancient urban civilization. My memories of the visit are still powerfully bound up in sounds. Starting at dusk each night, the noise that filled the air over the dusty floodplain was more insistent even than the loud chorus of crickets. Looters, most of them peasants armed with hoes and pickaxes, could be discerned in the shadows, flailing at the dry earth, hoping to prize away from it whatever kind of artifact they could find. By then, intact burial urns or unbroken sculpture, both quite rare, fetched many thousands of dollars on the frothy

---

* Since then, archaeologists have determined that Timbuktu is older than Djenné.

European black market that supplied unscrupulous collectors and even museums with African art.

The sounds of daytime were even more terrible than those of the night. To walk the grounds of the tell, the long, tear-shaped, sloping mound that revealed the contours of a walled city which faded mysteriously from existence six hundred or more years ago, was to wreak one's own damage to the sprawling site. Each and every footfall brought a sharp, crunching reminder of this as the already fragmented potsherds that densely littered the brown earth broke into ever smaller pieces.

Djenne-jeno, or "ancient Djenné," sprung to life roughly 250 years before the birth of Christ, on a floodplain near the banks of the Bani River, not far from where it joins the course of one of the continent's greatest rivers, the Niger, on its long, trundling arc through West Africa. In its early phases of growth, the city counted more than fifteen thousand residents, many of whom lived inside a high, 1.3-mile-long wall that was twelve feet thick at its base. Another thirty thousand or so people lived in related urban clusters nearby. Early in the Christian era, an aggregate population like this would have placed ancient Djenné among the ranks of world-class cities. There were bigger urban centers in China and in a few other places, to be sure, but not very many.

The public has long been conditioned to believe that Africa has little pre-modern history, or at least little of it that matters to the big picture of our world. As Western thinkers and politicians from Hegel down to the former French president, Nicolas Sarkozy, have argued from the dawn of time to the very recent past, African societies have lived, as it were, altogether outside of history. Accordingly, it has long been believed that people in sub-Saharan Africa were spurred to urbanize only by contact with Arabs, beginning sometime late in the first millennium. Following on this idea, the prevailing view has long held that it was only contact with Europe, which would come centuries later, that dragged what is fancied as "Black Africa" out of its supposed isolation and connect it to the big currents of change that began sweeping the rest of the world in the late Middle Ages.*

Djenné is the most prominent of many ancient cities in Africa that give the lie to this. It had urbanized hundreds of years before Arabs first swept into North Africa in the seventh century, never mind the arrival a century or two after that of Arabic-speaking travelers in the western reaches of the broad band of semi-arid land that stretches just south of the Sahara from Ethiopia to the Atlantic—a region known as the Sudan. Djenné thrived by trading fish, grains, and copper and other metals with places hundreds of miles distant, like the surviving cities of Timbuktu and Gao. (See map, page 14.) Intriguingly, digs have uncovered artifacts that date to the city's very beginnings, including glass beads that come from Han China, when that dynasty itself (202 BCE to 220 CE) was scarcely a century old, as well as other trade goods from the eastern Mediterranean. Items like these bear witness to the fact that West Africa was never so cut off from the rest of the world or lost in time as is commonly imagined.

What had brought me to the floodplain of the Niger in 1995 to walk the ground with archaeologists was to write about the monumental challenges that conservation poses in a poor environment like this. But what I have come to appreciate since then is how this region was anything but a passive or inert presence in the affairs of the Middle Ages. Indeed, as the following account demonstrates, African initiative in this region was every bit as important as Europe's in spurring the creation of the world we inhabit today.

Sometime during its first half millennium of existence, Djenne-jeno became an important southern terminus in a highly lucrative trans-Saharan trade in gold. Rumors of this trade first appear in writings from antiquity in the Mediterranean. The first real evidence

---

* The problematic idea of something called Black Africa is a convention so deeply embedded in our culture that it is hard to avoid, never mind overcome. As it is most often used, it is roughly coterminous with the notion that a large part of the continent is composed of senselessly warring tribes who are without literacy or history, views that this book confronts head-on. As a term, Black Africa also strongly overstates racial distinctions between societies located on either side of the Sahara Desert, overlooking their heterogeneity.

of a trickle of sub-Saharan African gold to that part of the world, though, dates to the early centuries of the Christian era. This commerce became plentiful around the sixth century, as parts of what would later become the Ghana Empire began to trade gold with Berbers from the north for salt, cloth, and other goods. All of this was aided by the recent introduction into the region of the desert-hardy camel, which revolutionized transportation.

In addition to creating new stirrings of prosperity, camel-borne trade produced dramatic economic and religious changes in Sudanic Africa, resulting in the formation of geographically extensive empires. Ghana, the first of these, was a loose and sprawling confederation. It mixed both sedentary agriculture and transhumance for livestock. But the real power of Ghana's rulers was based on control of strategic chokepoints through which gold passed from south to north, and through which other essential goods—like salt, which was lacking in the rain forests to the south—traveled in the opposite direction. By the eleventh century, Ghana's wealth and prestige allowed it to field impressively large armies.

A major shift in the regional climate beginning in the third century CE ended a lengthy dry period in the Sahara and Sahel and gradually allowed North Africans to trade with peoples farther and farther to the south of the Sahara for both gold and slaves.

Through sustained contact with these northerners, Ghana's leaders began to Islamize, but only in a partial fashion. Ancient Ghana maintained twin capitals, separated by a distance of six miles. One was rigorously Muslim, while the other, the abode of the king, al-Ghāba (the Grove), honored older, ancestral religions, which were still practiced by the masses. For as long as it lasted, this unique approach favored both lucrative trade and peaceful relations with the Berbers, while also allowing Ghana's leaders to retain the allegiance of peasants and urban commoners.[*]

A striking tenth-century account by the Arab geographer

---

[*] Broadly speaking, Islam did not become a mass religion across the Sahel until a series of reformist movements swept the region in the nineteenth century.

and chronicler Ibn Hawqal gives a feel for the development of the remarkable networks of credit and trust that enabled trade across the Sahara to blossom:

> *I saw at Awdaghust a warrant in which was the statement of a debt owed to one of them [merchants of Sijilmāsa] by one of the merchants of Awdaghust, who was [himself] one of the people of Sijilmāsa, in the sum of 42,000 dinars. I have never seen or heard anything comparable to this story in the East. I told it to people in Iraq, in Fars, and in Khurasan [both in Iran], it was considered remarkable.*

On the basis of this trade, Ghana became known throughout North Africa, Mediterranean Europe, and as far away as Yemen as the "country of gold," and for cause. In time, it would generate as much as two-thirds of the supply of the metal known to the inhabitants of medieval western Eurasia.

The gold that flowed out of the Sudan played a crucial role in the Arab golden age, a period of explosive growth and political expansion that began around 750 CE and extended until the Mongol invasions of the thirteenth century. As a result of this trade in the precious metal, the hard currency of the Arab world, the gold dinār, became prized everywhere it circulated. This included medieval Christendom, where Arab coins were often copied. And the existence of a quasi-universal currency greatly facilitated the growth of Arab commerce from the Levant to Andalusia, the name given to the Muslim empire that flourished in what are now modern Spain and Portugal.

The question before us is why, beginning in the first half of the fifteenth century, did Europeans, led principally by the Portuguese, begin to mount a determined push for trade opportunities and political relations with what had previously been regarded as impossibly remote and inaccessible regions of Africa? What drove them to overcome their long-standing fears and superstitions to do so? Obscure though it may be to contemporary readers, little-known Djenné constitutes an important piece of this story. Early centers of urbanization like this one—city-states, in effect—became swept up in a process of empire formation in a part of Africa that would soon become as outward looking as Portugal or Spain, only long before the oceanic explorations of the Iberians. In fact, the most famous of these Sudanic empires, Mali, which succeeded Ghana in the thirteenth century, and gave the present-day country its name, was ruled at the turn of the fourteenth century by an emperor named Abu Bakr II, whose personal obsession was reaching the western limits of the Atlantic Ocean by boat. This was more than a century and a half before Columbus set out for the New World from Andalusia.

Although the surviving documentary record of Abu Bakr II is frustratingly scant, there can be no doubt as to his existence, nor any reason not to credit his fixation on maritime discovery. This is because his much more famous successor, Mansā Mūsā, gave the governor of Cairo a detailed account of Abu Bakr's life and attempts at oceanic discovery during a pilgrimage to Mecca in 1324–1325, which was recorded contemporaneously.

> The ruler who preceded me did not believe that it was impossible to reach the extremity of the ocean that encircles the earth, and wanted to reach that (end) and obstinately persisted in the design. So he equipped two hundred boats full of men, as many others full of gold, water and victuals sufficient enough for several years. He ordered the chief (admiral) not to return until they had reached the extremity of the ocean, or if they had exhausted the provisions and the water. They set out. Their absence extended over a long period, and, at last, only one boat returned. On questioning, the captain said: "Prince, we have navigated for a long time, until we saw in the midst of the ocean as if a big river was flowing violently. My boat was the last one; others were ahead of me. As soon as any of them reached this place, it drowned in the whirlpool and never came out. I sailed backwards to escape this current." But the Sultan would not believe him. He ordered two thousand

boats to be equipped for him and for his men, and one thousand
more for water and victuals. Then he conferred on me the regency
during his absence, and departed with his men on the ocean trip,
never to return nor to give a sign of life.

How could so few people be aware of something like this today?
one might reasonably enough ask. To be sure, an important part of
the explanation lies in the near total lack of further documentary or
archaeological evidence beyond the details presented here. But that
is not all. Of equal importance is the fact that our understanding of
the world still comes down to us in many cases as hagiography. This
is combined with an often deliberate and pervasive neglect and erasure of the role of Africa and of Africans in the creation of a modern
Atlantic world. This cultural bias if not eradication has dulled our
senses to matters of both provable fact and tantalizing possibility,
helping ensure that the postulated ocean ventures of Abu Bakr are
ever so rarely mentioned at all, much less taught.

To be fair, certain important details do not jibe. If they existed,
these "ships," for one, would most likely have been something more
akin to very large dugouts, and almost certainly not sailing vessels
with tall masts, since the craft of shipbuilding seems never to have
been developed indigenously in West Africa. The number of boats
is another question. One must understand, though, how common it
was in antiquity in many cultures for a round number like a thousand to be used metaphorically—i.e., simply as a stand-in for "a great
many"—rather than literally.* Perhaps the most intriguing question,
but one that will probably forever remain unsolved, is: What under-
laid Abu Bakr's theory of the world? Did the earth have only a modest diameter, meaning that to reach the far shore of the ocean might
require only a daylong voyage, however daring or unprecedented, or
was it unimaginably vast, truly making it a fool's errand to venture a
crossing in mere high-end canoes?

---

* This is a numbering convention still much used in China today, where the figure 10,000 is
a metaphor for something nearly countless or infinite.

Despite such reservations, Abu Bakr's story nonetheless contains logical elements that argue strongly for taking it seriously. The first is that by virtue of spending time in the Canary Islands, off West Africa, we know that Columbus discovered the existence, at a fixed latitude, of powerful winds and ocean currents that circulate in a counterclockwise fashion and swiftly bear ships off to the west. The waters off the coastal region of West Africa controlled by Abu Bakr II's Mali are dominated by these very effects, helping make sense of a possible survivor's account of a big river flowing violently in the midst of the ocean. Indeed, just to the north of this large system, which in modern times has been fittingly known as the Canary Current, lies an equally large and powerful clockwise current that thrusts all in its path in an eastward direction. In fact, this system helps explain why Europeans had believed for centuries that sailing westward across the ocean was not only impractical but also suicidal.

Other reasons not to hastily dismiss this account draw on what we know of medieval science in the Islamic world, as well as the complex geopolitics of those times. Mali's rulers had been conducting pilgrimages to Mecca since the mid-thirteenth century, and throughout this period, they had also sent embassies to Cairo and to other cities in the Arab world. In the Middle East, unlike the Europe of that era, the earth's roundness had been taken for certain at least since the work of al-Masūdī, a tenth-century Arab geographer and historian. This makes the idea of a voyage of ocean discovery for Africans, or at least the harboring of such an ambition, seem like less of a blind leap into the unknown than it would remain even a century and more later for the Portuguese and Spanish.

Sheer persistence of the sort attributed to Abu Bakr II still demands powerful motives. Here, one can easily imagine that by Abu Bakr's time, a ruler in command of such vast supplies of gold would have been eager to overcome his realm's dependence on the Berbers who ruled North Africa, and through whose hands almost all of his precious metal passed, but presumably only after a hefty markup.

Seeking to eliminate the so-called middleman in order to maximize Mali's profits would have been a normal goal, but beyond this, there were other possible incentives. Mali had come together as a polity early in the thirteenth century on the basis of a political pact among clans from the Mande language group.* In the initial phase of empire, it shared key features with its long-lived precursor, Ghana: it was an ethnically based polity that embraced castelike divisions, and its elite also practiced an African ancestral religion alongside Islam. Already by the second generation of its existence, though, its rulers had begun conquering and absorbing other non-Malinke peoples in a widening radius, quickly transforming expansionist Mali into a richly heterogeneous realm. With equal alacrity it had also begun a broader and more enthusiastic conversion to Islam. This latter choice was likely to have been a matter not only of spirituality, but also of pragmatic adaptation to the changing politics of regional trade and security.

By converting to Islam, an ascendant religious movement that had strongly universalist aspirations, Mali's rulers were, in effect, achieving two purposes. On the one hand they were bidding to enhance their legitimacy among the peoples they conquered and absorbed. As with most empires, especially in their formative phases, this meant concocting various forms of cosmological bluster. The clan at the center of Malian power, the Keïtas, went so far as to claim direct descent from Bilāl, the Black companion of the Prophet Muhammad and Islam's first muezzin, the figure whose duty it was to call the founding generation of Muslim faithful to prayer.

By the same token, a deeper commitment to Islam than previously shown by Ghana helped position Mali favorably in the broader world. In the middle of the fourteenth century, the famed North African historian and global traveler Ibn Battūtah approvingly described the worship he witnessed among Malians this way: "The people come out, dressed in their white clothes, to the place of prayer, which is close to the palace of the Sultan. The Sultan came

---

* This group sometimes goes by a number of related names, including Malinke, Manden, Manding, and Mandingo.

mounted, with the preacher and jurists in front of him, called 'There is no God but Allah, and Allah is Great.'"

Through the development of networks of business and learning, the embrace of Islam by Malinke traders strengthened relations of confidence with those who controlled North African commercial networks. The supple form that the religion took in the region, meanwhile, helped hasten its spread among the common folk. Nonbelievers were not disparaged as wicked, but regarded, rather, as merely ignorant. It was accepted that God would accord them time to gradually change their ways.

For all of this, Mali's leaders would have nonetheless been keenly aware that adherence to Islam by itself, no matter how enthusiastic, was far from a sufficient guarantee of their security. Less than two centuries before the rise of Mali, Ghana had paid the ultimate price for its isolation and dependence on camel-borne traders from the north. Its power crumbled after 1076, when the Almoravid Berbers, fervent Muslim ascetics from North Africa, seized control from Ghana of Awdaghust, a critical southern terminus of the trans-Saharan gold trade. Espousing a severe creed of what the historian David Levering Lewis has termed an "undeviating Qur'anic literalism bent on the propagation of 'righteousness,'" the Almoravids soon went on from this victory to take over southern Iberia. It was an intervention by these Africans that secured Islam's hitherto vulnerable presence in Europe for another four hundred years. The clear twin lesson of Ghana's demise was that never again would either ambivalence toward Islam or geopolitical aloofness be viable options for the rulers of empires in the western Sudan. Like it or not, their region had been permanently drawn into a thickening web of connections involving power centers north of the Sahara and beyond, along with all of the benefits and perils that this portended.

The sole surviving written account of Abu Bakr's bid for ocean exploration, the one provided in Cairo by his successor, Mansā Mūsā, includes the critical detail that his expeditionary fleets included numerous boats heavily stocked with gold. Two possible motives for carrying such a prized cargo, among many, stand out:

one would have been to assess new markets for the precious metal in the unknown lands awaiting discovery somewhere across the ocean, while the other would have been awing the rulers of these faraway lands with Mali's great wealth and thereby winning their respect. These, indeed, are quite close to the known motives of Mansā Mūsā during his Cairo mission itself. It is unnecessary and even unhelpful, meanwhile, to imagine that Mali's doomed explorers were looking for anything even remotely akin to the Americas, or even less Columbus's true objective, India. It is enough to know that Mali's rulers were by then already keenly aware that on the far shores of the Mediterranean lay another landmass, this being Europe. Their bid for westward discovery may have simply been aimed at finding something analogous to this: new territories for them to trade and diversify their relations with and that were within manageable reach somewhere off the West African coast. And this much more limited objective intriguingly foreshadows and anticipates what the Iberians themselves would attempt to establish with their maritime expeditions to Africa during most of the fifteenth century. Their goal was an end run around Muslim-controlled lands in the Maghreb in search of new sources of wealth, and perhaps also in search of allies among the Blacks in what they sometimes fancied as Ethiopia.

2

BLACK KING, GOLDEN SCEPTER

I T IS WORTH ACKNOWLEDGING here that some historians and anthropologists regard the legend of Abu Bakr II with great skepticism, with some even arguing that the tale of doomed ocean discovery was little more than a cover story for an abrupt shift in the line of Malian imperial succession, which may possibly have involved a violent struggle for power or a coup d'état. One needn't speculate any further on the mysteries of Abu Bakr II, however, because Mansā Mūsā was acting upon many of the same impulses that we have conjectured for the doomed Sahelian voyages of discovery when he undertook the 3500-mile overland pilgrimage to Cairo. It is there that he bequeathed the story of his predecessor's exploration bid to the annals of history. Mūsā assumed power in the year 1312, a time that historians regard as Mali's golden era. At its zenith, the empire controlled the nexus of three of West Africa's most important river valleys: the Senegal, the Gambia, and, most important of all, the Niger. The combined population of Mali's subjects and vassals may have been as large as fifty million, an impressive number in the world of this era. Gold production was booming. Whereas Ghana had principally relied upon goldfields at a place called Bambuk, which was connected via western caravan routes that lead to Morocco, Mali diversified its sources of gold and was able to greatly boost production. In addition to Bambuk, already by then an ancient source of the metal, Mali obtained ore in even more abundant quantities from a place called Bure, which was located in forestland to the southwest of Djenné that was controlled by non-Muslims who paid tribute to the empire in gold. Mali also began to extend its gold-trading networks even farther afield to the southeast, tapping production from areas controlled by the Akan ethnic groups of present-day Ghana, a name adopted by the former British colony, the Gold Coast at independence, and not by connection to the Ghana Empire discussed above.

In addition to gold, each of the three major Sudanic empires that succeeded one another in controlling the most important river valleys and the savannah to the south of the Sahara—Ghana, Mali, and Songhai (this empire is discussed below)—aggressively pursued a trade in slaves. Some slaves were acquired for domestic purposes (i.e., used in armies, in administration, and for labor), and others were sold to Tuaregs and Berbers, who conveyed them into bondage in North Africa and beyond. "The emperor could ensure his cut in the trade of gold and slaves more readily than the extraction of surplus production from 'his' people. He could use the profits of trade to buy slaves, who could fight on his behalf as well as produce. His wealth and military could attract the support of young men who had become detached from or sought an alternative to their own kinship group," Frederick Cooper, a historian of the continent, wrote in *Africa in the World: Capitalism, Empire, and Nation-State.* Cooper was speaking of Ghana, but his observation holds equally well for any of these Sudanic empires, and this deeply entwined economic background of gold and slavery, as we will see, would have profound consequences for our story—meaning for the birth of a transatlantic slave trade, beginning in the early sixteenth century.

Rather than pursuing Abu Bakr II's costly dreams further by once again attempting the seemingly impossible at sea, Mūsā set off in 1324 for Egypt and Mecca, after twelve years in power. Although still only in his midthirties, he was obsessed with a dramatic geopolitical gambit of his own: diversifying Mali's foreign relations. In doing so, he was substituting bold diplomacy to the moon-shot approach attributed to his predecessor as a solution to what was essentially the same problem. Mūsā needed to preserve close relations with the Marinid Empire, the eventual successors of the Almoravids, who controlled the entire Maghreb, and thereby enjoyed a chokehold on Malian trade. At the same time, however, he hoped to ease Mali's utter dependency on North Africa by forging strong ties with Egypt, which was then ruled by the Mamluks, a Turkic sultanate that was at the height of its prestige in the Islamic world.

Mansā Mūsā arrived in Cairo on horseback on July 18, 1324, "under very large banners or flags with yellow symbols on a red background." As the following account aims to make clear, this date, remembered by virtually no one save for historians of medieval Africa, merits consideration as one of the most important moments in the making of the Atlantic world. The reasons for this have less to do with anything Mūsā himself could have possibly imagined, let alone foreseen, resulting instead from the momentous ways that the unintended consequences of his diplomacy played themselves out on the grandest of global stages.

On its own terms, Mūsā's astonishing entrée into Cairo for a three-month stay on his way to Mecca was filled with enormous drama, so much so that even two generations later it is said to have still been the talk of Egypt and far beyond. No one had ever witnessed such scenes of pomp and largesse, establishing a reputation that has followed this Malian leader down to the present as the richest man in history. Even the quickest perusal of the most basic evidence makes it easy to understand why: Mūsā was accompanied by a sixty-thousand-person delegation, including twelve thousand slaves, each of whom reputedly carried a wandlike fan of gold weighing four pounds. Mūsā's senior wife, Ināri Kunāte, is said to have been catered to by five hundred maids and personal slaves devoted to her needs alone. Camels and horses carried hundreds of pounds of gold dust. In all, some estimates of the amount of highly pure gold that Mūsā brought on his pilgrimage range as high at eighteen tons.*

Gifts of the metal were dispensed to rich and poor alike all along the pilgrimage route, seemingly in order to create a sensation and announce Mali's grandeur to the world. Gold in the form of ingots and sacks of pure metallic dust were donated to mosques and handed out as patronage to officials high and low. And as a result, the price of gold throughout the region is said to have plummeted by between 12 and 25 percent for the next decade or longer.

As the intricate organizational demands of mounting such a vast entourage suggest, Mali's rulers by this time had a very highly developed sense of the theater of power. Before any supplicants could approach Mūsā, for example, they were required to press their foreheads to the ground repeatedly and toss soil over their shoulders and onto their heads and backs while they awaited permission to speak. For his part, the Malian ruler would address others only indirectly; all communication flowed through an official spokesman and interpreter. No one was allowed to see the monarch eat, and the penalty for sneezing in his presence was death. The Moroccan chronicler Ibn Battūtah went so far as to claim that Mūsā commanded more devotion from his subjects than any ruler in the world.

By far, Mūsā's most lavish gesture in Egypt was the gift he personally bestowed upon the ruler of the Mamluks, al-Malik al-Nāsir, from whom Mūsā evidently craved recognition as an equal. This reportedly amounted to the extraordinary sum of fifty thousand dinārs, or more than four hundred pounds of pure gold.

The surviving accounts of Mūsā's audience with al-Nāsir, following a three-day stay near the Pyramids, on the outskirts of the city, vary in some of the finer details, but in all of them, the Malian comes across as both prideful and shrewd, even though he was ultimately frustrated in his bid to be considered a peer of the Mamluk sultan. A retainer of the sultan named al-Umari wrote, for example:

---

* For perspective, in all of human history, only 161,000 tons of gold have been mined, more than half of it in the last fifty years.

*When I went out to meet him . . . I tried to persuade him to go up
to the Citadel to meet the sultan, but he refused persistently. . . .
He had begun to use [a religious] argument but I realized that the
audience was repugnant to him because he would be obliged to
kiss the ground and the sultan's hand. . . .*

*When we came into the sultan's presence, we said to him:
"Kiss the ground!" but he refused outright saying: "How may
this be?" Then an intelligent man who was with him whispered
to him something we could not understand and he said: "I make
obeisance to God who created me!" then he prostrated himself and
went forward to the sultan. The sultan half rose to greet him and
sat him by his side. They conversed together for a long time, then
sultan Mūsā went out.*

Other accounts of the encounter with his Egyptian host deny
that Mūsā prostrated himself at all, saying that he was made to sit
at a substantial distance, or even stand, while the Mamluk leader,
who never rose to greet him, spoke. For a man of such grandiose
gestures who had arrived from afar with such grand ambitions,
even arm's-length protocol like this would have to count as a huge
comedown. In the end, the distribution of gold on such an unheard-
of scale had failed to secure the desired result of respectful parity
that Mūsā had so ardently sought for his land. The blow may have
been softened a bit, though, by the sultan's loan of a palace to house
Mūsā throughout his stay in Cairo. "Insofar as the Mamluk ruler
was concerned, the two men were not in fact peers," the historian
Michael A. Gomez wrote in *African Dominion: A New History of
Empire in Early and Medieval West Africa*, adding that "the whole
of the evidence suggests meeting al-Nasir was a major disappointment for Mūsā."

It is probable, in fact, that the many acts of profligacy by the visiting king and his vast retinue actually undermined Mali's image. And
this is where our tale of perverse outcomes properly commences.
One commentator of that era wrote that when the visitors from the
Sudan arrived in Egypt, they never imagined their money could run

out, and yet incredibly when the time came to return to Mali, Mūsā had to borrow funds at usurious interest rates in order to finance the homeward travel. Along similar lines, ibn a-Dawādārī, an Egyptian historian, wrote: "these people became amazed at the ampleness of the country and how their money had become used up. So they became needy and resold what they had bought at half its value, and people made good profits out of them. And God knows best."

Another pernicious consequence of the trip, and not one to be underestimated, is the way that Mūsā's extravagant use of slaves, which was every bit as eye-catching as his flaunting of gold, may have reinforced sub-Saharan Africa's reputation throughout the Near East as an inexhaustible source of Black bondsmen and women. And such a legacy would come to haunt the region for the next five and a half centuries. Between 1500 and 1800, approximately 3 million Black slaves were trafficked across the Sahara Desert or via separate routes from eastern Africa into the Red Sea and Indian Ocean regions. Another million or so were sent to the Americas from the areas of the Senegambia and the Upper Guinea coast, both of which constituted core zones of influence of the medieval era's great Sahelian states. Most of these deportations into bondage occurred well after Mali, though, accelerating rapidly following the demise of its successor empire. That polity, Songhai, which was based in Gao, an ancient urban center located just beneath the big, southward bend of the Niger River, 260 miles downstream from Timbuktu, succumbed in 1591, just as Ghana had before the rise of Mali, to a trans-Saharan invasion from Morocco. This specter was likely to have been a principal motivation behind Mansā Mūsā's Near Eastern diplomacy. The defeat of Songhai was an immensely critical historical watershed for West Africa. If one imagined something like the significance of the Battle of Hastings' influence on the history of Europe, the scope of impact would not be far off. The demise of Songhai, an amoeba-shaped geographic giant that ruled over parts of present-day Mali, Niger, Senegal, Gambia, Guinea, Liberia, Ivory Coast, and Nigeria, set off a process of rapid political fragmentation in West Africa and ushered in an era of almost constant warfare between an ever shifting kaleidoscope of petty states and chieftaincies. And this state of near permanent chaos and strife, in turn, later helped feed the nascent transatlantic slave trade.

In the short term, Mūsā's pilgrimage seems to have left a more positive legacy. The Malian leader secured the training of clerics in Islamic theology and law and brought home with him a vast library of Islamic texts. After distributing untold amounts of gold in Mecca, the Malian sovereign requested that two or three descendants of the Prophet be assigned to return to his kingdom with him. When this was politely declined, Mūsā offered one thousand mithqāls of gold (4.5 kilograms) for any sharīf who would accompany him, and four sharīfs from the Prophet's Quraysh tribe, together with their families, returned to Mali with him. On this voyage, Mūsā also hired some of the best architects of the day, including the Andalusian Abū Ishāq al-Sahilī, to help design and build great mosques in Timbuktu and other important cities in his realm. His camel caravan also carted home sumptuous silks, carpets, ceramics, and all manner of other fineries snatched up in Egypt's rich markets. He is also said to have brought home with him numerous Turkish slaves, both male and female, the latter to be employed in his harem.

Mūsā had discovered that money alone could not place him on a par with a Mamluk sultan, but gestures like these may have nonetheless helped him secure recognition for Mali as an integral part of the Islamic world and a significant "transregional" power in its own right. Be that as it may, as ever, it is the historical quirks that loom over Mali that generate the most intriguing resonances. As a matter of timing, Mansā Mūsā missed by a mere few decades the coming widespread introduction of firearms to Egypt and the Near East. Had they been in use during his sojourn in Cairo, all sorts of alternative paths for Africa's subsequent history are imaginable. With unlimited specie at his disposal, the most intriguing among these is the possibility that Mali could have imported gunpowder-based weaponry on a large scale, and not only architects, clerics, and exotic Turks for the imperial harem. Mali already boasted long-standing traditions of advanced iron- and other metalworking, and Mansā Mūsā conceivably might have even acquired the know-how for arms manufacture of modern firearms of his own. This could have positioned Mali (or Songhai) for further consolidation or even expansion of its power in Sudanic Africa and, plausibly enough, even enabled it to resist the recurrent menace of aggression from the north.

What Mali would experience instead over the next two centuries were sharp swings, up and down, including less spectacular bids by other rulers in Mūsā's wake for global recognition via yet more pilgrimage diplomacy. What would ultimately doom its rulers and indeed the entire polity was a weakness fatal to so many empires, including the great Inca Empire, as well as those of the conquering Iberian world, which was just then about to make its presence felt in Africa: chronic, internecine disputes and civil warfare over rules of succession. With Mali's demise, though, the brief and little-known era when large imperial formations in West Africa mounted ambitious strategic diplomacy on the biggest of global stages came to a quiet close.*

A century or so after him, Mūsā's successors belatedly learned that the fame of Mali had spread with astonishing speed in the wake of his sojourn in Cairo, reaching the capitals of Europe, whose kings and sovereigns expressed awe over this African kingdom's prodigious stores of gold. As a result, they were determined to find its source. Although Black African states of the Sahel like Ghana, Mali, and Songhai would soon cease to be vessels for the boldest of imperial projects, the era in which Africa was profoundly shaping human affairs had in reality only just begun.

---

* This is not to say that kingdoms and states in sub-Saharan Africa undertook no further serious diplomatic initiatives. Kano, a Hausa city-state in present-day Nigeria, for example, later sought but failed to secure an alliance with the Ottoman Turks. In the sixteenth century the Kingdom of Kongo maintained an extensive diplomatic presence in Latin Christendom and also played a key role as an ally of Holland in the intercontinental Atlantic conflict it waged against Portugal known as the Thirty Years War.

3

RETHINKING EXPLORATION

I N THE SPACE OF LESS THAN two hundred years, from the early
fourteenth century to the end of the fifteenth, the course of world
history changed in more lastingly transformative ways than it
had during any comparable period in previous human experience.
Since that time, perhaps only the Industrial Revolution has changed
human life more.

It was during this time span that all the world's major population centers on each of its continents were brought into permanent
and sustained contact with one another for the first time, generating the most profound of consequences. Societies, nations, and
entire regions were jolted into motion as a result, their trajectories
careering like ping-pong balls in a lottery machine as they collided,
with some that had earlier shown no exceptional promise suddenly
rising fast and others left behind or sent reeling in sharp decline or
violent demise. Vast new empires were launched, and with them
were born immense movements of people and of goods, as well
as plants, animals, foods, and also diseases transferred from one
part of the world to another. More than any other fact, mobility
on a scale never witnessed before in all of history became the new
name of the game. And at the heart of this movement lay a terrible phenomenon, the mass trafficking of human beings who were
transported in chains from the continent of their birth, Africa, to

new and utterly unfamiliar places, first to Europe, and then to what quickly came to be known as the New World. Its handmaiden, of course, was the idea of race as a principle for determining a person's enslavability.

When we hear that term, "the New World," it immediately conjures familiar geography, bringing to mind vast territories in the Americas that were inhabited by indigenous races but hitherto unknown to Europeans, or for that matter to Africans or Asians. But this New World was more than an assemblage of places. It must also be seen as a project: something created through the projection of power and investment of energy by Europeans, and through the long-term sacrifice and destruction of human lives and the appropriation of vast quantities of human labor. This meant, of course, devastation on an unheard-of scale for many native societies from crusading, conquest, and disease. "Holocaust" is not the perfect metaphor, but it was alongside of this massive dying that the lives and the labor of Black people transported in chains from Africa, millions of whom perished along the way, made new European schemes of plantation agriculture possible. And these, in turn, would sweepingly revolutionize the global economy, not only becoming viable but hugely lucrative. No one at the start of this era could have possibly fully imagined the consequences of this immense project, but it was on the basis of these brutal arrangements that a global economy was invented and our "modern" world was born.

To fully make sense of the profound changes wrought in this era, we must first address the question of how these transformations got under way. For centuries before this time, Western Europe had earned for itself only a modest stature on the world stage. It had been a relative sideshow on an unbroken landmass that stretches all the way east to China. The biggest developments in human civilization mostly seemed to arise elsewhere, whether in religion and philosophy, science and technology, or navigation and warfare. Due to Europe's modern history, many imagine the continent as having always been a leader in thought, initiative, and creativity. But before the moment of its breakout, Europe was a big net recipient of ideas

that flowed to it, mostly from points east, just as it was the last refuge
for people migrating from points east to its Atlantic seaboard.

Classroom lessons and many traditional histories depict the uni-
fication of the Atlantic world as the result of quasi-miraculous feats
in what is fancied as an Age of Discovery. By this time, however,
many other parts of the world had already experienced eras of deep
discovery of their own. The most famous of these is perhaps that
of the Ming Dynasty, where an admiral named Zheng He led seven
exploratory maritime expeditions to places as far away from China
as East Africa and the Red Sea. From the very outset, these were
huge ventures. The first of them, in 1405, comprised nearly twenty-
eight thousand men aboard more than 250 ships. Zheng He's biggest
vessels were enormous, nine-masted affairs that were as long as four
hundred feet, which is out of all proportion to Columbus's flagship—
the *Santa Maria* measured less than twenty yards long and carried
a mere fifty-two men.

The Chinese stand out as the most spectacular explorers before
the western Europeans, but they were by no means the only ones.
The peoples of South Asia and of Arabia were already deeply familiar with the monsoon cycles of the Indian Ocean. Malay peoples had
long ago mastered exploration of the entire South China Sea and the
Indian Ocean, even settling the African island of Madagascar. Indigenous navigators in the South Pacific had logged extremely long-
distance voyages while peopling islands throughout that ocean and
even visiting South America. DNA analysis has recently revealed
that eight hundred years ago Polynesian populations were infused
with Native American genes, presumably borne by early Americans
brought to those islands on the return trips of those South Pacific
explorers. Genetic studies have also shown that native populations
in the Amazon have strong ties to people indigenous to Australia,
New Guinea, and the Andaman Islands, which is possible only if
there were transoceanic voyages in prehistoric times. Carib Indians, meanwhile, also conducted long-distance trade and navigation
in the western Atlantic between present-day Colombia, Florida, and
Mexico. And the Incas, too, may have mastered long-distance sea

travel. Finally, let us not forget the maritime mystery of the Malians. However lacking we are in material evidence for their long-distance ocean voyages, it appears that by the fourteenth century even empires centered deep in the interior of the African continent were already dreaming of the possibilities of faraway discoveries.

The elements that are usually given pride of place in explanations of how our world came together in a burst of Iberian-led exploration each contain grains of truth, and yet all fall short of reflecting the central verity behind the Europeans' motives.

Most intriguing is the unshakable belief that it was Europe's yearning for a maritime route to Asia, and that obsession above all, that drove the European breakout, creating what became known as the Age of Discovery. This explanation, long emphasized from American grade-school curricula onward, says that it was Asia's coveted markets in spices and silks that compelled European kings and queens of the late Middle Ages to invest in seaworthy ships and to empower figures like Columbus to brave the unknown and find a way by sea to the East.

Associated with this idea is a historiographical trope that one encounters so often that it suggests a kind of preprogrammed explanation, a writing of history as if by function key. Its sheer simplicity and appearance in text after text lend it a hard-to-resist feeling of weight, and yet it is not even a scintilla, but a mere facsimile of truth, not truth itself. Basically, it ascribes the earliest, little-discussed phases of the Age of Discovery—meaning, the first few decades of the fifteenth century, when the Portuguese led in efforts to edge their way southward down the coast of West Africa, beyond the lands of the Moors and into the world of Blacks—as nothing less than a whole-cloth bid by Europeans to navigate around Africa. The continent is rendered a mere obstacle, and if trade with it is mentioned at all, it is merely as a sideshow. Typically, in this rendering, once the Cape of Good Hope is reached by Bartolomeu Dias, in 1488, Africa drastically recedes from the narrative or disappears altogether. Few such accounts bother to explain why, though, if Portugal was truly caught in the grips of a feverish obsession with discovering a route to

Asia, nearly a decade elapsed after Dias's feat before Vasco da Gama was commissioned to follow in his wake, ultimately allowing the Portuguese to reach Calicut.

In fact, there were no early efforts to follow up on what modern historians have long treated as one of the most singular voyages of Iberian discovery. Nor do historical archives reveal any great signs of interest in Dias's accomplishment on the part of the Portuguese king of the time, João II. A strong clue lies in the sobriquet enjoyed by this monarch. He became known in his time as João the African, because of the abundant wealth his men gained access to in West Africa, which was no mere accident. Portugal had been looking for riches there from the outset.

This idea of finding a way around Africa, rather than acknowledging anything of interest there, persists in book after book on the topic of the Age of Discovery, providing an important foundation for a phenomenon that persists to this day. It is a bedrock feature of the way the West has explained its path to modernity by erasing Africa from the picture. Take, for example, *The Silver Way: China, Spanish America and the Birth of Globalization*, by Peter Gordon and Juan José Morales, which appeared in 2017. It likens the competition between the two Iberian countries over discovering a route to Asia to the U.S.-Soviet space race of the mid-twentieth century, and calls Dias's rounding of the southern tip of Africa Spain's "Sputnik Moment." "Portugal," the authors say, "had by then been inching down the coast of Africa for several decades, something that didn't much matter if Africa, as some suspected, went on forever southwards." The implied meaning here, of course, is that Portugal's engagement with Africa, both prior and subsequent, was of little consequence.

Among countless other examples one might finally cite the generally admirable *The Worlds of Christopher Columbus*, written by William D. Phillips Jr. and Carla Rahn Phillips. In its opening pages these authors write, "In just over thirty years, mariners from the Iberian Peninsula tied the world together in unprecedented ways. Dozens of voyages figured in this rush to explore, but the most famous were Bartolomeu Dias's rounding of Africa's southern cape in 1488, Columbus's first voyage to the Caribbean in 1492, Vasco da Gama's arrival in India in 1498, and the first circumnavigation of the earth in 1519 by Fernão Magalhães," who is better known in English as Magellan. A few dozen pages later they declare that "Europeans of the fifteenth century would come to see the circumnavigation of Africa as their best hope for reaching Asia and challenging the Muslims from behind." Such a conclusion betrays an unwillingness or inability to think of Africa as having any intrinsic interest or value.

Another commonly encountered explanation for the Iberian breakthrough is bound up in crusading, and is centered on the story of Portugal's 1415 conquest of Moroccan Ceuta, a tiny spit of African land then controlled by the Marinid dynasty, just opposite Gibraltar, near the mouth of the Mediterranean. This theory amounts to a version of empire acquired in "a fit of absence of mind" the famous phrase of the English historian John Robert Seeley, which he used to explain how Britain had come to take over much of the world, as if by serendipity, as opposed to strategic pursuit or self-interest. Applied to Portugal, what this notion means is that the lust for victory over the infidels of Morocco and the plunder and booty that went with it led the Portuguese in a more or less unconscious way into expansionary pursuits both in the Atlantic Ocean and in Africa. These began with Portuguese moves into the Canary Islands in the fourteenth century, and proceeded through the takeovers of Madeira and the Azores, and then gradually down the coast of Africa. In this narrative, the continent is usually given just as cursory a treatment as in the last. It too barely alights on stopovers in Africa before shifting to the Dias breakthrough to the Indian Ocean and the lucre of Asia.

Another traditional story line has long attributed Europe's rise to global empire to newfound progress in science and technology. According to this school, it was advances in shipbuilding—and, in particular, in the Iberian adoption of the caravel and its lateen sail—that finally made it easy for Europeans to tack against the wind and avoid hugging coastlines in pursuing long-distance sea journeys. This helped them to cast aside fears of not being able to sail back home once they reached the Canary Current. In turn, this permitted European mariners to pursue their route downward along the West African coast, then cross the Atlantic to the Caribbean, and finally, under the captaincy of Pedro Álvares Cabral, accidentally "discover"—or probably better put, locate—Brazil, in 1500. Technologically driven narratives of how Europe discovered rich new territories in the west and forged lucrative new sea routes to the East emphasize how this breakthrough at sea fundamentally relied upon navigational advances, such as the use of more advanced compasses, astrolabes, and sextants, as well as upon much more sophisticated mapmaking, with the emergence of the portolan. These were charts that displayed increasingly accurate navigational bearings and emphasized the disposition of ports, where ships could safely call. Advances like these played an important enabling role, to be sure, but they receive much less emphasis nowadays than they once did. At least in part, this, one might suppose, is because most of the developments cited, including the tacking method of sailing, were the innovations of non-Europeans, and of Arabs in particular. Such a background detracts from the historical determinism of a Western ascendancy based on science and reason that lay at the heart of many traditional accounts of the era.

Despite these objections, there are grains of truth of varying sizes in each of these explanations, as we will see. But neither taken separately nor even in combination do they constitute a truly satisfactory basis for understanding a so-called European breakthrough, lacking as they do a sufficiently powerful central motive. That people have clung to these explanations for so long is surprising, given that a much more compelling primary motivation has been hiding in plain sight all along. It revolves around the singular figure of our recent acquaintance, Mansā Mūsā, and his otherworldly wealth in gold.

An abundance of modern scholarship shows that more than any other cause or explanation it was the sensation stirred by news of

Mansā Mūsā's 1324 sojourn in Cairo and pilgrimage to Mecca, more than any of the more traditional theories, that set the creation of an Atlantic world into motion. One important gauge of the impact of Mūsā's diplomacy is the speed with which word of it spread. We know, for example, that by the late 1320s historical accounts told of maps already in circulation in Europe that announced the existence of a gold-rich empire called Mali, or "Melly," situated somewhere deep in the West African interior, south of the Sahara.

Just fourteen years after Mansā Mūsā completed his famous pilgrimage, a surviving 1339 map attributed to Angelino Dulcert described Africa, hitherto either a mapmaker's blank slate or a projection screen for wild fantasies, with a modicum of accuracy. It has been called the founding document in the so-called Majorcan school of cartography, which played a vital role in launching what would become the Age of Discovery. This map depicts the "the road to the land of the Negroes" and shows a light-skinned "Saracen King" ensconced beyond the Atlas Mountains who is said to rule over "a sandy country" and to possess "an extraordinary abundance of gold mines." (In this age, "Saracen" was often used in Europe as a generic term for dark-skinned Muslims.)

In 1346, maps fueled dreams of a land of unlimited wealth in gold that was simply awaiting discovery in Africa, and prompted a Genoa-born Majorcan adventurer named Jaume Ferrer to set out amid great fanfare for a southward voyage hugging the West African coastline aboard an "uxer," an awkward hybrid-powered ship that combined features of a rowed galley and square-rigged sailing vessel. This is the first known European attempt to explore beyond what had long been considered a navigational point of no return, Cape Bojador, located on the coast of modern-day Mauritania.*

Ferrer's explicit aim was to journey to a spot that had begun to feature widely on fourteenth-century maps of the world, in which Africa suddenly enjoyed pride of place: the Rio do Ouro (River of

---

* In 1291, a pair of Genoese brothers, Vandino and Ugoline Vivaldi, had sailed aboard two galleys in search of India, disappearing without a trace. There is no evidence that they got any farther than Cape Nun, on the coast of Morocco.

Gold), postulated in *Libro del conosçimiento* (The Book of Knowledge), a mid-fourteenth-century book that enjoyed widespread circulation in the courts of Europe. This text, written by an anonymous Spanish Franciscan and presented as a travelogue, freely mixed what is easily identifiable today as pure fancy with nuggets of seemingly well-informed details about Africa.

A few years later, Latin Europe's interest in prospecting for gold in Africa was further boosted by news of a series of lectures by the famous Berber scholar Ibn Battūtah about his travels in the region known as Sudan, given in Granada, in 1355.

The geographical feature that was then the focus of feverish speculation on these earliest of maps was almost certainly the Senegal River, which was imagined by the Europeans of this age to be a western branch of the Nile. The Senegal, a 1015-mile waterway, cuts southeastward from the coast of the modern-day nation of Senegal to headwaters in the very gold-producing heart, as it happens, of what was then the Mali Empire. Ferrer, about whom sadly little else is known, was never heard from again after setting off for West Africa, and it would be nearly another century before Europeans successfully sailed beyond the forbidden point of Cape Bojador, the locus of the powerful, westward-driving Canary Current that navigators so feared.

Although few other maps of similar scope as early as these survive, they may all be regarded as precursors to what many historians of this form say ranks among the most important and beautiful maps ever made, the so-called Catalan Atlas of 1375, a lavishly hand-drawn and -colored six-panel *mapamundi*, or map of the known world. Even though this famous product of the Majorcan school contains elements of astrology, myth, and superstition, it is the oldest surviving map from the European Middle Ages that mostly eschews long dominant church dogma in an attempt to establish a scientific geography of the true world. In it, Asia appears as an entire continent for the very first time in European mapmaking, even if the contours of that continent were still both vague and, to our eyes today, obviously speculative.* The most interesting highlight of this extraordinary document, though, is Africa: not only does one find coastal locations identified in great number, both in North and West Africa, as befits a portolan, but there is also a tremendous amount of detail about the interior of the continent, which was exceedingly rare before this map was created.

New maps like these were more than mere practical representations of the world; in this era they became, above all, compendia of new discoveries, eagerly bought up in European capitals and circulated widely. And in this regard, the most interesting feature of the Catalan Atlas is its identification of Mali and its famous king, who is called Musse Melly. The ruler is depicted as unambiguously Black and glowingly described in the following terms: "sovereign of the land of the negroes of Gineva [Ghana]. This king is the richest and noblest of all these lands due to the abundance of gold that is extracted from his lands."

By the time of the Catalan Atlas, European mapmakers had already spent the middle decades of the fourteenth century busily outdoing one another in embellishing Mansā Mūsā's imperial legend. The irony here is that in life, as we have seen, the old king of Mali never quite managed to achieve his dream of parity with the most powerful emperors and monarchs of the wide world. Posthumously, though, through the Catalan Atlas, his hopes of recognition and attention were more than realized. In fact, seated atop a throne, as seen on this book's cover, his crowned and serene likeness is rendered in much the same manner as a European monarch. In one hand, he holds a golden scepter, symbolizing his authority, and in the other, a golden orb, which represents his enormous wealth. The principal novelty is his unambiguous Blackness. Surrounding him, arrayed in every direction, are the great cities of his realm, Tim-

---

* Maps that depicted the continents of Asia, Europe, and Africa, along with the oceans and internal continental seas, began appearing in the Islamic world by the tenth century. A prominent example is the map of Ali al-Masudi, who had traveled from Spain to Turkistan; it mentions East African polities, as well as China.

buktu, Gao, and Mali itself, as well as numerous mosques. Against this backdrop he is depicted as giving audience to a turbaned Tuareg dressed in a jade-green robe who has arrived in Mali from the west astride a camel in order to take part in the lively and lucrative caravan trade for African gold.

The Catalan Atlas did more than alert European royalty to the suspected location of the world's greatest source of the precious metal. It drove an explosion of a new kind of mapmaking that had the mysteries of African geography as its focus. This, more than dreams of India or technological advances in and of themselves, gave the incentive for ever bolder exploration. In some sense, though, the atlas must have also acted as a key to a puzzle. For one thing, the map's panels offer guidance to those who might seek to cross the desert to trade in gold, indicating routes through the daunting Sahara Desert used by traders: "Through this place pass the merchants who travel to the land of the negroes of Guinea, which place they call the valley of the Dra'a."* Of even greater relevance is a detail that purports to show the most distant point along the western coast of Africa that the Majorcan Jaume Ferrer reached in his search for the River of Gold, albeit with no further record left to history confirming his return. The atlas seems to situate the terminus of Ferrer's voyage near Cape Juby, in the extreme south of present-day Morocco, near the border with Western Sahara.

By Ferrer's time, to be sure, there had already been a long and abiding interest in India among Europeans, but "India," just like the word "Moor" or "Saracen," meant profoundly different things in different contexts and was long used, confusingly, as a toponym for both northeastern Africa and points beyond. As for China, meanwhile, at least since the celebrated (and in some of its details fantastical) account of Marco Polo's travels, published in the thirteenth century, it could no longer be considered a real mystery. In this same

---

* Guinea, or Guiné, had begun to turn up in European maps and documents in the early fourteenth century, as in the 1320 map of the Genoese chartmaker Giovanni da Carignano as a generic name for the entire sub-Saharan realm inhabited by Black peoples in Africa.

era, during the rule of the Mongols, overland travel between Europe and Asia had, in fact, been all but wide open, contributing to a very lively trade along the Silk Road. The history of maritime exploration during the hundred years after the publication of the Catalan Atlas would be dominated not by thoughts of Asia but by the emphatic desire to nail down the source of West Africa's wealth in gold.

4

ENTER THE AVIZ

THE EXACT ORIGINS OF the Catalan Atlas itself are still disputed. The document is most commonly attributed to a certain Abraham Cresques, a Jewish man residing in Majorca who is believed to have been from Catalonia or North Africa. Others theorize, however, that the document was the work of a commonly postulated mathematically and scientifically inclined "Jewish school" of mapmaking in Majorca that included Abraham's son, Jehuda. As sketchy as they are, even details as incomplete as these nonetheless impart to us a world of deeply significant information. Indeed, as frustrating as it is for us today and for our story, there is nothing particular to Africa in this era about the lack of surviving, firsthand written sources about documents like this, or even about events of world-historical importance. Only a single personal letter survives from the famous "navigator," Prince Henry, for example. What is known about his actions, or imputed about his mind-set, reposes overwhelmingly on a single source, the accounts of a Portuguese royal chronicler and hagiographer, Gomes Eanes de Zurara, who seems to have taken dictation about events from Prince Henry long after they took place.

In the fourteenth century, the island of Majorca, then a possession of the crown of Aragon, was a richly multicultural commercial entrepôt, where the worlds of the European and African Mediterranean came together almost as one. At a time of mounting hostility toward Jews, Aragon treated the people of this faith with a rare relative hospitality. "From 1247, Jaime I encouraged [Jews] to enter his realms 'for the sake of dwelling and settling in our lands,'" the historian Felipe Fernández-Armesto has written. "They remained welcome in Aragon's peninsular dominions for most of the next century and a half. They found refuge there from sufferings in outlying parts of the Aragonese world, when they were expelled from Roussillon or Montpelier, for instance, in 1307." And it was this openness that gradually positioned the Jewish community of Majorca to play the crucial and little-known role of intermediary between two adjacent continents, Africa and Europe. This was due in part to the long-standing commercial traditions of the Jews, and in part to the fact that members of their religion, unlike Christians, were allowed to travel freely and even dwell in Islamic North Africa, often without being required to wear special clothing identifying them by their faith.

Jews had been trading in small numbers in North Africa in this manner since the middle of the thirteenth century; at the same time, Genoa, which was then among Europe's most outward-looking powers, began to establish commercial outposts both there and in the southern Iberian peninsula. In all probability, already by the end of the fourteenth century, Jews, possibly accompanied by Genoese, had already crossed the Sahara repeatedly, reaching the trading cities of the western Sahel. In the words of a modern-day historian, "Antonio Malfante, a Genoese who travelled to the Tuāt oasis [in modern Algeria] in 1447, refers to the 'many Jews who lead a good life here, for they are under the protection of the several rulers, each of whom defends his own clients.'" Jews residing in places like these employed letters of credit as they traded southward for gold with Muslim participants in the trans-Saharan caravan commerce, often exchanging clothing woven by their coreligionists of the Maghreb for gold supplied by West African empires like Ghana, and later Mali. Such mechanisms formed part of what the historian of the Sahara Ghislaine Lydon has called the "paper economy of faith" that first

Jewish and then Muslim merchants had set up in commercial networks that spanned the great desert beginning centuries earlier.

卍

BY THE TWELFTH CENTURY ALREADY, visions of African gold had led
the Genoese to also establish trading enclaves, then known as "factories," on Ceuta, with Muslim consent. This small Moroccan peninsula projecting into the Mediterranean faced Islamic-ruled Iberia to
the north and Muslim North Africa to the south, and was an important northern terminus of the lucrative caravan trade in African gold.
It was against a backdrop of growing knowledge of the sources of
African wealth (whether furnished through expanding Muslim and
Jewish trading networks, or through increasing European profi-
ciency in mapmaking and navigation) that the early history of Portugal and of its precocious search for overseas empire would play
out. The starting point for this expansion can be plausibly dated to
the Battle of Aljubarrota, in 1385, when the armies of an illegitimate
prince, João I, routed the forces of Castile amid a contest over disputed succession and established the throne of a new imperial line,
the Aviz dynasty.

Separated by just ten years, the production of the Catalan Atlas
(1375)—with its details about the rich, worldly realm of Mansā Mūsā
(albeit by then already dead, circa 1335)—and the establishment of
Aviz rule over Portugal arrived at a critical transitional moment in
European history. The second half of the fourteenth century would
be profoundly marked by two grand phenomena, one of them widely
recognized and the other much less so. The first of these was the
Black Death, which peaked in Europe during the middle years of
the century, killing between one-third and three-fifths of the western European population. This medieval pandemic resulted in dire
labor shortages, which almost certainly fueled interest in Italy and
Iberia in acquiring African slaves. Then, shortly before the century's close came a dramatic balance of payments crisis as output
from Europe's silver mines, possibly due to those labor shortages,
and supplies of Sahelian gold simultaneously declined. Disruption

in these gold supplies has been linked to political instability in the western Sudan amid succession crises in Mali.

Periodic balance of payments crises involving trade via the Levant with the East had been a destabilizing factor in Europe from antiquity. This was because Europe, as an economically marginal part of the slowly emerging world economy, had few manufactured products to offer richer trade centers in China, the Indian subcontinent, and Southeast Asia in exchange for such highly prized luxury goods as silks, fine cottons, and spices. In the fourteenth and fifteenth centuries, chronic shortage of specie was so serious as to even render religious pilgrimage, itself a tremendous drain on reserves of precious metals, prohibitive.

As the great French historian Fernand Braudel wrote, since the rise of the Sahelian Ghana Empire in the early High Middle Ages, gold sourced in Africa had been Europe's providential solution to these vexing problems: "Since the thirteenth century, the Maghreb evidently played the role of the gold mine without which commerce in the Mediterranean and in the rich and powerful Levant would have ground to a halt, or at least been jeopardized."

Between the 1340s and 1370s, during the heyday of the Mali Empire, vast quantities of African gold poured into European coffers; from four hundred to eight hundred kilograms of Sudanese gold, mostly in the form of dust, were registered annually by Genoa alone. As Mali declined in the waning years of the fourteenth century and during the first decade of the fifteenth, however, mints across Europe experienced acute shortages of gold, with some of them, such as Flanders, which halted production from 1402 to 1410, forced to suspend their operations or shut down altogether. Gold coinage in England cratered in this era, from an annual average of £56,064 during the 1360s to a yearly average of £4,715 in the decade from 1401 to 1410. This led to a severe contraction in liquidity and the reversion with a vengeance to a more primitive economic system based on barter. By midcentury, Pope Pius II summed up the general sentiment of the day with regard to the shortage of specie in Europe saying, "The problem of money predominates, and without it, as they commonly say, nothing can be done aright." For Europeans, of course, "money-changers" often meant Jews, and this gold crisis became an important factor in the wave of ferocious riots and pogroms against Jewish adherents that swept many parts of Europe during this era.

The establishment of the Aviz dynasty and Portugal's early quest for overseas empire in Africa must be seen in this light in order for it to be properly understood. A peace with Castile, Portugal's larger and richer neighbor, would not be signed until 1411. The intervening years of back-and-forth conflict across the border left Portugal, a poor, scarcely urbanized land to begin with, thoroughly depleted economically and in urgent need of new sources of revenue.

The country's population, numbering barely a million, lived in a state of generalized subsistence and social immobility, with most of João's subjects barely getting by via barter and never straying far from their rural homes. Beyond the salt of Setubal, wine, and dried fish, Portugal had few products worthy of trade. And the new crown desperately needed to find the wherewithal to ensure its continued survival, especially against the persistently covetous designs of Castile.

After many years of upheaval and conflict on the Iberian peninsula, others might have judged that what was most needed at this time was a period of peace to establish a stronger footing for Portugal's new rulers, but the Aviz clan had different notions. After winning power in what was essentially a coup backed by an armed uprising, João saw his task as having to hurriedly construct a new elite virtually from scratch. To accomplish this, he enthusiastically embraced the violent ethos of an era of crusading and chivalry. As he pursued this approach, João leaned heavily upon his own six sons, including the most famous of them, Henry, born in 1394. Portugal was too small and poor to fulfill the ordinary aspirations to wealth of a royal clan like this based on its own land and resources, and for this reason, Henry, the third born, with no realistic hope of ever inheriting the crown, trained his gaze outside of the immediate realm, posthumously earning him the title the Navigator.

In the early fifteenth century, at Prince Henry's nearly constant prodding, the Aviz would adopt the famous watchword of Pope Urban II at the Council of Clermont four hundred years earlier and apply it with a vengeance to lands that lay both outside of Europe and the traditional crusading grounds of the Near East. Urban had urged southern Europeans to venture out beyond their own lands, which were surrounded by mountains and "shut in by the sea." Wariness about challenging Castile on Iberian soil and Europe's loss of initiative in crusading in the Levant both pointed the Portuguese toward overseas conquest. And as we have seen, conquest initially came to mean Ceuta. Hitherto little known to the Portuguese, this projection of land at the mouth of the Mediterranean became an attractive target due to a strong confluence of both interests and circumstances. As targets go, it had the merit of being modest in size and close by, situated only 160 miles from the Portuguese coast. With Castile pushing into the Canary Islands, Portugal seems to have feared being left behind by its biggest Iberian rival in the very opening phase of the struggle for overseas empire, and Ceuta offered the prospect of a conquest of its own.

The Portuguese had other objectives still, such as currying favor with the all-powerful Catholic Church by waging war against infidels. But at a time of dire, Europe-wide thirst for gold, it was probably the prospect of gaining access to African sources of the metal by seizing the terminal point of the rich trans-Saharan trade that ranked highest of all among the Portuguese priorities.

Word of the Portuguese capture of Ceuta, which was won in the space of a mere thirteen hours by a large assault fleet on August 21, 1415, reverberated thunderously throughout Christian Europe, announcing that Lisbon was an important new power to be reckoned with. Prince Henry, then all of twenty-one, did not direct the assault, but nonetheless played a leading role, charging out in front of the invading troops early in the attack at some personal risk, and thus providing vivid material that would be used as the foundation for an expanding personal legend of chivalry.

The Portuguese soon discovered to their dismay, however, that control of Ceuta alone did little to ensure mastery of the trade in African gold. The North African terminus of the trans-Saharan commerce in gold remained in Muslim hands, shifting fifty kilometers westward; Tangier, the new terminus, was a much more daunting military target than Ceuta, as Lisbon would later learn at great expense. In the meantime, merely holding Ceuta would require garrisoning troops there and building costly fortifications.

In wholly unanticipated ways, though, for Portugal the exigencies involved in retaining control over Ceuta turned that small territory into an important site of early experimentation in both colonization and empire building. It was an unpopular deployment for Portuguese troops, and even the Order of Christ, the offshoot of the Knights Templar that Henry headed, resisted calls for it to help defend Ceuta against the Marinids of Morocco. With few other options, Lisbon deployed prisoners and other social undesirables there from Portugal instead. This gave Ceuta the dubious distinction of being a pioneer of this tactic to populate and police overseas outposts. It was a practice that would be repeated in one new Portuguese colony throughout this dawning age.

5

ISLANDS IN THE OFFING

H ENRY MAY HAVE REVELED in the glory that came with conquering Ceuta, but it is not for nothing that his personal attentions soon shifted—indeed lastingly—toward another objective. The Canary Islands, although far more distant and already partially controlled by Castile, would become much more prized in Henry's eyes and would replace Ceuta as the premier domain of imperial experimentation until the 1470s. At its closest point, this island group, nowadays a part of Spain, sits only sixty-two miles off the farthest southern reaches of Morocco's Atlantic coast. The Canaries seldom feature in world history books, and even less in discussions of current affairs, but this was the very first European colony in the Atlantic, and indeed the place where Portuguese, Spaniards, and others deepened their taste for overseas empire, along with many of the darkest methods of achieving it. These included chattel slavery, genocide, violent religious indoctrination, and settler colonialism, all of which saw their Atlantic debuts on these islands.

By the time Portugal had seized Ceuta, the indigenous peoples of the Canary Islands had already experienced decades of atrocities at the hands of the Europeans. The islands were mercilessly raided throughout the fourteenth century, and their inhabitants, a Stone Age culture whose natives are currently thought to have been distantly related to the peoples of nearby Saharan Africa, themselves onetime rulers of Muslim Spain. The Canarians were ruthlessly abducted and shipped off to Europe, where they fed a highly lucrative market in slaves; later, they were traded as chattel on nearby islands in the Atlantic for work on early sugar plantations.

Despite this, Spanish efforts to settle some of the Canary Islands were fiercely resisted by the native population. In fact, European efforts to fully overcome the inhabitants of the Canaries would not reach fruition until 1496. By that time, though, the doors of West Africa had already been flung open wide by the Portuguese, with world-transforming effects. Dias, by then, had also sailed into the Indian Ocean and Columbus had "discovered" the Americas.

At first, it had seemed certain to their Iberian conquerors that the Canarians would be easy prey. The Europeans had immediately judged them to be primitive because they lacked any tradition of seafaring, and also because they wore few clothes and possessed implements made of only wood or animal horns. It is not hard to imagine how cultural features like these powerfully flattered European beliefs in their own superiority. In 1393, a heavily armed Castilian expedition captured a local king and queen on the island of Lanzarote, along with 160 prisoners, many of whom were shipped off to Spain as slaves. The leader of the raiding party, Gonzalo Pérez Martel, told the Castilian king the Canaries would be "easy to conquer . . . and at small cost." One hundred years later, Columbus, arriving in a land the locals called Ayiti (Haiti), would express the same overweening confidence. According to the Spanish missionary and historian Bartolomé de las Casas, Columbus wrote in his diary, "We saw naked people. They were a people poor in everything." Shortly thereafter, he wrote this of an island that is believed to have been populated at the time by three million people: "with 50 men all of them could be held in subjection and can be made to do whatever one might wish." This was chillingly prescient, given what would befall the Taino indigenes of Haiti, whose population would be reduced to a mere five hundred within fifty years, hastened by exposure to new infectious diseases. For our purposes, though, Lanzarote and Haiti are best seen as bookends, with a steep European learning curve coming in Africa in between them. Sheer arrogance and superficial impressions, based on ignorance about the languages, religions, and governments of native peoples, would lead to conflict and devastation throughout the Atlantic world. Less well known because the "winner's" history seldom speaks of it, they would also serve up frequent and dramatic humblings of the European newcomers as well.

The Canarians, for example, often fought off large-scale attacks and defended themselves with remarkable effectiveness against Iberian forces, employing sharpened staves made from honed tree branches, and especially by throwing rocks, "with enough force to knock an armored knight off his horse." Alvide da Ca' da Mosto, a fifteenth-century Venetian slave trader and chronicler of maritime explorations employed by Prince Henry who has become widely known as Cadamosto, sounded like an eighteenth-century British officer complaining about the frustratingly "irregular" and yet effective tactics of George Washington's fighters when he complained of the Canarians: "They leap from rock to rock, barefooted, like goats, and clear jumps of incredible width. They throw stones accurately and powerfully, so that they can hit whatever they wish. They have such strong arms that with a few blows they can shatter a shield in pieces. . . . I conclude that this is the most dexterous and nimble race in the world."

In 1424, an indigenous militia routed the first large-scale attempt, and merely the first of many, by men sent by Prince Henry to enforce his claim to the islands, which was disputed with Spain. Later, in 1468, inhabitants of another island, now known as Gran Canaria, even defeated something that was exceeding rare in the early annals of European imperialism in the Atlantic: a combined offensive by Portuguese and Spanish fighting together as allies. This time, the islanders prevailed using wooden swords and shields, copying the weaponry of the invaders.

Completely unheralded nowadays, these were the very first of what was about to become an almost endless series of colonial wars fought by Europeans against native peoples around the world over the next half millennium. Many more of them than we hear about ended in humiliating defeat for the colonizers, and none more so than the victory of former slaves over European armies in Haiti a little more than three centuries hence.

I flew into Las Palmas from Madrid on an evening in March, on my first visit to the Canaries, eager to see what traces, if any, of this history remained. The balmy evening air immediately attested to the fact that I was not in Europe, and yet every subsequent experience would say that I was—politically, legally, and above all, culturally, whatever the geography suggested. After breezing through the tourist-filled airport, a taxi took me into the city, following a coastline lit up by oil rigs just offshore, twinkling in the distance like casinos. Finally, we pulled into the old city at the very center of town, a world of cobblestone pavement and terraced hillsides, first laid out more than half a millennium ago. It could not have been more typical of Spain, down to the narrow streets lined with iron-railed balconies, as well as the restaurants full of typical dishes like paella with chorizo and tortilla española. I knew there would be no Canarians for me to see, but found there was little to remember them by, either. Not even so much as a prominent plaque. Over the next few days, that left long walks to visit public squares dominated by old cathedrals, where I encountered haggard-looking Africans who had made their way here by perilous boat trips from Senegal and Mauritania, desperately hoping to reach the European mainland. I wondered if the Spanish into whose midst they had fallen registered the irony that their forefathers, many of them penniless and scorned at home, had made the opposite journey long ago. As I wandered other highlights, like the mustard-colored home with orate entranceways and high wooden ceilings that Columbus had visited in 1492, when it was the governor's residence, there seemed little hint of that. This had been his place of stopover while repairing the helm of *La Pinta* and replacing its sails in preparation for his groundbreaking voyage. And to cash in on the hordes of tourists bearing euros, it had been turned into a museum in his honor.

Once Europeans had fully conquered the islands, the Canarian population and culture were wiped out with a rare thoroughness, a grim event that remains little recognized, least of all, I discovered, in the popular museum to Columbus. There are many ways to think of the commencement of the modern era. And as I dodged the tourists posing for pictures, it occurred to me that this genocide, which befell the Canarians decades before the extermination of the native population of Hispaniola, was as plausible a milestone as any to rival the voyages of the Genoese admiral as the dawning event of a new age.

Few notions have remained so persistent and unexamined as the belief that Europe's subsequent global rise was due to superiority of one form or another. This is true whether one considers technology, belief systems, or a notion that has become widely but not universally repudiated today: innate racial qualities. Nowadays, the idea that medieval Europeans enjoyed any lead whatsoever in science and technology over Muslims, South Asians, or East Asians doesn't withstand even passing scrutiny; as we have already seen with navigation, in many areas Europeans, in fact, lagged quite significantly. Equally dubious is the once common belief that there was something unique about Christianity that inclined Europeans to advantageous cultural virtues like reason, enterprise, and thrift. Confucianism, to pick but one of many possible counterexamples, clearly suffers nothing by comparison with Christianity in any of these regards. But the difficulties in overcoming the Canarians described above also help illustrate why any advantages that Iberians enjoyed over West Africans early in the fifteenth century were also far less dramatic than most people today might expect—that is, when these advantages existed at all.

Few pause to consider, meanwhile, why Prince Henry or his Spanish rivals so desperately desired to control the Canary Islands. Reading backward in time from the present, already knowing the history of Western empire, there is a subtle temptation to imagine that the man who came to be known as the Navigator was already prosecuting with bold forethought some comprehensive vision of maritime expansion, and that the Canaries were seen by him as a stepping-stone to India or even to the Americas. (The latter existed then only at the level of fantastical speculation. Brazil, for example, was a name used beginning in the fourteenth century for a phantom island rumored to exist somewhere in the Atlantic.) Henry's motives, however, were altogether more practical and down-to-earth, and the importance of the Canary Islands to him, like that of Ceuta, was entirely bound up in Africa, and more specifically in the prince's undying dreams of establishing a stranglehold on the trade in the continent's gold.

The Canary Islands were thought to be located at roughly the same latitude as the forbidding Cape Bojador, which Europeans took to be a navigational boundary beyond which no one could safely travel. And it was imagined that control of the islands with such proximity to the continent might offer the Portuguese (or Spanish) a staging ground from which they could tap the ancient caravan trade in gold and perhaps tempt their chances in the world beyond. The Canaries' latitude does roughly coincide with the southern boundary of the Sahara Desert and the commencement of the geographic region we have already spoken of often, the Sahel. (The word "Sahel," incidentally, derives from the Arabic word *sāhil*, which means shore.) This broad and arid belt of scrubland, home to the great Sudanic kingdoms of the African Middle Ages was, in effect, a shore lapped by the dunes of the world's largest desert. Having failed to control the gold trade by seizing Ceuta, Prince Henry now set his sights on finding a way to intercept the gold of the Sudan even before it entered the desert, which is to say on the Sahel's metaphorical shore.

The existence of a "pagan" race of inhabitants on the Canary Islands was a further incentive for exploration of Africa, if one were needed. In a typically economical assessment of this question, Prince Henry's official chronicler, Cadamosto, condescendingly wrote of the Canarians whom he witnessed: "They have no faith, nor do they believe in God: some worship the sun, others the moon and planets, and have strange, idolatrous fantasies." This gave Henry the hope that somewhere farther to the south, along the African coast, there might exist other peoples who, distinct from the Moors, did not embrace Islam; peoples who could be converted to Christianity and perhaps enlisted in Lisbon's struggle against the powerful infidels of North Africa and the Near East. In his *Crónica de Guiné* of 1450, Gomes Eanes de Zurara, Prince Henry's devoted biographer, listed five motives for Henry's push down the coast of Africa, one of which was to "find Christian princes, in whom the good nature and love for Christ were so manifested, who would want to help against enemies of the Catholic faith."

Thinking like this, which persisted well into the sixteenth century, thrived alongside the profound geographical misunderstandings that still prevailed on the Iberian peninsula and throughout Europe in the 1450s. Like many others of his time, Henry believed that beyond Cape Bojador, somewhere along the African coast lay an immense east-west river, a *Sinus Aethiopicus*, which cut into the heart of the continent and provided a shortcut to the Red Sea and to Abyssinia. This was the land imputed to be the home of a Christian African sovereign named Prester John. This figure of legend supposedly led a vast and powerful kingdom whose armies the Portuguese dreamed they could enlist in a crusade together to crush the Mamluk Turks, whose power sat astride the old Silk Road routes of the Near East. A quest to find Prester John stands alongside the other motives cited earlier, which have been traditionally stressed (and, I would argue, overemphasized), in explaining Europe's Iberian-led engagement with Africa in the fifteenth century.

According to one careful study of Portuguese navigation during the era of Prince Henry, common allusions to the Indies and to Indians in Henry's time were nothing less than references to Africa itself:

> The "India" that Henrican documents have in mind is in fact north-east Africa. Ever since the supposed location of Prester John's legendary Christian empire had been transferred by southern European publications from Asia to Africa early in the fourteenth century, the area of the African continent lying east of the Nile and south of Egypt had become known to cosmographers as "India Tertia." Thus, when Henrican documents speak of "Indians" it is to the Black Christian inhabitants of the Prester's

*empire in north-eastern Africa that they refer. The inhabitants
of that empire were regularly referred to by Europeans in the fifteenth century as Indians.*

Campaigns to subdue and dominate Morocco and to capture the
Canary Islands would consume Prince Henry for much of the rest of
his life. But the military and diplomatic efforts to enforce claims over
the Canaries, which ended in complete failure, are best understood
as being more about the gold of continental Africa than about the
islands themselves. Their real purpose was to help pull an end run
in the bitter, ongoing struggle against Muslims in northern Africa.
What the Portuguese sought was not a way around Africa, as has
been frequently supposed, but a way into it that sidestepped the hostile Maghreb region.

PORTUGAL'S FAILED EFFORTS to wrest control over the Canary
Islands from Spain would spur it in ironic ways to become the most
successful explorer of the Atlantic world in the fifteenth century,
with the first of its many collateral breakthroughs coming in the
early 1420s. First came Madeira in 1424, and shortly thereafter, the
Azores. Although tiny, these islands provided Henry considerable
new sources of political patronage and income. Most important,
working in tandem with Genoese operators, the prince came into
ownership of what was probably the first sugar mill of the Atlantic
world on the newly conquered island of Madeira; it proved to be
both a lucrative investment and a profound harbinger of the future.
By the middle of the century, Madeira was producing almost 70
tons of sugar per year, and in 1456 a British ship landing from there
provisioned the parlors of Bristol with one of their first supplies of
this new luxury commodity. At the time, it was still mostly prized
as an exotic medicinal.

The Portuguese determined that the only practical way to produce sugar in volume involved copious inputs of slave labor. Free
peoples, white or otherwise, including even the most disfavored ele-

ments of society, would simply not put up with the endless brutality of cane work. As one historian has attested, "the plantation production of sugar was among the deadliest innovations known to humanity." Slaves were initially brought to Madeira from the Canaries, but as sugar production soared (reaching 200 tons a year by 1472, and then quickly doubling and doubling again by the turn of the century), those rapidly depopulating islands proved to be inadequate sources. Portugal itself was too lightly peopled to provide large numbers of laborers. Madeira's extraordinarily heavy forest, meanwhile, provided cheap and abundant timber, and this could be used both to fire mills and to build ships on the island that were used to mount slave raids against the Imraugen, a tribe of fishermen who inhabited the northwestern coast of Africa.

In 1433, Henry personally ordered a mariner named Gil Eanes to sail down the West African coast with instructions to try to venture past the psychological barrier of Cape Bojador. Freely confessing his own terror, Eanes ignored the order and returned home directly after reaching the Canary Islands. Nearing his destination after being sent back the following year, he was surprised when his men didn't mutiny. Approaching the continent, they had seen that the seas around what they thought was Bojador (in reality, they'd reached Cape Juby, 175 miles north of their goal) were neither black nor churning with whirlwinds, as legend held, but rather "as easy to sail in as the waters at home." Eanes, for all of his troubles, failed to bring back anything of greater note than a sprig of rosemary found on the shore. Another mission to the same region, in 1435, reported news of tracks of men and camels in the coastal sands. Yet another expedition, in 1436, claimed to have reached the Rio do Ouro, which turned out not to be a river at all, but rather, a bay. Unfortunately there was no sign of gold whatsoever.

Despite all of this and no doubt driven in part by the Catalan Atlas, Prince Henry retained a conviction that, with persistence, a mission to the River of Gold or beyond would win him access to the mines of Mali and their untold wealth. Others in the Portuguese court were more skeptical, and amid competing priorities, such as the contest with Castile over the Canary Islands and an ongoing war in Morocco, they opposed the southward push along the African coast as an exorbitant distraction. Even Zurara, normally the most compliant of hagiographers, hinted at this in his 1434 account:

> *for in the first years, seeing the big fleets the Prince [Henry] put together with such expense, they neglected the care of their own properties, and busied themselves with sharing what little they knew. The longer the thing took to produce results, the bigger the accusations grew. And the worst of it was that beyond the vulgar ones, even important [people] spoke of it almost in a scornful manner, believing it was a waste of resources and labor from which no profit could return.*

This second-guessing of Henry's leadership, as well as of his interest in costly and thus far entirely speculative economic ventures in Africa, deepened with a major Portuguese defeat in an attack on Tangier, in 1437, which was aimed at seizing control of the northern terminus of Africa's gold trade. The debacle transformed the political climate in Lisbon, forcing a long slowdown in southward expeditions down the African coast. And this hiatus raises a fascinating historical comparison and counterfactual scenario involving roughly contemporaneous events and oddly parallel circumstances between Ming Dynasty China and Aviz Portugal.

Between 1405 and 1433, Zheng He, a Muslim eunuch in the employ of the Ming emperor, Yongle, undertook seven great voyages during which he displayed China's colors and its unmatched maritime power, returning home with African giraffes and immense stores of other treasure and exotica from a broad swath of the Indian Ocean stretching to the eastern coasts of Africa. Zheng He's fleets were typically composed of two hundred or so vessels, making them seventy ships more numerous than the famous Spanish Armada of 1588 (in addition, its vessels were far larger on average than the Spanish Armada's and they carried twenty thousand crack soldiers on board). For reasons that will probably never be fully grasped, however, these enormous missions in search of trade and tribute were judged not to be worth the candle, and they were abruptly called off.

Some have argued that austere and inwardly turned Confucianists in the Ming court prevailed in a contentious debate against rival factions about the costs and rewards of exploration and of the projection of naval power on the high seas. This caused China to abruptly withdraw from the world of maritime exploration and even destroy Zheng He's fleet, a startling shift given its enormous size. Little more than a decade afterward, following a brief period during which they constrained him, Prince Henry's conservative skeptics, by contrast, were resoundingly defeated in a very similar debate. Henry's austerity-minded critics had wanted to recenter Lisbon's power in the western Mediterranean and nearby Atlantic, focusing their small kingdom's limited resources on crusading and plunder in Morocco.* But after 1448, others took note of the fast-rising numbers of Black slaves being taken from the shoulder of Africa, and with once reliable sources of slaves in eastern Europe and the Middle East drying up or cut off after the Muslim capture of Constantinople in 1453, sentiments shifted back fatefully in the Navigator's favor. This critical turnabout in Atlantic history is documented in Zurara's *Crónica da Guiné*, the officially sanctioned account of the voyages of discovery down the West Africa coast under the auspices of Prince Henry between 1434 and 1448. After noting the ease with which the Portuguese took captives, whom they identified as "Moors," Zurara wrote those who had opposed Henry's order to push southward down the African coast confessed their foolishness. Outdoing themselves to flatter their patron, some went so far as to predict that because of the haul in slaves Henry would go down as another Alexander the Great.[†]

---

* An extensive account of the Zheng He voyages and their implications, including an exploration of the counterfactual involving a possible encounter with the Portuguese, is contained in my *Everything Under the Heavens*.

† In the same vein, a generation hence, advisers to Ferdinand and Isabella, Spain's monarchs, similarly briefly groused that the "Enterprise of the Indies" was a waste of time and money.

6

THE AFRICAN MAIN

BY THE 1450S, ACCORDING to Henry's chronicler Cadamosto, the slave-trading station built at Henry's behest at Arguim, an island off modern-day Mauritania, was supplying eight hundred to a thousand slaves a year to a burgeoning Portuguese market in Africans. As ridiculous as a comparison to Alexander now sounds, in terms of human capital, this amounted to an immense bounty for those times, and ships began departing Portugal for Africa in large convoys to partake in the traffic. The rush to get in on the slavery business was such that even the bishop of Algarve outfitted a caravel to acquire slaves on the continent's coast, helping launch the Catholic Church's long history of profiting from African bondage.

The early Luso-African encounters around slavery of the 1440s were purely constructed around coastal raiding. The Aviz dynasty was built upon the foundations of a predatory military class, and at the heart of its young expansionary project lay one essential idea: war should always be made to pay for itself. Henry's costly search down the coast of Africa for gold had so far yielded little of the metal, much less the control over its supply he coveted. As the expenses underpinning the drive for gold piled up, other sources of income needed to be found in order to justify sustaining exploration. Framed at its simplest, gold had led the Portuguese to slaves, and slaves drove the expansion of a lucrative new industry, sugar, which would transform the world like few products have in history, and in doing so would also produce one of history's greatest human tolls.

While this decade was marked by a relative lull in expeditions, it should not be taken to suggest that nothing important was happening in terms of Portugal's gold-prospecting efforts, nor indeed in terms of giving shape to the budding political project of Iberian imperialism or to ideas about race that would shape the Atlantic world for centuries. Quite the contrary. Along the coast of present-day Mauritania, the squires and other minor nobles who dominated the exploration business—and business it was—sent ashore small teams of men, often with a horse or two and dressed in full armor, to ensnare local residents for sale into slavery. To the befuddlement and certain terror of their victims, the raiders often charged toward their quarry shouting "Santiago," the name of the patron saint of Spain, but also honored by the Portuguese, whose supposed miraculous apparitions in moments of conquest like these were believed to confer blessing on any crusading enterprise. It was in this manner that in 1441 the leader of one expedition, a man named Antáo Gonçalves, skirmished with a man identified as a Moor who was walking with a camel, and then returned to the same site at nightfall, where he captured a woman he described as a "black Mooress." Some consider this woman of unknown name to have been the index case, or first victim, in the formation of the transatlantic slave trade centered on dark-skinned Africans. This is not because she was sent to the Americas, which of course was then still undiscovered, but because of the significance apparently attached to her race, which from this point onward became an increasingly important criterion of eligibility for enslavement among Europeans.

Gonçalves returned to Portugal with a yield of only ten slaves, which might seem to be a derisory "catch." And yet even this was enough for him to be made the governor of the Portuguese town of Tomar and granted a knighthood in Henry's powerful Order of Christ. For the Portuguese, far from a disappointment, this was an encouraging start and, as no reader will doubt, far more lucrative seizures of Africans were soon to come.

Three years later, after receiving permission from Henry, who by that time enjoyed rights to all of Portugal's Africa trade, a party of six caravels set out for Africa hoping to capture more slaves, netting 235 after repeatedly mounting ambushes in full armor in which they, too, screamed phrases like "Santiago" and "São Jorge." When the returning ships docked at the southern Portuguese port city of Lagos, their arrival back home caused a sensation. Word spread quickly of the presence of Black captives, and large crowds turned out to witness what was the very first large sale of sub-Saharan Africans in Europe. In fact, even Prince Henry, who by that time had taken up residence in the nearby town of Sagres, turned out in person, observing the novel spectacle of an African slave market from "upon a powerful horse, accompanied by his people, looking out for his share."

This sole surviving account of the event was provided by Zurara, whose words reflect a surprising amount of moral ambivalence, especially for an author whose ordinary mode with regard to Henry, his lord, was outright sycophancy: "I pray to you that my tears are not damaging to my conscience, not because of your law over them, but [because] your humanity compels mine to cry piteously over their suffering. And if these brute animals, with their savage feelings, by virtue of natural perception can tell the hurt done to their like, what do you expect from this my human nature, seeing in front of my eyes, as I do that miserable people, reminding me they are of the generation of the sons of Adam."

Zurara went on to invoke even more explicitly the emotional difficulty he experienced witnessing the suffering of fellow human beings who were victims of abduction from faraway lands, long transit at sea, and sale into bondage. Judging by his words, he was particularly affected by the horrors of separation of husbands from wives, and mothers from their children, things that would quickly become pillars of the transatlantic slave experience. "Who could finish that apportionment without great struggle," he asks, describing women who threw themselves onto the ground in lamentation, only to be beaten or whipped.

In nearly the same breath, though, he spoke in ways that drew a bold line under the distinction that had begun to be made with Antáo Gonçalves's capture of a "black Mooress" three years earlier. "It was a marvelous sight to behold," he said of the freshly disembarked captives. "For among them there were some of a reasonable degree of whiteness, handsome and well made; others less, who resembled leopards in their color; others as black as Ethiopians, and so ill-formed, as well in their faces as their bodies, that it seemed to the beholders as if they saw the forms of a lower hemisphere."*

In this way, the notion that the Black peoples who inhabited this part of Africa, which was coming under exploration by Europeans for the first time, were uniquely wretched and lacking in the redeeming attributes of civilization by virtue of their color was first mobilized in the 1440s. And this idea was married with another, equally damning thought: these were pagans, perfectly distinct in religious terms from the Moors whom the Portuguese recognized as Muslims, and hence, even though mortal enemies, people who were, like themselves, nonetheless "of the Book." From this early date, the Portuguese had begun to actively employ both of these ideas to provide justification for their impressment of Blacks as slaves. But as they encountered African societies with robust states in the decade ahead, the European newcomers would have to temper these views, recognizing the real limitations of their power in far-off lands and bowing to local laws about human bondage, at least temporarily.

For now, though, it is worth observing how Zurara took advantage of the opportunity to return to his normal role as unstinting hagiographer, to celebrate the rationale—or alibi, really—for the birth of a trade in Black slaves under Henry's auspices. There was legitimate "delight," he wrote, in "the salvation of those souls which

---

* A common belief in the Western Christendom of that era held that the region south of the Equator was almost unbearably hot and that the peoples who inhabited these reaches were burned and disfigured by the sun.

before were lost," meaning condemned to a life without faith in a Christian God and hence outside of His Grace.

卍

THE IDEA OF BLACKS as stateless and godless brutes, bereft not only of civilization but also of any effective means of collective defense, may have served as an important juridical European rationale for Black slavery in the late Middles Ages, but Portugal's real-world experience of Africa and of Africans in the ensuing years could not have been more different. The image that prevails in the public understanding of this history is nicely captured in the phrase "savage to slave," used by the historian Herman L. Bennett. Bennett's words describe the radical elision or compression usually employed to explain how the world went from the era of first maritime contacts between Europeans and "Guinea," i.e. the land of Blacks, in the 1440s, to the takeoff of a true transatlantic slavery roughly a century later.

The intervening decades of Afro-European contact were foundational to the birth of the modern world, to the development of the West, and to Africa's subsequent condition down to this day, and yet they go scarcely mentioned in most accounts of Western history. Western culture has labored long and hard to perpetuate ideas of precolonial Africa as a space of unadulterated primitivism and lack of human capacity for advancement. Therefore, this leap from savage to slave—meaning a supposedly seamless progression from the Iberian-led "discovery" of sub-Saharan Africa to the birth of a trade in slaves into the New World—feels for many like a transition that hardly merits explaining. The Europeans were manifestly superior in every way that mattered, and with the takeover of the Western Hemisphere and mass death of that part of the world's (also supposedly primitive) indigenous population, a large new labor force was needed to supplement the efforts of white settlers. Europeans alone were the avatars of reason, enterprise, and progress. Under the circumstances, the Blacks of "Guinea"—uncivilized and more or less without defense—loomed as if naturally as available victims and as the obvious solution to an impending severe labor shortage.

According to this paradigmatic trope, the Africa of this era is bereft of meaningful history or consequence; it is merely a cipher.

Where this narrative begins to completely derail is in 1448, when Prince Henry officially ordered a halt to the raiding and crusading that had generated African bodies for sale into the slave trade; in its place he initiated an approach that can only be described as conventional diplomacy. And although one rarely hears about it, this mode, one that would involve not just palaver, but mutual recognition of sovereignty and the full and complex range of statecraft, would dominate European relations with sub-Saharan Africa well into the seventeenth century, and involve the dispatching of ambassadors, the creation of alliances, formalized trade arrangements, and even treaties.

This shift in strategies came about in part from the Portuguese realization that an expanding African frontier was the most important overseas maritime theater and potentially biggest "prize" for Europe anywhere. This was not because no exploratory breakthrough to Asia had been achieved yet, as some might pretend, though. It was due, rather, to the critical contributions that Africa began to make to European wealth and prosperity in the second half of the fifteenth century, including driving big economic changes, such as the capitalization of Iberian economies and the launching of a new gold coin, the *cruzado*, in 1457. These contributed strongly to the acceleration of both urbanization and social mobility on the continent. Partially in reflection of this, early in the sixteenth century, Manuel I became the second Portuguese royal, after Afonso V, to adopt the sobriquet "the African."* West Africa was of such import that it was referred to as the "New World" decades before the discovery of the Americas, and tapping the wealth of this region was so vital to Lisbon that it considered Black Africa to be the Portuguese Main, in much the same way the Spanish would come to regard the American mainland. And lest one imagine this to be an obscure detail, Portugal,

---

* Manuel called himself in full King of Portugal and of the Algarves on This Side and Beyond the Sea in Africa, Lord of Guiné and Lord of the Conquest, Navigation and Commerce, of Ethiopia, Arabia, Persia and India.

as we will shortly see, waged the first naval battles in history fought between European powers outside of that continent's own waters off West Africa in order to retain preeminence over its rivals there.

Prince Henry's order to abandon the raiding approach to capturing slaves can also be explained, in part, because substantial numbers of Portuguese were getting killed in the fray, despite or maybe even because of their armor. Heavy metal plates worn for protection inevitably slowed them down and would have made those who wore it unbearably hot in the tropics. In addition, it seems that word spread rapidly through coastal African communities about the strange and violent new ship-borne outsiders. So fast, indeed, that it forced the Portuguese to venture farther and farther south and then eastward along the continent's coast in order to ensure a sufficient yield in captives. That is because once they had raided any spot along the coast, on learning the news, villagers far and wide would have been made wary of further visits by whites. What is more, the Blacks who didn't simply avoid contact with the Europeans defended themselves quite well—a good deal better, in fact, than even the plucky Canarians. This was not just a matter of supposedly unprincipled tactics or nearly superhuman physical abilities,* as sometimes alleged by the Portuguese, but because of the array of technologies at their disposal. These ranged from swift dugout canoes as large as eighty feet long that were capable of carrying as many as 120 men and were sometimes deployed in fleet formations, to sophisticated ironworking skills, archery, and the use of arrows and darts loaded with potent herbal poisons. As Zurara, who often invoked the strength and skill of West African combatants, said, "their dangerous way of fighting would be frightful to any reasonable man." Indeed, in one of this era's early raids, in 1445, Africans wielding poisonous arrows killed twenty of the twenty-two Portuguese who went ashore, including the leader of the expedition, Nuno Tristão.

Defeats like these obliged the Europeans to quickly come to

---

* Africans were said to be able to evade capture by swimming as well as cormorants, for example.

terms with the fact that realities on the ground in the region they called Guiné were radically at odds with their initial prejudices. Black Africans did not, by and large, live in unorganized societies without clear and well-established hierarchies and elaborate belief systems of their own devising, as the newcomers had initially imagined. In fact, along the coast of present-day Senegal, they learned that many Blacks lived under the rule of kings, and where not kings, usually formal chieftaincies. More than mere customs, whether or not preserved in writing, many of these African societies had what we would recognize today as laws. They also had the means to enforce them—and under most circumstances, the Portuguese, relatively few in number and lacking any great technological advantage, simply had to comply with them.

The Jolof, of present-day Senegal, was the first of the Black societies to strike up a sustained and complex relationship with the newcomers. Portugal's fortune seekers, in fact, had some advance knowledge of the Jolof via trans-Saharan trading networks, even before they ventured south beyond Cape Bojador. In the mid-fifteenth century, the Jolof had only recently freed themselves from vassalage to Mali, and they were therefore deeply familiar with the great empires of the nearby Sudan. This partially Islamized society would have also possessed clear knowledge of the dynasties that had long controlled the Maghreb, as well as a large part of Iberia. No small number of Arabic-speaking traders lived in their midst, and if only for that reason alone, the Jolof almost certainly had some advance notion or knowledge of the Europeans as well.

In 1488, a Jolof prince named Bumi Jeléen traveled to Portugal to seek Lisbon's support amid something Iberians were intimately familiar with themselves, a raging succession struggle. Bumi Jeléen was attempting to face down an attempt to unseat him by the son of a former king. Four years earlier, in 1484, Portugal's King João II had just faced down a plot by his own brother-in-law, as is detailed below, so he may have felt extra sympathy for his African counterpart. On that basis, Lisbon obliged, receiving the Jolof royal in Lisbon with full honors, knighting him and converting him to Christianity, under the name Dom João. Bumi Jeléen then demonstrated his deference to Portugal's king in the traditional manner of the Mali-centered Sahel by prostrating himself and throwing dust repeatedly over his shoulder. Urged to stand, he then gave a lengthy speech, stunning the audience who had expected neither articulateness nor grace. A court chronicle described him as having "all the eloquence of a Greek prince of [ancient] Athens." Sometime thereafter King João dispatched a fleet of twenty-eight caravels, replete with soldiers and priests, to support the prince's claim to the Jolof crown. Just short of their destination, however, Bumi Jeléen was stabbed to death by the captain of the fleet, Pero Vaz de Cunha, whom historians suspect was motivated by fear of a dangerous deployment. Although this maiden experiment with alliance building and intervention in local succession disputes went badly awry, this was a strategy that Portugal would employ again and again as a means of enhancing its influence and later fueling conflict between African states all along the coast of the continent from the fourteenth through the seventeenth centuries.

The Portuguese also found many of the kingdoms of Guinea, including the Jolof, more than willing to trade for slaves, which was already well established both among Black African societies and in trade across the Sahara. Of course, this was far easier and more lucrative, not to mention much safer, than headlong, sword-waving attempts to capture other human beings, and the Jolof went on to become Portugal's biggest suppliers of humans in bondage during this early phase of the trade.

It is a small irony of history that Portugal's big advances in Africa came only on the heels of Prince Henry's death in November 1460. By that time Portuguese ships had advanced as far down the African coast as modern Sierra Leone, close to where the continent's coastline begins to veer almost due eastward, but this had been achieved only at tremendous cost. What this meant in practice is that Henry had personally financed many of the expeditions, supplementing his own funds with monies he derived from the Order of Christ, which he led. Gold was still ardently hoped for, but returns in the metal had fallen far short of expectations, even if Portugal's outlay was increasingly compensated for by the growing trade in slaves. To supplement this human traffic, Portuguese ships began bringing brasswares in the form of thick bracelets they called *manilhas*, as well as *neptunes*, large brass tubs and basins used in food preparation and cleaning, or sometimes unworked brass ingots for sale to Africans, who were eager to obtain them. The other trade good that the European newcomers discovered was in high demand along the West African coast was cloth of various kinds, an item that will come to play an immense role later in our story.

According to both Portuguese accounts and ample archaeological evidence, many West African societies already possessed sophisticated metalworking techniques, as well as the ability to weave fabrics of impressive quality. The problem that local African populations faced in many of the places the Portuguese stopped, though, was a lack of abundant ores and sometimes natural plant fibers with which to manufacture these items. Seventeenth-century visitors from several European states wrote often about the high quality of African cloth and, especially, about dyeing technique using indigo in the regions of Senegal and Upper Guinea, as well as in the lower Niger River Valley, in present-day Nigeria. Clever Dutch traders even copied these techniques and sold small quantities of the cloth into New World markets.

Metalwares and textiles for onward export to Africa started to play an important but little heralded role within Europe itself as Portuguese merchants began selling goods acquired in Africa to northern Europeans. These included the prized "grains of paradise," or *melegueta* pepper, a hot spice that the Portuguese bought in large quantity near Sierra Leone and in what is modern-day Liberia, a region they called the Pepper Coast. In exchange, northern Europeans sold the Portuguese the textiles and metal goods that were in heavy demand in the newfound African societies. Although little remembered, this merits recognition as the first of the so-called triangle trades, long before the famous transatlantic pattern that goes by this name was established. By virtue of its commerce with Africa, southern Europe now became more economically linked with northern Europe than it had ever been before, particularly with Germanic lands and the Low Countries.

A second triangle trade, also earlier than the transatlantic one, and almost equally neglected among historians, came into existence almost as soon as the Portuguese "discovered" India at the end of the fifteenth century. Although often no better than the best local African cloth, Indian textiles were far more advanced than European ones in this era, and cottons (still a rarity in Europe) from India were particularly prized in tropical Africa, leading the Portuguese to create another circuit that linked Africa with South Asia. A European trade with Africa in Indian cottons, commonly known as chintzes (a corruption of the Hindi word *chint*, for spotted cloth), peaked toward the end of the seventeenth century, but in certain regions, such as western Central Africa, a prodigious source of bound Black labor, Europeans could scarcely trade for slaves without large amounts of Indian cloth, which remained the local preference throughout the century that followed.

In 1469, King Afonso launched a novel arrangement for sustaining Portugal's involvement in trade and exploration with Africa; one that would impose no drain on the royal treasury: he leased the rights of exploration to an established Portuguese merchant and minor *fidalgo* named Fernão Gomes for five years for the sum of 200,000 *reis* a year. But in a creative twist, the contract required Gomes's ships to advance at least one hundred leagues annually along the African coast beyond Sierra Leone, charting new territory as he went. The importance that Lisbon attached to expanding African trade under Afonso prior to the discovery of gold was still relatively low. This can be seen in Afonso's licensing terms. According to one historian's calculations, the value of this contract amounted to a mere 0.4 percent of the crown's revenues at the time. Such things were not as simple as they might first seem, however. Under these arrangements, the crown retained exclusive rights for the lucrative existing trade in slaves at the island of Arguim, as well as a royal monopoly in the region's most profitable luxury items, things like civet organs, used in the making of perfume, and the prized *melegueta* pepper, whose trade value at the time was nearly as great as the spices that reached Europe overland from the East.

One might still surmise that the modest price of the Gomes contract reflected the low state of expectations that Lisbon held of a big breakthrough anytime soon in the search for African gold. Those expectations would change, however, with stunning swiftness. Gomes launched his first expedition in 1470, as soon as his contract took effect, and he sent a second convoy of ships around the bulge of Africa the following year, venturing past the lagoons of what is today the Ivory Coast and onward into the waters of modern Ghana. Along the way, they passed "some tall red cliffs along the coast which lasted four or five leagues." (These happen to be the same red cliffs that form the headlands that loom above Bonyere, my wife's ancestral village in far western Ghana, offering a sweeping view of the sea that I took in on my first visit there in the early 1980s.) From that point, Gomes's ships proceeded eastward for another few miles until they reached a village called Shama, where they found safe anchor. As they came ashore, the signs of gold were so abundant there was no need to search for it; indeed, it was worn as jewelry, seemingly even by rank commoners who inhabited the villages along the coast. Assuming the existence of a major mine nearby, the Portuguese adopted the name El Mina for this site of such long awaited good fortune.

With sufficient samples in hand, Gomes's ships made a swift return to Portugal bearing news that would change the world as nothing else in this transitional era between the late Middle Ages and modern times would. Nearly sixty years of Portuguese efforts to win access to African gold had finally paid off. This breakthrough fulfilled even older European dreams of finding maritime routes that could unlock the continent's wealth, dreams most notably held by the Genoese that dated at least as far back as the thirteenth century. Gomes's contract, which had once looked stingy, suddenly seemed like a ridiculous steal, and even while establishing regular trade with the Akan societies of Ghana the newly rich *fidalgo*'s fleets pursued other African discoveries farther to the east, all the way to the Bight of Benin and the island of São Tomé.

Under the terms of his contract, Gomes was only required to surrender one-fifth of his bounty in gold to the crown, but even this was
enough to breathe life into Portugal's anemic currency. Recognizing
the importance of this windfall, King Afonso, until this point in his
life reserved toward Africa, placed his son, Crown Prince João, in
direct control over the booming new trade and, most important, its
rich proceeds in bullion. The Portuguese profit margins must have
been very handsome. The mariner-traders who first showed up on the
shores of what quickly came to be known as the Gold Coast, a stretch
of West African coastline mostly contained within modern Ghana,
located between the town of Assinie in the west and the mouth of the
River Volta in the east, found that the local peoples possessed a rich
material culture based on intricate and high-quality dyed cloths and
finely worked metals. In both of these fields, though, the problem
faced by the locals, as the Portuguese had seen in other parts of the
coast, was scarcity, of cotton, or of iron or brass, with which to make
sufficient weapons or farming implements. Some of the Gold Coast
textiles had arrived via a coastal trade with Dahomey and other societies to the east, as well as from North Africa. Quick to identify market opportunities, the Portuguese stepped in as suppliers of both
cloth and brass basins and ingots, which were snapped up avidly by
the locals in exchange for their gold nuggets and dust. Almost nothing about the Portuguese trade goods was new to the peoples of the
Gold Coast except their abundant quantity, and on that basis, a regular, large-scale, and history-shifting trade was established.

But for one problem, trade with the Gold Coast might have
seemed like perfection realized for the Portuguese crown. The difficulty in question, though, was a major one: it was impossible to
keep such a good thing secret, especially in the richly incestuous
and intrigue-laden world of the southern Europe of that era. There,
as the example of Columbus best illustrates, men of ambition as well
as pure adventurers worked for whichever crown would pay them,
irrespective of their birthplace, and spies abounded in every major
port and capital. Word about Lisbon's immense windfall therefore
quickly spread, and it took little time for others to activate plans of

their own to seize some of the action. Before long, Spaniards, Frenchmen, Genoese, and others began turning up on these shores in dribs and drabs, all attempting to horn in on Gomes's transformational find. In 1475, a Flemish ship under the command of a Spanish pilot is said to have reached the coast of present-day Ghana. Focusing its trade in the area surrounding a place they called the Village of Two Parts (Aldea de Duas Partes), or what would soon become known as Elmina,* the crew took in a haul of between five and six thousand *dobras* worth of gold before setting sail for home. The ship was lost, however, in a wreck hundreds of miles to the west.

To protect its discovery, in August 1474, Portugal proclaimed it illegal for "foreigners" to trade with Mina, promising the death penalty for all who were caught doing so. At about that same time, King Afonso decreed that what the Portuguese called the Mina trade would become a royal monopoly at the end of that year. Gomes, who by then must have accumulated a major fortune, was honored for his role in securing such an important new source of wealth for the crown with a title and feudal coat of arms, which depicted the heads of three Africans, with the word "Mina" inscribed just below. Henceforth he would be known as Fernão Gomes da Mina, and he was granted membership in the prestigious Royal Privy Council.

It is tempting to imagine that Afonso's motive in taking the Mina trade away from its discoverer and turning it into a crown monopoly was solely a matter of economic interest: No longer would Afonso and the Portuguese crown be limited to the royal fifth of the proceeds from this almost unbelievably rich source of African gold; it would all belong to the king. But Afonso also had good reason to fear that if the crown did not exercise tight control over its African gold bonanza, it would be snatched away by its rival Castile, which had already begun to manifest a keen interest in it.

---

* Upon discovery of large quantities of gold along the coast of what is today modern Ghana, the Portuguese named the region La Costa da Mina (the Coast of the Mine). In most references in this book, I have adopted the contemporary name of the town, where the Portuguese first set up trading operations in the region and built a major fort: Elmina. However, in many contemporary accounts, this place-name was shortened to Mina, a form that also appears herein.

In fact, over the next five years an intense struggle would unfold over El Mina, one that played a crucial, if largely overlooked part not just in the economic fortunes of Portugal and Spain, but in the very destinies of Catholic monarchs. On December 11, 1474, the king of Castile, Henrique IV, died, setting the stage for another violently contested Iberian succession. Isabella, Henrique's plump and girlish younger half sister, known for her sad eyes, immediately declared herself his heir. The problem was that so did Afonso of Portugal, who promptly married his own niece Juana, who was Henrique's daughter, in order to strengthen his claims to the Castilian crown. Relying on Elmina's gold to field a large army, Afonso invaded Castile in March 1475, hoping to prevail by force, but his troops were repulsed at the Battle of Toro, turning Afonso's bid into a major political debacle for his own kingdom. With his hold on power now in jeopardy, Afonso traveled to France to seek support from his neighbor. Isabella, who had not been raised with an eye to ruling, having received only a narrow, "domestic" education, nonetheless sensed a grand opportunity in Portugal's weakness and began to target Lisbon's new holdings in West Africa, and Elmina in particular. This reflected her keen understanding that it was the gold of Ghana that had provided Lisbon the wherewithal to mount its bid for the Castilian crown. As the Spanish chronicler Alonso de Palencia wrote, "the [Portuguese] crown was able to gather an invasion army to march into Castile in 1475 and pay for the soldiers with 600,000 cruzados, each equal to a Venetian florin," attesting to the belief throughout Iberia, and probably already far beyond, that Africa was the key to Portugal's strength.

Up to that point, Spain had made little serious effort to explore West Africa—certainly nothing comparable to Portugal. Now, suddenly, though, the Catholic Monarchs, as Isabella and her spouse, Ferdinand II of Aragon, were known after their marriage in 1469, were loudly stating their intentions to revive vague but nonetheless decades-old Spanish claims to the region and to enforce them with naval power. Because Castile lacked a centralized maritime force that was up to this task, Isabella commissioned privateers to sail to the waters off the West African coast both to pursue trade with

the gold-rich communities near Elmina and to attack Portuguese
shipping. Those who took up her call were stringently required to
surrender to the crown a fifth of whatever commerce or booty they
could generate, but many evidently calculated that this would still
guarantee a sufficiently rich prize to make the long and dangerous
voyage worthwhile. Mimicking the recent move by Portugal, Isabella decreed that all others lacking special official permission were
henceforth forbidden to trade with Guinea "under penalty of death
and loss of all your goods."

Some of the early Spanish Castilian convoys duly returned with
rich yields of gold and pepper, and with hundreds of slaves as well.
With greater central direction and far more experience in the distant
reaches of the West African coast, however, Lisbon was far better
prepared for the unfolding contest, which involved multiple naval
engagements in the waters of this region. Most decisively, in 1478,
probably after having gotten advance word of their rivals' movements, Portuguese ships wielding big naval guns sprung an ambush
on a Castilian convoy of thirty-five ships just as it was returning from
Elmina, sinking or capturing many of the vessels. The haul in gold
alone from this battle is said to have been equal to the entire cost
borne by Portugal during its failed invasion of Castile three years
earlier. It was in the aftermath of this battle off Elmina, history's first
intra-European colonial war at sea, that the rival Iberian powers
agreed to sit down for peace negotiations mediated by the Catholic
Church. Their conflict had produced a rough stalemate: Spain had
clearly won close to home, meaning on land, while Portugal had triumphed in the distant but suddenly strategically important seas off
West Africa. And this set the stage for a papal-sanctioned division
of the known world with immensely far-reaching consequences for
the early modern era and well beyond. Under the Treaty of Alcáço-
vas, of 1479, Portugal would abandon its claims to the Castilian
crown. But more to the point, it would also henceforth enjoy rights
to "all the islands already discovered and to be discovered, and any
other island which might be found and conquered from the Canary
Islands beyond toward Guinea . . . excepting [the Canary Islands

themselves] and all of the other islands of Canary, conquered and to be conquered, which remain to the kingdom of Castile."

After a little heralded naval war for control of the gold of modern-day Ghana, Portugal, in other words, had won Church-sanctioned control of all of sub-Saharan Africa, while Spain had finally won control over the long contested Canary Islands. Within a decade, Portugal was obtaining 8000 ounces of gold annually from Elmina, an amount that would nearly triple by 1494 and continue to rise thereafter. Lisbon's new monopoly over West Africa's tremendous supplies of gold then left the Spanish with little choice but to venture out far beyond the Pillars of Hercules and push new exploration efforts into the westward extremities of the Atlantic Ocean. In other words, Portugal's newfound wealth further fueled Spain's obsession with finding its own sources of the precious metal. It was a matter of keeping up. We know this, in part, through the many references to the search for gold in Columbus's journals. In fact, in conversation with Queen Isabella, he justified his project of crossing the Atlantic by saying that the rich supplies of gold at Elmina meant it would be found at the same latitude in the "Asian" lands awaiting his discovery, an idea he seems to have genuinely convinced himself of. As C. L. R. James wrote in the opening lines of his landmark 1963 work *The Black Jacobins: Toussaint L'Ouverture and the San Domingo Revolution*: "Christopher Columbus landed first in the New World at the island of San Salvador, and after praising God enquired urgently for gold." Columbus was not driven only by belief, however. This was his clear mandate from the Spanish monarchs who had commissioned him, and theirs, to be certain, was a thirst fired by envy of the Portuguese breakthrough at Elmina. The Canary Islands, meanwhile, would soon serve as a critical springboard for the Columbus voyages and for Spain's subsequent Church-sanctioned control over almost all of the new New World.* The geographic situation of these islands, astride the Canary Cur-

---

* Prior to the "discovery" of the Americas, West Africa had been frequently called the New World.

rent, all but assured Spain's success in this incomparably more famous breakthrough of its own. Ships that set sail from the Azores, the Portuguese launching point into the Atlantic, by contrast, were always stubbornly blown back toward Europe.

In its most familiar telling, the history of this era has been heavily skewed in favor of Spain and its spectacular conquests in the Americas, giving it possession of almost unlimited new territory and, soon enough, undreamed-of amounts of silver and gold. Portugal's acquisition of rights to Africa, by contrast, has traditionally been reduced to a mere footnote. This is clearly not how the Portuguese themselves experienced the breakthroughs of this period. Nor is it how we should see them today. It was in the wake of his maritime victory off Elmina that João II began celebrating West Africa as the "Portuguese Main," and proudly appending Lord of Guiné to his other titles. In most standard accounts, Lisbon returns to narratives about Europe's irresistible rise over the rest of the world only with its belated leap to Asia, under the command of mariners like Vasco da Gama and Afonso de Albuquerque late in the century. The theater and the telos of the narratives built up around conquistadores combine to make this understandable, but they don't make it correct. And in the section ahead, as we consider the birth of a Black Atlantic, we will have to "disremember" some of the traditional accounting of this era, in the phrase of the scholar of modernity Lisa Lowe, in order to understand it better. This means showing that Portugal did not really lose out to Spain at all in the great bargains reached during a series of world-dividing treaties brokered by the Vatican at the end of the fifteenth century, beginning with Alcaçovas. In fact, of the two Iberian powers, Portugal became the much more powerful engine of modernity. And in demonstrating this, we will see clearly that it was Portugal's far deeper connections with sub-Saharan Africa, first through gold and then through slaves, that more than any other factors in this era, bequeathed to us our familiar world.

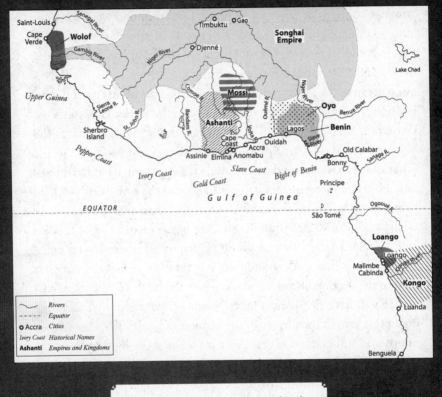

West and Central Africa, with major kingdoms
and European-named trading zones

PART II

THE ESSENTIAL PIVOT

People who meet occasionally remain
friendlier than do neighbors, on account
of the nature of the human heart.

KWAMENA ANSA (CARAMANSA),
1471

7

THE MINE

F ROM ATOP THE STEEP HILL that overlooks it, Elmina today is the very picture of a sleepy African town. The shanty-style dwellings that house many of its thirty thousand residents crowd the lower reaches of the incline and extend all the way to the sea. On the roughly cemented pathway that leads to the summit, where the cool nighttime air gives way to a quick-rising morning heat, mothers wash their children in flimsy plastic basins, the cheap, contemporary Asian substitutes for the brass *neptunes* people here once traded for with the Portuguese. At the summit, blackbirds wheel in the sky above a rampart that is more than three and a half centuries old. Somehow, although abandoned, it has remained impeccably whitewashed.

The Dutch-built fort, St. Jago, is certainly far less well known than the older Portuguese-built fort that looms in the distance below, at water's edge. Almost no one comes to Elmina nowadays with the purpose of climbing this hilltop. There aren't even signs pointing the way. But there is certainly no better place for understanding how the seaside settlement down below went from being a tiny fishing village, undistinguishable from hundreds of others strung along this coast, to one of the most important hinges, albeit almost never celebrated that way, of the modern era.

After 1479, Spanish designs on the gold of West Africa did not disappear; they merely became clandestine. The Catholic Monarchs, Isabella and Ferdinand, continued to encourage private expeditions to Elmina, hoping in that way to retain control of at least some portion of the fabulous wealth pouring forth from this region. Not stopping there, Isabella supported a plot by the Duke of Braganza, then the richest and most powerful noble in Portugal, to mount a coup against his relative King João II, in hopes of eventually absorbing her neighbor. In exchange for her help, Isabella was to be granted full access to the so-called Guinea trade, meaning the gold of Mina, if the usurping duke succeeded in taking over. The plot was discovered, though, and after conviction on twenty-two counts of treason, the duke was publicly beheaded on June 20, 1483. By this time, even the covetous English were also rumored to be busying plans to trade with Mina.

In 1481, not wishing to leave control over Elmina to chance, King João waved off the concerns of his court about the expense and ordered the construction of a fort along the Ghanaian coast to protect Portugal's booming supply of gold from European rivals and pirates. Lisbon had already tried policing these waters with a kind of distant-seas coast guard, once sending a convoy of ships led by Fernão Gomes himself. Not only had such an approach proven costly and logistically challenging, given Spain's persistent efforts to capture some of this region's gold trade in the previous decade, it was also less than completely effective. Proponents of the idea argued that the amount of gold that Portuguese ships could purchase and ferry back to Lisbon had always been limited by matters of chance—for example, how much of the metal local traders had on hand whenever a Portuguese vessel arrived. But with the construction of a fort, gold could be bought from the locals on a continuous basis and accumulated there, behind high and well-defended walls, for safekeeping. Ships could thus arrive there on a regular schedule and be relatively sure of acquiring enough gold to fill their holds, justifying the expense of each voyage.

João placed the construction of a fort at Elmina under the leadership of Diogo de Azambuja, a court nobleman and trusted military officer who had already proven himself in a variety of past roles, including campaigns against both Morocco and Castille. One of his crewmates was Bartolomeu Dias, the nobleman who seven years later would become the first European to reach the southern tip of Africa and sail from there into the Indian Ocean. Over the next few years, a number of other giants of what would become known as the Age of Discovery would also be enlisted in supplying or administering Portugal's first major outpost south of the Sahara, attesting to Elmina's role as a linchpin in Lisbon's budding global project. These included Afonso de Albuquerque, who later blazed a trail of imperial conquest in Asia, and Diogo Cão, who "discovered" Kongo, a major kingdom far to the southeast. For now, it suffices to say that in Lisbon Cão's Kongo mission took strong priority over searching for a route to India, and for many years afterward, he was a more celebrated figure in Portugal than Dias. Cão was elevated from esquire to a knight in the king's household and granted a generous annuity and a coat of arms. Dias, by contrast, was granted no special honors for proving that one could sail from Portugal into the Indian Ocean, nor is there any record of a royal audience for him upon his return. And then there is Christopher Columbus himself, who at the time was also in Lisbon's employ. In his correspondence he attested encouragingly to the fact that European worries about the inhospitable conditions of life in this part of Africa, just a few degrees north of the Equator, were greatly overstated. "I was in the castle of La Mina of the king of Portugal . . . and I am good witness that it is not uninhabitable, as is said," Columbus wrote of a visit that took place in 1482, the very first year of the completed fort's existence.

That December of 1481, when a convoy set sail for the Mina coast, the level of attention to detail evident in the planning of staffing and supplies spoke volumes about the importance the mission held for Portugal; Elmina had come a very long way indeed since the first royal contract for trade there had been let between the crown and Gomes for a relative pittance. In all, there were ten caravels carrying five hundred military men, plus one hundred more stonemasons and other specialists in a variety of construction trades. Two heavier and slower transport ships had been dispatched some weeks in advance with instructions to await the main contingent at a pre-designated point well off the African coastline. These cargo vessels carried not only lime, brick, nails, and timber, but also the principal pieces of the foundation and cornerstones for the fort, all of which had been precut and carefully marked. Nothing had been left to hazard including the structure's defense, for which cannons and plentiful ammunition were also stowed on board.

Diogo de Azambuja's expedition reached the waters off today's Ghana in the middle of January. Thus far, most of the Portuguese gold trade had been concentrated around Shama, but that village was deemed to be an unsuitable port for large ships and was also lacking in readily available supplies of fresh water and in the large stones that would be needed to complete the masonry of a proper fort. Late in the afternoon of January 19, after sailing another twenty-five miles to the east, the convoy reached the Village of Two Parts, a settlement that was cut in two by a narrow, slow-moving river. From the breezy hilltop that overlooks Elmina, the attractiveness of this site can hardly be more evident. On approach from the west, the rough and boulder-strewn coastline gives way to the arc of a broad bay that is so well sheltered that its curving fringe of sandy beach is lapped only by the gentlest of waves. There, at a safe distance from the shore, a Portuguese convoy would have the luxury of parking peacefully at anchor without fear of either attack by locals or running aground. What is more, the estuary of the river, which they learned was called the Benya, was navigable for a short distance beyond its mouth, giving immediate access to the lively fishing village and colorful market that still crowds the river's banks today.

When Azambuja eased his ship into the mouth of the Benya that day in early 1482, he and his men were probably surprised to find a sailing vessel belonging to an unauthorized Portuguese trader already anchored there, out in front of the flag, as it were. Due to either a prolonged stay or repeated visits, the captain of that ship, João Fernando, had already spent enough time in the area to communicate reasonably well in the local Fante language. Azambuja, therefore, enlisted his compatriot to send word to the local king at dawn the next morning that the leader of a major Portuguese expedition wished to meet with him.

Azambuja and his men immediately set about organizing a landing party with a particular eye to managing the proper sort of theater of awe for the hoped-for encounter with the king. The stakes were sky-high, but in their actions one finds consummation of the swing to diplomacy as opposed to raiding that we have spoken of earlier. The Portuguese had come not for quick and dirty trade, but for the previously unheard-of idea of building a permanent outpost in this gold-rich country, something that no outsider had ever attempted before. The team that disembarked the next morning included a squadron of men armed with harquebuses and swords carefully concealed under their clothing to avoid provocation, but despite this precaution, the clear hope was to avoid having to use them.

It is worth emphasizing here that we are limited in the recounting of these events, as with so many others in this era, to the accounts of Portuguese chroniclers. The stories they left, though, say that Azambuja awaited the local king next to the site that he had chosen for the construction of his fort. This was on a spit of land that rises above the western bank of the Benya, near the very point where the rocky coast gives way to the placid bay. The Portuguese knew that if they built their garrison on that spot, the thirty cannons they had arrived with, including six large guns that could hurl 14-kilo stones at least six hundred yards, could make easy sport of any enemy ships that attempted to enter the bay. The foreigners said Mass first thing that morning on their chosen ground and raised the royal banner of João II on a high branch of a large, solitary tree. Afterward, Azambuja, dressed in some of the best European finery of the day, including "a jerkin of brocade, with a golden collar of precious stones," sat in a great chair on a hastily erected scaffold and awaited the king, surrounded by his officers.

No one could have been fully aware at the time that an entirely new era of European relations with Africa, and indeed with the wider world, was commencing then and there. The experiences that

Africans and Europeans had with each other on this ground would become a formidable pillar of modernity: vastly consequential, but today all but unrecognized or even recalled. Here began a new, largely improvised, and highly tentative experiment with imperialism—i.e., the building of a permanent, fortified garrison in the African tropics, which for the time being remained Europe's sole and unique New World. Through this project, Europeans would discover both the possibilities and the limits of their power and take part in the formation of distinctive new identities, not least including for themselves. As this was happening, and while African gold powered Lisbon's rise, the initiation of a major Atlantic trade in slaves that grew out of Portugal's experiences here would soon make a coming revolution in plantation agriculture possible, along with the utterly transformative new wealth that it produced in the North Atlantic.

More immediately, this was an era when the visitors were obliged to come to terms with the fact that in place after place along the western coast of this continent, there were sophisticated societies with fully developed politics and protocols of their own, as well as the means to robustly defend themselves. The Portuguese were in the midst of discovering something they had ardently hoped to find: a new African realm endowed with great wealth, well beyond the land of the Moors. But many of the Africans they encountered were anything but new to the idea of the rich diversity of the world beyond their immediate horizons. Gold from these Akan-controlled regions, for example, was already being traded with Europe via Muslim networks in the Sudan, and for a century or more these same networks had been sending a growing volume of non-African goods southward in exchange. As a result, when the Portuguese began to make their move at Elmina, the inhabitants were anything but surprised, never mind overawed.

The first signs of this came with the very emergence through a thicket of trees of Kwamena Ansa, the local king, or *omanehene*, whose name the Portuguese would record as Caramansa. No stranger to the theater of power himself, he approached the appointed meeting spot preceded by a royal marching band that employed kettle drums, trumpets, and many other instruments. According to the Europeans, who had surely never witnessed a sight anything like this, the music was "more deafening than pleasing to the ear." Next came members of his court, including squires and the like, also dressed in the best finery of their culture, backed by men in arms, not at all concealed. "In general, they were all armed in their manner, some with short spears and shields, others with arches, and sheaths of arrows," wrote João de Barros, a member of Azambuja's party. His account continues: "Their king, Caramansa, came in their midst, with his legs and arms covered with golden bracelets and rings, and he wore a necklace from which some small bells hung, and in his plaited beard some strips of gold, that in this manner held his hair, which from being twisted turned smooth." From the description of this first "official" encounter, it is clear that for the king, gold was not just a means of exchange, but also an important marker of political and spiritual power.

As Ansa drew close to the Portuguese who were arrayed around their captain, Azambuja climbed down from his chair to approach him with the deference proper to a king or chief. Ansa took his hand briefly, releasing it so as to "touch his fingers and then snap the one with the other, saying in his language, 'Bere, bere,' which in ours means 'Peace, peace.'" As any visitor to West Africa can attest, this finger-snapping handshake survives as an emphatic form of greeting even today. After these initial welcoming formalities, an exchange of salutations and gifts ensued. Then Azambuja got down to business, announcing that his king had entrusted him with the construction of a permanent trading center, or "strong house," in this immediate area for the purpose of establishing regular commercial ties. Seeing that Ansa was noncommittal, the Portuguese captain repeatedly emphasized the wealth and new goods that would accrue to the African leader and to his people. These included, according to the visitors, conversion to Christianity and baptism, which they said would make him a "brother" and ally of the king of Portugal.

Ansa was already aware of the purported benefits and at least some of the inconveniences of trade with the Europeans, who had already been showing up in these parts in dribs and drabs for about a decade, all seeking their fortunes in West African gold, and he was unimpressed. "The Christians who have come here until now have been very few, dirty and base," he said tersely. One imagines that only a serenely self-confident African leader would have uttered words like these. This, nonetheless, can also be read as a compliment by way of comparison. Ansa seemed to be saying that he didn't realize that the Europeans could be as civilized as the fancily tricked out representatives of João II appeared to be. Whether flattered or simply undaunted, Azambuja continued to press his request, upon which Ansa issued a parable of a kind still so favored among the Akan and many other peoples of West Africa. "People who meet occasionally remain friendlier than do neighbors, on account of the nature of the human heart," he replied. Azambuja overcame this apparent demurral with yet more promises of lucrative trade opportunities, but when Ansa finally assented to the captain's proposal, his permission came with a warning: the Portuguese would be held strictly to all of their commitments and, in case of trouble, the king's people would simply abandon the area, leaving the Portuguese with no one to trade with.

A vivid thread that begins to unspool in this encounter runs all the way to the late Western imperial era. In what would become a familiar pattern, importuning Europeans arriving from afar sought to bid their way into local trade opportunities, offering up promises of great shared profits, of novel goods, and of salvation through Christianity and protection. The local power usually tried to accommodate the strangers, while limiting their freedom of action on the ground. But, in place after place, chaos soon followed.

Trouble at Elmina, as it happens, arrived almost instantly, and initially appeared grave, but would prove manageable. It was only in the far longer term, roughly a century and a half hence, that the prescience of the king of Elmina would be fully borne out. The following morning, even before Azambuja's men delivered their promised gifts, the convoy's stonecutters broke ground on the new fort, infuriating residents of the village. There were also complaints that the high ground where the Portuguese had begun their work was sacred terrain for the Africans. Amid inflamed tempers, a violent skirmish broke out, and with injuries on both sides, the Europeans were forced to scramble into their landing craft and regain their ships. A party returned the next day, though, and managed to appease the locals by doubling down on the gratuities they had offered: cloth, copper basins, conch shells, which were prized by the people here, and *manilhas*, bracelets. Once permission had been restored, Azambuja's men wasted no time throwing up their fort—long called a castle by the people of Ghana. Working under armed guard, masons built the inner walls of the fort in twenty days, and the outer wall, with its much larger circumference, was completed just a few weeks later. São Jorge da Mina thus became the first of sixty or so such outposts built over the next three centuries by a diverse assortment of European nations along the coast of modern-day Ghana. The first wave of these was created in order to procure gold. Only much later, beginning in the 1640s, did this region become a major source of slaves, long after such other regions as Upper Guinea, Kongo, and Luanda (now the capital of Angola). In the twenty-first century, Elmina Castle, as the fort of São Jorge da Mina is called today, is every bit as solid and well constructed as it appears to be from the distance of the hilltop I scaled to admire it.

Nowadays, streams of visitors come to take guided tours of the castle's breezy upper floors, which housed the governor and his top officers, and the dungeons situated just off the courtyard below, and most famously the "Door of No Return," from which slaves were shipped to the Caribbean, Brazil, or, later, Britain's North American colonies. Metal had been the engine of history that led the Portuguese here. This set in motion all that followed, from the New World discoveries of Spain to the launching of plantation economies that almost literally vacuumed up enchained Africans for shipment off to the far shores of the Atlantic, but today the fort at Elmina has become almost entirely reduced to a mnemonic of slavery; a place where there is scarcely any mention of the gold trade at all.

8

ASIA SUSPENDED

THE BUSINESS IN GOLD was of such urgency for Portugal at the tail end of the fifteenth century that the commerce was up and running from the very moment the construction of the fort was complete in 1482. Lisbon typically received a caravel's shipment every month from this prized new outpost, with its ships usually spending about a month in transit. And it was not long before these volumes grew so huge that they transformed the economic life of this small nation-state. Indeed, Elmina was everything its sovereigns had been dreaming of since the earliest voyages of Prince Henry—and more. From the completion of the fort at Elmina until the mid-sixteenth century, Portugal's caravel runs back and forth to the Gold Coast averaged between 46 and 57 kilograms of the precious metal per month for deposit in royal coffers. The kingdom's treasury—previously known as the Casa da Guiné, reflecting what was already considered the primary importance of trade with Black Africa—was renamed Casa da Mina and moved into the very edifice of the royal palace in Lisbon. There could scarcely have been more direct recognition of the importance of Elmina's gold to the prosperity of the realm. By itself, trade with Elmina caused royal revenues to nearly double in Portugal during the last twenty years of the fifteenth century. By 1506, with the tentacles of Portuguese empire already enveloping Brazil and reaching deep into Asia, gold from the

Elmina region still constituted fully a quarter of crown revenue. The Gold Coast was generating about 680 kilograms of gold per year for Portugal or, it has been estimated, about a tenth of the entire known total world supply around that time.

This river of gold refloated Portugal's chronically weak currency, making it universally respectable for the first time, while helping catalyze a shift in the kingdom's economy away from salt, dried fish, and wine, and toward a much more sophisticated mix of trade goods. This was, in effect, a replay of a much earlier history of African gold, which had had similarly stimulating impact on other rising empires in the distant past, including Arab, Carthaginian, and Roman. With Portugal, though, gold bounty from Elmina had even more sweeping effects, ones that were fundamental to the newly emerging modernity of this age: it propelled complex economic integration based on long-distance trade in an increasingly diverse range of high-value goods, from the brass and copper goods, iron bars, cloth, and high-quality Indian textiles we have invoked to crude firearms. Goods like these were used to procure African gold, and in the latter case, to stoke warfare between small kingdoms that made it easier to purchase slaves. Meanwhile, in Lisbon, life in the royal court became swathed in material luxury of a level only recently unimaginable.

These new trade circuits were not limited to Europe, either. The African kings and chiefs who freely traded with the Portuguese quickly became discriminating consumers of foreign imports themselves. They scorned most European cloth, for example, which was then made of wool or flax and was mostly unsuitably heavy for the tropics. In response, the Portuguese began using some of their African-sourced gold to buy Indian cottons, which were prized in West Africa. And it even led to a growing cabotage trade in West Africa, where the Portuguese bought African cloth from one place (especially Benin) for sale in another for gold.

Once it had finally been found in quantity in the 1480s, African gold gave such a significant boost to Lisbon that the vaunted search for a route to Asia, long preferred as the standard explanation of Europe's expansionary motivations during the Age of Discovery, was all but suspended. By now enjoying papal sanction for almost all of Africa, Lisbon was instead in a hurry to protect the gold that it had secured, as attested to by the construction of the trading fort at Elmina, and by the elaborate supply and defensive logistics it rolled out for its commerce there. Beyond the Gold Coast, though, Portugal's main priority remained identifying other sources of gold in Africa, a continent that it initially believed generally abounded in the metal. Decidedly, gold was the sort of good of which there could never be too much, and toward this end the Portuguese sent embassies two hundred miles upriver in Senegambia to Timbuktu, still hoping to corner the market in gold from the Sahel.

If opening a route to India had been Lisbon's driving preoccupation in the closing years of the fifteenth century, it is even stranger to see how much energy and effort was expended in sending another major embassy to the Kongo kingdom in Central Africa in 1491. This was a project replete with priests and artisans, dispatched in order to establish economic ties on a scale beyond even Elmina. Kongo was a vastly larger and more impressive polity than the modest kingdom the Portuguese had entered into trade with at Elmina, and Lisbon imagined that it could generate big, immediate commercial gains under royal monopoly. India, or even the farther reaches of southern Africa, by contrast, seemed more speculative.

As we have seen, Portugal would not follow up on Dias's breakthrough to the Indian Ocean in 1488 for nearly nine years. It was simply too busy in Africa, where the returns remained extraordinarily high. Moreover, when Lisbon finally did follow up on Dias's explorations, the captain it chose for the new expedition was no decorated veteran of this new maritime age, someone whose status would reflect the highest of royal motivations, but rather a minor court figure named Vasco da Gama.

There is another and altogether different way of appreciating the historical impact of West Africa's gold, though. It helped make possible the financing of new fleets and hence Portugal's most famous missions of exploration—first continuing down the coast of Africa, and then, after 1497, to India. The gigantic boost that Mina gold provided the crown did more than fuel the desire to discover yet more gold in Africa. It made it possible for Lisbon to keep pace with Spain in their headlong course into ocean faring, discovery, conquest, crusading, and intercontinental trade. An intriguing marginal note in a book from Christopher Columbus's personal library, d'Ailly's *Imago mundi*, has been taken to suggest that Columbus himself was in Lisbon at the time of Dias's return from the southern extremity of Africa, and took keen notice, even though this event transpired without great celebration:

> *And he told the most serene king of Portugal how he sailed 600 leagues beyond what had been sailed before, that is to say, 450 to the South and 250 to the North [sic], as far as a promontory he called the Cape of Good Hope. . . . The voyage itself [Dias] drew and wrote down on a sailing chart, to present it before the eyes of the most serene king. In all this I was present.*

Just four years later, Portugal received news of Columbus's return from his first voyage to the Americas, in the most direct way possible. The explorer's famous ship, the *Niña*, anchored off Lisbon before its return to Spain, and by almost incredible coincidence was met in the harbor of the Portuguese capital by an armed craft captained by none other than Dias, who then escorted Columbus to port. Soon thereafter, João II, who was naturally impatient to learn of the Genoese sailor's discoveries on behalf of rival Castile, received Columbus at court. Bartolomé de las Casas recorded their meeting, although one may assume he rendered it theatrically and not exactly verbatim, in his *Historias de las Indias*:

> *Then the king, understanding clearly the greatness of the discovered lands, and the riches that had already been imagined in them, not being able to hide the great pain which he felt . . . for the loss of such inestimable things, which through his own fault he had let slip through his hands, with a loud voice and an impulse*

*of anger against himself, beat his fist upon his chest saying; "Oh,
man of poor understanding, why did you allow such an enterprise of such importance to get out of your hands?"*

For all of the palpable chagrin attributed to João in this moment
of drama, when the record is fully considered, there is no objective reason to consider that Portugal was squarely bested in this
era's geopolitical scramble by its larger, more celebrated, and near
constant Iberian rival. That we find it so easy to believe so reflects
more than anything our contemporary devaluation of Africa. In the
1494 Treaty of Tordesillas, Portugal and Spain divided newly discovered lands outside of Europe according to a meridian located
370 leagues west of the Cape Verde islands, which by then already
belonged to Lisbon. Portugal would have rights to anything to the
east of that line, nominally including sub-Saharan Africa. Spain, to
be sure, won most of the Americas, save for Portuguese Brazil, while
at least for a time Lisbon secured control of much of Asia, which
is conventionally assumed to have been Europe's greatest preoccupation all along, as well as perhaps the biggest prize in the Age of
Discovery. And yet, careful calculations of the costs incurred in the
much longer-distance trade routes to Asia in the early sixteenth century show that Africa generated as much as twice the amount in real
returns for Lisbon than even the long coveted trade in spices and
early textiles with the East did.

The historian Felipe Fernández-Armesto has also expressed a
similar thought, but even more strikingly, in part because of his use
of an accessible contemporary analogy, making him one of the rare,
prominent contemporary historians of the Hispanic world to do so.
Most historians have treated Europe's trade and human contacts
with Africa in this era as "an aside in the formation of the West."
Fernandez-Armesto, by contrast, likened late-fifteenth-century Portugal to the economically weak nations of the so-called developing
world today, which drill in deep waters offshore in the desperate
hope of a breakthrough discovery of oil or gas that can alleviate their

poverty and lift them onto a more promising path for the future. This works out well for remarkably few countries, of course, and for none that come to mind the way it did for Lisbon nearly six hundred years ago.

However impactful, Portugal's discovery of African gold would merely constitute the first prize in a series of dramatic payoffs. It was superseded by a lucrative new trade in African slaves, and then by a boom in Portuguese sugar production on islands located just off the African continent. Soon afterward, this sugar boom would enter a drastically bigger phase, one of truly world-historical significance, and this was based entirely on African slave labor, starting on the tiny island of São Tomé. Fernão Gomes's men discovered that island in 1471, after their meeting with Kwamena Ansa, and it became a Portuguese colony in 1485, creating the vastly profitable template for plantation agriculture in Brazil. Surely, by any reasonable calculation, this would all amount to at least as much of a windfall as Spain received from the Americas, but that lay slightly ahead in time. For now, though, the essential pivot around which all this good European fortune turned was the fort of São Jorge da Mina, and the bountiful gold that it disgorged. Understanding the emergence of modernity in this era requires not only that we explore the early Afro-European contacts in depth and with greater patience, but that we ask ourselves: How is it that this story has gone for so long being so seldom examined or told?

9

WEALTH IN PEOPLE VERSUS
WEALTH IN THINGS

AKING THE MOST OF Portugal's discovery of the Mina coast required labor and, given any number of contemporary realities, increasing gold output meant acquiring slave labor. What use, one must ask, would it have been to build a trading fort at Elmina if the supplies of gold were, however promising, still irregular? By the same token, from the African perspective, what use was there in putting up with the meddlesome presence of the new white strangers from afar along the Mina coast if the best they could do was to produce a trickle of familiar metalwares, along with textiles from North Africa, an item that West Africans already enjoyed existing supplies of?

White-Arab and white-on-white slavery (mostly involving Slavs, a name that shares an obvious common root with the word "slave") had survived in Italy, southern France, and Iberia into the sixteenth century. And while slavery was in sharp decline in those regions by the late fifteenth and early sixteenth centuries, it would remain, as the historian Philip Curtin has observed, "at least a minor aspect of economic life throughout the Mediterranean world until the eighteenth century."* It was the Blackness of Afri-

---

* As Orlando Patterson has written, "There is nothing notably peculiar about the institution of slavery. It has existed from before the dawn of human history down to the twentieth century, in the most primitive of human societies and in the most civilized."

cans that offered the convenient rationale of a categorical difference from whites, something that became a prime justification for a new and soon to be dramatic expansion of slavery. Here, too, in this very same essentialization, or categorical thinking, lay the origins of modern racism.

Slavery in this part of Africa (as elsewhere in the sub-Saharan regions of the continent) was an age-old practice, albeit one that bore almost no resemblance to the chattel model that was just then set to emerge on sugar plantations, hand in hand with the flourishing of Western imperialism. For the Akan, a sprawling collection of ethnic groups whose languages shared a high degree of mutual intelligibility, slaves had traditionally been acquired during internecine competition, as well as during expansionary drives against unrelated groups. The captives in these conflicts were sometimes put to work in agriculture, road building, and even soldiering, but much like the Ottomans, the general emphasis was on assimilating them into society as rapidly as possible. Slaves were married into Akan families, especially females, and integrated in other ways, too, often as concubines and domestics, with little stigma attaching to them.

The Akan, who controlled the richest sources of gold located inland from Elmina, had recently established lucrative trade ties with the empires of the western Sahel, like Mali and Songhai, using them as an outlet for their precious metals. These they sold in exchange for goods from North Africa and even Europe. The value in the proposition of contact and the expense or bother for each side, Portuguese and Akan, was premised on both greater and more regular volume. But until India's coveted cloths became available, the Portuguese goods were not deemed desirable enough to the Akan to warrant the large-scale diversion of their own indigenous workforce to gold production. As a French slave merchant noted scornfully, the Portuguese "have only trifles [bagatelles] for their trade." At the time of European contact, the Akan had already begun applying remarkable technical ingenuity to the challenges of gold production, sinking mine shafts to a depth of nearly 230 feet, among the deepest anywhere. But generating yet more of the metal for trade with the Europeans necessitated substantially more labor, for both mine works and for porterage. Using draft animals like horses, long so integral to life in Europe and Asia, was not an option because West Africa south of the Sahel was infested with the tsetse fly, bearer of the trypanosome parasite. And the region lacked any type of native beast of burden of its own that could be employed in meaningful numbers.

This shortage of draft animals combined with other factors to make the Akan supremely reluctant to sell their ethnic fellows, or even war captives from neighboring peoples, for that matter, to the Europeans as slaves—at least in this period. One of the primary measures of wealth and power in the African kingdoms of this era was the number of one's subjects, with a premium often placed on the head count of men. It is not giving away anything to say that this reluctance would no longer hold once European traders became much more numerous along the coast. Higher demand for slaves then led in turn to the supply of vastly greater quantities and variety of trade goods, eventually including the sale of guns, especially by the Dutch and English in the seventeenth century. This, as we will see, fueled widespread political violence and instability in the region, which proved more effective than anything else in generating a new market for slaves.

Nearly a half century before the trade in slaves to supply the plantations of the New World began to ramp up, the main quandary the Portuguese faced in West Africa was how to boost the flow of gold from Elmina. This problem found its solution when it was discovered around 1480 that the peoples of the Gold Coast were willing and even eager to sell their yellow metal in exchange for African captives brought to them from afar. Here it should be emphasized that up until this time, the people of this continent had little notion of a collective identity of themselves as being "African," as anyone might understand the term today. Put another way, among the people of the continent in the fifteenth century, "African" was a label for a moral or political community that was still awaiting invention. It is safe to say that the Akan, both those on the coast at Elmina and in the interior, where most of the gold supply originated, would have felt quite differently about a traffic in other Africans with Europeans if they had had any inkling that the future held the same thing in store for them.

If for the Portuguese, and for the other Europeans who followed in their wake into this region, "Black African" was already becoming a categorical form of identity, one readily imagines that the sight of chiefs from Elmina eagerly buying Black slaves from whites, human beings whom chiefs and native traders in Benin had sold just as eagerly to those Europeans, went a long way toward "normalizing" this new form of commerce in the European imagination.

A Flemish sailor named Eustache de la Fosse recorded the first example of this new type of intra-African trade in slaves. In 1479 or 1480, he purchased a woman and her son from the coast of present-day Sierra Leone in exchange for a brass barber's basin and three or four large *manilhas*. Farther east, at Shama, the two captives were sold for fourteen gold weights. In the chronicle he wrote about his voyage, de la Fosse tells how, later, while he was being held prisoner by the Portuguese at the Village of Two Parts, the future Elmina, he witnessed two hundred slaves arrive there by boat from yet farther east for sale against local supplies of gold.

The story of the Flemish sailor accords with other accounts that say there were societies farther east along the coast that, at least initially, appeared to have no great hesitancy selling Africans into bondage to the Europeans in exchange for our by now familiar mixture of goods, including cloth and metalwares. In 1486, Portuguese ships exploring the eastern end of the Niger River delta, which their countrymen had first reached in 1471, found five snaking channels nested in a vast mangrove-forested water world. They called them the Slave Rivers, giving a clear sense of what they were looking for.

There, the newcomers were welcomed at Gwaton, a thriving port on the River Osse, which they used as their base. Gwaton, they soon discovered, was a commercial satellite of the Bini Kingdom (henceforth Benin, as it came to be known in most European languages), whose origins dated to the eleventh century.*

The Benin the Europeans encountered was nothing like the polity ruled over by Kwamena Ansa, whose diminutive territory was surrounded by substantially larger, if still fragmented Akan statelets. Benin was the preeminent power of the day in a broad swath of coastal West Africa. When the Portuguese showed up in 1485, they were impressed with the large rampart that surrounded the main city. Archaeological surveys conducted in the 1990s revealed this structure to be part of a complex network of walls, some of them towering, that extended for some ten thousand miles. The kingdom was also endowed with a highly centralized government, regulated trade, a police system, and an army that could field more than 100,000 soldiers. The Benin monarchy, led by kings who bore the title oba, maintained tight control over economic affairs through royal guilds that oversaw the production of both arts and high-value commercial products, like the fine textiles that it traded throughout the region.

The Portuguese instantly recognized the rich potential for trade in a savory local pepper that was sold in Gwaton and quickly became prized on markets in Flanders, but nothing could match the main draw of slaves. And the Portuguese were pleased to discover an existing supply in slaves rooted in Benin's wars with neighboring peoples. Initially, Benin, too, was powerfully intrigued with the commercial possibilities that contact with the European newcomers seemed to offer, and in 1486, the Beninese oba sent an embassy headed by the chief of Gwaton to Lisbon, where he was warmly received. This was two years, in fact, before the mission to Lisbon of the Jolof king previously mentioned. Chronicles from the court of João II described the Beninese ambassador as "a man of good speech and natural wisdom," according to the historian David Northup. "Great feasts were held in his honor and he was shown many of the good things of these

---

* Not to be confused with the modern-day country that bears the name Benin, the Bini Kingdom was located in what is now Nigeria.

kingdoms" and given presents of "rich clothes for himself and his wife" to take back on his return journey. More to the point, the ships that returned the emissary to Benin carried clerics whose job it was to try to convert the ruler of this affluent kingdom, along with traders to begin purchasing spices and slaves.

The Portuguese were not the only ones, however, who through such court receptions and diplomacy were forming new ideas of self-awareness in relationship to the perceived "other," another essential building block of what we commonly think of as modernity. The people of Benin were doing much the same. We know this by virtue of their distinctive artistic traditions, which had begun to flourish as early as the twelfth century, and were both aesthetically and technically highly refined. By the time of the contact with the Portuguese, artists in Benin were able to cast plaques in brass using the elaborate so-called lost wax technique at a thickness of only one-eighth inch, surpassing even the metalworking skill of European artisans during the Renaissance. This involved sculpting a model in clay, which was then covered in a finely detailed layer of wax. This wax layer was then carefully covered with another layer of clay. Once fully formed, molten metal is poured into the mold, replacing the wax, which drains away.

The demand for ceremonial art that, among other things, conserved a record of events at court and history, appears to be one of the principal reasons the Beninese coveted trade with foreigners for copper and for bronze *manilhas*, which they melted down to use in the creation of friezes and busts. (These are collected nowadays in the museums of the rich world today and although predominantly made of brass are collectively known as the Benin Bronzes.) A slave sold to the Portuguese in Gwaton in 1500 would have fetched between twelve and fifteen *manilhas*, but the price for human labor would rise smartly as the trade developed. The Portuguese appear frequently in the sublimely executed Benin art of this period, almost as human curios or novelties, with their long hair and beards and exaggeratedly pointy noses—just as Africans and, soon thereafter, Native Americans and other "exotics" would begin appearing in European figurative art and literature. This was all part of what scholars have called the "transformation in subjectivities" that began to take place in this era, when Afro-European contact began changing the way that people everywhere—not just Europeans—saw the world and understood their own humanity, in increasingly relativist ways.

After such promising beginnings, though, the trade with Benin would soon disappoint. For the first few years of this human traffic, Lisbon assigned a single ship to assure a dedicated service between Elmina and Benin. Round trips typically took between two and three months, with the bulk of that time at sea consumed in the westward, return passage to Portugal's fort on the Gold Coast, fighting adverse prevailing eastward ocean currents; this limited the initial supply to a paltry 300 slaves a year or so. By the turn of the sixteenth century, the men who ran Elmina were clamoring for more slaves, in order to compete with the Akan's older, rival outlet for gold overland via the Sahel. Once they were able to persuade Lisbon to dedicate three more ships to this slave route, this simple but incredibly vital economic circuit had a much stronger impulse, since slaves brought to Elmina from points east could be sold to the Akan. At its peak, which still lay a few years in the future, the profit the Portuguese realized from the sale of slaves alone, equaled 15 percent of their profits from the trade in gold itself. Thus, a second set of ships was assigned to making regular runs from Elmina to Lisbon carrying African gold one way and European functionaries and trade goods the other.

The Portuguese had other goals, as well, beyond the strictly mercantile; they were especially keen on associating religious conversion with their trade arrangements, and unlike Kwamena Ansa in Elmina, the oba in Benin showed at least a passing initial interest in the unfamiliar spiritual practices of the Europeans. There is nothing in the historical record to suggest that if Africans had widely adopted Christianity it would have materially altered the trajectory of the transatlantic slave trade. In Benin, and then Kongo, the Portuguese made early, earnest efforts at conversion. The overall impression one gets, though, is that the missionary work of the late fourteenth and fifteenth centuries was mostly about providing religious and ideological cover for the horrors of the recent innovation we now know as chattel slavery, not to mention an intra-European competition for legitimacy and prestige in which the Catholic Church and a global contest with Islam played outsized roles.

In their early encounters with Europeans bearing religious agendas, it must be said that Africans similarly suffered from no lack of ulterior motives. The Beninese oba seems to have calculated that indulging the whites in a discussion about their faith, and even allowing some modest and carefully controlled experiments in conversion, was a small price to pay if this could win him access to Portuguese weapons and other forms of assistance in fighting an ongoing war against a neighboring people, the Idah. Motivated in this way, the oba sequestered some of the Portuguese missionaries in his war camp near the battlefront to discuss Christianity. After returning to his capital, he announced that he would allow one of his sons and a number of other nobles to undergo conversion. Benin won the Idah war without great difficulty, though, and the seemingly open-minded oba then died soon thereafter. A series of successors showed far less interest in the Portuguese, whether for their trade goods or their religion. Then, around 1514, Benin began restricting the commerce in slaves, first by banning the sale of male war captives, who were probably deemed of greater value to Benin as assimilable subjects. For African rulers, adding people in this way was the only realistic solution to increasing one's power in the near and medium terms.

Deprived of a supply of slave labor, the Portuguese, whose agents in the Bight of Benin were dying by the score from endemic tropical diseases like malaria and yellow fever, eventually had to close their *feitoria*, or "factory." What is most noteworthy about this episode in Afro-Portuguese relations in the early sixteenth century is that Benin always remained firmly in control of the terms of engagement with the Europeans, obliging the outsiders to broadly conform to its customs and protocols, and ultimately shutting off the supply of slaves when it no longer perceived the trade to be in its interest. In fact, with the Portuguese playing the game of bilateral relations for the most part on Benin's terms, successive obas may have imagined the foreigners as their vassals, even if the Europeans did not share this view.

Portugal would nonetheless come back to the river delta region, helping to turn it into one of the most prolific sources of African captives sold off to the cash crop plantations of the New World between the last quarter of the seventeenth century and the first quarter of the eighteenth, when nearly half a million people were shipped into slavery from the coastal area known as the Bight of Benin. For now, though, Lisbon's attentions were shifting with huge consequences to the equatorial island of São Tomé, which was located off the coast of Central Africa.

10

CIRCUITS OLD AND NEW

M AKING A MODERN COMMERCIAL virtue of its bygone imperial marauding, the Portuguese national airline, TAP,
names many of its long-haul planes after some of the country's most famous navigators. During the research of this book, I
endured a long, uncomfortable layover at the Lisbon airport, watch-
ing as these aircraft berthed at their gates and eventually trundled off
to their assigned runways for takeoff. Their fat bellies were embla-
zoned with the names of the country's most celebrated men of discovery, people like Bartolomeu Dias, Vasco da Gama, Fernão de
Magalhães (Ferdinand Magellan), and Pedro Álvares Cabral. It was
exciting enough to be flying off to São Tomé, one of the few African
countries I had never visited before, but there was an added delight.
The airplane would be making a brief stopover in Accra, the capital
of Ghana, which meant that TAP was operating an airplane route
today that re-creates a nearly five-century-old itinerary that retraces
one of the most important economic circuits in the history of the
world. It did so by linking Portugal, Ghana, and São Tomé, much as
slave- and gold-carrying ships of the sixteenth century had. Alas, the
airline was doing so with a total lack of fanfare and, as far as I could
detect, even awareness. Such is the state of recognition of the importance of Blackness to the history of the Atlantic.

For a variety of convergent reasons, by the second decade of the sixteenth century, the Portuguese had shifted their priorities from maintaining the factory operating in Benin since 1486 to fully colonizing the then uninhabited island of São Tomé. Endowed with black, volcanic soils and with plentiful tropical rainfall, São Tomé, which lies practically on the Equator about 200 miles west of present-day Gabon, was discovered in 1471. The Portuguese had learned some lessons from the death toll on the mainland in places like Benin and from the political problems attendant to dealing with strong, and sometimes fickle African states. They had also learned from their experience (and that of the Spanish) of other islands off the African coast—places like Madeira, the Canary Islands, and the Cape Verde islands—where the ability to produce lucrative cash crops, especially sugar, was making early African imperialism so financially profitable. For Portugal, there was an additional advantage to settling São Tomé that related to the kingdom's small population. There were only so many men that it could dedicate to new foreign adventurism, and in island environments it could get a lot of bang from deploying even modest numbers of settlers. Using a launchpad like Cape Verde, Lisbon learned furthermore that it could conduct a lucrative trade in slaves in nearby coastal areas of the continent without fear of being attacked or overrun. When São Tomé was formally decreed a colony in 1485, some historians have argued that the island was envisioned as a stopover point for long voyages to Asia, which were just then being dreamed about. For navigational reasons, this never turned out to be the case, even after Dias's 1488 breakthrough to the Indian Ocean. Such speculation, however, distracts from much more immediate Portuguese priorities for the island (and for the smaller nearby island of Príncipe). From the very first royal decrees establishing its legal basis as a functional colony, Lisbon had three practical goals in mind: supplying Elmina with foodstuffs and other provisions that could sustain the small population that resided at the São Jorgé da Mina fort, supplying slaves obtained from nearby continental Africa to supplement and eventually replace Benin as a source of Black labor, and producing sugar for European markets to supplement Portugal's output from Madeira, which had been highly profitable, but was already peaking and would soon decline.

A fourth important purpose that São Tomé would serve was more a matter of accidental timing, and not deliberate strategy. In 1492, Spain expelled an estimated 100,000 Jews, mostly from Castile and Granada, who streamed into Portugal; for a time afterward Jews may have amounted to as much as a tenth of the Portuguese population. The country's rulers were highly ambivalent about this sharp spike in the Jewish population, at once eager to benefit from the absorption of new wealth and the skills and knowledge that they brought, but aware of the deep currents of antisemitic sentiment that existed throughout Iberia. Thus, Jews were given a terrible choice: convert to Christianity or leave the country. Many chose the latter, with some going to Cape Verde or the Upper Guinea region of the African mainland, where some of them went on to mix with local communities. Others eventually made their way to the New World, which was just then about to be opened up, with some of them becoming important to the story of booming sugar production.

With São Tomé being so far away from Europe, and with Europeans sent there suffering very high mortality rates from tropical diseases, even if not quite as high as Benin, the biggest initial challenge to building a new colony there lay in peopling the place in order to make it economically viable. To do so, Lisbon relied in part on deporting *degredados* (prisoners), prostitutes, and other "undesirables" to the island, but also by sending as many as two thousand Jewish youths, who were to adopt new names and live there as so-called New Christians, meaning new and involuntary converts to that religion. The surviving documentary evidence from this period is thin, but that record suggests as many as six hundred of the Jewish newcomers perished soon after their arrival on the island. The remainder, however, would form an important constituent of an entirely new and important social hybrid that emerged as a by-product of Portuguese-African contact in the early crucibles of the trade in gold and slaves: Creole culture.* This Jewish population seems to have played an important role in São Tomé's innovations in sugar production, and in sugar's subsequent commercialization in Europe. From an early date, Lisbon took care to supply African women for the pleasure and convenience of the settlers, and with an idea to breeding more colonists. Beyond that, Creole peoples, who were racially mixed and spoke new languages and dialects that derived from the blending of their varied origins, would play an essential role in the creation of the new, ocean-spanning civilization of the Atlantic world. By doing so, they came to constitute another important brick in our rising edifice of modernity, but the first place for us to look at this phenomenon is Elmina, to which we will return shortly, and not São Tomé.

São Tomé began sending its first shipments of slaves onward to Elmina before the close of the fifteenth century. The early human traffic along this circuit seems to have been mostly generated from trade for slaves with Benin. But the first two decades of the sixteenth century saw the rise of the Kongo as a leading source of bound labor for Elmina, and by the 1530s, enslaved people were being sent from Kongo via São Tomé to the New World, as well as to thriving markets for Black labor in Lisbon and Seville. From the Portuguese perspective, Kongo had the advantage of greater proximity to its new outpost at São Tomé than Benin. The leaders of Kongo, which became the first and only major African polity in the fifteenth and sixteenth centuries to embrace Christianity in a wholehearted way, also cooperated politically with the Portuguese, at least initially. The trade in slaves on the continent that began almost immediately with the settlement of São Tomé was so lucrative, in fact, that European *degradados*, sent there under a form of indentured servitude, quickly began trying to flee the island in order to set them-

---

* The term "Creole" has taken on different meanings in different times and settings. In the Old World, including modern Africa, it generally refers to mixed-race societies and their linguistic offshoots. In early New World historiography, and particularly in the United States, meanwhile, Creole is often held to mean either the descendants of Europeans or of African slaves born in the New World.

selves up on the African mainland to enter the business illegally on their own accounts.

In 1504, 900 slaves were shipped from São Tomé for sale at Elmina, and by the early 1520s, the island was importing roughly 2000 enslaved people a year from the African mainland, and year after year shipping about a quarter of those captives onward for trade with the Akan of the Gold Coast in slave vessel runs that Portugal legally mandated to operate every fifty days. The remainder, the roughly 1500 Africans acquired in nearby Kongo and its surroundings, were sold off to the New World or to Europe. Although it was only met in the breach, this prescribed rhythm set in motion some of the most notorious innovations in modern slaving. These included the mercilessly tight packing of bound slaves on ships, sparse feeding routines for slaves at sea, and the steep pricing bias in favor of captives between their early teens and early twenties. Young slaves were prized for reasons of labor productivity and, in the case of women, fertility. Given the gruesome conditions of the traffic, a final consideration was the sheer ability to survive the barracoon, or stockade, where slaves were held while awaiting shipment to faraway markets. These holding pens would go on to be deployed in nearly every major slave trade market along the West and Central African coasts as the European reliance on chattel labor spread from Brazil and Spanish America to the Caribbean and North America over the succeeding centuries.

We have argued that Elmina deserves a much more prominent place in history for the way that the specie traded there strongly buoyed Portugal, helped accelerate Europe's economic integration, and helped fuel a continent-wide price revolution, meaning an era of steady growth and moderate inflation after a long period of near stagnation. As a purchaser of slaves from elsewhere in Africa, Elmina was equally important as a catalyst for what became the Atlantic slave trade. In this, though, São Tomé deserves an equal, if distinct renown—or infamy, one that has so far largely eluded it. This 330-square-mile island would be the last stop in the Eastern Hemisphere for sugar cultivation. The practice arrived after a long and halting westward migration, which began in prehistory in New Guinea and moved to India and then to the Near East. Finally, with the Crusades, it took hold in the extremities of southern Europe. With the progress of Iberian navigation, sugar cultivation expanded into the Atlantic world, notably the Canaries and Madeira. Those islands, located off the African continent, were sites of modest innovation. They were home to far larger plantations than what had been typical anywhere in the Europe of their time, growing a specialized product for faraway markets, and doing so under the domination of distant, imperial powers. These new-style plantations further distinguished themselves from anything analogous in Europe by the larger numbers of workers they employed—a mixture of indentured servants and slaves, altogether numbering several hundred at any time, with a functional minimum of one slave per every two acres. Just as unusual for their time was the highly regimented nature of the labor performed on them. In the approach to sugar cultivation practiced on these Atlantic islands, which depended on lots of specialized roles for workers, one can also find an early seed of the intense division of labor that is more commonly identified with capitalism and the beginnings of industrialization.

But it was not until São Tomé that the modern plantation model based on sugar production came together in its more or less definitive form. Bosses on this island did most of the new things that cane growers had done on Madeira or the Canaries, but they added a series of final flourishes. São Tomé's plantations were larger still and more industrial in nature than those on these other islands. Their most important innovation, though, stands out both in terms of its impact on the lives of the human beings brought by force to work there and in the way it shaped the global economy, society, and geopolitics of the next five hundred years. Here, for the very first time, we find fully racialized slavery for the production of processed agricultural exports into foreign markets. São Tomé's plantations, in other words, were designed for and run exclusively on the basis of the violent domination of Black African slave labor. This would prove to be the indispensable killer apparatus of modernity. And it was from the harbors of São Tomé that the model soon spread to the New World, with all of the grotesque inhumanity inherent to it.

On the strength of its ready access to abundant supplies of slaves from nearby continental Africa, the output from plantations on Portuguese São Tomé helped launch the sharpest ascent that any food crop had seen in human history. When production of sugar on the islands off Africa had begun, early in the fifteenth century, the crystalline sweetener was less a commodity than a medicinal, a tonic that was affordable only to royalty and other elites. São Tomé put sugar on the road to becoming the mass consumer product we nowadays take for granted. Portugal had only recently been hoisted by its trade in Elmina gold. By the middle third of the sixteenth century, it had gone on to figure out how to bring together sugar production, bound Black labor, and largely private enterprise, in order to dominate the South Atlantic and Europe's commercial relations with Africa. Crucially, this positioned Lisbon to use the great wealth and expertise gained in these endeavors to launch its subsequent expansion into the New World and beyond.

As if all of this was not remarkable enough, the history of São Tomé stands out for even more important but widely overlooked features. It was the first in a long run of Black slave societies created for and lucratively run by Europeans, places where slaves vastly outnumbered their masters (think Barbados, Jamaica, parts of Brazil, and the cotton-growing heartland of the American South). This pattern would become the norm in most places where Europeans and their descendants built plantation economies during the first two centuries of the slave era in the Americas. Overall, until 1820, four times more Africans were brought across the Atlantic to the New World than Europeans. Relatedly, São Tomé was the first place conceived from the very outset as a site for the conversion of Black men and women into chattel. Not for nothing, this word shares a common root with "cattle," and it means dehumanized beasts of burden. São Tomé was the site from which the first Portuguese shipments of commoditized slaves from Africa to the New World took place. It was also the scene of some of the earliest Black slave revolts, including a poorly remembered event that was nonetheless one of the few in history that can be considered successful. As we will see, these unheeded lightning bolts foretold an earthshaking thunderclap that would come with a delay of more than two and a half centuries in the form of a singularly transformative event in world history, the Haitian Revolution. Curiously, despite all of this, one can spend days driving around São Tomé, as I myself found during the work on this book, searching in vain for prominent landmarks or public memorialization of this history.*

---

* In 2018, a statue of Amador, the leader of a slave revolt in 1595, was installed in front of São Tomé's main library, and a likeness of Amador features in the watermark of the country's banknotes.

11

UNTO THE END OF THE WORLD

OBVIOUS RELICS OF THE physical legacy of slavery and of the era in which it was built are surprisingly scarce in São Tomé. The "great houses" of the plantation society are few, even as ruins, and those that survive are secreted in mountains on heavily forested cul-de-sacs. On People's Square, in the very center of the island's dusty and forlorn little capital, which bears the same name as the island itself, one finds Our Lady of Grace, the dowdy, twin-spired descendant of the colony's founding cathedral, originally built in 1534. Given the seminal role the Catholic Church played in Lisbon's launching of the slave trade, by providing sanction for the activity and even trading in human captives itself, one feels walking past it there should be some kind of statue or monument for the slaves right here.* Instead, five minutes further along, passing through deeply potholed streets, one finds a tiny national museum housed in the original 1566 fortress, at water's edge, with its original old guns strewn along its base, that the Portuguese built to secure their prize. (In 1599, São Tomé would be raided by the Dutch as Portugal's empire came under pressure from European rivals eager to end its domination of trade with Africa.)

* In one of the first acts of direct church involvement, in 1446, the bishop of Algarve invested in a caravel to partake in the African slave trade, alongside other ships given license by Prince Henry.

Actually, "museum" is a bit of a misnomer. This airless and ill-lit place offered scant information about slavery, the central fact about an island whose history is central to modern slavery itself. The modest exhibits inside speak, instead, mostly of the twentieth century. Most incongruous of all, though, just outside the museum's doors, on a sandy patch of ground by a beach where young people throng to swim by day, loom giant statues of three Portuguese explorers who helped establish this colony, and the trade that came with it. One of them is of João de Santarém, who sailed on one of the Portuguese ships that found gold in Ghana, in 1471, while another is of Pêro Escobar, who crewed with Diogo Cão aboard the ships that made the first contact with Kongo in 1482. The third statue is of João de Paiva, who was granted possession of the island in 1485 by the Portuguese crown. It was in their era that the verb *descobrir*, "to discover," begins to enter common usage in Portuguese in association with far-flung societies in Africa. The very concept signaled the emergence of a new way of thinking about identity, which was becoming multiformed and highly relativist. In a remarkably short period of time, the idea that an endless succession of other worlds, each with its own transformative potential, lay just beyond each horizon became a commonplace. This all started with the gold of West Africa, followed there by a human traffic in slaves. Escobar later sailed on da Gama's first expedition to India, in 1497, and on Pedro Álvares Cabral's accidental discovery of Brazil, three years later.

As I traveled around the world researching this book, I gained a profound new appreciation of how monuments like these, balanced against the absence of memorials to the African experience to slavery and to the millions who died in the production of wealth for Europe and in New World, have become a kind of global norm. Paradoxically, this seemed true even in nominally independent countries ruled by Black people. I saw it throughout the Caribbean, in places like Bridgetown, Barbados, for example, where the main statue in the center of town is a bronze likeness of Horatio Nelson, as if you happened to be walking through London's Trafalgar Square. Famously, Lord Nelson fought the French and Spanish in the late eighteenth century to preserve British dominance on the high seas and in the Caribbean, in particular, at the very height of the American slave trade. The vice admiral was a fierce defender of the transatlantic traffic in Africans in his private life as well.

A year and a half after my visit to the island, Barbados finally removed the statue from its pedestal just opposite Parliament, a mere 207 years after it had been installed. Two weeks later, in another move that was at once symbolic and yet full of import, the island rescinded its recognition of British royals as its head of state. In one of his biggest hits, "Redemption Song," the visionary Jamaican artist Bob Marley had famously called on Africans and members of the Black diaspora to "emancipate yourselves from mental slavery." The lesson of Barbados is how difficult and protracted a process that can be, especially for a country so economically dependent on tourism.

The clearest manifestations of slavery in São Tomé lay not in the converted sixteenth-century fort-museum, but rather in the timelessness of the little towns and villages that hug the sharply winding mountain roads that go around the north of the island, where the direct descendants of enslaved sugar workers now live in unbroken poverty. Almost no one I asked in these tiny settlements seemed to recognize the names of the most infamous of the historical plantations of the early slave era. With a bit of persistence, however, driving on flooded, unpaved roads, I found some of those sites in the unmarked beyond, places like Playa das Conchas, where long, green plains that slope downward almost to the very edge of the sea provided land of sufficient expanse to make profitable sugar plantations with. Today, the fields lie fallow, overgrown with high, windblown grasses.

Where sugar was concerned, São Tomé burned incredibly brightly but, as such things tend to go, only briefly. It rose as a mighty force in the nascent Atlantic economy and then, its soils giving out and then spent, gave way to Brazil, the sugar plantation-complex's

new and incomparably bigger center of gravity.* From there, the
island entered a phase of irreversible decline. This all took place
in the space of a mere seventy years. Sugar had been launched to
great profit in Madeira around 1425. Production in Madeira topped
out at about 300,000 arrobas, (an arroba, a customary weight mea-
surement of the era in Portugal, is equal to 32 pounds). By 1496,
when São Tomé was being settled, Madeira's production was down
to about 120,000 arrobas. By 1530, São Tomé had seized the baton
and was the leading supplier of sugar to Lisbon. In 1555, there were
between sixty and eighty mills for the crop on the island, producing 150,000 arrobas, and production was rising steeply each year.
Twelve thousand or so Africans worked the land and kept the mills
churning at any given time, performing labor so arduous that the
working life expectancy was probably no more than a handful of
years. This required constant resupply of Africans from the mainland. Not only did these slaves have to keep the insatiable mills fed
with cane, but on their one day off per week, they also had to somehow produce enough food to feed themselves. By contrast, the small
community of whites on São Tomé were supplied with staples and
luxuries alike ferried in by the twenty or so ships a year that called
from Portugal.

The slave plantation innovations that came together in their near
final form in São Tomé, terribly inhuman though they were, would
be of far greater economic consequence over the long run than even
the much more famous expansionary pursuits of Spain in the same
era. That is because the violently marshaled labor of Blacks led to
much more lasting productive economic activity—with far more
opportunities for what economists call virtuous feedback loops—

---

* In speaking of a sugar plantation-complex, I have adopted the term "plantation complex"
derived from the writings of the historian Philip Curtin. Curtin used this term to describe
the unprecedentedly large farms that Europeans began to operate in the early sixteenth
century, using enchattled slaves in large numbers to grow tropical commodities. I have
appended the word "sugar" to the Curtin term, because sugar was the crop in places like
São Tomé and Brazil, whose production needs drove the creation of these entities. Later in
this work I speak of the "slave plantation-complex" to accommodate the fact that the model
of large slave-labor-dependent plantations was widely adopted for the production of other
crops, from coffee and cacao to rice and cotton.

than the mining that drove Spain's acquisition of wealth from the New World ever would. However fabulous, Spain's silver and Brazil's gold booms, moreover, would eventually peter out, their peaks extending less than a century;* on the other hand, plantation agriculture powered by Black slaves would continue far into the nineteenth century in the Portuguese-speaking world and would be emulated by many others. Here and there around the Atlantic world, including in São Tomé and Cuba, plantations that operated with near-slave-like conditions would not be completely extirpated until well into the twentieth century. Directly or indirectly, the essence of the slave plantation model that arose here would be responsible for the two most significant mass agricultural revolutions in modern history, both of which we will look into in detail: Big Sugar and Big Cotton, with the straight line that connects them running right through the cultivation of indigo and tobacco here and there as well as South Carolina rice and coffee and cacao, as the slave plantation experience was extended to wherever it could be made to work in the New World.

One cannot move on from São Tomé without considering one final feature of the deep and unheralded history of this island. Nowadays few bother to ask the question of why the Europeans did not focus their energies on building plantations on the African mainland itself, especially given Africa's proximity to their home continent compared with the New World they would soon discover. This question is lent additional urgency because of the abundance in Africa of finely suited land on which to grow sugar and, later, cotton and all the plantation crops that came in between them. Africa, after all, was the very source of all the labor so indispensable for this enterprise, labor long considered by Europeans to be inexhaustible. Such views obtained even a century after the founding of the São Tomé slave colony, and would persist among Europe's slaving powers long thereafter. In 1591, when upward of twenty thousand slaves a year were being shipped from Angola alone, a Portuguese official there wrote

---

* Potosí, the Bolivian mine that was the single richest source of silver in the New World during this period, essentially went dry by 1700, whereas Brazil's gold boom, which commenced in earnest somewhat later, had essentially wound down by the end of the nineteenth century.

in a letter to the crown that this colony could be counted upon to supply slaves to Brazil "until the end of the world."* As it turns out, carving out plantation lands to produce sugar or other commodities on African soil was rarely attempted before the nineteenth century, and even then only haltingly, and only as the slave regime in the New World was finally being wound down. Disease provides some of the answer, but only part of it. It would be a long time before Europeans understood exactly why, but on the soil of the Americas they held an enormous epidemiological advantage: the native populations that lived there had thrived for thousands of years in isolation from the maladies of the Old World, and began dying in extraordinary numbers almost immediately upon contact with whites for lack of any biological resistance to the diseases that they and the animals they brought from Europe, especially swine, introduced. For the natives, even what we call today the common cold was deadly. One recent demographic study has suggested that the total population of Native Americans at the time of first contact with Europeans (1492) was roughly 60 million, or 10 percent of humanity's global total, and that by 1600, as a result of contact with white people, 56 million of them were dead.

In tropical Africa, though, the epidemiological balance swung in the opposite direction. There, it was the Europeans who enjoyed no immunity to lethal diseases like malaria and yellow fever, and to a host of other less invoked sicknesses. In the early modern era, no fewer than 25 percent, and sometimes as many as 75 percent, of Europeans arriving in West Africa died within the first year. Even after white mortality declined sharply, as notions of hygiene took hold, death rates of 10 percent per annum in Africa remained common. And this, naturally enough, strongly tempered any desire

---

* From the sixteenth to the late nineteenth century, Central Africa, comprising modern Congo, Angola, and Gabon, would be the largest source of slaves overall for the American slave trade. In the eighteenth century alone, 2.5 million Africans were shipped across the Atlantic from this region, a number that perhaps helps explain the cruel and horrific European delusion that the supply of Black bodies was basically without limit.

to control territory that Europeans might have had in the Gulf of Guinea or Central Africa in the age of empire.

Deadly disease was only part of the story, though. During the life of Prince Henry the Navigator, the Portuguese had already switched from a strategy of terror and pillage along the West African coast to one of diplomacy and equal trade; they had done so because this was the only thing that made sense for them to do, the only thing that was truly feasible. After Henry's death, as they sailed farther and farther down the coast, aside from skin color, the most important societies they encountered—meaning ones that dominated their subregions, such as the Akan, Benin. and Kongo—could not have been deemed so terribly different from their own, either in political organization or in military power. And whatever small advantages the Portuguese may have had in swords or crude firearms were nullified by the long lines of resupply from home and by the limited numbers of men they could field in any given African setting.

Given the enduring depth of both public ignorance and primitive stereotypes about Africa's present and past, readers might be even more surprised to learn that by the late medieval and early modern eras, even literacy, especially in the Sahel and on its fringes, was not so different from medieval Europe.[*] The continent had any number of states that boasted their own formal institutions and processes of learning and scholarship. Make no mistake. There would be a real divergence between Europe and Africa, but for the most part it still lay in the future, and it would ride on the backs of the violent disruptions of plantation agriculture and chattel slavery.

For Portugal, the attractiveness and logic of São Tomé were premised as much on these realities—of a rough social and not easily breached hard-power equilibrium with large states on the African mainland—as they were on the island's abundant rain and extraordinarily fertile volcanic soil. Slave production, it was believed with

---

[*] Even as late as the nineteenth century, the literacy rate of enslaved Muslim Africans was often higher than that of their slaveholders in the Americas.

reason, was best secured through the isolation of captive Blacks on islands, which almost by definition were places from which one could not easily escape, and where acts of revolt would bring only merciless repression, and hence no real relief.

That the plantation-complex made a giant leap from São Tomé to the Americas and not to nearby Africa, despite its enormous reserves of both land and population, was an expression of Europe's relative weakness in this era. Taking slaves away to the far-off Americas was a "second-best alternative," in the words of the historian David Eltis. And it was a path taken not only for reasons of a hostile disease environment, but because of African agency.

As Eric Williams, the late prime minister of Trinidad and Tobago, wrote:

> On plantations, escape was easy for the white servant; less easy for the Negro who, if freed, tended in self-defense, to stay in his locality where he was well known and less likely to be apprehended as a vagrant or runaway slave. The servant expected land at the end of his contract; the Negro, in a strange environment, conspicuous by his color and features, and ignorant of the white man's language and ways, could be kept permanently divorced from the land.

Williams's Caribbean, which had begun its vocation in plantation agriculture with white indentured labor, would become the most direct inheritor of this new model, but even Brazil, a vast territory with a seemingly unlimited hinterland, should be understood as another implementation of this basic scheme. In the New World, Portuguese and, then later, other whites elsewhere learned they could count on the skin of Blacks—its very Blackness—to automatically betray these laborers as slaves (unlike Native Americans, who could sometimes merely melt away), thus helping foreclose potential paths of egress. In other words, in these new environments opened to chattel slavery, Blackness itself became a kind of island.

The other device favored by Europeans was the deliberate

mixing of African captives of wildly diverse ethnic and linguistic groups, thereby avoiding the concentration of too many people from any one source. This was done with the obvious aim of limiting the slaves' ability to communicate easily among themselves and therefore, it was hoped, to organize and conspire. It also seems to have been undertaken with the aim of hastening the forgetting of their social identity, who they had been as a people, instilling in them hopelessness about resistance, and forestalling the emergence among the captives of what we might call political thought. It was in São Tomé, where these ideas first germinated, however, that the captives delivered the first eloquent and historically vital refutation of this strategy. By their actions, the captive and trafficked Blacks of São Tomé sent the Europeans who would control them the message that you can take Africans out of Africa, but you cannot so easily take Africa, and all of what that signifies, starting with memories of freedom, away from Africans.

12

PATHWAYS OF RESISTANCE

T HE DRIVE TO THE NORTH of the island was not the only
foray into history I had made by road during my stay in São
Tomé. On a quiet Sunday afternoon, I set off in the equatorial torpor in the opposite direction to look for reminders of the first
of two recorded events involving slaves or would-be slaves on this
island. Lost to the history books, these were experiences that had
early on refuted the notion that Africans could so easily be alienated
not just from themselves, but from all ideas of freedom.

São Tomé, the city, is about as ragged and unpretentious a capital
as one can find anywhere in West Africa, and on this day, just before
New Year's Eve, everything was closed but the large, low-slung sea-
food market. It seemed like the town's center of gravity, with smoke-
belching taxis and crowds of pedestrians swelling around its dirty
pink columns, with buyers and sellers clamoring, all bartering over
the most extraordinary variety of freshly caught fish that I have ever
seen. As one heads south, following the sea, the city seems to peter
out amid a jumble of old neighborhoods that crowd busy, narrow
roads. Poverty in this ragged skirt of the city was more acute than
what I had seen elsewhere in the capital. For want of space in tiny
ramshackle, single-story dwellings and perhaps of air conditioning,
life here was mostly lived in the street.

After that, the drive, during which for long stretches mine was the only car on the road, turned into what seemed like an interminable scroll of idyllic but empty beaches, and steep mountains that climbed through forests so brooding that one could observe the steam wafting up from the ground as it coalesced into pillow-like clouds. Ninety minutes or so after I had set off, I finally arrived at a village whose green road sign announced its name as São João dos Angolares. I made a sharp turn off the two-lane highway onto a steep side road that rose to a lofty plateau, atop which sat a large, bright-red house. At first, I thought I was all alone, but suddenly a broad-shouldered man in his late twenties emerged from the forested roadside and eagerly beckoned for me to drive all the way up the hill. Within another instant or two, before I could resolve my own question about whether it was wise to do so, a file of children appeared, now climbing the hill. I immediately sensed their excitement about eyeballing the rare foreigner. I explained to the man in my Spanish-infused attempt at Portuguese that I was looking for the Sete Pedras, a group of rocks offshore where a shipwreck took place in 1554; the young man, now my enthusiastic and inseparable guide, urged me to park and to follow him to the top of the hill. Once there, with the two of us surrounded by the children in their brightly colored tattered clothes, he pointed, grinning cheek to cheek, into the middle distance just off the coast, where I could plainly make out a cluster of seven black boulders rhythmically washed over by incoming whitecaps.

Right there upon the Sete Pedras, as the long recounted story goes, a ship carrying captives from the African mainland had run disastrously aground, but somehow enough of the freshly enslaved people had swum to the shore and managed to regain their freedom. In the nearby *matos*, the heavily forested south of the island, far from any European settlement, they supposedly formed the embryo of a viable community. It is unknown whether this was a simple maritime disaster or the result of a revolt. Twenty-two years earlier, in 1532, the 190 slaves aboard the well-named *Misericordia*, a ship bound from São Tomé to Elmina, rose up and murdered all but two of the crew (who somehow managed to escape) and were never heard from again.

Points of uncertainty still linger about the details of the Sete Pedras story, which some historians now dismiss as a mere oral tradition. But heavy traces of the Angolan language that the escapees would have likely spoken, Mbundu, still resonate in the localized Portuguese Creole spoken by the young people who surrounded me on the hilltop that day and elsewhere in the south of this island, reinforcing the idea of a historical connection. Noticing it immediately, I understood why many have taken this for a sign of a link with the African mainland.

The lineaments of this story about the wreck upon the Sete Pedras are like a photographic negative of the adventure stories that generation after generation of whites spun and novelized: tales of catastrophic arrivals in strange and distant climes during the burgeoning imperial age. Prototypes of the genre like Daniel Defoe and *Robinson Crusoe*, his 1719 novel, come to mind, as do *Gulliver's Travels*, published by Jonathan Swift a mere seven years later, as well as *The Swiss Family Robinson*, which appeared nearly a century after Defoe's classic. Crusoe was in fact shipwrecked while on a slaving expedition from Africa. At one point in the narrative, Crusoe climbs a hill hoping to spy a glimpse of rescuers, only to sink into despair. "I could not forbear getting up to the top of a little mountain, and looking out to sea, in hopes of seeing a ship; then fancy at a vast distance I spied a sail, please myself with the hopes of it, and then after looking steadily, till I was almost blind, lose it quite, and sit down and weep like a child, and thus increase my misery by my folly." It seems never to have occurred to authors like these, or others in the genre, to explore the storytelling potential inherent in a real-life catastrophe like the Sete Pedras incident. The possibilities of Black freedom, both dramatic and moral, escaped them completely, just as this episode seems to have largely escaped the attention of all but a few historians.

For nearly twenty years, the white residents of the Portuguese *povoação*, or city of São Tomé, are said to have known nothing of the existence of the free Blacks. The two groups had been living their lives in parallel: the one community consisting of accidental settler-colonists from nearby continental Africa, and the other, purpose-driven ones from Europe. The former came to be known as Angolars. Theirs was among the first autonomous settlements formed by African escapees from slavery, or maroons, as such people were broadly labeled in the wake of Europe's Atlantic slave trade. In Brazil, where they proliferated, these communities would become known as *quilombos*.* The ignorance of the Portuguese about the presence of free Black settlers would end, however, with a devastating Angolar surprise attack on São Tomé city, which the Africans virtually destroyed in 1574, only to melt away back to their base in the southern *matos*. In those reaches of the island, the rugged mountainous geography, the lack of natural ports, and the absence of the flat farmland needed for plantation agriculture combined to make settlement unattractive to the Portuguese.

Much remains unknown about this attack on what was then Lisbon's principal outpost and slaving entrepôt in Central Africa. It stands out nonetheless as the first major organized act of violent resistance by Africans against Europe's mounting imperial project. Historians like Robert Garfield have postulated that the Angolars, from the outset few in number, were under mounting demographic pressure, in desperate need of replenishing their population, and especially of increasing the number of women among them in order to ensure their survival. As this theory goes, the Angolars had probably already been absorbing a trickle of runaway slaves during their two decades of isolation and would have learned a great deal from these escapees about the Portuguese and their brutal plantation economy. It is more than plausible to imagine that their hostility toward the whites originated in the Angolars' oral traditions about the Sete Pedras or the *Misericordia*. I had been treated to a sort of live testimonial to these traditions when I was swamped by village children almost from the moment I pulled my car off the road that day while searching for the shipwreck site. São Tomé is an island that receives scant tourism, but in that scene, everyone present intuited what had brought me that way. And even the smallest children

---

* On São Tomé these communes became known as *mocambos*. They did not begin to dissolve until the early nineteenth century, after negotiations with colonial authorities.

among them could recite elements of the story of disaster at sea and survival. But even if memories of the escape from bondage after the Sete Pedras had not prompted the surprise attack against the Portuguese on the island, the accounts the Angolars surely heard from runaway slaves about the deadly regime Blacks were subjected to as they cultivated and processed sugar would have been enough. Thus, as tenuous as they are, details like these make this story a candidate for one of the first acts in a long history not just of revolt, but in pursuit of a nascent if tentative Pan African ideal, a tradition that one usually thinks of as entirely modern.

For years after that first assault on Portuguese power suddenly ended, little was heard from the Angolars, and for the European community on the island, life quickly went more or less back to normal. This meant back to the booming business of extracting fabulous profits from the flesh and blood of the slaves who produced sugar there, as well as from a now fast-growing New World traffic in slaves itself. It is reasonable to expect that the whites redoubled their vigilance against future attack. The history of subsequent revolts throughout the Atlantic world suggests they would have treated their own slaves to harsher supervision and work regimens, too. But this early return to prosperity was a mere reprieve, for in 1595 there was a much more devastating uprising that lasted twenty days, this one not by the mysterious Angolars, but by São Tomé's plantation laborers themselves. That July, led by a man named Amador, who took on the titles of king and captain-general, the mutinous slaves burned more than half of the island's mills along with many great houses in the cane-rich north, killing their masters and seizing their weapons. Amador divided his army into four separate companies, which proceeded to encircle and lay siege to the city, finally entering the heart of São Tomé on July 28, where a pitched battle ensued. His attempted revolution was defeated, though, thanks, it appears, to a betrayal of Amador's plans by one of his key associates. The would-be Black king escaped the scene of the battle but was captured alone sometime later in the countryside, and hanged and quartered as a warning against all others of his race about the certain perils of revolt. Despite Amador's defeat, the resistance of escaped slaves continued in sporadic and less organized fashion in São Tomé for years, helping sound its death knell as a main grower of the green gold that was sugarcane.

By this time, São Tomé was already being usurped by Brazil, which was on its way to producing far more of the commodity than such a small island ever could. But just as surely as Brazil inherited the sugar business, it would inherit Black rebellion and revolt, only on a far larger scale. It has been estimated, furthermore, that active rebellions took place on as many as one-tenth of the thirty-six thousand shipments of slaves across the Atlantic during the ensuing centuries. Other shipboard uprisings have been more famous, like the revolt on the *Amistad*[*] in 1839, or may have made more noise in their time, such as the *Little George*, a sloop sailing from the Guinea coast with a cargo of ninety-six Africans in 1730. Escaping from their shackles at four thirty in the morning, when their ship was six days out of port en route to Rhode Island, enslaved men broke through the bulkhead, captured three white crew members, and threw them overboard. A pitched battle ensued between the Africans and the surviving crew. The whites improvised an explosive device, but instead of killing many rebellious captives, it ravaged the ship. After much struggle, the men and women marked for slavery finally triumphed, managing to steer the limping vessel into the Sierra Leone River, where it ran aground, surely making the *Little George* one of very few ships bearing people sold into slavery to return them to Africa.

From the *Misericordia* onward, a lesson for Europeans was encoded deeply in the history of São Tomé, a place of enormous significance to the Atlantic world despite its tiny size and even smaller repute. For one, slave uprisings were inseparable from plantation sugar production. In the ensuing centuries, as many as 70 percent of the slaves shipped in chains to the Americas would go on to be employed in this singularly cruel pursuit. Seen in one

---

[*] The *Amistad* was carrying fifty-three Mende slaves from Havana to the small Cuban port of Guanaja when they revolted.

light, the history of sugar's migratory spread, driven by devastating deforestation and soil exhaustion, as well as by the relentless search for greater and greater scales of production, was a remarkable, if terrible economic story. Seen in another, though, it was essentially the history of violent rebellion. In places like Palmares, Brazil, *quilombos* would swell to a size of 11,000 people or more. There and in Jamaica, when their survival was threatened, maroons waged fierce and protracted wars against colonial armies.

In the 1640s, Barbados became the site of a revolution in slave-powered agriculture that would turn the entire Caribbean region into a sugar-producing archipelago and the boiler room of the North Atlantic economy. Along the way, the West Indies became home to a group of colonies that were each in turn the richest in the history of humanity. Nonetheless, while Barbados lacked mountains or forests for escape, even that island experienced rebellions from the earliest days of big sugar.

When a young George Washington traveled to Barbados in 1751, seeking relief in the island's warm sea air for his half brother's tuberculosis, he kept a diary in which he faithfully recorded his impressions of the place, most of them favorable. In one entry, he described himself as "perfectly enraptured" by the beauty of the island. At the time, although slaves represented three-quarters of the population of Barbados, nowhere did Washington even mention their presence except to say that some whites had adopted what he disparagingly called "the Negro style." As a slave owner himself, first by inheritance from the age of eleven, the most glaring part of this omission was the failure of America's future first president to remark upon one of the most common Barbadian sights of that era: the rotting heads of rebellious slaves erected on sharpened pikes at busy crossroads, bloody emblems of a regime of plantation terror and mortal warning to would-be rebels. We are frequently urged not to judge the Founding Fathers by the standards of today. But I am reminded here of a phrase from James Baldwin: "It is the innocence which constitutes the crime." The very least one can say is that Washington's failure to see something this grotesque as worthy of note constitutes an onion-

skin leaf in the thick and bulging book of silence on the place of the
Black experience in the making of our world.

卍

THE EARLIEST SURVIVING RECORD of the use of the word "maroon"
in the English language dates from Barbados in 1666, when John
Davies, an Englishman translating a young history of the island,
wrote that slaves "run away and get into the Mountains and Forests, where they live like so many Beasts; then they are call'd Mar-
ons, that is to say Savages." This kind of usage, which crept into
French as well (*marrons*), derived from a Spanish term that had been
employed at least as far back as 1535 (almost from the very outset of
the American slave trade). That Spanish word, *cimarrón*, was, in the
description of the scholar Joseph Kelly, "coined to describe domesticated cattle brought to Hispaniola that escaped into the wild parts of
the island," and it speaks bluntly to the abject dehumanization that
is the root and essence of the concept of chattel. The first enslaved
Blacks had been brought to Hispaniola in 1501, and already by the
following year, some of them had escaped their bondage.

The first blacks to escape in mainland North America employed
the oldest and most common form of slave resistance there is: running or melting away from a failing Spanish settlement on the South
Carolina coast in 1526 and taking up residence among Native
American communities. This made them, and not the latterly more
famous enslaved residents of Jamestown, who arrived ninety-three
years later, in 1619, the first to settle a part of what would eventually become the United States. I traveled to Jamestown during my
research, pausing in silence under a leaden sky before the site of an
ongoing excavation of the home of a wealthy planter named William Pierce. Pierce owned one of the initial thirty or so people to be
enslaved in Virginia, a woman called Angela, who was sold to the
English in 1619. The house is long gone, but researchers still sift the
earth looking for artifacts, including from the kitchen where Angela
was made to work. These Africans, who embarked from present-day
Angola and were brought to this early Virginia settlement, have only

recently—and very grudgingly—been centered in the early colonial history of what became the United States, thanks to the efforts of a team spearheaded by Nikole Hannah-Jones, of *The New York Times*. The 1526 maroons, though, remain broadly unknown to the public.

From the first known acts of rebellion in São Tomé right up until the liberation of Haiti in 1804, the people who ran or profited from the slave trades, whether directly or indirectly, would generate all manner of rationales for racial slavery that were meant to salve their consciences or justify the brutality of the system that underpinned their lives and prosperity. One theory popularized by pseudoscientific thinkers of the late eighteenth century like the white Jamaican Edward Long, held that Africans were not really humans at all, but rather the product of a process of polygenesis. According to this shibboleth, the genus *Homo* merited subdivision into three species: Europeans and similar people, Negroes, and "orang-outangs." Others, from the Portuguese in Prince Henry's time to the Puritans of New England, sought moral refuge in the claim that enslaved Africans were being Christianized, and thereby saved from savagery and the damnation that it inevitably led to. Others still solemnly insisted that slaves were "happy," a word not infrequently used, and thankful to have entered into the trusteeship of whites, with all of the supposed benefits, like freedom from the need to care for oneself, that this implied. In the late eighteenth century, a delegate to the French Colonial Assembly testified:

> *Let an intelligent and educated man compare the deplorable state of these men in Africa with the pleasant and easy life which they enjoy in the colonies. . . . Sheltered by all the necessities of life, surrounded with an ease unknown in the greater part of the countries of Europe, secure in the enjoyment of their property, for they had property and it was sacred, cared for in their illnesses with an expense and attention that you would seek in vain in the hospitals so boasted of in England, protected, respected in the infirmities of age; in peace with their children, and with their family . . . freed when they had rendered important services.*

Stripped of its most ornate features, this was nothing more than the "happy" slave narrative, which (as history would show everywhere) had no basis in truth. Frederick Douglass, among others, famously denounced this idea repeatedly and at length, as in this dialogue, which appeared in the African American newspaper *The North Star*.

> *I once passed a colored woman at work on a plantation, who was singing, apparently, with animation, and whose general manners would have led me to set her down as the happiest of the gang. I said to her, "Your work seems pleasant to you." She replied, "No massa."*
>
> *Supposing she referred to something particularly disagreeable in her immediate occupation, I said to her, "Tell me then what part of your work is most pleasant."*
>
> *She answered with much emphasis, "No part pleasant. We forced to do it."*

What the events in São Tomé, the first European plantation society, had proven three centuries earlier, if only there had been an audience then that was willing to take heed, was that the will to freedom and the willingness to die in pursuit of this goal was an inherent feature of chattel slavery, and attempts to contain these energies not only were doomed in the long run but would also produce, from the perspective of whites who wished to forestall liberation, deeply perverse outcomes at every step along the way.*

---

* The myth of the "happy" slave survived well into the twentieth century, as attested to in this passage from *A History of the United States*, a high school textbook published by the recent former Librarian of Congress, Daniel J. Boorstin, in 1989: "Though most slaves were whipped at some point in their lives, a few never felt the lash. Nor did all slaves work in the fields. Many may not have even been terribly unhappy with their lot, for they knew no other."

13

BECOMING CREOLE

E ARLY IN THE SIXTEENTH CENTURY, in the very same era that
São Tomé was beginning to piece together its vocation as a
leading sugar-growing plantation society and crucial entrepôt
for the early American slave trade, Elmina was laying another foundational piece in the construction of a new transatlantic civilization.
There, beginning in the aprons of São Jorge, the Portuguese fort,
sprung up a large village that went on to become a bustling town and
eventually, by the standards of the middle of the seventeenth century, an unusually cosmopolitan global city. To begin to get a sense
of what this means, Elmina's fifteen to twenty thousand residents
made it considerably larger than the New Amsterdam (soon to be
New York) of that day, or even the New Orleans of a century hence.

But what was most novel and important about Elmina in this
age was less its size than the unusual nature of the society that
emerged and thrived there for decades; more specifically still, it was
its unique makeup, composed not just of Blacks and whites, but
also of a new social category that had just begun to arise in places
like this, where "at African sufferance" Europeans and indigenous
populations remained in deep and extended contact in the pursuit
of mutually profitable commerce exchange. Here, we are speaking of a population that went by the name "Creole," a polyvalent
term that can lend to some confusion. In the Americas, as we have

seen, Creole often came to mean simply born in the New World. In other usages, Creole would become a linguistic term, signifying hybrid languages that were spawned in places where Europeans and Africans traded, especially among the enslaved. Here, though, we intend for it to mean a distinctly new class of culturally and frequently racially mixed people who were the literal offspring of these sorts of intercontinental contacts. Elmina was by no means the only—nor for that matter even the first—place where members of this new class of people arose. In the fifteenth century, both Portuguese Catholics and New Christians had used the island of Cape Verde as a base to prospect for trade throughout the western bulge of Africa, from Senegambia to Upper Guinea. As some white traders prospered building solid networks in areas that lay inland from the African coast, they began to produce children with local women, sometimes as a matter of official alliances with chiefs. These Luso-Africans provide perhaps the earliest example in the formation of Afro-European Creole cultures. The experience of French trader-explorers on the Senegal River likewise generated its own class of Creoles, as did São Tomé a bit later.

Coastal West Africa, of course, was not the only place that brought Blacks and whites into extended contact. A Nuremberg physician named Hieronymus Münzer, who visited Lisbon in 1494, was surprised to discover that people from south of the Sahara were being tutored there in special schools set up to teach them Latin and theology. (It seems unlikely that he would have known that this was being done largely at the behest of the sovereigns of the Kingdom of Kongo, which had dispatched the children of its own nobles there.)

By the time Portugal banned the importation of slaves into its territory, in 1761, four hundred thousand Africans had been brought to the kingdom in bondage, and yet even numbers this large paradoxically did not bring about the kind of racial and cultural mixing and cross-fertilization that one saw in new Creole societies in places like Elmina. Africans in Lisbon, Seville, and elsewhere in Europe undoubtedly interacted with Europeans as domestic servants, agricultural workers, blacksmiths, and masons, but on that continent the African presence remained relatively marginal, and over time mixed-race people weighed relatively little in the balance.

Elmina, by contrast, had produced many generations of culturally polyvalent operators by the middle of the eighteenth century—many, but not all of them, mixed-race people who went on to help seed virtually every economically important port of call in the Atlantic world. What made Elmina and its surroundings the right kind of platform for the emergence of a distinctive culture like this was the persistence of contacts between Europeans and Blacks under circumstances that the Europeans could never fully control. A Creole subculture had taken root during the long period of Portuguese trade that began at Elmina in the late fifteenth century, only to be followed by another stable period of Dutch commerce after that country captured the São Jorge da Mina fort in 1637.

Awareness of the importance of early Creole communities in places like Elmina has become widely associated with the scholarship of Ira Berlin, the late American historian of Africa and slavery. Berlin emphasized the liminality, or role as intermediaries, of members of this group, who inhabited many coastal towns in Africa. In port environments like Elmina, Creoles proved their supreme adaptability, a polivalency that would serve both European trade with Africa and the early settlement of the New World.

In some ways, hurricanes serve as an apt metaphor for transatlantic slavery. Just as those systems form on the western fringes of Africa before hurling their energy upon the distant shores of the Americas, the mass traffic in Africans violently yoked together the millions of victims gathered on its western shores before scattering them in the distant hemisphere to the west in sometimes random-seeming ways. In the early phases of Europe's New World imperialism, these Creoles operated somewhat differently. They filled the interstices between the worlds of Blacks and whites, moving back and forth across long distances and often sustaining their own networks of transcontinental communication, or brotherhoods (*cofradias* in Portuguese). This was facilitated, most of all, by their strong presence among workers on ships and in and around ports.

At the very outset of the modern age, men drawn from these Creole communities accompanied Columbus to the New World; others marched with Balboa, Cortés, de Soto, and Pizarro during their historic conquests. As such, Creoles became the grease that made the commercial and social machinery function. They were the ultimate go-betweens.

This was as true in the preindependence colonies that would form America as it was anywhere. Berlin named the Creoles who established themselves there the "charter generation," meaning African Americans who played indispensable roles before the widespread establishment of plantation slavery and without whom the European imperial project would have faced vastly steeper odds. Creoles were among the first settlers of the Chesapeake region, in what would become the United States, as well as New Amsterdam, where Blacks—enslaved, free, or occupying fluid intermediate categories—had been present at least since 1625 and accounted for roughly 30 percent of the population in 1640.

Other Creole communities quickly formed in places as varied as Cap François (in Saint Domingue), Cartagena, Havana, Mexico City, and San Salvador. Intimate with cultures on both sides of the Atlantic, they could be found speaking pidgins and Creole tongues that were (and in many places remain) heavily laced with Portuguese, even in non-Portuguese colonies. This positioned them to perform a unique and indispensable form of cultural brokerage.

Although Berlin made this idea famous among scholars of the African diaspora, one finds important, earlier descriptions of the importance of these strikingly cosmopolitan Creole communities in Africa, and especially in Elmina, in the scholarship of others, including those of African origin. In 1970, for example, the Ghanaian scholar Kwame Yeboa Daaku wrote of the racial, social and cultural transformation of Elmina society: "There were people who came to the towns to sell their commodities and then returned to their states, and there were others who had nothing but their services and skills to sell." The acquisition of a common trading language threw up a new class of enterprising middlemen, local men like John Kabes and John Konny, so-called merchant princes, who grew rich and powerful, provisioning the foreigners' fortified outposts with food grown on their plantations and ferried to their slave ships with fleets of canoes they operated. What is more, to preserve their autonomy they frequently switched allegiances from one group of Europeans to another and even built forts of their own. "Side by side with the new class was the emergence of a new group of people—the mulattoes, who were the direct progeny of European traders and African women."

Recent scholarship has emphasized the importance of west Central Africa in the formation of Creole identities—indeed, to a degree far greater than anything suggested by Berlin. This region generated more than half of all slave shipments of the New World, with huge numbers coming not just from Kongo and the neighboring kingdom of Ndongo, but from traditionally more obscure regions like Benguela and the Loango Coast. Benguela, a port located in southern modern-day Angola, alone shipped off seven hundred thousand people in chains. This recent scholarship has complicated the picture of creolization by emphasizing that many captives from west Central Africa had a long-standing relationship with or awareness of Christianity even prior to their enslavement, as well as by demonstrating how persistent even older, African traditions in agriculture, religion, language, and culture generally have been in many parts of the Americas.

I do not wish to detract from insights of Berlin, Daaku, and other scholars on this topic by suggesting the following revision—or, perhaps better, expansion—of the Creole thesis, a significant broadening, in fact. In an influential 1996 article, "From Creole to African," Berlin wrote, "Black life in mainland North America originated not in Africa or America but in the netherworld between the continents. Along the periphery of the Atlantic—first in Africa, then in Europe, and finally in the Americas—African-American society was a product of the momentous meeting of Africans and Europeans and of their equally fateful encounter with the peoples of the Americas."

What one wishes to reply, though, is that everything Berlin has argued here about a new type of descendants of Africa—some Black, many mixed race—is almost equally true of the whites who would come to populate the New World. They were just as much transformed by intercourse with new "others" as Black people, and would be no more "European" as a result than the people with a dominant African ancestry in the New World would continue to be "African." More than anything else, it was these contacts and the resultant *brassage*, or mixing, culturally, racially, socially, economically, through innumerable dislocations, unions, and traumas, that made the Americas a new and utterly distinctive realm, a truly New World, and ultimately the most powerful engine of modernity there's ever been. Processes like these were at the origins of everything unique and original about the Americas, down to jazz and the blues.

This is not to say there has not been a toxic side to this reality. As widespread as it is, the *brassage* in America's cauldron has always been partial or incomplete. Blacks were the catalyst that made an American society possible, but a catalyst that for the most part went selectively unabsorbed in the mixing process. Their presence and their persistent relegation to limited and secondary roles served to bind the others, including the rankest of newcomers. And in doing so, it served to create and to elevate whiteness, producing a legacy that we have powerfully suffered from and still struggle to emerge from today. As Toni Morrison once put it:

> *Blacks were steady. Everybody could look down on them. Immigrant Italians. Immigrant Polish. There was always a bottom that you could be hostile to. And that was what brought the country together as a melting pot. . . . What was the basis of the cauldron, the pot? Well black people were the pot. Everything else was, you know, melted together and, what, American. That's how you get to be American.*

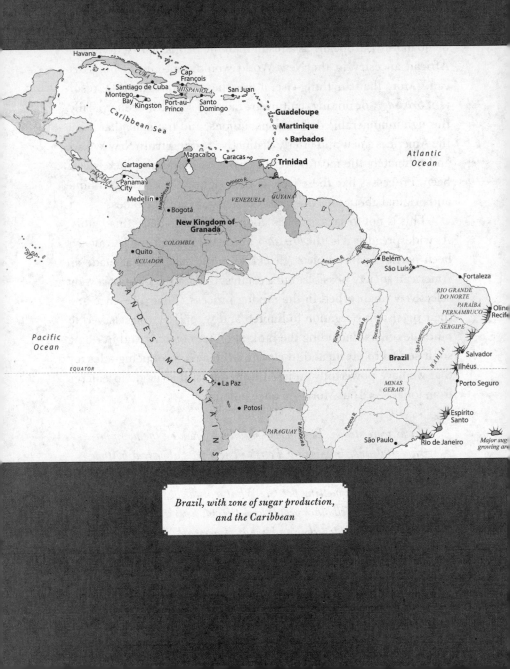

Brazil, with zone of sugar production,
and the Caribbean

PART III

THE SCRAMBLE FOR AFRICANS

Nothing is more favourable to the rise of politeness and learning than a number of neighboring and independent states, connected together by commerce and policy. The emulation, which naturally arises among those neighboring states is an obvious source of improvement.

DAVID HUME,
Of the Rise and Progress of the Arts and Sciences,
extract 14

14

FOR A FEW ACRES OF SNOW

T HE MODERN HISTORY OF Africa as a geopolitically contested landmass full of parcels of territory that were sliced up by covetous outsiders formally began in Germany in 1884, at a famous event known as the Berlin Conference. At the time, Europeans barely controlled 10 percent of the continent, mostly in its northern and southern extremities. By 1914, as a result of decisions taken in Berlin, Old Continent monarchs and other rulers held sway over 90 percent of Africa. The borders these European leaders agreed to among themselves remain the borders in force across most of the continent today.

As they seized control over the continent, Europeans took almost no account of African history, the legacy of indigenous empires, or preexisting African states. They ignored considerations involving the mosaic of local languages that prevailed as they divided and then subdivided regions. They took little heed of long-standing patterns of local identity, local trade, or even ethnic rivalries and animosities. Africans themselves were not consulted.

The notion of a Scramble for Africa, as the late-nineteenth-century push by Europeans to lay imperial claim to virtually every part of the continent is called, is one of the most powerful images that the public retains of African history, and for good reason. It left an enduringly debilitating legacy for the continent: a plethora of puny and scarcely functional states, with conflict among and between ethnic groups, and with some once coherent groups left pointlessly straddling borders and others with far less in common, just as illogically, jumbled together in an artificial confection.

As harmful as its legacy was, this period was preceded by an even more consequential, not to mention deadly, scramble, one whose consequences remain largely unknown to the public and poorly understood by experts. We will call this earlier and longer-lasting scramble a Scramble for Africans. And it was this centuries-long scramble, which followed Portugal's construction of the fort at Elmina—messy, drawn out, and mostly unplanned—that delivered to us our modern world.

Europe's competition for Africa, the geographic void that it was supposedly fixated on circumnavigating, has taken many forms. These merely began with the major sea battles fought by Spain and Portugal on the Gold Coast in order to dominate the region's rich gold supplies toward the close of the fifteenth century. By the seventeenth century, intra-European competition over Africa and the new wealth that its labor generated on plantations in the New World had fueled a prolonged, multifaceted contest over the South Atlantic, indeed, a quasi-world war that is seldom taught about or discussed. This struggle was fought simultaneously on opposite shores of the Atlantic and drew in complex, shifting alliances of both European and African states, as well as their Brazilian allies and proxies. A forgotten but critical part of the Thirty Years War, it placed tremendous demands upon the national resources of the combatants and involved dramatic, high-stakes gambits on land and at sea.

This contest for the South Atlantic would soon be followed by what must have long seemed like interminable war over what subsequently became the Atlantic's most coveted sea: the Caribbean. This began in earnest when Oliver Cromwell, who took power as Lord Protector of the Commonwealth of England, Scotland and Ireland in 1653, conceived of something he called the "Western Design." Its avowed aim was to oust the Spanish from the Americas, beginning with the West Indies. Cromwell's England scored its first great

For a Few Acres of Snow   149

success in this venture when it managed to capture Jamaica from the Spanish in 1655, but that was only after a failed attempt to capture Santo Domingo. Both expeditions were led by Admiral William Penn (the father of the Quaker who founded Pennsylvania a quarter century later). This made Jamaica England's consolation prize, albeit one that was eighteen times bigger than Barbados, its most important foothold in the Caribbean until then. The English wasted no time applying the lessons of their experience on that smaller island and soon Jamaica replaced it as the world's biggest sugar producer.

England had carefully studied Holland's early imperial successes, all the while hoping to eventually supplant it. The Royal African Company was a mercantile company created by the Stuart family and City of London traders in 1660 to win a share of the era's growing commerce with West Africa from European rivals.[*] As such, it was a rough copy of the Dutch West India Company, and the Western Design drew similar inspiration from a Dutch blueprint for conquest at the expense of Portugal, its so-called *groot desseyn*, or Great Design, about which we will hear much more later. Having helped Holland secure independence from Hapsburg Spain, England then fought the Dutch in three wars in the latter half of the seventeenth century. Their fellow Protestants and rivals across the Channel had recently been weakened by losses in Brazil and in Angola against the Portuguese. As a result, by 1660 England emerged as the largest shipper of slaves across the Atlantic, and by 1700 would by itself account for nearly half of the entire Atlantic traffic in slaves.[†] An ancillary reward for England would be the rising value of its exports to Africa, which would increase tenfold during the eighteenth century. With the Dutch and the Spanish increasingly sidelined from the enormous wealth that flowed from sugar and slavery, this left

---

[*] The Royal African Company briefly existed under the name the Company of Royal Adventurers into Africa, and underwent a variety of name changes and reorganizations during its early years, as well as spawning spin-offs, such as the Gambia Adventurers, which was created to trade in slaves in 1668.

[†] According to the Trans-Atlantic Slave Trade Database, England (and subsequently Britain) exported 2.9 million Africans across the Atlantic between 1640 and 1807.

France and England to fight time and again for dominance over a region that is nowadays mostly thought of as a collection of sun and sand vacation destinations. At the conclusion of one of these conflicts, the Seven Years War, in 1763, Voltaire lent his voice to those in France who successfully argued for holding on to tiny Guadeloupe in exchange with England for the incomparably larger New France, as its possessions in Canada were then known. These he derided in his masterpiece, *Candide*, as a "few acres of snow."

To the modern ear, Voltaire's comment may sound like nothing more than a wit's lighthearted quip, but reasoning like this about such an eventful trade-off for France in the New World was carefully considered and speaks volumes about the scope and nature of the original scramble, which in fact was the Scramble for Africans. One easily imagines competition among European states in the age of empire as being about controlling giant swaths of territory, the bigger the chunk of real estate the more important. The Scramble for Africans, though, obeyed a very different logic. Its focus was less on sheer square miles than on control over the supply of Black labor and over the strategic patches of cane-growing soil that Africans could be made to work as slaves to produce previously undreamed-of wealth on the plantations of the New World. Until the age of Big Cotton, which still lay roughly a century and a half in the future, this strategy produced its biggest yields by controlling small coastal outposts like Elmina, narrow enclaves like Portugal's Angola colony, and the islands of the West Indies, most of them quite small, like the 629-square-mile Guadeloupe so prized by Voltaire.

Even the war between Britain and France over the Ohio River Valley in what would become part of the United States can be fully understood only in the broader context of competition between these two powers in the Caribbean, a reality that is scarcely touched upon in narratives that focus on battles in what is now known as the Upper Midwest and Canada. Much traditional historiography has emphasized an interpretation of this conflict as being centered on balance of power politics within Europe, where most of the Seven Years War's deaths indeed occurred. A particular American strain of analysis of what in the United States is usually called the French and Indian War, meanwhile, has centered attention on the Anglo-French struggle for control of North America, where the war broke out, to the exclusion of much else. In these accounts, for reasons that are easy to understand, the exploits and errors of the young George Washington, then a lieutenant colonel in the Virginia militia, receive greatest attention.

There is much to suggest, however, that shipping and trade, which were then seen by European rulers and publics alike as the keys to national fortune, were some of the most important motivations for both of the main parties in the war. For a century prior to 1750, the Caribbean had already been of greater economic and strategic importance in this regard than the northern colonies in continental America. When war broke out, the balance between these two colonial regions was just beginning to become less lopsided, but from the perspective of some influential voices in France, the most compelling reason to fight the British on the mainland was a defensive one: to keep their English rivals tied down there would prevent their trying to take over France's West Indies colonies, control over which was still seen as paramount. Despite an initial population of slaves that was considerably smaller than England's, the plantation sector in the French Caribbean expanded much more rapidly than its British counterpart in the eighteenth century, mostly on the back of the performance of Saint Domingue (later Haiti).

As the historian Daniel A. Baugh wrote, citing the advice of Roland-Michel Barrin, comte de la Galissonière, a governor of New France to the court at Versailles, "if the British in North America were no longer threatened by Canadians and Indians, they could 'make formidable *armements*' on that continent, and from there it would 'take them so little time to carry large forces either to St. Domingue or to the Island of Cuba, or to our Windward Islands' that defense would be very difficult and expensive."

Barrin's prognostication in fact proved remarkably accurate. When the British minister William Pitt rose to power in 1757, he conceived an ambitious plan to attack the sources of French wealth, which he understood to mean both its West African slave supply pipeline and the sugar-growing islands of the Caribbean that they kept furnished with manpower. The following year, Pitt's navy seized France's main slaving centers in present-day Senegal and Gambia, including Gorée Island just off Dakar. Victorious in the first stage of this assault on French prosperity, he directed a fleet of seventy-three ships, bearing nine thousand men, toward the West Indies. Within a month of reaching Barbados, four thousand of the British troops were dead or unfit for service, most due to the ravages of yellow fever, even before they had engaged the French. By another month later, the number of British healthy enough for combat had been reduced by nearly a third again.

Pitt's initial aim had been a takeover of Martinique. Despite being less than one-fourth the size of Long Island, its sugar production drew more imports of slaves than the total volume of Africans trafficked to the United States throughout its history, including the colonial era. But intimidated by that island's potent array of defensive guns, the English attacked nearby Guadeloupe instead. That they attempted this at all tells us something remarkable. Judging by their repeated actions, Europe's leading powers in this era had clearly deemed that control over the slave trade and over the plantation sector that it supplied was worthy of immense sacrifices. And the answer to why that was is not quite so elusive as some historians have seemed to pretend. Once they had captured Guadeloupe, the British immediately set out to restore the island to its original vocation: slave-produced sugar. With Britain dramatically increasing the number of slaves brought to the island, importing more in two years than France had during the entire eighteenth century, the number of sugar plantations in Guadeloupe leapt from 185 to 447. The results were not long in coming and were spectacular. Not only did Guadeloupe's plantation output quickly surpass that of Martinique, but "in 1761 it led the British Empire in exports of sugar, cotton, rum and coffee, as well as in its purchase of British and American products."

Just as Barrin predicted, this struggle for control over the immense productive power of enslaved Africans ultimately led to Saint Domingue, where plantation production reached its apotheosis late in the eighteenth century. The island of Hispaniola is large by Caribbean standards (forty-six times the size of Guadeloupe), but it is still smaller than South Carolina. By one estimate, France's Caribbean colonies, led overwhelmingly by Saint Domingue, accounted for roughly 15 percent of France's overall economic growth during the boom years between 1716 and 1787, lending a powerful boost to the country's transition to capitalism and industrialization. For both of the great European powers of this era, Britain and France, the prospect of control over profit centers as lucrative as this was simply irresistible, a prize they would expend extraordinary human and material resources to fight for. Unfortunately for both nations, the will to freedom of the large slave population in Saint Domingue and the tactical and political genius of a generation of revolutionary leaders who led Blacks to freedom there were even greater.

In their traditional recounting of the history of the modern world, the scholarly establishments of Western countries seldom invested serious attention in the role of Africa or of Africans, until a young doctoral candidate from Trinidad had the temerity to argue that without Africa, and the slave plantation agriculture of the Caribbean that derived from it, there would never have been the kind of explosion of wealth that the West enjoyed in the nineteenth century, nor such early or rapid industrialization.

These claims were put forward by Eric Williams in his 1938 doctoral thesis in history at Oxford, coincidentally the same year that C. L. R. James, another groundbreaking Caribbean thinker and Williams's former teacher, published his landmark book on the Haitian Revolution, *The Black Jacobins*. Williams later reworked and expanded upon his thesis in his 1944 book, *Capitalism and Slavery*, which also became an intellectual landmark. In *Capitalism and Slavery*, Williams wrote to boldly overturn the prevailing ways of understanding the economic revolution that turned the West into the globally ascendant force that it became and, in doing so, in the words of the twenty-first-century scholar Selwyn Carrington, "place the Caribbean at the center of the Atlantic economic system." In discussing the history of slavery with British intellectuals, I have frequently had the experience of a sudden or insistent desire to shift focus to the leading role that their nation played in the abolition of the slave trade. Such efforts, they say, were undertaken out of a commitment to an emerging doctrine of liberalism. Because of this, I can readily imagine the difficulties Williams must have had to overcome to get his thesis approved in the far more conservative academic climate that must have prevailed in the United Kingdom nine decades ago. In 2020, the popular Anglo-Jamaican author Zadie Smith wrote, "It is no exaggeration to say that the only thing I ever learned about slavery during my British education was that 'we' ended it." Prior to Williams's writings, after all, the dominant historical tradition had been something called the British Imperial School, which insisted "the development of the Caribbean colonies resulted from the riches of Europe," not the other way around.[*] Much the same, by the way, would be said about Africa as it emerged from European colonization.

Williams's persistence in the face of such intellectual headwinds paid off generations later, but not until after the empire, so to speak, had struck back. A huge outpouring of academic research into the questions at the heart of Williams's thesis soon followed, but not so much to test the Trinidadian's assumptions as to disprove them. The historian Scott Reynolds Nelson has reported, "Dozens of British political and economic historians from David Landes to Ralph Davis responded from the 1950s through the 1980s, arguing that the colonies had never been important to Britain's economic growth. Instead, machinery, international shipping, and liberal banking laws had been the 'engines' of economic growth in the mother country."

---

[*] Beyond the matter of liberalism as a theory of international trade, the British antislavery movement that is still proudly invoked today played an important role in elevating and ennobling wage labor domestically in that country, just as the poor were coping with large-scale forced removal from rural lands and being shunted into low-paying and often dangerous jobs in the rising industrial economy of the day.

Equally determined pushback also arose on the far shores of the Atlantic—i.e., in the United States.

What made Williams's thesis all the more remarkable is that Western scholarly traditions had devoted almost no serious thought to the fairly obvious possibility that plantation colonies, slave labor, the trade in slaves, or the sugar plantation-complex, whether taken individually or considered together, had ever made a serious contribution to the industrialization of Britain or to the ascension of the modern West more generally. Instead, in broad, theoretical terms, going back as far as the eighteenth-century Scottish economist and philosopher Adam Smith, the academy had tended to portray slavery as a historical dead end out of which nothing economically promising or worthwhile could have possibly emerged. There was, in other words, little shrift given to the idea that our present-day prosperity stemmed in any noteworthy way from the synaptic spark of African muscle, and from the sweat of Africans' brows, from the tears of Africans borne off into bondage, from their ingenuity or will to survival.

This is not to say that Williams's arguments were without their flaws, indeed serious ones. Even sympathetic critics have pointed out that he lacked formal training as an economist, that his methodological framework was somewhat archaic and that his arguments were not backed up by the kind of deep mastery of data and statistics that a topic like his, with such bold economic claims, deserved. The very breadth of his argument also proportionately expanded the size of the target for his critics. That the West Indian sugar plantation-complex and the slaves who worked it helped fuel the Industrial Revolution is just for starters. "The rise of Liverpool, the wealth of the British Empire, the triumph of the English navy, the success of Britain's banking families, and the success of English cotton mills all depended on the slave trade and slave-made commodities," as one summary of Williams has it. But for every refutation of claims like these, in recent decades modern historians who broadly endorse Williams's view have served up strong defenses of both the man and his arguments.

Where critics of the young Trinidadian scholar, who later became his country's first prime minister, have been most effective is in disproving the proposition most offensive to the Imperial School: the idea that Britain resolved itself to abolish slavery only once it had determined that the plantation-complex was no longer very profitable, especially compared to the "free trade" alternatives for the supply of commodities that were becoming available. "The whole world now became a British colony and the West Indies were doomed," Williams wrote. In fact, when abolition came, in 1807, as many of Williams's critics have pointed out, it occurred at the very peak of Britain's booming transatlantic slave business, with its plantation sector also still going gangbusters.* As a movement, abolition arose in the immediate wake of the American Revolution, and had numerous authors. These included the Quakers, tireless activists like Thomas Clarkson and Granville Sharp, and William Wilberforce, a member of Parliament. Also of great importance was Olaudah Equiano, a freedman, who informed Sharp of 132 Africans who were cast overboard from the *Zong*, a Liverpool slave ship that was bound from Cape Coast, near Elmina, and São Tomé to Jamaica in 1783. This atrocity occurred after a navigational error took the ship way off course in the Caribbean, leading the crew to fear a shortage of water. They later claimed insurance damages for the Africans they had massacred. Sharp helped publicize this shocking case.

The 1807 ban came about not so much out of overriding concern over the fortunes of Blacks as fellow human beings, however, than as a result of a crisis in imperial legitimacy. And this was sparked, in good part, by America's successful independence struggle. Reformist Islam movements then sweeping West Africa, and which began combating the slave trade, also played a part, making the pretense of relative Christian benevolence toward Africans (an argument as old as the early Portuguese slave trade) harder to defend. Another, more immediately practical spur was France's loss of Haiti, which

* The peak years of the transatlantic slave trade lasted from 1680 to 1830.

largely eliminated Britain's motive of competition with France over slave commodity production in the Caribbean.

Eric Williams misgauged the involvement of British self-interest in the slave business, taking this to mean something almost entirely material. As it happens, another kind of self-interest became paramount, one of self-regard, involving freedom from moral corruption and guilt. Protestant Britain had been so persistently victorious in its contest with Catholic France in the eighteenth century that it framed its successes as "part of a universal battle between parliamentary democracy and absolutist tyranny," in the words of the British historian Michael Taylor. In its own mind, liberty itself was at stake. The surprise victory of the Protestant-led, liberty-invoking Americans in their revolution, however, created a profound moral quandary for Britain and for the very idea of empire. As the historian Christopher Brown wrote, "Support for slavery could become an embarrassment if and when the virtue of imperial rule became a public question."

Williams's misfire aside, the phalanxes of critics who have worked so hard to refute his thesis have a problem so obvious and insurmountable that it is probably not a surprise that they tend to avoid it altogether. Some have insisted that the slave trade was in fact only marginally profitable and could not therefore have possibly constituted a decisive, or even a very important factor in England's, or Europe's sharp rise. What they do not explain, though, is why, if slavery was so incidental to the prosperity of Europe and of its New World offshoots, did the powers of the Old Continent invest themselves so heavily, for so long, and at such enormous cost in terms of their own blood and treasure in the mastery and control of both the main sources of slaves in Africa and the places they were transported to for work on plantations in the Americas. The most plausible answer, of course, is that they were convinced all along of the centrality of slavery and of the commodities it produced in their own prosperity, and had a rational understanding of the costs of empire needed to maintain the system.

This history, in fact, compels us to reconsider one of the most familiar lines of reasoning explaining the economic rise of parts of

Europe, and especially of Britain, in the eighteenth and nineteenth centuries, and their accelerating divergence from China, India, and the Ottoman Empire, as well as Africa, in terms of wealth and power. The usual argument invoked to explain these successes, concentrated in northern Europe, is that states of that region had become more capable than those of their would-be peers and rivals elsewhere, including the many states that Europe subjugated and eventually colonized. There is some truth to this, even though adopting such a claim comes close to outright tautology. Borrowing the famous notion of the American sociologist and political scientist Charles Tilly that "war makes states," I would propose extending this thought further while placing greater emphasis on competition among Europeans outside of the continent itself. The growing capacity of the state in this era was precisely a function of violent interstate competition in Europe over empire, and above all in the Atlantic world, which began, as we have seen, in places like the seas off Elmina in the late fifteenth century. Building a more capable state was a sine qua non of extending and securing lucrative new conquests, and as Tilly wrote, this meant, "as a by-product of preparations for war, rulers willy-nilly started activities and organizations that eventually took on lives of their own: courts, treasuries, systems of taxation, regional administrations, public assemblies, and much more." With such things as these, a state's extractive power and therefore its ability to mobilize and project force increased enormously, "as did the claims of citizens on their state," which had to expand the social contract and in turn provide yet more services to its citizens. Speaking of the state that eventually rose to preeminence in the Atlantic world via massive shipbuilding beginning in the seventeenth century, the historian Frederick Cooper wrote along much these same lines: "Empire was making the British state, not the other way around."

Tilly's iconic formula about war is good as far as it goes, but risks being interpreted too narrowly. War between European states in this era should not be understood only classically, in the unending scroll of alliances, counteralliances, tactics, and outcomes that fill history books. It must also be seen, more candidly, in terms of what it was so often about, something both novel and profoundly transformative. By this we mean the control of large, overseas empires. But even that term obfuscates. Over the span of four centuries this struggle consisted, in large part, of a long series of unconventional and largely undeclared conflicts that were waged for control over Africa and Africans and especially over the domination and exploitation of the Black body. Put to work in stringently coordinated and heavily policed ways, the rents extracted from Africans became far more valuable even than the yellow metal extracted from the continent in the sixteenth century had been as a natural resource. One could do worse than to think of the people shipped in chains across the Atlantic as black gold. The Scramble for Africans went beyond that, though. It was a global contest not just for the supply of slaves but simultaneously for the Guadeloupes of the world—meaning the tropical places where captive peoples could be put to the most productive use. And it was war over these things, above all, wars deemed worth endless fighting and armament and dying, that forged the most successful modern European states.

15

FIGHTING FOR AFRICANS

S ANTIAGO HILL, THE SOLITARY mountain that looms over the town of Elmina, is an ideal vantage point for understanding Europe's centuries-long struggle for control of Black bodies. When they first scaled these heights, the Portuguese erected a chapel atop the summit. Later they would build a small defensive rampart. In modern times, this hilltop would be used to house a sanatorium for lepers, and then as a school for the national tourism industry—sadly, now long closed. Santiago Hill's greatest significance by far, however (one surely missed by nearly everyone who visits Elmina), is that this was the spot where Holland defeated Portugal in 1637, finally allowing it to seize control of the Gold Coast after decades of trying, and bringing 155 years of Lisbon's hegemony over the gold trade in coastal West Africa to an end.

The Dutch had attempted frontal assaults on the fort before, as well as attacks from the sea, pounding São Jorge da Mina with shipboard guns and blockading the crescent harbor, preventing the Portuguese from either shipping gold out or being resupplied. But even as their governors died one after another and their overall numbers dwindled to a few dozen men, mostly due to the attrition brought on by malaria and other tropical fevers, the Portuguese held on. Their tenacity could be explained in part by the robustness of the fort, and also by the successful recruitment by the Portuguese of indigenous allies. These local Akan auxiliary forces supplied not only food but timely intelligence about Dutch ship and troop movements in the immediately surrounding area.

In August 1637, a Dutch fleet composed of nine men-of-war bearing eight hundred soldiers arrived in the waters off the Gold Coast to begin yet another bid for Elmina. Because of their local allies, the Portuguese learned of the Dutch plans to take command of Santiago Hill and pummel the fort from the heights. To prevent this, African auxiliaries guarded the approaches to the mountain and routed the Dutch on their first attempt to make the ascent. But the African fighters, most of them residents of Elmina, then left the scene, launching into a premature celebration of their victory in the town. This gave the enemy a chance to regroup and wheel their guns up to the summit. From there they struck São Jorge mercilessly, but because the construction was so stout, to little effect. What caused the Portuguese to finally surrender, after several days of this bombardment, was hunger, not the cannon barrage. The victorious Dutch allowed the remaining Portuguese to abandon the fort, but a condition of their surrender was they could take no belongings with them. Later, they were shipped off to Portuguese-owned São Tomé, but that island, far less well defended than Elmina, soon fell to the Dutch as well; so would Portugal's young colony of Luanda— temporarily, at least, as we will see.

In the period prior to their capture of Elmina, the Netherlanders had been acquiring as much as five tons of gold per year by just poaching on the Portuguese franchise up and down the Gold Coast. All along, the Portuguese had little doubt that it was this African-sourced wealth that had positioned upstart Netherlands to mount an all-out war on its empire. And with their capture of Elmina, the Dutch knew that the Portuguese—or if not them, other European nations—would try to oust them in turn, or otherwise horn in on the action. Taking no chances, the Dutch, doubtlessly enlisting African labor, constructed the whitewashed redoubt that still dominates this summit as a mountaintop base. It would prevent others from entering the harbor or from ever daring the kind of assault that they had managed on the fort below.

For the Dutch states, the strategic purpose in all of this could not have been clearer. In 1580, Portugal had been unified with Spain, which was then at war with the Netherlands, in order to retain its hold on the Low Countries against Protestant revolt. By this time, the vast empire of the Spanish king Philip II included much of the New World, running from present-day California to the southern tip of South America and even stretching across the Pacific to the Philippines, which were named after him. His coat of arms read, "The World Is Not Enough," and a measure of his ambition lay in the fact that he even contemplated invading China with eight thousand men. In order to punish the recalcitrant Netherlanders, Philip banned Dutch shipping from Iberian ports. This sent the Dutch, ardent seafarers whose wealth was built upon maritime trade, scrambling for commercial opportunities elsewhere, which led them into the waters of the Caribbean, where they found rich supplies of salt at Punta de Araya, off the coast of present-day Venezuela. As a pamphlet from the Dutch West India Company put it in 1630,

> West India can become the Netherlands' great source of gain.
> Diminishing the enemy's power as it garners silver plate.

Shortly thereafter, the Dutch expanded their scope of activity, following the same path down the coast of West Africa that the Portuguese had taken beginning with Prince Henry, nearly two centuries earlier; their clear aim was to seek a share of the action in that region's booming trade in gold.

In retrospect it seems abundantly clear that the Portuguese empire suffered grievously from its forced marriage with Spain, for the restive Dutch possessed a number of serious advantages. One of these was the fact that the Netherlands, with thriving, cosmopolitan commercial markets in places like Antwerp and later Amsterdam, was the leading source of many of the goods that Africans demanded in exchange for their gold. These included the ever popular *manilhas*, bar iron, and worked metal goods of various kinds, as well as textiles, both European and Indian. The Portuguese, by contrast, produced almost nothing that was highly prized along the African coast.

To support its trading ambitions, Holland also built up a huge shipping capacity, including a robust fleet of men-of-war. The most important advantage the Dutch had, though, was a paradoxical one. Because it had occurred so quickly, Portugal's extraordinary imperial expansion had left it badly overstretched. In pioneering imperialism Portugal had grown rich, but its model, based on scant human resources, given the size of the country's population, was dependent on mercenaries and was inherently self-limiting. As other powers sought fortune of their own overseas, Lisbon failed to improvise fast enough, and soon found itself unable to keep up. European rivals (notably the French and the English) had already begun to poach on Portugal's holdings during the sixteenth century. But as that century came to a close it was the Dutch who had the strongest political motivation to take on the Iberians in a concerted way, and they developed a strategy to match it: licensing merchants to organize colonial rule and hit Portugal where its overseas presence was thinnest or where it was most vulnerable economically, thus forcing it to make hard choices about which assets it could realistically hold on to. As the imperial sweepstakes over the control of Black bodies and the wealth derived from them continued to draw in other powers, the English would apply much the same strategy against the French a century and a half later.

When Dutch ships launched an assault against Portuguese Brazil in 1624, Henock Estartenius, a Calvinist minister who sailed with the fleet pithily summed up Holland's strategy in the Thirty Years War. The offensive against Brazil's Pernambuco, he said, was nothing less than "the means and route with which to divert the king of Spain's arms from our throats and to cut the nerves with which he sustains the wars in Europe." This campaign received an extraordinary boost three years later, when a Dutch admiral,

Piet Heyn, seized a large Spanish silver fleet in the Battle of Matanzas, off the Cuban coast, capturing a cargo of at least 11.5 million guilders worth of gold. The boon was so enormous that it allowed the West India Company, chartered in 1621, and still struggling, to finance a large new fleet as well as pay a 50 percent dividend to shareholders. As they are usually told, the subsequent chapters of this history have always emphasized the use of this expanded fleet to take over the biggest sugar-growing regions of Brazil, which the Dutch indeed accomplished. Given scant attention in most accounts, though, is the way that Holland's new merchant power was used to expand the country's influence up and down the African coast at Portugal's expense. In the Dutch mind, Africa and its slaves were most critical to defeating Portugal, and later to making Brazil profitable for Holland. And all of this began with the successful assault on Elmina, which was still seen in Europe as the key to West Africa's strategic gold markets.

The thrust against Elmina was the opening salvo in a new, quasi-global, and yet scarcely heralded conflict launched in an era when the dictum of war being politics by other means could have borne improvement via a tiny tweak: European trade in the early seventeenth century was war by other means. Practically speaking, what this meant was that simultaneous Dutch offensives in both Africa and in the New World presented Portugal with unprecedented choices, exposing just how far its commercial and administrative reach had each exceeded its grasp. As Tilly writes, "Its domestic supply of men, timber, and other resources for imperial adventure remained perilously thin, so much so that sixteenth-century 'Portuguese' ships often bore no native Portuguese but their commanders."

In the opening decades of the seventeenth century, in order to manage this crisis, some voices in Lisbon urged the crown to send detachments from the fleet that serviced its trade in Asian spices to fend off the Dutch in Africa. Others argued that the East Indies were simply too valuable to allow them to be exposed to greater risk in this way. Initially at least, the Asian interests won out. This is what had caused Elmina to go for years without adequate resupply and with a dwindling force of men to defend it. But the capture of Elmina in 1637, quickly followed by the seizure of São Tomé and Luanda, raised the sense of alarm in Lisbon to a whole new level, forcing a radical reassessment of the crown's imperial equities, and a shift back to the Atlantic. Luanda had been supplying twenty thousand slaves a year to the Portuguese before its fall to the Dutch, far from the sort of volume that the slave trade would achieve in later centuries, to be sure, but already for this day and age an extraordinary number.

A common saying of this era ran, "Without Angola no slaves, without slaves no sugar, without sugar no Brazil," and it would be hard to imagine a formula that packs more historical truth about the Atlantic world of this time. By virtue of its Angolan-supplied slave labor, Brazil had become a sugar powerhouse and a leading profit center for Portugal in an astonishingly brief period of time. For the first three decades following Pedro Álvares Cabral's landfall in South America in 1500, Brazil had occupied a lowly place in the economic scheme of Portugal's young empire. It was neither rich in gold like Africa, nor rich in spices like Asia. Virtually the only trade item of interest was an exotic tropical product, brazilwood, which was used to make brilliant red dyes. Because of this, many merely regarded Brazil as a mere stopping-off point on the way to the East for ships that followed the same zigzagging path discovered by Cabral, which involved tacking far to the west before crossing the Atlantic eastward again to round the Cape of Good Hope and enter the Indian Ocean. As the explorer Amerigo Vespucci lamented, "One can say we found nothing of profit there except an infinity of dyewood trees, *canafistula* . . . and other natural marvels that would be tedious to describe." Another chronicler of the time, Julius Caesar Scaliger, was even more scathing in his appraisal of the spices found in Brazil, calling them "scarce, ignoble, and bad." Historically speaking there is, of course, a supreme irony in this: sugar, whose production Brazil would soon dominate, was about to become the greatest spice of all, and incomparably so. Indeed by 1660, the value of sugar on world markets exceeded the value of all other tropical commodities combined.

As it happened, Lisbon's first gestures toward actual administration of Brazil did not come until the 1530s. That is when the crown moved to establish a series of feudal concessions called *donatorias*, or captaincies, more or less copying the blueprint from how São Tomé had been organized a few decades earlier. Unlike Castile, which could and did draw upon great revenue streams through local taxation, Portuguese absolutism depended for its lifeblood on imperial commerce and enterprise, which it entrusted not to direct state administration but to the financial ambitions of its nobility. In a system such as this, colonies had to be made to pay for themselves; by any such metric, Brazil was a laggard, producing scant income. This problem was gradually addressed by encouraging agricultural production, beginning with tobacco, which was first domesticated in Amazonia, and then sugar, as well as by collecting taxes on other trade. Just as important was fending off European interlopers, preventing them from challenging Lisbon's claims in South America. Here, the biggest threat came from French traders, whose refusal to pay royalties occasioned the dispatch of a Portuguese fleet in 1530 to defend Lisbon's holdings. The French persisted, however, and in the 1550s, French Calvinists even established the first of several attempted French colonies, this one strangely named, given its location in the tropics on Coligny, a small island off Rio de Janeiro, France Antarctique. Scarcely remembered today, it drew direct support from the king of France. But this prompted the dispatch of a new governor-general for the entire colony from Portugal; once he arrived in the colony, Mem de Sá became the founder of Rio de Janeiro, a pioneer in sugar cultivation, and one of the most important figures in early Brazilian history.

As commander of a fleet of twenty-six warships manned by two thousand soldiers, one of de Sá's first tasks was to disband the small French colony altogether. His administration of the territory directly on behalf of the Portuguese crown marked the start of Lisbon's more attentive governance of Brazil and roughly coincided with the beginnings of concerted efforts to develop sugar cultivation there. At the time, when sugar was still considered an exotic medicinal or luxurious spice in Europe, Brazil's output of the commodity stood at roughly 2500 tons, or about half of what São Tomé produced.

By 1580, nearly a decade into what is sometimes called Brazil's sugar century, production matched São Tomé's peak output, and by the end of the sixteenth century, with the island off Central Africa in steep decline, it reached 16,000 tons a year and was still fast ascending. Just as São Tomé's rapid takeoff had helped doom sugar production on Madeira, the rise of Brazil, both broader and sharper, helped kill off big sugar in São Tomé. By 1625, the colony had become the predominant source of sugar for virtually all of Europe. A little more than a century later, sugar would no longer be considered a luxury product at all. In a stunningly brief period of time, it had turned into a product of universal necessity throughout the North Atlantic world. But by then, like São Tomé before it, Brazil, which had done so much to establish sugar as one of the world's most traded goods, would also be relegated to an also-ran. The new tenor was an archipelago of emergent cane growing slave colonies in the Caribbean. By the middle of the eighteenth century, sugar and the various products made from it, from molasses to rum, had laid the foundations of mass consumerism, and utterly transformed eating habits in Europe; in no place was this more so than in England. Indeed, no other product did as much to shape and define the modern condition. As an abundant commodity that was newly affordable for all, sugar would have profound economic and social impacts, transforming trade, labor, worker productivity, leisure, and, of course, health. More grimly, sugar also became a proxy in tangible form for slave labor. Most of the stories that explain the hows and the whys of sugar's transformational impact on the world economy, on geopolitics, and on human society lie in the pages ahead. First, though, one must first take a closer look at sugar slavery itself in Brazil, because as the adage about Angolan slaves had it, it was Africa and the labor robbed from that continent that made every bit of this possible.

16

ENDLESS DEATH IN LANDS
WITH NO END

I N THE EARLY SIXTEENTH CENTURY, during the first decades of
the Portuguese presence in Brazil, enslaved Native Americans
provided almost all of the hard labor as the first sugar plantations, mostly modest in size, began to proliferate in Bahia and Pernambuco. This era ushered in an important transitional moment in
the economic development of the West, in which the first hints of the
capitalism to come flickered amid feudal modes of production, notwithstanding their theoretical opposition to one another. As Philip
Curtin wrote in *The Rise and Fall of the Plantation Complex*:

> *The planters owned the land, they owned the tools—the sugar*
> *mills—and they owned the labor [slaves]. But a sugar plantation*
> *was also a society consisting of 100 to 300 people—even more in*
> *later centuries. The plantations were scattered throughout the*
> *countryside in a new country where the web of government was*
> *not yet capable of dealing with individuals. These small societies*
> *needed some form of government. It was natural for the senhor de*
> *engenio, or master of the sugar factory, to begin settling quarrels,*
> *punishing offenders against the common interest, and taking on*
> *the powers that were otherwise those of police and magistrates*
> *courts. . . . Ownership carried with it the right to punish the*
> *slaves. The estates were self-contained and nearly self-sufficient*

in food, and the royal government was too far away to exercise
effective control.

With each successive migration of the sugar industry, first out
of the Mediterranean, then into the Atlantic and down the coast
of West Africa, and finally to Brazil, there would be other significant changes in the business of producing sugar like these; some
of them constituted important refinements, others utter transformations. In Madeira and the Canary Islands, the Portuguese had
relied on a mixed labor force that combined indentured servitude
for whites and slavery for both native Canarians and Black Africans.
São Tomé's most important innovation was the reinvention of the
sugar plantation in the late 1400s on a model that relied exclusively
on forced African labor. No one knew it yet, but this new factor was
about to become the most important generative force of this age, and
in the period just beyond it would propel the world onward to the
Industrial Revolution. On such a small and remote island, given the
state of technology at the time, the only practical way to increase
production was to increase the number of Black slaves and extract
the maximum quantum of labor from them at the absolute lowest
cost. The inherent logic behind this, of parasitism and rent collection, would quickly make São Tomé the first Creole plantation
society: a place with a sharply pyramidal social structure whose template would remain familiar centuries later, whether in the Caribbean or the Mississippi Delta. In its simplest form, this meant a
limited number of whites, an intermediary class of mixed-race people, and a large foundation of Black laborers, whose brutal exploitation produced soaring mortality rates and an unquenchable demand
for newly imported slaves to replace them. São Tomé's exclusive
focus on sugar production for export meant that nearly everything
that whites consumed had to be imported from afar. The governing
principle of a monocrop plantation economy like this, in fact, was
that the only people who were self-sufficient were the slaves. On this
island colony they built their own shacks for housing at the edge of
the fields they worked. And they largely fed themselves on a diet

of bananas they grew themselves and the pigs they were allowed to keep, which mostly fed on cane field refuse. In order to maximize sugar production, the time allotted to them for taking care of their own needs was limited to Sundays. Here lay the rudiments of the chattel system that would soon cross the Atlantic.

Brazil's most important innovation, by contrast, was immensity of scale. The coastal regions of Bahia and Pernambuco where the Portuguese established the sugar industry were endowed with vast expanses of flat, fertile, and plentifully irrigated land. Sugar may have been native to faraway New Guinea, as scientists nowadays postulate, but *massapé*, a soil found in parts of the Brazilian northeast, seemed to suit the crop better than anyplace it had ever been cultivated before. Besides capital, the only other essential was an abundant workforce. Sugar was a crop whose production necessitated nearly year-round labor, most of it both grueling and dangerous. Wherever it had been grown commercially, farming it necessitated some form of compulsion.[*]

꠸

AS WOULD HAPPEN ELSEWHERE in the New World, the arrival of fortune seekers, soldiers, traders, and settlers from Iberia triggered a period of death en masse for native peoples in Brazil. To the Portuguese, the indigenous population had initially seemed very nearly inexhaustible, much like their impressions of the potential slave supply in Angola during the early years of the transatlantic trade in human beings. But the diseases transmitted by the European newcomers caused astoundingly high turnover on sugar plantations and other Portuguese ventures, due to soaring mortality rates among indigenous slaves and indentured workers. The first documented epidemic, probably involving smallpox, was reported on the Brazilian coast in 1559; it rapidly spread northward, peaking three years later when thirty thousand natives living under Portuguese control

---

[*] Brazil also saw the introduction of an important technical innovation: a three-horizontal-roller mill used to extract sugary juices from raw cane with maximum efficiency.

perished, mostly in *aldeias*, Jesuit-run mission villages. Countless others living on the periphery of these areas of forced resettlement or in direct or indirect contact with them also doubtlessly died as a result. One year later, this epidemic was followed by a similarly devastating outbreak of measles. A Portuguese chronicler noted at the time, "The population that was in these parts twenty years ago is wasted in this Bahia, and it seems an incredible thing for no one believed that so many people would ever be used up, let alone in such a short time. Even those natives who didn't die quickly were often rendered listless when they were not incapacitated outright by infections for which these populations were like a virgin field," free of any natural immune resistance.

The astonishment and confusion of the Portuguese over this turn of events was only deepened by the recent history of early European imperialism. As numerous chronicles had attested by that time, Europeans had themselves inexplicably died off in startling numbers in tropical Africa, something that many explained in terms of what they imagined to be a mysterious miasma they associated with swamplands and rain forests. In the Americas, however, it was the natives who died in droves soon after contact with the newcomers. With modern science, of course, we know the culprit to be pathogens brought from the Old World, a long list that included smallpox, measles, whooping cough, chicken pox, bubonic plague, typhus, typhoid, diphtheria, cholera, scarlet fever, and influenza, none of which the native populations had ever been exposed to before. Even the common cold, newly borne to South America aboard European vessels, was deadly.

The Jesuits, however, responded to the widespread dying-off of Amerindians whom they sought to evangelize with a kind of superstition that we have too quickly sanitized with fancier language, by calling it dogma. Rather than as a medical problem, they interpreted the high mortality rates as a form of divine wrath for the nudity and for differing sexual and other social mores that they deplored in the native populations. This caused them to redouble their efforts to minister to the souls, as opposed to the bodies, of the populations they had corralled and put to work. "Stricter, more thorough Catholic instruction would forestall deviant behavior," one Jesuit report read. "And that, in turn, would keep so many bodily afflictions at bay." Treating this behavior by the Jesuits for what it was, a kind of irrational or magical thinking, is all the more important given the scorn poured by Europeans in this era and Westerners long since on the superstition of native peoples in the many regions of the world they colonized, and in Africa in particular.

The dramatic decline of the native population didn't only affect sugar production, which once it had started in earnest quickly became the be-all and end-all of the Brazilian economy. Because the Portuguese were dependent on indigenous labor, it also struck hard at food production. This led to famine among those natives who had been incorporated into the Portuguese realm, and conditions of increasing scarcity for whites as well. Governor-General de Sá responded to this situation by organizing military style expeditions farther and farther into the interior in order to capture indigenous people and press-gang them into plantation work. Often this was done in alliance with local Indian groups whom the Portuguese armed, allowing them to settle scores with traditional rivals.

Here, one finds striking similarities to the strategies that Europeans were just then beginning to roll out in many places along the West African coast, as they navigated a historic shift away from the era of mutually respectful trade and diplomacy practiced by the Portuguese beginning in the last decades of the fifteenth century. This gave way to deliberate efforts aimed to sow violence and chaos among Africans as a means of drumming up the traffic in slaves, starting in the seventeenth century. The Dutch actually lent firearms to rival states on the Gold Coast on the condition that their African clients would sell whatever prisoners they took captive to the Dutch as slaves, as the slave trade quickly overtook Europe's older commerce in African gold. A seventeenth-century saying favored among the Dutch at the time held that wars made "gold scarce but negroes plenty." In Africa, this approach was usually based on the trade in arms, alcohol, and certain prestige goods, especially Asian cloth. In

Brazil, where unlike West Africa, native peoples had little tradition of metal-tool making, the Portuguese sometimes traded guns, but usually favored axes and saws, because of the nearly revolutionary impact these tools could have on indigenous life in a heavily forested environment.

Felling a single four-foot tree with an indigenous stone axe would take 115 hours—nearly three weeks of eight-hour days. With a steel axe, workers could topple the same tree in less than three hours. Stone axes would clear an acre and a half, a typical slash-and-burn plot, in the equivalent of 153 eight-hour days. Steel axes would do the job in the equivalent of eight workdays—almost twenty times faster.

Despite the technological gap in metal tools and weapons, many indigenous peoples in Brazil responded to the Portuguese invasion of their lands and aggressive attempts to kidnap and ransom their people with counterraids of their own. These were often focused on destroying sugar mills, which reflects the natives' clear understanding of the centrality of the cane crop and of the finished product, sugar, to the Portuguese imperial project. Although it is scarcely emphasized in traditional historic accounts, this kind of resistance among Native American populations—often protracted—was seen virtually everywhere that European immigrants "settled" in the New World, from the islands of the Caribbean to the earliest continental settlements of the British Americas and later the Plains of the United States.

Out of the native resistance to the Portuguese takeover of their land and efforts to impress Amerindians into plantation slavery grew a wave of uprisings led by a messianic cult the colonists called Santidade. The leaders of this movement melded elements of rituals from the Tupinambá, a major ethnic group, and Roman Catholic symbolism, promising future redemption and a reign of peace on earth once the whites had been driven from the land. Some of these rebel communities grew as large as twenty thousand in number by the late

1580s, when Africans were just beginning to become a major source of labor. And, as would happen in many other parts of the Americas, some of them incorporated runaway Blacks, as well.

Unlike enslaved Blacks put to work on small islands, Brazil's so-called Indians were living and operating in their native lands and the Portuguese, to their great frustration, found it almost impossible to prevent their escape. Resistance by Indians took many other forms as well, from the armed raids just mentioned and a baffling (to the Portuguese) refusal to buy into European material values, including monetary inducements, to persistently low productivity, a classic form of resistance often misunderstood by the colonizers as laziness, a sturdy "weapon of the weak" in the phrase made famous by the political scientist and anthropologist James C. Scott.

Practical limitations on harnessing indigenous laborers like these led the Portuguese to consider substituting Africans for Indians in the first place. And without the arrival of millions of enslaved Africans, it is hard to imagine a whole chain of familiar historical developments that followed. The New World would not have been made viable anywhere near the extent that it did. Without their prosperous colonies, the major imperial nations of Europe, and indeed Europe overall, would have become far less rich and powerful. And without this wealth and power, coupled to growing European diasporas in the Americas, what would be left of the vague but by now unavoidable term "the West"? The heavy weight of the present is such that this is all hard to imagine. But without this interlocking suite of developments, Europe might very well have remained a kind of geographic and civilizational dead end. Without its hold on a New World made viable and profitable by enslaving Africans, there is little reason to believe the place nowadays fancied as the Old Continent wouldn't have continued to lag behind the leading centers of global civilization in Asia and the Islamic world.

It is in this stark light, finally, that one must consider the epidemiological advantage that Europeans arriving in Brazil (and many other parts of the Americas in the sixteenth and seventeenth centuries) enjoyed. Without it, they would never have managed to take over and settle the vast territories of the New World on anything like the scale, or with anything like the speed that they ultimately did.

Historians, demographers, environmental scientists, and experts in numerous other disciplines are still struggling to provide an exhaustive and definitive account of the tragic population collapse that befell the indigenous peoples of the Americas. A thorough review of the most recent findings is beyond the scope of this work, but a narrative like this cannot proceed without at least offering a big-picture sense of the native cataclysm. The waves of epidemic and expiration that followed the arrival of whites became part of what has been described as a hemisphere-wide Great Dying. One recent study has suggested that this event killed as many as 56 million people, or roughly 90 percent of the overall hemispheric population of indigenous Americans between the time of first European contact and the start of the seventeenth century. Such a number would make the deadly transmission of diseases like these by far the largest mortality event in proportion to the global population in human history, and second only to World War II in absolute terms with regard to the number of people killed. Others, meanwhile, have criticized what they regard as an excessive focus on pathogens alone, insisting instead on the effects of warfare and of constant, forced displacement, which resulted in both "material deprivation and starvation, conditions that favored disease." To give a clearer idea of what numbers of this magnitude might mean in practical terms in a given region of the Americas, though, when Hernán Cortés arrived on the shores of Mexico, scientists estimate there were 25.2 million inhabitants living there, occupying an area of roughly 200,000 square miles. By 1620–1625, the number of indigenous people had plummeted to a mere 730,000, or roughly 3 percent of its earlier size.

17

THE PERPETUAL OVEN

MY EXPECTATIONS FOR VALONGO Wharf had been strangely heightened by the well-known pleasures of Rio de Janeiro. I had come to the city in the middle of the northern winter and stayed at a friend's apartment a mere block from one of the world's most famous beaches, Copacabana. It was a research trip, but the ocean had an undeniable tug, especially in the hot, late afternoons. The hardest thing about exploring the slave past in this city was neither sand nor samba, though. While I had placed myself in the very epicenter of the Atlantic slave trade, the Rio I discovered was a city resolutely not focused on any aspect of this history—a history that had built not only Brazil, but the modern world itself. I had spent days touring favelas and the old, historic districts filled with grayed, colonnaded buildings that remained from the colonial era and engaging in conversations that spoke to the present invisibility of Blacks in the upper ranks of society, but these activities yielded little beyond boilerplate about the deeper past. I searched, as I had done in so many other places during this work, for monuments and archaeological remnants that spoke to the traffic in Africans that had transformed the society; here in Rio, however, it was largely in vain.

That is until we arrived at Valongo, a place I had read about before leaving New York, but which many of the Cariocas I met knew nothing of. Somehow, I had nonetheless expected something grand in dimension, a proper monument, or at least a place of remembrance with prominent signage. What I found instead, almost stumbling upon it by accident, was in effect a large hole in the ground. That spot, consisting of a long wall and sunken plaza paved with rough-hewn stones of different sizes covering what was once a beach, was excavated only in 2011, after being covered up for 168 years. There, as a plain and modest UNESCO World Heritage sign attests, nine hundred thousand Africans first landed in the New World, more than any other single point of disembarkation.

During Brazil's first decades of sugar cultivation, production was too small and the available investment capital from Europe insufficient to finance a large-scale trade in African slaves. The Portuguese in Brazil thus relied almost exclusively on forced indigenous labor until about 1560, when they began a gradual but fateful transition to Black labor that took forty years to complete. But once African slavery began to take hold, there would be no turning back. Brazil would eventually account for more traffic in slaves for plantation labor than any other country— roughly 40 percent of the total of Africans landed in the Americas. Surprisingly, given this, Africans were originally imported not as field slaves at all, but as manservants and as skilled workers, used in such roles as sugar master, purger (whose job was to remove impurities from the cane during the refining process), and blacksmith. But as forced African labor in Brazil came to predominate, most of the work performed by Blacks inevitably consisted of backbreaking plantation labor.

The product of their output made the sugar industry an important, if still unheralded building block of what became the industrialized West. First, it provided Europe with a powerful financial stimulus. Beyond the most obvious benefits from the sugar business—the revenues and profits that it generated directly—one must also look at what economists call multiplier effects, which stemmed from the many spin-offs and ancillary businesses that flowed from sugar, and from the rapidly expanding world of plantation economies. In terms of scale, perhaps the biggest of these was the exploding slave trade itself, which sugar drove like nothing else, before or after. Finally, there was the technically demanding nature of sugar's production. Harvesting, pressing of the cane, boiling, and other processing steps were all highly time sensitive and needed to be carefully synchronized in order to ensure both efficiency and quality. As they came to be integrated operations, sugar plantations and the mills they fed with cane, moreover, became some of the largest industries anywhere. The Caribbean still lies ahead in our story, but once sugar took off there, two thousand or more slaves per integrated plantation was not uncommon, making them far larger in size than almost any businesses known in Europe. As the historian Caitlin Rosenthal has written, "Only in the mid-nineteenth century would the largest factories begin to approach the scales of late eighteenth-century plantations. Josiah Wedgwood's famed pottery works, which some historians have described as the largest industrial factory of its time, employed only 450 people at his death in 1795. In Britain, most textile mills in Lancashire employed fewer than 500 hands."

By the time of sugar's initial expansion in Brazil in the second half of the sixteenth century, Lisbon already enjoyed advanced trade and diplomatic relations with the Kingdom of Kongo. Portugal had also just recently founded a new colony at Luanda, next door to the south. This was only one part of a perfect confluence of factors that set west Central Africa up to be the main source of slaves in Brazil during this critical period, the colony's so-called sugar century. Central Africa was close, relatively speaking, to Brazil, but that was not its only advantage for Lisbon. As we have seen, wind patterns and ocean currents have often played a decisive but underappreciated role in Atlantic history, and at that latitude they ensured a very rapid east-west ocean crossing. This resulted in lower slave mortality rates, higher volumes, and lower prices. Brazil's vast expanses of flat, extremely fertile, and well-irrigated land made labor the most important form of capital in plantation farming, amounting to perhaps 20 percent of the expense of sugar production in this era, and if one frames this only as a narrow economic problem, putting aside morality and ethics, Central Africa no doubt stood out as the best solution.

The nearly successful uprising of the enslaved in São Tomé in 1595, followed by attacks on the island by Portugal's covetous European rivals, culminating in a Dutch fleet's raid of São Tomé in 1599, was another element in the perfect storm that transferred the epicenter of slave-grown plantation sugar westward across the Atlantic. The recurrent turmoil in São Tomé fueled an exodus of both planters and technicians with expertise in sugar production from the island. Those determined to continue thriving in this lucrative business overwhelmingly made their way to Brazil, then still a fledgling colony, but one fast developing a reputation as the Portuguese world's new El Dorado.

In remarkably little time, the conjoining of these elements (the boundless fertile land of northeastern Brazil, and the cheap and seemingly inexhaustible supply of slaves from Central Africa) produced one of the most spectacular events in the economic history of the early modern Western world. Starting from a paltry output in 1570, soon after Blacks began to be trafficked to Brazil in substantial numbers, sugar production grew at fantastical rates. By 1580, slave labor in the Portuguese colony already was generating 180,000 arrobas of the commodity, or three times the output of Madeira and São Tomé combined. By 1614, the crop had surpassed 700,000 arrobas, orders of magnitude greater than what those small islands had ever produced. Output would soon hit 1 million arrobas, or roughly 14.5 long tons. To modern ears, this may not sound like such an impressive quantity, but for its day and age, this was an unheard-of deluge of a good that was just beginning to wreak transformational effects on diet, economy, and society in Europe.

Once it began to take off in earnest, those who profited most from Brazil's sugar industry felt as though they had been gifted an economic miracle, and indeed this was not far from the truth. Their giddiness was even reflected in the terminology of the business. They began calling northeastern Brazil's proliferating mills at the center of large estates—where capital, cane, and labor were brought together in industrially, if not morally virtuous synergy—*engenhos*, turning the adjective "ingenious" into a new noun. The first decade of the seventeenth century produced numerous wonder-struck accounts of the boom in Brazil like this: "The most excellent fruit and drug of sugar grows all over this province in such abundance that it can supply not only the kingdom [Portugal] but all the provinces of Europe, and it is understood that it yields to His Majesty's treasure about 500,000 cruzados and to private individuals about an equal amount." On this basis, one historian has estimated that Portuguese income from Brazil was about 50 percent higher than the costs of operating the colony paid by the crown.

In Brazil, as I discovered, one stills finds virtually intact a vast archipelago of once wealthy towns that arose on the back of sugar, places like Cachoeira, the second-oldest city in Bahia. There, the district's presiding sugar baron lived in an enormous plantation home on the top of a small mountain. From this vantage point, amid cooling breezes, he could take in views of the entire river town. Today, though nearly a ghost town, the center of Cachoeira still exudes bygone wealth. Its heart is cut as neatly as a jewel and consists of an opulently decorated cathedral, green but empty riverside parks, and a warren of streets shaded against the intense heat by their own narrowness, their cobblestones laid by seemingly unlimited sugar money more than two centuries ago.

By the 1630s, as many as 60,000 African slaves labored on Brazilian plantations, and their numbers were fast rising. Africans and Afro-Brazilians already accounted for virtually the entire sugar plantation workforce. Portugal, which remained semifeudal and which utterly dominated the American slave business, was sending Africans across the Atlantic at a pace of perhaps 15,000 per year, some for sale into new Spanish colonies, whether in the Caribbean, Mexico, or Bolivia, where many played important roles in mining or mining-related occupations. A Portuguese priest who visited Jesuit-owned plantations in Bahia in this decade was left with a searing impression of the human suffering endured by these slaves:

Whoever sees those tremendous ovens perpetually ablaze in the darkness of the night; the high flames rising up in gushes out of each of them, out of the two openings or vents through which they breathe in the fire; the Ethiopians or Cyclops bathe in sweat, as black as they are vigorous, who supply the thick and sturdy material to the fire, and the pitchforks with which they surround and rouse it . . . people all the very color of the night, working intensely, and moaning all the while, with neither a moment of peace nor of rest; whoever sees, finally, all the confusing and thunderous machinery and apparatus of that Babylon, will not doubt, even if they have Etna and Vesuvius, that it is the likeness of hell.

Traditional histories of both Latin America and of the rise of the West in the early modern period tend to emphasize the importance of New World mining booms. The most famous of these are the sixteenth-century stories of Spanish silver extracted from Potosí and from colonial Mexico. Three to five million pesos worth of silver was shipped annually aboard Spanish galleons, the largest ships of the age, to the Ming Dynasty. There it was traded for silk, porcelain, tea, and other goods.* Stiff European demand for these goods turned China into what has been likened to a "vacuum cleaner" of the metal. The Ming took to silver after the inflationary debasement of paper money in imperial China, where it had been in widespread use at least since the eleventh century. Insatiable demand for silver in Ming markets lifted the price of the metal to double what it fetched in the West, irresistibly opening up lucrative opportunities for arbitrage on a massive scale.

Spain's obsession with extractive mining strongly shaped its approach to the New World, resulting in what has been called "the highest stage of feudalism." Where the Portuguese favored commercial and maritime enterprise and took a comparatively hands-off approach to colonial economic management, Spain endeavored to micromanage its vast colonies and tightly monitored all economic

---

* One should also recall that this was, in effect, reprising the long-term historical pattern of European deficits in its trade for luxury goods from the East. In the time of the Mali and Ghana Empires, as we have seen, it was African gold that allowed Europe to finance this trade.

transactions. When the emphasis was not on direct extraction of gold and silver, it was on the exaction of tribute from newly conquered peoples, which was "easier to keep track of than the profits of enslavement." The historian Robin Blackburn has cogently analyzed these differing approaches to colonial management:

> *Unlike the Dutch, the English, and the Venetians, Portuguese rulers did not license merchants to organize colonial rule. Unlike the Spanish, they did not tolerate the creation of great autonomous domains in their overseas territories. But they could not stop colonial administrators, priests, and soldiers from trading on their own account, or from accepting payoffs for illegal uses of their official powers. Colonial revenues thus made Lisbon and its king relatively independent of powerholders elsewhere in Portugal, but dependent on frequently corrupt officials. Such a monarchy could only prosper when gold and goods flowed freely from the colonies.*

To be fair, part of the distinction with Spain here may be more a reflection of demographic realities than sheer ideology. Much smaller Portugal simply lacked the population to staff large settler bureaucracies. By contrast, not only could its Iberian neighbor send plentiful settlers, it routinely deployed nobles to occupy the highest posts of government in places like New Spain and Peru, carefully auditing them once their terms of duty ended. Starting in 1503, Spain mandated that all commercial exchanges with the New World be channeled through the formidable crown agency that managed Spain's sprawling empire, the Casa de Contratación in Seville. And from 1519, its large imperial bureaucracy, the Council of the Indies, met weekly to deliberate on and regulate colonial affairs, with the king often personally attending.

There is little doubt that the immense windfall that Spain derived from its business in New World silver had a profound impact on global economic history, famously binding East and West together more tightly than ever before. Less widely noted in accounts of economic change in this era, but also extraordinary in terms of the new wealth that it generated, was a prolonged eighteenth-century boom in gold production in Brazil, centered in the Minas Gerais region. And this, even more than the silver of Bolivia, was made possible largely on the basis of African slave labor. Saying that "almost all of our gold" comes from Portugal, Adam Smith, for one, credited the huge injection of specie into the European economy that resulted from the Brazilian gold boom with helping fuel the Industrial Revolution. Scarcely recognized in most historical accounts of the rise of the West, however, is the fact that Brazil's sugar crop, which by itself accounted for 40 percent of Portugal's total revenue by the late 1620s, generated more income than either of these metal booms, silver or gold. What is more, the world of slavery-driven plantation sugar production had far more extensive and deeper connections to other productive sectors of the economies of both the New World and Europe than did purely extractive mining. As Stuart B. Schwartz, a leading historian of Latin America, wrote:

> *It should be emphasized . . . that, despite a tendency in Brazilian historiography to speak of a sugar cycle followed by a gold cycle, even at the height of the period of gold production, earnings from sugar were always greater than those from gold or any other commodity. In 1760, when Brazil's total exports were valued at 4.8 million milreis, sugar made up fifty percent of that total and gold forty-six percent. Although after 1680 to say sugar was no longer to say Brazil, at no time in the colonial era did sugar cease to be Brazil's or Bahia's leading export.*

It was for precisely these reasons that Portugal calculated that a Brazil worked by slaves was worth substantially more to it than its holdings in the East. Under pressure from every quarter, particularly from the Dutch, this forced a painful, but necessary choice. Portugal lost Elmina in 1637 and soon began relinquishing control of its various Asian footholds as well. Within less than three decades, these came to include Malacca (in present-day Malaysia), Colombo

(Sri Lanka), and Kochi and Kannur (India), all key ports in the spice trade. These, of course, all went down as serious defeats at the time, but it was only by virtue of relinquishing some of its sprawling empire that Lisbon was able to clarify its strategic purposes and hold on to what was, in fact, deemed most essential. This meant that after an extraordinary series of seesaw wars fought simultaneously against the Dutch and against a pair of highly capable and resilient kingdoms in western Central Africa, as we will see, Portugal managed to restore its control over the twin jewels of its empire: Brazil and Angola, the first being almost worthless without the second. Had it attempted to hold on in the East, it seems almost certain that Lisbon would have lost everything.

18

THE COCKPIT OF EUROPE

I N THE 1640S, the epicenter of the mounting Atlantic sugar revolution began to shift away from the vastness of Brazil and back
to small and far more easily controlled islands, not so different,
in fact, from the island off Africa where it had begun. The first step
in this transition took place in tiny Barbados, in the eastern Caribbean. This island measures a mere twenty-one miles long and nineteen miles wide, slightly less than half as large as its progenitor, São
Tomé. But despite its modest size, among all of the relocations in the
migratory history of cane, this was arguably the most consequential
stop yet for the most important crop of the age when measured in
terms of the economics of empire. And for the English, it was here
that sugar, big landholdings, and plentiful Black slave labor all came
together for the first time.

When the first permanent settlers from England arrived there
in 1627, Barbados was completely uninhabited, having been abandoned by the Caribs, and before them by the Arawaks, possibly due
to slaving raids mounted by the Spanish in order to supply manpower
for their mines on Hispaniola. In the early seventeenth century, by
the time the English and the French set about occupying the Lesser
Antilles, Spain had already locked up control of the major islands of
the Caribbean. By then, places like Barbados or Saint Martin stood
out mostly as consolation prizes. Well before either Britain or France

had any notions of constructing rich empires on the basis of plantation agriculture, they saw the Lesser Antilles mainly for its strategic value. That is because the Caribbean Sea was situated well beyond "the line," meaning located in a zone south of the Tropic of Cancer and west of the mid-Atlantic, in which the diplomatic treaties, conventions, and other niceties governing relations among rival European empires on their home continent lost all legal force. In an era of rampant freebooting, this made the Lesser Antilles ideal bases from which to play hide-and-seek while poaching on Spanish shipping of treasure from the Americas. It was places like these that helped make the Caribbean Sea "the cockpit of Europe," in the memorable phrase of Eric Williams—in other words, a zone of ceaseless maritime jousting and warfare well into the nineteenth century.

When they landed at a place that came to be known as Holetown, situated on the western side of Barbados, the first task for the new English settlers was clearing the extraordinarily heavy forest that covered the island. In the zone of landfall, they reported, the trees grew virtually to the water's edge and reached a height of two hundred feet. Some accounts hold that sugarcane was brought to the island shortly afterward from a Dutch colony on the Essequibo River, in modern Guyana. But Barbados's unpromising early commercial life was based on the cultivation of tobacco, indigo, and cotton. In those early days, these crops were mostly farmed by English indentured servants, who were supplemented by a small minority of African slaves. By the mid-1630s, the takeoff of Virginia as a tobacco-growing colony and the relatively poor quality of the Barbados crop combined to foreclose early dreams of tobacco-driven wealth on the island. The pressure from Virginia on Barbados's tobacco earnings, however, coincided with a strong upward movement in the price fetched by sugar, propelled in part by continued instability in Brazil, where the rivalry between Holland and Portugal over control of the South Atlantic raged on. The confluence of these two factors set the stage for sugar's historic takeoff on Barbados. Planters began buying more slaves with money raised from willing creditors in England against future deliveries of sugar, and soon began laying the legal groundwork for the subjugation of Africans that would be widely copied throughout the English-speaking New World.

By 1636, civil authorities on the island decreed a rule that became common in chattel systems throughout the hemisphere: slaves would remain in bondage for life. In 1661, with the island now amid a full-blown sugar boom, the authorities formulated a fuller set of laws governing the lives of slaves, a Black code that one historian has called "one of the most influential pieces of legislation passed by a colonial legislature." Antigua, Jamaica, South Carolina, and, "indirectly," Georgia adopted it in its entirety, while the laws of many other English colonies were modeled after it. The law described Africans as a "heathenish, brutish and uncertaine, dangerous kinde of people," and gave their white owners near total control over their lives. The right of trial by jury guaranteed for whites was excluded for slaves, whom their owners could punish at will, facing no consequences even for murder, so long as they could cite a cause. Other rules barred Black slaves from skilled occupations, thus helping to reify race as a largely impermeable membrane dividing whites and Blacks in the New World. With steps like these, tiny Barbados became an enormously powerful driver of history, not only through the prodigious wealth it would generate, a wealth hitherto "unknown in other parts of colonial America," but by its legal and social example as well. The island colony stood out as a pioneer in the development of chattel slavery and in the construction of the plantation machine, as the originator of codes like these, and later as a crucial source of early migration, both Black and white, to the Carolinas, Virginia, and later Jamaica. Here was the seed crystal of the English plantation system in the New World, or in the words of one historian, its "cultural hearth."

In 1642, imperial conflict among Europeans took another violent turn with a fierce uprising against Dutch rule by *moradores*, the Portuguese-speaking settlers in Brazil who remained strongly loyal to Lisbon. Holland had taken over Brazil in order to deprive Portugal and Hapsburg Spain (with which Portugal remained conjoined) of the income produced by slaves working sugar. Not satisfied with

their initially limited objective of weakening Spain by attacking Portugal at the Brazilian source of its great newfound wealth in sugar,
the Dutch launched a short-lived but much more ambitious push
to become a world power in their own right. This Dutch scheme
had nothing of the ad hoc quality of early Spanish and Portuguese
conquest, but was based, rather, on high-concept plans for an integrated empire that would tie together disparate but complementary
holdings around the Atlantic Rim. Under this scheme, the Great
Design mentioned earlier, the Dutch hoped to use their country's
newly founded West India Company to construct a monopolistic
trading system in the Western Hemisphere, much in the mold of
what it had already accomplished in Asia. There, the Dutch East
India Company had become Holland's most important source of
wealth overseas by far.

Traditional Dutch histories have placed so much emphasis on
the Asian basis of new Dutch wealth in this period that they have
discounted, or overlooked altogether, what the Netherlands sought
to achieve in the West using African slave labor, shipping power,
and plantations. As Jan de Vries, a leading historian of Holland's
Golden Age, has written, "The 'Atlantic Reality' never came near to
fulfilling the high hopes of the early promoters, but this was not for
want of trying." Conceptually, the Great Design was premised on
synergies already inherent in Portugal's older imperial schemes, but
it sought to take them much further. While it lasted, Holland would
control many of the leading sources of slaves in both Central and
West Africa, meaning both Elmina and Luanda. In the space of a
mere twenty years after 1630, this allowed it to send 31,533 Africans
to produce sugar in Brazil. At the same time, it controlled the largest
and most ecologically promising zone for sugar production known
in the world—namely, the lands it had conquered in Brazil. Meanwhile, the Dutch also controlled settlements on the North American
mainland from present-day Massachusetts to Delaware, then known
as New Netherlands, and New York, then New Amsterdam. These
territories quickly moved beyond an early trade in furs to become
purveyors of foodstuffs for Holland's developing plantation econo-

mies far to the south. Both the New Netherlands and Brazil were to be populated by Dutch settlers and native peoples converted to Calvinism.

The Dutch never managed to completely fulfill their grand scheme, but this does not mean that their designs went unexecuted. Their implementation would be left, instead, to the English, whose fast-rising power, beginning in the mid-seventeenth century, was founded on pursuing the same kinds of synergies, only much further still. This meant an even deeper integration of economies that spanned the four corners of the Atlantic—Europe, Africa, the fertile tropics of the New World, and North America—than the Dutch had ever realized. The North American mainland, from which the English evicted the Dutch, came to play its role far more fully than had been the case with its previous masters, as we will see. From the early stages of this new integrated system, Britain's American colonies served as the larder of meat, fish, and grain, as well as horses, oxen, timber, and other natural resources for far wealthier colonies like Barbados, whose sugar industry gave it the highest per capita exports in the Americas, and where the high profits from growing cane quickly made other uses of scarce land uneconomical. As one mid-seventeenth-century colonist on the island wrote, "[M]en are so intent upon planting sugar that they had rather buy foode at very deare rates than produce it by labour soe infinite is the profit of sugar works after once accomplished."

In the end, no part of continental America was bootstrapped more dramatically than New England, whose farmers and fishermen focused heavily on supplying Barbados and the greater, sugar-growing Caribbean. In fact, as much as any Enlightenment ideals, it was the West Indian roots of New England's rising prosperity—freeing the merchants and farmers of places like Boston, Salem, and Providence from economic reliance on the English homeland—that fueled a nascent thinking about independence in this part of British America. As the historian Wendy Warren has noted, "[B]y the 1680s, more than half of the ships anchored in Boston's harbor on any given day were involved in West Indian trade, and almost half of the boats trading in the West Indies had set sail from New England home ports."

But what had tied each wave, from Portuguese to Dutch, then Dutch to English, of European empire building in the New World together in the first place was a common foundation premised on the game-changing, wealth-generating value of enslaved Africans. Without this, none of the Europeans' imperial ambitions made any sense. This reality is captured in the thoughts of the prominent late-eighteenth-century French antislavery thinker Abbé Raynal. On this topic, Raynal, who oversaw the publication of a multivolume history of European colonialism, wrote: "The labors of the colonists settled in these long-scorned islands are the sole basis of the African trade, extend the fisheries and cultivation of North America, provide advantageous outlets for the manufacture of Asia, double perhaps triple the activity of the whole of Europe. They can be regarded as the principal cause of the rapid movement which stirs the universe." By that last phrase, he of course meant Europe's fast and accelerating economic progress.

Raynal's insights mirrored those of William Burke, a cousin of Edmund Burke and a colonial official in Guadeloupe in 1760, then only recently seized by England from France. "It is by means of the *West-Indian* trade that a great part of *North America* is at all enabled to trade with us," he wrote. "[I]n Reality the Trade of these *North American Provinces* . . . is, as well as that of *Africa*, to be regarded as a dependent Member, and subordinate Department of the *West-Indian* Trade; it must rise and fall exactly as the *West-Indies* flourish or decay." We must cut through a bit of euphemism and indirection here to get at the true meaning of these words. In Burke's formulation, the Africa trade overwhelmingly consisted of the violent commerce in men and women who were shipped in chains across the ocean from that continent. The labors of the Caribbean colonists of whom Raynal speaks, meanwhile, were the toil of Black people being worked to death for big profits mostly in plantation sugar.

Returning to Holland's schemes, they would come undone in two stages. First, the Portuguese began copying the very playbook that the Dutch had used against them, as when rebellious Portuguese loyalists in Brazil sacked the Dutch-run sugar plantations of Bahia, depriving Holland of the income from slave labor it needed to make its new Atlantic empire pay for itself. With Holland substantially weakened, the English moved in for the pickings, seizing New Amsterdam in 1664 and rebranding it as New York, while also going from strength to strength in the Caribbean.

It was the devastation of the plantation worlds of Brazil during the back-and-forth contests between Portugal and the Dutch, though, that provided Barbadian sugar, and England in the West Indies, with decisive historic opportunities. Among the very first, and without a doubt the most important of the original Barbados cane planters was a tough and ambitious Englishman of Dutch extraction named James Drax. He had come to the island in 1627 at the age of eighteen, one of fifty passengers aboard the *William and John*, the first settler ship to arrive there from his country. Another of its passengers was Henry Winthrop, whose father, John, would lead settlement efforts in Massachusetts.

Drax arrived in Barbados armed with £300 and a dream: not to retire to England until he had built an estate that could produce an annual income of £10,000. Motivation like this was the rule, not the exception, among early English settlers in the Caribbean. And in the boom years to come, Drax would immeasurably surpass even this princely income. In this good fortune he was not alone: in a remarkable illustration of the power of perfect timing, two of the other settlers who arrived on the *William and John* would join him as kingpins of the sugar industry just a few years later.

Somewhere in the western Atlantic, before it had made landfall in Barbados, the *William and John* encountered a Portuguese vessel carrying slaves from West Africa en route to Brazil. The English ship attacked the other vessel and managed to seize ten of its African captives, thus making them the very first enslaved people on the island. I find the terror inherent in this incident thoroughly arresting and have often thought about how well it crystallizes the condition of countless other Africans who would be sold into bondage in the

American slave trade. No one will ever know their names, nor where they came from exactly, but it is likely that by that point these Africans had already changed hands between different owners at least three times. The first time would have been between African states or societies, perhaps as a result of conflict on the African coast. Then they would have been sold to white traders and either held in a barracoon or loaded directly onto a Portuguese ship anchored offshore. The captives would have had no prior experience of ocean navigation, nor would they have had any sense of where they were being taken, which would have meant terror enough. Finally, they would have undergone the trauma of a skirmish at sea between different tribes of whites whose causes they could not possibly divine, and with themselves, for reasons they could still not yet have known, as the prize. What is certain is that an abundance of horror lay ahead for them and the hundreds of thousands who would follow.

The surviving evidence suggests that Drax owed much of his early success, beginning in the early 1640s, to a labor force of "Portugal negroes," in the words of Richard Ligon, a seventeenth-century author who wrote an important early chronicle of sugar's takeoff on the island, *A True and Exact History of the Island of Barbadoes*, published in London in 1657. The most likely connotation of the word "Portugal" here is that Drax had gotten a head start in building the most advanced sugar operation on the island, which would eventually allow him to dominate the early trade in the commodity. That is because he had had the foresight to purchase slaves who were already expert in the growing and processing of cane in Brazil's richest sugar region, Pernambuco.[*]

When I set out to find the remnants of the Drax estate on Barbados, I was marginally more successful than I had been in locating the slave cemetery mentioned in this book's introduction. It took me only the better part of a day to find it. This meant driving into the heart of the island from the beaches of the coast, crossing parishes whose

---

[*] Similarly, the know-how of slaves brought from Madeira and São Tomé had helped establish the early sugar plantations and build the first mills in Brazil in the 1530s, if not before.

fields of rich, black soil, once thick with forests, were planted high in sugar that season that swayed with the wind. From there, I took narrow roads past pastel-colored homes with frilly Victorian touches that were built on the hillsides, zigzagging into the verdant uplands. There, under a comfortable breeze, the earth turned more reddish in color from the higher clay content that makes it especially suitable for growing cane. The GPS on my phone was of little use in these parts and I made several false turns. To my surprise, the Barbadians I repeatedly stopped to seek directions from had only hazy notions of how to find the place, many of them contradictory. It turned out to be located down a sloping, gravelly unmarked path that cut through a muddy field just off a main road. I knew that James Drax himself had been commissioner of roads in the early days of the colony, so there was a strong chance that all along I had been riding over routes that he had traced. There, as I approached it, what finally wheeled into view was the oldest Jacobean mansion in all of the Americas: the baronial house that Drax built sometime in the early 1650s. With even a quick glance, one immediately understood this stout, fortress-like three-story dark stone home, with twin gables on each side and a bright red roof, had been built to last; however, not long after its completion, for reasons that remain unknown, at the height of his success, Drax decamped for England, never to return.

Off to one side of the mansion, no more than one hundred yards distant, stood a tall furnace, the robustly built boiler of the old sugar mill that had once generated such tremendous profits for its owner. In another direction lay the crumbled stone ruins of the quarters that housed the slaves who both grew the sugar and fed the mill. One of Drax's great insights had been to push the development of an integrated sugar plantation to its logical conclusion. Although he bought some of the crop of smaller planters who grew sugarcane nearby (as had most of the early mill operators in Brazil), in an important innovation, the brunt of his business, by design, was the vertical transformation of his product, all the way from replanted cane cuttings of his own to the white, granulated loaves of sugar that he shipped off to England. This, he had determined, was the most efficient way to run a plantation, if only one could acquire enough land and slaves. Integration was the route to maximum added value. It was the secret to Drax's great fortune, and to that of other great planters who would follow his example. What is more, it was the future of the industry in the Caribbean, turning this region into one of the greatest wealth engines the world has ever known.

THE INTEGRATION OF sugar production on Barbados quickly took on other forms, beyond the mere incorporation of mills on active plantations. In 1660, as mentioned earlier, elites in London had formed the Company of Royal Adventurers into Africa, which the historian Christopher Brown pithily has characterized as "an incorporated band of robbers." The founding mission of the Company of Adventurers, though, had been to devise a way to muscle in on the gold trade along the West African coast. The answer was state-sanctioned raiding, or piracy, conducted for the most part against the ships of rival European nations. In the Company's early years this proved so lucrative that the Royal Mint created a new unit of currency, the guinea, struck with an African elephant on one side (this coin, worth one pound and one shilling, remained in use until 1967). But even despite this early success with gold, just three years after the Company's founding, the one-thousand-year charter for this royal monopoly was changed in order to place slave trading at the heart of its activities. At the time, the Duke of York, the king's brother and heir, led the Company, and its other eminent investors included several members of the royal family, beginning with the new queen, Catherine of Braganza. One other subscriber of note was a young professor at Oxford named John Locke.

It was but a short step from muscling in on the gold trade to capturing as much of the traffic in Africans as possible, whether from the Portuguese or from the Dutch, who had established themselves at Elmina and elsewhere along that continent's coast since the late 1630s. For this purpose, almost straightaway after the change in the Company's charter, a convoy of forty English ships were dispatched to Africa where, as the historian Hugh Thomas wrote, they "conquered the Cape Verde Islands, and recaptured Cape Coast [eleven miles from Elmina] along with several other Dutch possessions on the Gold Coast, before crossing the Atlantic to seize New Amsterdam, in New Holland, in North America, a city soon after renamed after the leading shareholder in the Royal Adventurers, the duke of York." As the effectiveness of the Company's monopoly eroded, however, as Christopher Brown has observed, the slave trade in West Africa "took on the character of an open, unpoliced bazaar," with many English fortune seekers taking to the coast in search of Black captives.

The Company's original aim was to "supply slaves to Barbados at a price of £17 per head, and between 1663 and 1666 it landed over 5,000 slaves on the island at an average price of £18," just barely missing that mark. An estimated 32,496 Africans were delivered to the island in the 1660s. By then, the price of slaves delivered to Barbados had fallen by 35 percent from the highs of the 1640s, when roughly 10,000 fewer Africans were sold. Of far more lasting importance than any short-term fall in price, though, was the breaking of the Dutch stranglehold on this human traffic. This put Britain on a path to dominate the slave trade outright, as it would for the next century and a half, propelling its imperial expansion throughout the Caribbean, and its widening empire generally. By the end of this period, the Company of Royal Adventurers, and its successor, the Royal African Company of England, founded in 1672, would ship more men, women, and children from Africa to the New World than any other entity or institution. Britain would easily best Holland, but it did so by way of emulation, with actions that closely followed the contours of the Great Design, only infused with even greater ambition.

Among the most important innovations that began taking shape in Barbados were new models of finance. Building the kind of big plantations with incorporated mills that James Drax helped pioneer required access to copious amounts of capital, and this in turn contributed to the development of what has been called England's "empire of credit." Lured by the prospect of big returns, enthusiastic lenders in the home country began extending loans against future harvests. For their part, plantation owners took whatever profits they earned and plowed them back into the acquisition of more slaves in the pursuit of ever higher productivity and output. Commercial credit from London provided the grease that kept the wheels turning and drove the expansion necessary to meet the ferocious demand for sugar and its by-products back home.

19

DUNG FOR EVERY HOLE

T O FULLY COMPREHEND THE revolution that now began moving into high gear requires one to think about sugar as something far bigger and more important to the changing economic fortunes of the West than a mere comestible or commodity. As Sidney W. Mintz wrote in his seminal *Sweetness and Power: The Place of Sugar in Modern History*, "[S]ome people in power in Britain became convinced that commodities like sugar mattered so much to their well-being that they would politick fiercely for the rights of capital invested in developing the plantations and all that went with them." By the latter decades of the seventeenth century, in fact, sugar was becoming a central driver of economic activity in England. And, in the early twentieth century, it was observed that "[o]ne thousand pounds spent by a planter in [the Caribbean] produced in the end better results and greater advantages to England than twice that sum expended by the same family in London."

New commercial outfits like the Company also became critical innovators in the sense that they were formed on the basis of association of capital by disparate investors, not unlike a modern corporation. This is just one of many ways that the slave trade of this era, as it ramped up quickly, would drive the modernization of business, politics, and society in Mother England, while steadily touching a wide variety of associated industries, including banking, shipping, and insurance. More than has been recognized, slavery even contributed to the emergence of a system of rival political parties, Whigs and Tories; to the growth of the City of London as a financial center; and to the blossoming of British power and prosperity more generally. In the words of the late historian of Atlantic slavery Joseph C. Miller, plantations, monopoly companies, and new sugar colonies like Barbados constituted "controlled laboratories for early investment and management," that were responsible for "creating golden modernity from monarchical lead."

To return briefly to the story of the Drax family, the accumulation of slaves and of land under the reign of James Drax, and later, his successor in Barbados, Henry, had run together in close tandem. James Drax was the first big slave owner on the island, with twenty-two Africans in 1642—a huge number for the time; he added another thirty-four in 1644. By the early 1650s, as two hundred Blacks were farming his fields, Father Antoine Bier, a French visitor, remarked that the Blacks operating Drax's mill made for "quite a sight." By contrast, it took another decade for most other planters on the island to fully embrace the use of Black slaves, by which time African labor "was not only cheaper but also much easier to procure" than white. By the early 1640s, Drax had stitched together 400 acres, and a decade later he owned 700.

The sort of plantation James Drax ran is revealed in the writing of his grandson, Henry, who left a detailed memo, a twenty-four-page instruction book to his overseer, which was duplicated and studied by other aspirational sugar barons on the island for more than a century. The picture it paints of the Draxes is one of "book farmers," or pioneers of capitalism, whose rigorous accounting practices and focus on labor organization sought to leverage careful bookkeeping and the harnessing of data to steadily improve productivity.

Given the island's small size, once the early waves of land grabbing and fevered investment in sugar had passed, there was little left for newcomers to acquire, least of all the penniless indentured whites who had been the island's main source of labor in the early years of the colony. For ex-servants, this made Barbados "the worst poor man's country" in British America, a place that almost every white person who didn't quickly prosper desperately wanted to escape, which usually meant onward migration to other English colonies in the Caribbean or on the North American mainland. In order to sustain a supply of whites into indentured servitude on the island, as many as fifty thousand political prisoners had been shipped to the island by 1655, along with Scottish and Irish soldiers captured during Cromwell's campaigns and many other victims who were inveigled in cities like London and Bristol and shipped off involuntarily to the Caribbean. The slang for this has been largely lost to the English language, but back then people spoke of being "Barbadosed," a term that was used in much the same way the word "shanghaied" came to be employed in the late nineteenth century. These and other factors, starting with the substantially lower cost of African labor, but also including crude racial notions that fancied Blacks as being better suited physically and temperamentally for unremittingly grueling work in the tropics, helped incline planters toward a preference for African labor, and within less than a generation this is what turned Barbados into an archetypal slave society.

Between 1630 and the 1680s, Barbados went from being an island with a tiny Black presence to one where people brought in chains from Africa constituted 75 percent of the population, and 95 percent of the workforce. In the West, new slave societies like these were largely confined to the Caribbean, where Barbados became both avatar and model. Even though Brazil received the largest number of slaves of any single country by far, at no point did it ever have a demographic majority composed of slaves, or even of slaves and mixed-race Creoles combined. In America, meanwhile, a racial composition so thoroughly dominated by Blacks was witnessed only in the Carolina Low Country, where rice was farmed. There, by the way, the earliest recorded instance of African slaves being put to work on plantations was that of the third governor of the colony, Sir John Yeamans, founder of Charleston, who brought slaves from Barbados in order to clear his land and commence planting. To a significant degree, the populations of Carolina, Virginia, Maryland, and even Rhode Island and Massachusetts would be seeded by white people from Barbados as well.

Sugar planters in Barbados, and then later in much bigger production centers like Jamaica and Saint Domingue, were relentless tinkerers, searching through constant innovation to increase yields and profits, not just through farming techniques, per se, but through strict and exacting management of labor, as well, making them some of the most "accomplished capitalists of their time." It is hard to us to reconcile this with the fact that their wealth, as well as the very prosperity of the age, was built on the cruel foundation of bondage, but therein lie the roots of our common modernity.

New notions about the ethical basis of labor and social values that today we might call humanist were just then beginning to arise in England, but Black slaves benefited little from this, if at all. It was permissible for Europeans to exploit African labor in maximalist ways, much "like a horse or a cow," that would not be socially acceptable in the case of whites. This extreme racial exploitation began with unremitting fieldwork, with workdays commencing before sunup and continuing until dusk and often beyond. The Royal African Company originally aspired to a ratio of two males for every female on its slave shipments but was never able to approach this target, possibly due in part to African resistance, and to the premium some African societies themselves placed on males. To make up for the shortage in men, the plantation regime as it emerged on Barbados and other islands began to assign women to some of the harshest of tasks, such as the heaviest roles in the field. By the early modern era, these practices were already inconceivable among whites, even for indentured laborers, whose harsh treatment has sometimes been likened to that of African slaves. And as they planted, weeded, and harvested, Black women, even while pregnant, were almost equally subject to the lash.

More than tactics aimed merely at boosting productivity, the subjection of Blacks to such brutal and degrading regimes very early on became a key psychosocial factor in elevating white identity in the new mixed societies of the Americas; they became proof for whites, in a tautological sense, that people of European stock were a fundamentally different type of human being, people of an inherently superior nature to Blacks. As the historian Peter Thompson wrote, "The nature of labor on a sugar plantation was without parallel in the European experience, and even writers who prized its end product characterized the work itself, and hence the workers who carried it out, in animalistic terms." By being exempted from the most flagrant indignities inflicted on enslaved Blacks, even the lowest of whites gradually began to identify with "the strong sense of honor the experience of mastership generated," in the phrase of the sociologist Orlando Patterson.

One of the most dehumanizing tasks was the seasonal handling of manure, an unavoidable requirement for successful sugar cultivation. Intensive dunging was another one of Drax's innovations. "Theire is No producing good Canes without dunging Every holle," he wrote. Roughly a ton per acre was applied on his lands each year. This involved the conveyance of large, sloshing eighty-pound vats of feces, both animal and human, into the fields atop the heads of slaves, inevitably washing over the faces of the people who bore them and drenching them, followed by the pouring of feces into the individual holes in which cane seedlings were planted. As one would expect, this produced soaring disease rates in the manure porters. In seventeenth- and eighteenth-century Barbados, female slaves from Africa generally dominated the ranks of those who performed this task, and indeed field labor in general.

During the grueling harvest season many slaves were obliged to work nearly all-night shifts, feeding cane into the boilers and keeping their fires stoked. "The only break in the work week was from Saturday night till Monday morning. Otherwise, the twenty-five men and women in the factory worked continuously in shifts lasting all day and part of the night, or the whole of every second or third night." Slaves were sometimes kept going with cane juice, due to its high sugar content, and sometimes with cane spirits as well. And the dead-on-your-feet effect this produced in them led to many deaths of slaves by extensive burns or by crushing after being pulled into the

rollers by their fingers. This latter type of incident occurred so frequently that it was common to keep a hatchet on a chain within reach
so that an unfortunate slave's arm could be chopped off before the
machinery consumed his whole body. These sugar-mill labor practices helped burn an image so deeply into the English language that
it survives in our popular culture down to this day as a staple of pop
music à la the Michael Jackson hit "Thriller" and Hollywood and
television, think *The Walking Dead*, that of the zombie.

Although overseers were sometimes warned against excessively
harsh treatment of slaves, the world of sugar plantations accepted
the high mortality rates for Blacks driven in fields or put to work at
the boiler in unabashed fashion; this was considered an ordinary
part of the business, an ordinary fact of life. If Henry Drax's Black
workforce included 327 slaves, for example, his writings assume a
death rate of 3 to 5 percent per year. Other Barbados planters of that
era spoke of 6 percent as being common. A common estimate for the
average life expectancy of slaves ensnared in sugar production was
seven years or less.

Mortality rates on Brazilian sugar plantations were undoubtedly
also high, but the approach of Drax and other members of the founding generation of big planters on Barbados marked a sharp break
with the practices in Pernambuco and Bahia, one that reflected
the industry's important but unheralded role in the early stages of
a shift from feudalism toward capitalism. As the historian Richard
Dunn observes, "In Brazil the senhor de engenho, or lord of the mill
was, as his name implies, a grandiose manor lord. He owned a huge
tract, maintained a large force of salaried artisans, tenant farmers,
and slaves, lived nobly in his Big House, and presided over a self-
sufficient, paternalistic community complete with church, court,
police force, and social-welfare agencies." In contrast to this *sei-
gneurialism*, the big, early success stories among Barbados growers
were men who, like Drax, followed a much narrower, more hard-
nosed pursuit of profit and specialization, quite close, in fact, to the
ethos of modern business. Significantly, many of them had commercial roots back in England, and hailed from families with experi-

ence investing in Atlantic trading and privateering. Dunn continues, "The English planter combined the roles of mill owner and cane grower. He did not attempt to produce food, clothing, and equipment for his work force on his own estate, but depended on outside suppliers. He offered a minimum of social services."

As Britain came to see the abundant and regular provisioning of slaves to its sugar colonies as essential to its Atlantic empire and stepped up its involvement in the trafficking of Africans to the West Indies, what inexorably followed was a further de-emphasis on slave longevity or indeed even on their reproduction. Beginning no later than the 1660s, short life expectancies and low reproduction rates became a universal feature of plantation economy regimes as sugar spread throughout the Caribbean. In a region where the Barbados model became the leading template, including for the French, it was widely considered "cheaper to work slaves to the utmost, and by hard fare and hard usage, to wear them out before they became useless, and unable to do service; and then to buy new ones to fill up their places," as one Antiguan farmer put it in 1751. Robert Robinson, a clergyman-planter on the colony of Nevis, considered that in light of the low survival rate of infants, the loss of work to pregnancy by females, and the expense of feeding and clothing children before they could contribute much to the plantation, the gain from reproduction "cannot be great," so there was little point in encouraging it.

As anecdotes like these are meant to suggest, the emergence of the Caribbean as the beating heart behind Britain's economic rise (and arrayed just behind it, that of France) was predicated on a system of exploitation grounded in human churn. As surely as the manufacturers of the phone you carry around expect it to become obsolete, slave owners in the islands expected the burdens of labor, poor nutrition, and disease to bring the members of their Black workforce to an early death. This was what Malachy Postlethwayt, the influential eighteenth-century British thinker on slavery, trade, and empire, had in mind when he called the ample and continual supply of new slaves from Africa "the fundamental prop and support" of his country's prosperity.

Between slavery's modest start in Barbados in the 1630s and the last decade of that century, 95,572 African lives were ground up in the fields and mills of that tiny island alone. By 1810, the toll for Barbados had reached fully a quarter of a million. To broaden our sense of the scope of atrocity, altogether some 2.7 million Africans were carried off into slavery in the British West Indies in the century and a half before London abolished this transatlantic human trafficking in 1807. The largest volume, moreover, was skewed toward the end of this period. Nonetheless, by that terminal year, as the historian Randy Browne has reported, "the total British Caribbean slave population was barely a third that number—about 775,000."* Even after the trade ended, the slave population continued to die far faster than they could reproduce. Again according to Browne, by 1834, "only 665,000 slaves were still alive."

This was somewhat different from the pattern that obtained in Brazil, and radically different from how slavery would unfold in the United States, which was largely cut off from re-supply from Africa following the British abolition on the trade in 1807, followed by a similar American prohibition that took effect the very next year. These developments coincided with the takeoff of Big Cotton, which we will explore later. For now, suffice to say that as brutal as slavery on the mainland could be, American plantation owners, who benefited from easier crops to grow and a more benign disease environment, generally took a keen interest in the reproduction of their human property.

Barbados was the site of yet one other key so-called innovation, gang labor, which relied on armed "drivers" to compel people to sustain a desired pace. Although it wouldn't be universally adopted on the island until the closing decades of the seventeenth century, when African slaves had completely replaced white indentured servants, this system also saw its initial implementation in the early experiments of Richard Drax. The original idea behind these small work

* In 1790, it is estimated there were 675,000 slaves in the French Caribbean, which experienced similar rates of life expectancy and mortality.

units, or gangs, as Henry Drax wrote, was to "prevent idleness and make the Negroes do their work properly." This resulted in more than merely constant surveillance and merciless discipline for slaves; it also led to an increasingly fine-tuned system for matching slaves to the tasks they were thought best suited for—whether by gender, age, physical strength, dexterity or endurance—and for measuring their productivity. Drax made a practice of having these reports brought to him every fortnight, which allowed him to provide rewards or, likely more often, administer punishment to both slaves and overseers as he saw fit. Slaves who worked in specialized roles tended to outperform those who floated from one task to another, developing little expertise. It wasn't enough to muster slaves in formal work teams, however. An obsession with record keeping, first seen on the Drax plantation, allowed owners to organize work gangs in a numbered hierarchy.

The first gang was typically constituted of the strongest and ablest slaves, both men and, in large and sometimes dominant numbers, women. It saw to the arduous digging of cane holes (the most physically trying of all the tasks), the planting of each new crop, and its harvest, all using crude hoes and scythelike tools called billhooks. The British historian of slavery Simon Newman has determined that "[a] first gang slave was expected to dig between sixty and one hundred holes each day, and a slave who dug an average of eighty holes per day was moving a daily total of between 640 and 1,500 cubic feet of soil." Those who fell behind could expect to feel the lash. A second gang was made up of workers who were less fit, but still deemed capable of hard labor. This included planting, weeding, and harvesting, usually along with some dunging. A third gang was composed of whatever older people had survived this regime, together with numerous children; together they fulfilled an assortment of less demanding tasks.

Drax's system closely anticipated industrial-style division of labor and regimentation and record keeping, elements that would not fully come together in England for another century or more. A contemporary observer of a plantation in early-nineteenth-century Barbados remarked, "It has often occurred to me, that a gang of

Negroes in the act of holing for canes, when hard driven appear to be as formidable as a phalanx of infantry by the rapid movement of their hoes . . . while I have been astonished how such habit could enable beings to persevere, so many hours in such violent effort." These management techniques, emphasizing specialization and the time-sensitive coordination of tasks, anticipated the modern assembly line, and were applied in the sugar mill just as eagerly as in the field.

> *Slaves fed the cane into three-roller vertical mills, with one slave feeding cane in through the top gap, and another slave on the other side feeding it back through the bottom gap, with brown cane juice flowing from the rollers into a trough, and thence through pipes into a holding tank in the boiling house. The cane juice had to be boiled within a few hours before it fermented and became useless.*

Features like these challenge our traditional notions of how industrialization arose in the first place. Standard histories generally place its origins in England's Lancashire region, where investor-entrepreneurs began paying people who worked with looms in their own homes to produce textiles for their companies. This so-called put-out work generated big profits and with them, gradually, investment in newer, bigger scale production using better and better technologies, including waterpower, followed by steam.

Historians seldom look outside of England for other roots of these processes. An argument on behalf of the Caribbean as an important precursor need not negate the main outlines of the traditional narrative in order for the big, integrated sugar mills of this era to be recognized as places where the worlds of the farm and factory first came together, making for some of the biggest enterprises of their era. The precocious contributions of the integrated sugar mill to the transition to industrialization merely begin, though, with division of labor, specialization, and careful synchronization, all of which are widely recognized hallmarks of industrialism. Other features include the aforementioned heavy involvement of commercial credit, as well as the sheer scale of their operations. To put these developments in sharpest relief, they should be appraised in contrast to the parallel legacy of Iberian extractive industries, especially the mining of silver and gold in the New World, the other sources of this age's great economic windfalls for Europe. Speaking of Spain in this regard, Marie Arana wrote in her history *Silver, Sword and Stone*, "No industrial advances came of [its] silver windfall; no bridges, no roads, no factories; no true betterment of life for the ordinary Spaniard."

We should not limit ourselves to the assessments of historians and economists in these matters, either. These words spoken in 1676 by an anonymous Barbadian slave speak most eloquently of the industrial essence of any slave laborer's work life: "The devil was in the Englishman that he makes everything work; he makes the negro work, he makes the horse work, the ass work, the wood work, the water work and the wind work." Every type of what a modern economist would call an input, in other words—and with sugar there were many others beyond this enslaved man's cursory list—was exploited in careful and complex synchrony with every other type in the interest of rationalizing production and maximizing output. The relentless exploitation of Black labor, as in the gang system (or *atelier* in French) was, of course, the master stroke within this devil's symphony, its crux and pivot. And the result was a source of wealth and productivity that cemented the new and emerging Atlantic economy and helped place Europe itself on a new footing. As the historian David Eltis has written, "[I]t is inconceivable that any societies in history—at least before 1800—could have matched the output per slave of seventeenth-century Barbados."

20

CAPITALISM'S BIG JOLT

FOR EUROPE, THE WEST INDIAN takeoff of plantation sugar, initially centered in Barbados in the mid-seventeenth century, was a matter of strongly fortuitous timing. Spain's boom in New World silver had already begun to flag by around 1620. Coincident with this was a downturn in the Baltic grain trade, in the woolens that were the mainstay of northern European commerce, and in the French wine trade. As a result, in the British historian of slavery Robin Blackburn's words, as slave plantations gathered economic momentum, they "not only swam against the stream of the seventeenth century crisis; they became a dynamic pole of the Atlantic economy in period 1700–1815."

Sugar thereafter quickly became that rare kind of product whose supply could rarely match its demand, and yet for which prices nonetheless declined dramatically over time. This came about mostly as a result of the ever larger acreages of planted cane as the plantation-complex took over bigger and bigger islands. England seized Jamaica in 1655 and eventually re-created the Barbados experience on that much larger island, importing about 1.2 million kidnapped Africans there over time, more than it would anywhere else in the Caribbean. But after an initial lag, France, determined not to be left out of this boom, began to catch up with British production on the islands it controlled. Between 1651 and 1725, slave departures from Africa bound for the French Caribbean increased from around 5500 to roughly 77,000 per annum. And in the quarter century that followed, with the rapid emergence of Saint Domingue as the largest sugar producer of all, the volume of French slave shipments doubled again.

We will return to the story of sugar and to slavery's spread throughout the Caribbean shortly, culminating with the liberation of Haiti via the determined uprising of that society's slaves. But first one must contemplate the profound nature of global change that slave sugar had already begun to wreak during its first big Caribbean wave. During the forty years after James Drax founded his plantation, consumption of sugar increased fourfold in England, overwhelmingly on the back of Barbados's production. By the 1620s, Brazil's combined trade in sugar and slaves had eclipsed Portugal's Asia trade in overall value, and had equaled the value of Spain's haul of American silver. In 1600 Brazil had supplied nearly all the sugar consumed in Western Europe. But in a striking measure of just how the sugar revolution progressed in the West Indies, by 1700, Barbados alone was producing more of the commodity than the Bahia region of Brazil, supplying nearly half of Europe's consumption—despite its later start and vastly smaller size. By 1660 it is estimated that tiny Barbados's sugar production alone was worth more than the combined exports of all of Spain's New World colonies. And this was just for starters. From 1650 to 1800, as major new sugar islands came on line in the Caribbean, sugar consumption in Britain would increase 2500 percent, and over this time, the market value of sugar would consistently exceed the value of all other commodities combined.

It stands to reason that a boom so large and so sustained would have been enormously stimulative, in ways both direct and indirect. In London the number of refineries shot up from five in 1615, to thirty in 1670, and perhaps to seventy-five by 1700; many other sugar refineries set up operations in smaller port cities and provincial centers. And these were not, by a long measure, the only commercial and growth-inducing effects of the sugar and slave complex.

In fact, the sugar boom created a long succession of strong, systemic economic waves that were felt throughout the Atlantic world. We have spoken already about how the early Portuguese trade with West Africa strengthened circuits of trade in Europe and beyond, with African gold being used to buy *manilhas* and other metalwares from northern Europe, usually via Dutch markets. As Holland temporarily usurped Portugal's imperial outposts in Africa and Brazil, and even as it later largely abandoned territorial empire in the Atlantic world in order to specialize in the shipping of goods and slaves, it managed to outcompete its Iberian rivals through not only superior firepower but lower costs. The Dutch produced the goods Africans prized most and could supply them more cheaply than the Portuguese. This included textiles, which were about to become the most important product of the industrial age. West Africans loved India's high-quality lightweight dyed cloths, so the Dutch busied themselves making passable knockoffs, which they sold in large quantities along the African coast. In its early empire, England assiduously followed the Dutch commercial example, even as it set about expanding its power at sea in order to muscle out its close neighbor and rival.

African markets would play a vital role in the growth of English manufacturing in general, albeit mostly indirectly. This included everything from guns to ships and from rope to sails, among many items required for long-distance maritime trade. But as their fledgling Caribbean empire grew based on the expropriation of African labor, the English found especially important new markets for the next big industry of the future, textiles, in the form of clothing for slaves. The importance of slaves in the rise of English textiles was not limited to the sale of cloth at England's African slaving outposts, like Cape Coast, or on its own sugar islands, either. As part of its contest with Holland in the mid-seventeenth century, England provided support to Portuguese efforts to throw off Dutch rule in Brazil. This came at the price of opening Brazil's markets to English manufactures. By the mid-eighteenth century, this turn of affairs had brought the Marquis of Pombal, the Portuguese king's chief minister, to rue that "[g]old and silver are fictitious riches; the negroes that work in the mines of Brazil must be clothed by England, by which the value of their produce become relative to the price of cloth."

Barbados and the other Caribbean sugar colonies that followed in its wake not only provided a direct boost to the European economy in the seventeenth century, but perhaps even more critically, they threw a lifeline to the struggling colonies of British America, which were restricted from selling many types of manufactures into the protected English market. To the Americans' good fortune, they found avid buyers on Barbados for products both rough and finished. As we have seen, these included furniture, livestock (both for its meat and manure, which was highly prized as fertilizer), and lumber. Barbados imported such things and many more because once sugar monoculture had taken over on that booming island, productive land was deemed simply too valuable to farm for food or put to any other use and so, like a modern petro state, pretty much everything required for local consumption was imported. In time, this even came to include New England rum. As Eric Williams wrote in *Capitalism and Slavery* of a time just a few decades later:

> *In 1770 the continental colonies sent to the West Indies nearly one-third of their exports of dried fish and almost all their pickled fish, seven-eighths of their oats, seven-tenths of their corn, almost all their peas and beans, half of their flour, all their butter and cheese, over one-quarter of their rice, almost all their onions; five-sixths of their pine, oak and cedar boards, over half of their staves, nearly all their hoops; all their horses, sheep, hogs and poultry; almost all their soap and candles. As [an earlier historian] has told us, "It was the wealth accumulated from West Indian trade which more than anything else underlay the prosperity and civilization of New England and the Middle Colonies."*

To better understand North America's dependence on trade with the sugar islands, it helps to put a figure on the kind of wealth disparities that existed within the British Empire. Taking Jamaica as an example, one historian has estimated that annual per capita income among whites on that island in the decade that Williams wrote of was more than thirty-five times higher than in Britain's mainland colonies, £2201, compared with £60.2.

⌘

UNDOING THE GROSS UNDERSTATEMENT of the contributions that Africa and Africans made to the creation of the modern world and restoring them to their proper place requires multiple approaches, or lines of argumentation, drawing in evidence from many directions. So far, we have emphasized the direct impact of the labor of slaves taken from Africa (as well as that of their offspring). In the sixteenth century, when the American slave trade took off in earnest, 370,000 Africans were brought in chains across the Atlantic. This number would increase fivefold in the century that followed, which saw the launching of Caribbean sugar. And in the eighteenth century, the slave traffic increased another threefold, landing a further 6.1 million into New World slavery.

In addition to the vast output—not just of sugar, but of many other commodities—created by this labor, in the immediate prior chapter and elsewhere, we have spoken about the large new markets, or demand, created by the need to clothe, feed, and transport slaves. As we have already seen, these were responsible not just for boosting business, but for integrating markets, first between northern and southern Europe, and later elsewhere. Most important, perhaps, was the effect on New England and others among Britain's American colonies, whose economies were made viable in large part by demand from the slave societies of the Caribbean. This, in turn, made them "the key of the Indies," in the phrase of the historian Wendy Warren. To give an indication of the degree of complementarity that was struck up between these two regions of the British Empire, a scholar has estimated that "of colonial shipping trading to Barbados in 1686, 80 percent of tonnage was registered in New England, more than a third of it in Boston."

Two decades ago, Kenneth Pomeranz, an economic historian who specializes in China, made a powerful contribution to our understanding of Europe's transcendent rise in the nineteenth century by investigating how Britain in particular managed to surpass the longtime previous incumbent as the world's richest nation, China. Pomeranz's landmark study, *The Great Divergence: Europe, China, and the Making of the Modern World Economy*, opens the door for deepening our understanding of the contribution of Africa and Africans to the modernity we share. It credits two main factors for Europe's sharp, British-led ascent. The first of these, he said, was the "ecological dividend," the windfall that Europe reaped by completely taking over the Americas in an astoundingly brief period of time, effectively integrating many millions of square miles of agriculturally productive land into the European economic sphere. Pomeranz's second factor was Europe's expropriation of African labor on an immense scale through slavery, or what he rather delicately called "the fruits of overseas coercion."* Pomeranz's joining of these two factors, land and labor, greatly improves our picture of slavery's central role in the emergence of a new global capitalist economy centered on the Atlantic.

The Great Divergence argued that Britain received a tremendous dietary boost from the takeoff of commoditized sugar, which injected dramatically more calories into the daily fare of its population. Just as critically, it managed to do so remarkably cheaply, especially once Barbados and the follow-on English sugar islands of the Caribbean hit their strides as producers. The caloric boost furnished by cheap sugar, Pomeranz postulated, fueled the long, intense workdays of England's early industrial mill laborers. Without it, the country would have been required to devote vastly more of its own land and labor to the provision of these new caloric sources. Fifteen years before Pomeranz, in *Sweetness and Power*, the anthropologist Sidney Mintz emphasized the huge impact of cane and its by-products on eating habits in England. Mintz estimated that sugar accounted for a mere 2 percent of Britain's caloric intake in 1800.

---

* One historian has gamely sought to affix numbers to this, estimating that by 1800 Britain was acquiring the output of a million slaves working in sugar, tobacco, and cotton alone, thereby effectively stealing 2.5 billion hours of labor from them.

But by the end of that century, the very century of Britain's historic ascension, this number had risen to 14 percent—far more than any of its European rivals. Measured another way, the takeoff of sugar consumption may seem even more impressive:

> *Per capita consumption of sugar in England rose from about 2 pounds per person in the 1660s to 4 pounds per person by the 1690s and continued to expand in the eighteenth century. By the time of the American Revolution, every man, woman and child in England on average consumed 23 pounds of sugar a year. . . . British colonists on the North American mainland imported less than half as much sugar, about 14 pounds per person in 1770, but made up for it with a much higher consumption of sugar's by-products, rum and molasses.*

Dietitians today may frown, but as Pomeranz reasoned, these caloric developments helped boost domestic productivity in critical ways. The entry of cheap sugar into the English diet did far more than produce an onslaught of cakes, tarts, and other confectionary goods. It paved the way for caffeine-containing beverages like coffee, which was also slave grown in the Americas (as well as cocoa, another stimulant), and tea, which followed the coffee craze to become the national drink a century later. Because water supplies were often unhygienic, many English had hitherto favored ale, consuming it even during daytime work hours, which inevitably produced lethargic if not disorderly behavior. The era of Big Sugar therefore ushered in a new age of alertness based on drinks that had the additional benefit of being hygienic, because their preparation required boiling water. And at roughly the same moment, with these new stimulants came yet another, tobacco, which had the additional merit for the workplace, if not for long-term health, of suppressing appetite. As the historian of the Caribbean Randy Brown told me in summing up the shift that underpinned the Industrial Revolution, "they switched from downers to uppers."

There is yet another crucial and surprising dimension of sugar's impact, however—one that Pomeranz leaves unexplored. In speaking of the modern, we must consider much more than just economics, and sugar and its stimulant companions played a role of outsized importance in developments in another sphere altogether: the nature of society itself. The era of Barbados's takeoff and of the sugar revolution that it produced was one of fundamental change in the development in Britain of what we now call civil society. The availability of hot, sweetened, stimulating drinks gave birth to the first coffee shop, which opened its doors in Oxford in 1650. From there, coffee shops quickly spread to London, where they proliferated, and this in turn helped rapidly establish a medium only recently invented in Germany: the newspaper. Gathering places like coffee shops and the availability of regularly printed political news in this format are what gave birth to a modern public sphere, to employ the terminology of the German philosopher and sociologist Jürgen Habermas. This is a fancy way of referring to the emergence of a richly enhanced shared sense of public affairs and citizen participation that emerged during the Enlightenment. For Habermas, conversations over caffeinated drink and newspapers in places like the coffee shop marked "the first time in history [that people] came together as equals to reason critically about public affairs."

Describing the London of the mid- and late seventeenth century, the historian of early modern Europe Brian William Cowan wrote, "The numerous coffeehouses of the metropolis were greater than the sum of their parts; they formed an interactive system in which information was socialized and made sense of by the various constituencies of the city." The coffeehouse, in other words, became "the primary social space in which 'news' was both produced and consumed," and "no coffeehouse worth its name could refuse to supply its customers with a selection of newspapers." This transformation in the social life of England was pithily captured in a couplet from a satire called "The Student," published in 1751.

Dinner over, to Tom's or to Clapham's I go.
The news of the Town so impatient to know.

Through major historic social transformations like these, we come finally to the understanding that the Enlightenment itself had vital roots in the toil and sweat of African captives, trafficked and put to work in gangs on the integrated plantations that were becoming the dominant model of sugar production in the Caribbean by the mid- to late seventeenth century. Anticipating the objection that Britain could have eventually acquired its calories from alternative sources, Pomeranz carefully demonstrates just how extraordinary a boon in metabolic and, just as critically, environmental terms New World sugar amounted to for Britain:

> *[A]n acre of tropical sugar land yields as many calories as more than 4 acres of potatoes (which most eighteenth-century Europeans scorned), or 9–12 acres of wheat. The calories from the sugar consumed in the United Kingdom circa 1800 (using figures from Mintz) would have required at least 1,300,000 acres of average-yielding English farms and conceivably over 1,900,000; in 1831, 1,900,000 to 2,600,000 acres would have been needed. And since the land that remained uncultivated in Europe (and especially in Britain) by this time was hardly the continent's best, we could plausibly make these numbers still larger.*

Pomeranz employs the same kind of logic involving opportunity cost to demonstrate that without its millions of square miles of fertile newly appropriated farmland in mainland North America and the slave labor that made its cotton the dominant global commodity in the nineteenth century, Britain would have been hard-pressed to sustain the kind of textile boom that lay at the heart of the Industrial Revolution:

> *By 1815, Britain imported 100,000,000 pounds of New World cotton; by 1830, 263,000,000 pounds. If one replaced this fiber with an equivalent weight of hemp or flax, the extra acreage needed would be comparatively modest: 200,000 acres in 1815, 500,000 in 1830. But hemp and flax—especially hemp—were both considered inferior fibers for most purposes and were much*

Reclining figure, Djenne-jeno, Mali, twelfth–fourteenth century. *(Metropolitan Museum of Art and Musée National du Mali, Bamako [R 88-19-275])*

Equestrian figure, Mali, twelfth–fourteenth century. *(Metropolitan Museum of Art, Collection of James J. and Laura Ross)*

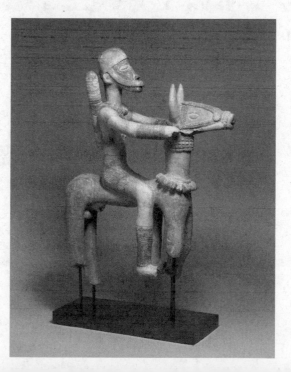

Dinar of as-Shakir li-Allah (r. 933–958 CE), struck at Sijilmasa, AH 334. Gold, diameter 19 mm.
Bank al-Maghrib, Rabat, Morocco, 515455. *(Photographs by Fouad Mahdaoui. Courtesy of the Block Museum of Art, Northwestern University)*

Dinar of Abû Bakr ibn 'Umar (r. 448–480 CE), struck at Sijilmasa, AH 477. Gold, diameter 25 mm. Bank al-Maghrib, Rabat, Morocco, 520162. *(Photographs by Fouad Mahdaoui. Courtesy of the Block Museum of Art, Northwestern University)*

Elmina Castle, shown from hilltop site of Dutch-built fort, St. Jago, Elmina, Ghana. *(Photograph by Howard W. French)*

Tourists inside Elmina Castle. *(Photograph by Howard W. French)*

São Sebastião Fort and Museum, with statues of Portuguese conquistadors, São Tomé. *(Photograph by Howard W. French)*

Brazilian landscape with sugar mill by Frans Post. *(SMK Photo/Jakob Skou-Hansen. Statens Museum for Kunst, National Gallery)*

Sugar mill ruins in Bahia, Brazil. (Engenho Sergipe do Condo, "Queen of the Recôncavo")
(Photograph by Howard W. French)

Casa de Angola, Angolan cultural center, in Salvador, Bahia, Brazil. *(Photograph by Howard W. French)*

Newton Slave Burial Ground in Barbados, one of the largest known burial sites for enslaved Africans in the Western Hemisphere. *(Photographs by Howard W. French)*

The SlaveRoute

NEWTON SLAVE BURIAL GROUND

This area of about 4500 square metres was used as a cemetery for slaves on Newton Plantation. An estimated 570 slaves were buried here, some in low earthen mounds, others in non-mound graves.

In the 1970s, excavation of this burial ground revealed valuable archaeological information of slave life in Barbados. Artefacts found here, including jewelry and eating utensils are on display at the Barbados Museum and Historical Society.

This site represents the only excavated communal slave burial ground within a plantation setting in the western hemisphere.

Drax Plantation boiler ruin, Saint George, Barbados.
(Photograph by Howard W. French)

Emancipation Statue, Barbados.
(Photograph by Howard W. French)

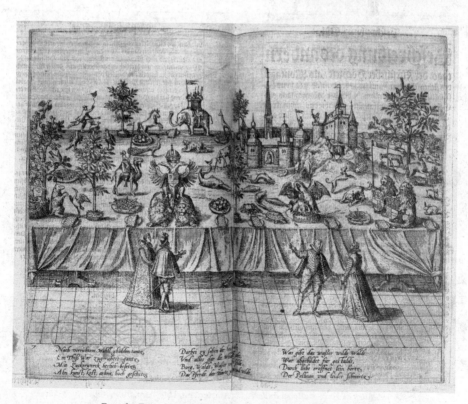

Feast, by Franz Hogenburg. *(Getty Research Institute, Los Angeles)*

Bronze panel with
Portuguese soldiers, Benin.
(Metropolitan Museum of Art)

Kongo Kingdom capital, San Salvador (Mbanza Kongo). In O[lfert] Dapper, *Naukeurige Beschrijvinge der Afrikaensche Eylanden: als Madagaskar, of Sant Laurens, Sant Thome, d'eilanden van Kanarien, Kaep de Verd, Malta en andere* . . . (Amsterdam, 1668), pp. 562–563.
(Caroline Batchelor Map Collection, David Rumsey Map Center, Stanford Libraries)

Letter from Afonso I of Kongo to Manuel I of Portugal, requesting Portuguese religious paraphernalia. June 8, 1517. *(Carta do rei do Congo para D. Manuel, rei de Portugal, a pedir uma cruz de prata, uma custódia, retábulos, breviários, entre outros, tudo para sua capela real. Corpo Cronológico, Parte I, maço 22, no. 5. PT/TT/CC/1/22/5. Arquivo Nacional da Torre do Tombo/DGLAB, Ministério da Cultura, Lisboa, Portugal)*

Official coat of arms of the Manicongo kings, 1528–41. (Godinho) *(Detail from* Livro da nobreza e da perfeição das armas dos reis cristãos e nobres linhagens dos reinos e senhorios de Portugal, *by António Godinho. Casa Real, Cartório da Nobreza, liv. 20 PT/TT/CR/D-A/001/20. Arquivo Nacional da Torre to Tombo/ DGLAB, Ministério da Cultura, Lisboa, Portugal)*

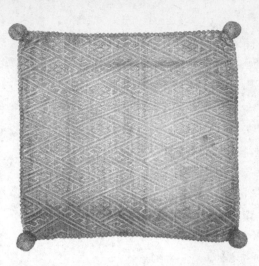

Raffia or pineapple fiber prestige hat, Kongo Kingdom, sixteenth–seventeenth century. *(Photograph by Kit Weiss, National Museum of Denmark)*

Raffia cushion case, luxury cloth, Kingdom of Kongo, seventeenth–eighteenth century. *(Photograph by John Lee, National Museum of Denmark)*

Dutch ambassadors at the court of Garcia II, king of Kongo. From O[lfert] Dapper, *Naukeurige Beschrijvinge*, p. 580.

Don Miguel de Castro, emissary of the Count of Soyo Kingdom in Dutch Brazil, ca. 1640–47. *(Photo by SMK Photo/Jakob Skou-Hansen. Statens Museum for Kunst, National Gallery of Denmark)*

Lieutenant-Admiral Pieter Pietersz Heyn (1577–1629), by Paulus Moreelse, 1630. (Het Sheepvaartsmuseum, Amsterdam.)

Akan measuring weights used in the regional gold trade, Gold Coast (Ghana).
(Collection Nationaal Museum van Wereldculturen)

Toussaint Louverture, Chef des Noirs Insurgés de Saint Domingue, c. 1800. (John Carter Brown Library, Brown University)

Building where a woman given the name Angela, who arrived in Jamestown, Virginia, in 1619, worked the kitchen. *(Photograph by Howard W. French)*

Evergreen Plantation, Saint John the Baptist Parish, Louisiana. *(Photograph by Howard W. French)*

Slave quarters, Evergreen Plantation. *(Photograph by Howard W. French)*

Clarksdale, Mississippi, cotton-growing lands of the Delta. *(Photograph by Howard W. French)*

Club Paradise blues poster
with Muddy Waters and
Howling Wolf, 1964.
*(Photograph by
Howard W. French)*

Riverside Hotel, Clarksdale, Mississippi, formerly the Afro-American Hospital, where Bessie
Smith died following an automobile accident. *(Photograph by Howard W. French)*

Point of disembarkation in 1738 of 126 enslaved Africans from the ship *Martha & Jane,* Middletown, Connecticut. This site is part of UNESCO's Slave Route Project: Resistance, Liberty, Heritage. *(Photograph by Howard W. French)*

Barboursville Ruins, home to James Barbour. Designed by Thomas Jefferson. *(Photograph by Howard W. French)*

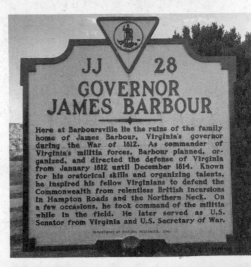

James Barbour Road Marker. State Route 33, Barboursville, Virginia. *(Photograph by Howard W. French)*

*more difficult to work with, and processes for spinning them
mechanically emerged later than that for cotton. More important,
both hemp and flax were extremely labor-intensive and manure-
intensive crops: so much so that most people only grew them as
garden crops. Even three centuries of government schemes and
subsidies had failed to promote larger-scale production in either
England or North America.*

*This leaves wool, long Europe's main clothing fiber. But rais-
ing enough sheep to replace the yarn made with Britain's New
World cotton imports would have required staggering quantities
of land: almost 9,000,000 acres in 1815, using ratios from model
farms, and over 23,000,000 acres in 1830. This figure surpasses
Britain's total crop and pasture land combined.*

Even if one grants that such a replacement in quantitative terms
could somehow have been arranged, which is unlikely, one encounters yet other problems. Ever since the thirteenth or fourteenth century, England's leading export had been woolen textiles, which it
had always sold to Europe. European markets for English woolens
grew more restricted with the rise of mercantilism in the seventeenth
century and with competition from French production in the late
eighteenth century. Tropical markets, whether in Africa or the New
World, could not replace European demand, because wool was so
unsuited to hot climates. England's economic takeoff and industrialization prior to its neighbors was contingent upon overcoming the
limitations bound up in dependence on wool-led growth. This it was
able to achieve via the new Atlantic markets, which only slavery and
sugar had made possible. This Atlantic world was one of economic
diversity and wealth-producing opportunities based on division of
labor and trade.

English manufactures found their way to markets so rich in
mainland North America that they quickly matched and then
exceeded the value of trade with Europe. As we have seen, England's
American colonies financed their trade with the mother country by
selling a wide range of their own goods first to Barbados and then to

England's other commodity-producing plantation-economy islands, such as Jamaica. Despite the nominal mercantilism of the era, opportunities for trade with others were numerous, whether between English slavers and the Spanish in the New World, or American colonies selling their wares in the Caribbean to the French and others. This triangular boom is what relieved England of the need to devote so much of its land for the sheep pasturage needed to produce wool, and it was all built on the solid foundation of African slavery.

The belated but growing historical consensus about the importance of trade in goods that were grounded in or financed by slave plantation labor to Europe's ascension has also received important support not just from historians but also from historically minded economists and political scientists. In an important paper issued five years after Pomeranz's *Great Divergence*, three prominent MIT scholars, Daron Acemoglu, Simon Johnson, and James Robinson, placed the roots of this divergence, or of Europe's economic "miracle," further back in the past, while also complicating the story substantially. Their study, "The Rise of Europe: Atlantic Trade, Institutional Change and Economic Growth," establishes a robust statistical connection between accelerated urbanization and economic growth in Europe and Pomeranz's "fruits of overseas coercion" in the New World between 1500 and 1850. What clearly emerges through their data is that the differential in growth between Western Europe compared with other regions during this time period is almost entirely accounted for by the growth of nations with access to the Atlantic Ocean, or what the authors call "Atlantic traders." Strikingly, this differential already begins to show up almost immediately after Columbus's breakthrough to the New World (hence their use of as early a date as 1500). The data deployed by Acemoglu, Johnson, and Robinson sets apart economic growth in Atlantic port cities in western Europe not only from Mediterranean cities and landlocked eastern European cities, but also from Asian cities.[*] It is in the early seven-

---

[*] The patterns noted by the MIT scholars would also hold up on the American mainland, where the greatest centers of economic growth and new wealth were precisely the places most directly connected to the slave-production-driven economic centers of the Atlantic world.

teenth century, however, when the most dramatic divergence begins, which seems unlikely to be a matter of happenstance. This was the precise moment when the Dutch and, right on their heels, the English became active in the pursuit of the wealth of Africa. This they did, of course, through trade in gold and slaves: for the Dutch, in Brazilian plantation agriculture and slave trading and related commerce in the West Indies; for the British, in Barbados and subsequently in other emerging sugar islands in the Caribbean, which resulted in Britain's becoming the Atlantic's dominant slave-trading power.

By situating the beginnings of this European divergence as far back as 1500, the authors compel us to briefly return to our story of the emergence of gold-rich kingdoms in Africa's Sahel region in the medieval era, including the visit to Cairo and pilgrimage to Mecca of the Malian emperor Mansā Mūsā. That voyage caused the existence of abundant sources of African gold to be highlighted on European maps, prompting Portugal's long quest down the coast of West Africa in search of the source of this great wealth. This is yet another way of demonstrating how Portugal's breakthrough in discovering gold at Elmina became a critical milestone in European history—one that has been widely overlooked in standard narratives of this period, which fast-forward to the discovery of sea routes to Asia, treating Africa as if it were of no intrinsic interest or benefit.

For the post-sugar period of the eras they examine, Acemoglu, Johnson, and Robinson make no claim that, whether taken alone or together, the value of new trade with Africa (textiles and other goods for slaves) or with the Caribbean (for sugar and other plantation products) or with the North American mainland (British manufactures) constituted enough of a windfall to provide a one-stop explanation for a further acceleration in the economic rise of Europe's major Atlantic powers beginning in the seventeenth century. The idea they advance instead provides a different theory of modernizing change, at once more subtle and complex. Early in this period, they say, Madrid and Lisbon garnered important new sources of wealth from mining (especially Spain) and plantation agriculture and slave trading (especially Portugal). These spurred meaningful increases in intra-European trade, as well as greatly increased imperial competition between these Iberian neighbors, and subsequently among a broadening array of European powers. The nations that benefited most from their burgeoning connections to the New World, however, were Holland, England (later Britain), and, subsequently, France. This argument is especially nuanced because it goes far beyond narrow measurements of income from trade in its assessment of the benefits and effects of empire.

The authors postulate that the fact that the Dutch and English were far less absolutist in their political structures compared with the Iberian powers put them in a better position to seek out and develop wealth, and to profit more deeply as the Atlantic economy became more and more integrated. By the same token, they argue, the growth of new private fortunes, especially those bound up in the slave trade and in its plantation agriculture offshoot, helped limit the power of monarchs, thus curtailing royal monopolies, strengthening political pluralism, and encouraging the emergence of stronger, more business-friendly institutions. Nowhere was this truer than in England. There, the slave trade became the central issue in the seventeenth-century debate over whether, in the words of the British historian William A. Pettigrew, "the legitimacy of the English state [ought] to derive from the crown or from the subjects of the crown." The opponents of the royal monopoly over African slavery became highly adept at lobbying Parliament and giving vent to their views in a free press. So much so that Pettigrew has called these struggles "not the relics of a traditional, precapitalist society [but] the distillate expressions of modern society's dynamic founding moments." This, however, was just the beginning. As this lobby helped propel Britain to the status of a slaving superpower in the century that followed, it would crystallize into something more formal known as the West India Interest, which fought to defend slave plantation agriculture well beyond abolition in Britain in 1807.

The role of new business elites whose prosperity was bound up in slavery became important features of the English Civil War of 1642–1649 and of the Glorious Revolution of 1688–1689. Ironically, both of these events, when viewed from the narrow perspective of the English themselves, were fundamentally struggles aimed at expanding "freedom" by restricting the power of the monarchy. Acemoglu, Johnson, and Robinson draw upon this history to make a broader point about Europe's ascension: "The evidence weighs against the most popular theories for the rise of Europe, which emphasize the continuity between pre-1500 and post-1500 growth and the importance of certain distinctive European characteristics, such as culture, religion, geography and features of the European state system. Instead, it is consistent with theories that emphasize the importance of profits made in Atlantic trade, colonialism and slavery." The authors go on to add, however, that

> *the rise of Europe reflects not only the direct effects of Atlantic trade and colonialism but also a major social transformation induced by these opportunities.... Atlantic trade in Britain and the Netherlands (or, more appropriately, in England and the Duchy of Burgundy) altered the balance of political power by enriching and strengthening commercial interests outside the royal circle, including various overseas merchants, slave traders, and various colonial planters. Through this channel, it contributed to the emergence of political institutions protecting merchants against royal power.*

In arguments like these we thus see a corollary to the picture of how European societies were changed through the arrival of mass-consumed sugar and its accompanying stimulants, coffee and tea. In that example, the major change brought about to Europe as a by-product of African sweat and productivity was to civil society and the emergence of a modern public sphere. Acemoglu, Johnson, and Robinson's insights offer a better understanding of how Europe's connections with Africa and, via African labor, to the plantation economies of the New World also helped impel modernizing political change in Europe at more elite levels in crucial yet seldom recognized ways. This brings us back to Tilly's theory that the more the fiscal-military state developed its powers of extraction in this era, the more it had to respond to the claims of its own citizens via political reforms and new notions of accountability.

Much work remains for economically minded historians, as well as for historically minded economists and others in order to fill in this story and further consolidate an emerging picture that highlights the pivotal role that Africa and Africans played in launching Europe on its path to modernity and an economic divergence compared to other regions of the world that has only now begun to close. One of the most remarkable features of this history, however, is how slowly and reluctantly the academy has come to considering the crucial African contribution in the first place. In the decades that followed Britain's abolition of the slave trade in 1807 and for nearly the next century and a half, Western attention toward Africa was broadly consumed with what Europe claimed to be its civilizing mission on the continent, of the "white man's burden." It took a non-European, and a Black man from the West Indies at that, Eric Williams, to turn traditional debates on their head, belatedly shifting them from a focus on the supposed great good that Europe has done for Africa to advancing the proposition that it was in fact the so-called Dark Continent, via Atlantic slavery, that provided the critical boost that had made Europe's takeoff possible. Relatedly, and equally worthy of note, is the curious fact that in the half century that followed the 1944 publication of Williams's *Capitalism and Slavery*, Western scholars poured vastly more energy into attempts to find fault with or outright debunk his arguments than they had ever previously invested in considering the possibility that Africa and Africans had played an important role in the story of Europe in the first place. It is a credit to the fertility of Williams's ideas, though, that in the decades that followed scholars in fields as varied as dependency theory, Marxist history, British cultural studies, and postcolonial studies have continued to draw on his writings. One should also cite the ongoing Legacies of British Slave-Ownership project at University College London, which, drawing inspiration from Williams, has identified the 47,000 Britons who claimed and received £20 million in compensation from their government after slave ownership in the British Caribbean was ended in 1833. This payout amounted to 40 percent of the government's budget at the time, or the equivalent of roughly £17 billion today.

In broadly dismissing Williams's critics, Pomeranz summarized some of their key objections to his ideas:

> *Some deny that coercion (i.e., slavery) allowed above-average profits in the first place. Others concede at least the possibility of above-normal profits but argue that the accumulation of these profits was trivial compared to the accumulation of profits from economic activity within Europe itself. And others point to . . . the relatively small capital requirements of the early Industrial Revolution and argue that this makes whatever above-normal profits there might have been largely irrelevant to industrialization.*

Frames like these, however, miss what is most vital to understanding this history. The most important contribution of African slavery to the West was not whatever fillip it may or may not have provided for industrialization, which even most sympathetic scholars today feel Williams fundamentally miscast and overstated.* Rather, it was something far larger and yet hiding in plain sight, something in fact that is indisputable: Africa, and the human resources drained from that continent via the greatest forced migration in human history, had provided the most essential input of all by far to making the New World economically viable. Africans, in other words, became the ingredient sine qua non in this vast project. Doubters must ask themselves, What would the European newcomers have done without them? But we needn't await an answer. To a degree that has never been recognized, it was upon the bedrock of their strength and their

---

* Williams has also been strongly refuted for his so-called decline theory, a thesis that held that Britain conceded an end to the slave trade and to slavery only because its empire in the Caribbean had ceased to be profitable. Historians like Seymour Drescher have convincingly shown this not to have been the case. Indeed, abolition in Britain followed on the heels of a particularly intensive period of slave trading, as well as the opening of ambitious new plantation sugar domains in Guyana.

will to endure and survive the horrors of slavery that much of the wealth and power of subsequent centuries of predominant Western capitalism was founded. The Atlantic world was not just made viable through their labor. Yes, as we have claimed here, it was this appropriated toil that generated nearly all of the commodities and much of the gold and silver that helped fuel the ascension of the West. But that is not all. Far from it.

More important still, it was the very founding of this Atlantic world, an unprecedentedly large geographic sphere spanning four continents, that created what we now think of and understand as the West, and this is what made the very greatness that we associate with this geographical notion possible. Without the Americas and their long and deep connections to Africa, what would Europe have weighed in the historical balance of the last half millennium? To answer the question is to not only challenge our understanding of modern history, but to fundamentally reconsider Western identity itself. What has most distinguished modern Europe from other regions of the world is not so much any qualities intrinsic to it, as cultural chauvinists and those who fixate on race profess, but rather the fact that its peoples spanned the Atlantic at a particularly opportune moment in time, utterly transforming life on every shore, thanks to the indispensable contribution of Africans. And in doing so, Europe was itself transformed as well, and not merely the agent of transformation as is often imagined. Later, we will further explore Africa's essential hand in the invention and construction of this new creation we call the West, paying particular attention to the American colonies that became the United States and to Haiti, the former plantation colony that—after the only successful large slave revolt in world history—became the second republic in the Americas. Before we arrive there, though, in the pages that follow we must first turn to the story of how these interactions impacted Africa, the overlooked cornerstone of our Atlantic world.

21

MASTERS OF SLAVES, MASTERS OF THE SEA

THERE IS ONE FINAL THING to be said about Eric Williams moving on, and it is a reply to those who have argued that slavery and the plantations of the New World were never so valuable to Europe as people like the Trinidadians have pretended them to be. Perhaps as effective as any of the arguments that have been explored to this point is an interrogation. As the historian David Geggus wrote of the Caribbean, "No other part of the world was ruled from Europe for so long or had such a large proportion of its population living as slaves." Europeans waged extraordinary struggles among themselves throughout this period for control of the region. A long era of Spanish dominance that began with Columbus was followed by a chaotic scramble that in turn drew in the Dutch, the English, and the French, and this was followed, lastly, by a period of quasi-British hegemony, but one punctuated by enormous wealth production by French slaves on Saint Domingue. Throughout, maritime forces, both formal navies and privateers, were the main instruments of commercial expansion, with each power determined not only to outcompete its rivals, but to subvert or evict them. Some have wrongly preferred theories for this behavior that depend on abstract motivations, such as the pursuit of glory. In reality, the imperial contest over the Caribbean was driven by a realist understanding that power flows in good part from wealth, whose sources must be controlled lest one's rivals seize them to one's detriment or peril.

As the historian Robin Blackburn wrote:

> *The commercial and naval strategies of such statesmen as Walpole and Chatham, Choiseul and Pombal, concentrated on the New World as much as the Old. Britain's rulers wished to avoid the domination of continental Europe by a single power, but were themselves quite prepared to aim at hegemonizing the Americas. However important Europe might be to France, its rulers never felt that they could allow the British a free hand in the New World. To do so would have been to renounce not only fabled riches but also something that held out extraordinary promise for the future and distinguished the modern from the classical age.*

Blackburn was writing about the eighteenth and nineteenth centuries, but he might well have extended his chronology further into the past, because the violent and costly European contest over the slave and plantation trades of the Caribbean seventeenth century usually receives far too little attention in accounts of the era. In 1690, an era when England had only recently begun making its move on the region, Christopher Codrington, a wealthy Barbadian planter, slave owner, and trader, and later English governor of the Leeward Islands, wrote: "All turns on mastery of the sea. If we have it, our islands are safe, however thinly peopled; if the French have it, we cannot, after the recent mortality, raise enough men in all the islands to hold one of them." But in his classic *The Command of the Ocean*, N. A. M. Rodger writes of what the European powers that coveted control of the Caribbean would soon learn: "The great fleets of which everyone had hoped and expected so much, proved to be difficult to use effectively in unforeseen circumstances. [It was] easier to fight battles than to win them, and easier to win them than to achieve any lasting advantage."

Enormous fleets were duly mustered and deployed to the Caribbean basin at extraordinary cost in treasury, and for a century and a half there was great loss of life in battle as well. But what did these "unforeseen circumstances" refer to? Principal among them was disease—most particularly, yellow fever and malaria. Both of these maladies originated among African slaves and devastated the European forces who operated in this environment, performing an ironic flip of fate's coin on the whites whose diseases had so devastated the Native American populations. Campaigning at sea was roughly limited from December to May in the West Indies, where it was followed by the so-called sickly season, when death rates as high as 85 percent were not uncommon among European sailors, laying low entire fleets.

In 1741, when the British admiral Edward Vernon set forth at the head of a squadron to the coast of present-day Colombia to besiege Cartagena, 22,000 men were lost to disease, again mostly yellow fever and malaria. Two decades later, in 1762, Britain mobilized more than 230 ships and 26,000 soldiers, sailors, and African slaves in order to seize Havana from the Spanish. In six weeks of active fighting and the eleven months of occupation that followed, Britain lost more men than it did during the entire Seven Years War in North America.

Even as the power of these nations ebbed and flowed in the region, they kept investing vast amounts of naval resources, of treasure and human lives, doubling down in attempting to advance their hold over the West Indies, or limit the hold of their rivals. For England and France, this meant deploying sixty to eighty ships of the line each, together with an abundance of smaller ships, in the Caribbean Sea. Despite each side's repeated huge losses, they just kept coming until their showdown over what had become the biggest prize of all in the entire sea: Saint Domingue. This is where the imperial jousting over plantation islands and the wealth they produced finally entered its terminal phase. But the beginning of the end came in the form not of a triumph by one European nation over another, as those protagonists might have expected, but rather of the victory of a nation largely composed of people who were actually born in Africa and abducted from there or pawned into slavery on the far side of the Atlantic. When France was finally forced to permanently relinquish its control of Haiti, a writer of the time called its defeat at the hands of Blacks "the worst catastrophe ever to befall an empire." It was, in fact, something of even greater consequence than that. It was a defeat for empires throughout the New World *tout court*, as we will come to understand better later; it would lead to the defeat of the idea of Black slavery itself.

In the opening lines of the preface to the first edition of his classic history of the Haitian Revolution, C. L. R. James captured this best:

> *In 1789 the French West Indian colony of San Domingo supplied two-thirds of the overseas trade of France and was the greatest individual market for the European slave trade. It was an integral part of the economic life of the age, the greatest colony in the world, the pride of France and the envy of every other imperialist nation. The whole structure rested on the labor of half-a-million slaves.*
>
> *In August 1791, after two years of the French revolution and its repercussions in San Domingo, the slaves revolted. The struggle lasted for 12 years. The slaves defeated in turn the local whites and the soldiers of the French monarchy, a Spanish invasion, a British expedition of some 60,000 men, and a French expedition of similar size under Bonaparte's brother-in-law. The defeat of Bonaparte's expedition in 1803 resulted in the establishment of the Negro state of Haiti which has lasted to this day.*

This final expedition was led by General Charles-Victor-Emmanuel Leclerc, who had been dispatched to Haiti with the aim of restoring white supremacy on the island, to return its Black population to slavery after they had already won their freedom, and to pursue further conquest in the Caribbean once that was achieved. Instead, as we will see in detail ahead, it ended up costing Napoleon's France the entire Louisiana territory, and even spurring the end of New World slavery altogether, although that would take a few more decades to accomplish. Why again would Europeans have consented to so much expenditure and submitted themselves to so much bother if slave-based empires in the New World were not deemed vitally important to them? Why is it that the leading nations of Europe had been so willing to fight and die for these islands for so long, if this new mode of empire building based squarely on slave power had not been immensely profitable, as some have pretended?

The answer is that during the moment in history where it had mattered most, the Caribbean seemed to possess the things most vital to empire in the Atlantic world. As one historian has written, this meant "territories cleared of native peoples, fertile land, good harbors, favorable winds, high-yielding local subsistence crops, appropriate climatic conditions, manageable security problems— the only thing missing was a labor force." But as every reader will know already by this point and will now see in detail, Africa, the most important factor of all, was there for that.

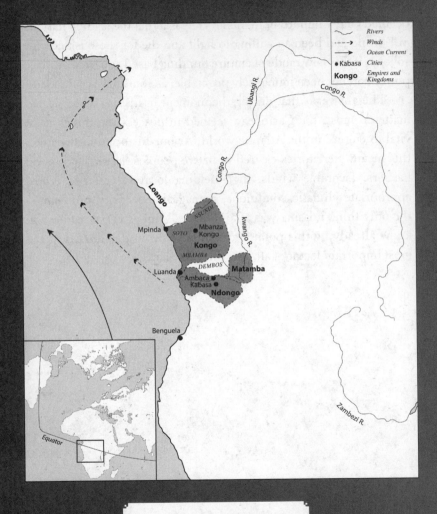

Kongo and other selected kingdoms of west Central Africa

PART IV

THE WAGES OF THE PYTHON GOD

Our memory is the only help that is left to them [the dead]. They pass away into it, and if every deceased person is like someone who was murdered by the living, so he is also like someone whose life they must save, without knowing whether the effort will succeed.

THEODOR W. ADORNO,
"Marginalia on Mahler"

22

SHATTER ZONES

T O ENTER THE ELMINA CASTLE one must first cross a narrow bridge over the moat that was dug around its perimeter for protection against attack, whether foreign or local. At one end of this gangway there is a marble plaque that reads:

> In Everlasting Memory of the anguish of our ancestors may those who died rest in peace. May those who return find their roots. May humanity never again perpetrate such injustice against humanity. We the living vow to uphold this.

Once they've paid their entrance fee, most visitors linger in the castle's large, open courtyard, where one feels a deep and inevitable sense of disorientation. At one end of the yard rises a grand double balustrade leading to a pillared entrance to the two elevated floors above, which once housed the governor and his officers. Around the circumference of the whitewashed courtyard, meanwhile, lie the doorways to dungeons that separately held male and female captives. There, they awaited shipment across the sea into a world bounded by pain and occluded by unknowns: the world of enslavement.

I followed a group of about a dozen visitors, most of them fellow African Americans, ducking into the most infamous of these rooms, a dark and humid dungeon referred to as the Door of No Return.

When a similar holding pen at the nearby slaving fort at Cape Coast was excavated in 1972, archaeologists scraped away from its floor eighteen inches of compacted waste, much of it feces, blood, and skin. Inside that low, dim space, I awaited my chance to stick my head out its single slit opening and gaze into the piercing sunlight. The glimpse one obtains is of a narrow strip of land that separates the castle from the shore. This was the waiting spot for small boats that gathered nearby to ferry the frog-marched captives in their heavy chains to the large, seaworthy ships that had come to bear them off to the Americas. As frightful as the captives' forced and stumbling steps toward the shore must have been, their departure from Africa served up one more moment of sheer terror. It came when those who had been chained together by twos, to prevent them from jumping overboard, were seated in the ferrying boats. The muscular rowers who manned the local crews were expert in timing the serried incoming waves, some as large as ten feet high. They had to be. The final separation from the continent for their human quarry involved running as fast as they could as they pushed their long dugouts into the ocean at the occasional appearance of a less formidable crest, and hoping not to be sunk or capsized. Climbing out of the darkness of the dungeon of the fort at Elmina and into those waves was like leaving the womb in a strange and backward birthing ritual. By clambering aboard the ship that would carry them to the Americas, the survivors were completing "the first leg of their journey from humanity to cattle."

Later, from a terrace on the castle's upper floor, I got a clearer view of what I had barely been able to make out from the dungeon's dismal portal. In the near distance I could see the village clustered on the banks of the Benya River, its mouth crowded with wooden fishing boats that could not be very different from the ones employed here at the time the Portuguese arrived, in 1471. Also, there in the beyond, rendered hazy by the ocean spray, lay the bay with the crescent beach where Diogo de Azambuja sought safe anchor for his ships before coming ashore to secure the history-changing supply of abundant gold here.

The story passed down by the Portuguese discoverers said that the villagers they had first encountered at Elmina wore so much gold jewelry and other gilt adornments that the Portuguese instantly knew they must be near the source of West Africa's fabulous wealth in the metal, whose legend in Europe dated from the voyage to Cairo of Mansā Mūsā. The day after I visited the castle, I took a late afternoon walk alone from my modest hotel, which sat by the rusty bridge that spans the mouth of the Benya, to the end of the beach that lines Elmina's crescent bay and back. At that quiet hour, the fishermen were busy mending their nets, having already returned from their daily foray at sea. But as the sun engaged its descent toward the horizon and the afternoon heat palpably faded, here and there one could detect another kind of activity, albeit almost furtive: women and children were digging holes in the wet sand, sifting what they had excavated with their hands over wobbly screens framed in wood. They were looking for gold.

This ocean-fronting stretch of West Africa, now located in modern Ghana, had returned to its old vocation. That was not because of this artisanal prospecting, which locals readily acknowledged is illegal, but because gold is once again a pillar of the country's economy, even though common people are no longer so richly adorned in the metal. Instead, the nation's mines are a major source of employment in this region, like the one at Nsuta, an hour away inland by road, where my brother-in-law, Ngamah, works as an engineer for a multinational producer of the metal.

Gold, in fact, has never ceased being a big deal in these parts. It never went out of production, and, as the presence of Ngamah's company attests, Europeans never abandoned their efforts to acquire it. But in a remarkably brief period of time, beginning in the mid-seventeenth century, it came to be rapidly eclipsed by another commodity; one that would change the course of the world economy in its wake even more profoundly than gold itself had: the transatlantic trade in Black people.

As the slave trade first began to ramp up in the first half of the sixteenth century, its early volume was mostly sourced in an area that the Europeans called Cape Verde, a region that comprises not just the island of that name, but stretches from the baobab-studded scrub-lands of modern-day Senegal and Gambia all the way to Guinea-Bissau and the rain forests and swamp of Sierra Leone. To a large extent this choice reflected convenience, since this area was the part of the West African coast that was closest to both Europe and the Americas. For these reasons, Upper Guinea, as this region is also known, became the first part of sub-Saharan Africa to become integrated into the emerging Atlantic world. Some historians have gone even further, calling it the true birthing ground of an Atlantic economy.

The trade in slaves by Europeans that began with a relative trickle here after the mid-fifteenth century was largely conducted from the Cape Verde Islands. That brand-new Portuguese colony received its first slaving charter from the Portuguese crown in 1466, a decade before the remainder of the West African coast had been explored, and almost immediately began drawing seekers of fortune through trade with Africa from the home country.

Portugal's hoped-for bonanza in gold never materialized in Upper Guinea. But as a staging ground for the slaving business, Cape Verde Islands and Upper Guinea would come to fulfill a variety of convergent interests for Lisbon. The first of these was a desperate need for people in Portugal itself, which in this era was still recovering from a major episode of the Black Death a century prior. By the early sixteenth century Lisbon's population of about 100,000 was fully 10 percent Black, while Portugal as a whole contained 40,000 people of African descent. Nicolas Clénard, a Belgian traveler to the country in this era, wrote, "In Evora, it was as if I had entered a city in hell; so frequently did I encounter blacks, a race that I detest." In 1472, the Portuguese parliament sent a petition to King Afonso V, "the African," urging him to prohibit the export of enslaved Blacks from the kingdom to other lands, and most particularly to Spain, where there was an equally avid market for Africans.* The justifica-

---

* Of a total population slightly greater than 85,000, a 1565 census of the city of Seville counted 6327 slaves, most of whom were sub-Saharan Africans.

tion for this read, "because sir, [the slaves] constitute a great part of the population in your Kingdoms, and are responsible for making new lands clearing woods and opening swamps and of other benefits. And these people of Africa have surrendered [to Portugal], and it will be better that they surrender to your Kingdom than have foreigners take advantage of [the lands of Guinea], who did not spill blood to find them."

The most pressing and constant challenge for the crown in this era, in fact, was how to maintain control of a business that generated such lucrative revenue streams. Toward this end, Lisbon introduced increasingly restrictive statutes and codes aimed at regulating business on the African mainland. Soon, travel to the continent without authorization was made a capital offense, according to a law that read, "no person, irrespective of rank or station, should throw himself with the Negroes, on pain of death."

By the start of the sixteenth century, a contemporaneous assessment by the Portuguese explorer and trader Duarte Pacheco Pereira stated that 3500 slaves were being purchased each year on the coasts of Upper Guinea. Just a few years earlier, in 1497, after Columbus had visited Cape Verde, he wrote to Spain's Catholic Monarchs, Ferdinand and Isabella, that "in these past days when I went to Cabo Verde, where the people have a great trade in slaves and are always sending ships to obtain them and receiving them in the port, I saw that even the cheapest slaves in the worst condition were being sold for 8,000 maravedis."

For reasons that the Portuguese probably did not fully grasp at the time and certainly could not have anticipated, the Upper Guinea region was a highly propitious ground upon which to found a transcontinental business in slaves. That is because it had already become a kind of "shatter zone" over the previous two centuries; this occurred as Kaabu, a Malinke empire, expanded coastward, both to the west and south, from its heartland in what is today southwestern Mali and collided with other kingdoms that lay in its path, creating a "mêlée of peoples," in the phrase of the historian Walter Rodney.

"Indeed, the whole of the Upper Guinea offered ample opportunities for conflicts between ethnic groups, localized wars being fought specifically to procure slaves for export." Widening conflict frequently meant bulging markets for slaves, a commerce that long had been traditionally directed in this region toward Islamic markets, whose biggest outlets were situated on the far northern side of the Sahara Desert and in the Near East. And it is reasonable to postulate that Africans who already had a long history of selling members of rival groups into slavery via circuits like these would have just have eagerly sold them to newcomers from Europe.

As other European nations dove into the trade for African slaves, the stiffening competition, in addition to other factors that we will explore, drove the Portuguese farther and farther down the African coast until they reached the region of Kongo and Angola, where they would soon begin to acquire slaves in much greater numbers than ever before. Others, meanwhile, especially the Dutch and English, concentrated on Elmina and the stretch of coastline extending eastward into modern-day Nigeria, which experienced an enormous boom in slave trading itself.

23

NEGROS SEGUROS

WITH ITS RANK AND centuries-long exploitation of Africans, the plantation-complex was the most important driver of wealth in the New World, and indeed in driving the ascension of the West. As readers have seen, far more than silver and gold, it was agricultural commodities procured through Black suffering and effort that lofted the North Atlantic onto an entirely new trajectory, allowing it to dominate the new modern age.

But before we visit the regions of sub-Saharan Africa that supplied the greatest parts of the forced labor that made such developments possible, it is important to explore how enslaved Blacks themselves became the dominant commodity of the New World in the first place. To an extent that will surprise many readers, this is a story whose early roots lie as much in Spain's new imperial conquests as it did in the plantation economies of Portugal or England.

The first Black man to arrive in the Americas, Alonso Prieto, landed in 1493 on a Spanish vessel, as a free member of Columbus's second expedition. By 1501, the enslavement of Africans had clearly been introduced into the New World, beginning in the settlement that Columbus founded, Hispaniola. That was nearly a quarter century before the first direct shipment of slaves from the continent to the New World, via São Tomé, which did not occur until 1525.

In the sixteenth century, approximately 277,000 Africans were brought in chains across the Atlantic, with nearly 90 percent of them going to Spain's newly conquered American territories, led by Cartagena, New Spain, and Veracruz. Over its long course, this human traffic would bring an estimated 2.07 million people to the Spanish Americas, either by direct shipment across the Atlantic, or via a lively intra-American trade, trafficked onward from places like Dutch Curaçao or English Jamaica. This made the Spanish Americas the second most important zone of forced permanent African migration, after Brazil. As a region, it places well ahead of either the British or French Caribbean, and it saw vastly greater slave traffic than what, somewhat paradoxically, is the most heavily documented region of the trade by far: the English colonies that later became the United States. In no other part of the New World has the trade in Africans been so little studied, and nowhere has the historical erasure of Blacks been so shockingly complete. And yet the available evidence shows that Africans were just as indispensable to making Hispanic Latin America viable as they were in the domains of the hemisphere's other major European colonial powers.*

In the face of the Great Dying of native peoples, the Spanish quickly grasped the urgent need of a stable workforce in order to sustain their new colonies. In 1517, the Dominican friar Bartolomé de las Casas had already written to Spain to urge that the crown send Blacks to Hispaniola in order to relieve and supplement the native population, which was fast disappearing. The advocacy of Las Casas and others would lead to an abolition of the trade in Indians throughout the Spanish Americas in 1542. Even though this ban was respected only in the breach, it greatly heightened the

---

* In 1976 the African American scholar Colin A. Palmer published a pioneering work on this topic, *Slaves of the White God: Blacks in Mexico, 1570–1650*. In their important 2015 article "Atlantic History and the Slave Trade to Spanish America," the scholars of slavery Alex Borucki, David Eltis, and David Wheat observed: "Not a single monograph or even article on the slave trade to Mexico has appeared since the partial treatment in Colin Palmer's work. For countries such as Peru, Venezuela, Colombia, and Ecuador, scholars have yet to fully exploit the abundant documentary sources on the connections with Africa. And very little is known of the Africans shipped to Iberia, the Canary Islands, and the Philippines during and after the Iberian Union."

urgency for the crown to provide African labor to work its newly conquered lands.

As enslaved Africans largely sourced in Upper Guinea poured into New Spain, they were put to work to help generate production in that colony's most famous source of wealth, its silver mines. Blacks were also made to toil in two other important kinds of enterprise, however, both of which have been generally passed over in accounts of the European settling of the New World. These were the basic industries created to provide shoes, clothing, and other goods for both settlers and slaves, and Mexico's own extensive sugar plantations. By 1645, just when sugar was getting started in Barbados, the Society of Jesus, or the Jesuits, a leading producer of slave-grown sugar, boasted that it possessed two plantations in the archbishopric of Puebla with an output of 1.5 million pounds of the commodity per year.* Three years earlier, Hernán Cortés, the Spaniard who led the 1519 expedition that brought down the Aztec empire and brought most of Mexico under the rule of Castile, had contracted for 500 African slaves to work his personal sugar works near Oaxaca, which was reputedly the first such plantation in New Spain. The other large-scale form of employment of these Africans was in brutal sweatshop-style factories producing textiles and other manufactured goods. This production arose from the realization that Spain was unable to supply the colony with sufficient clothing, shoes, leather goods, and many other items of routine necessity. These early *obras*, or factories, were concentrated in urban areas, where Blacks in Mexico lived in large numbers in the sixteenth century. For example, Vázquez de Espinosa, a visitor to Mexico City in 1612, reported there were 50,000 Blacks and mulattoes living in the city, as well as 80,000 Indians and 15,000 Spaniards. By 1600, Potosí, in Bolivia, had a population nearly as large as that of London or Tokyo. By the turn of the eighteenth century, Spanish America would have half a dozen cities that were larger than the biggest cities in British Amer-

---

* During this period, the Jesuits were probably the second largest corporate owner of slaves in the Spanish Americas, after the Catholic Church itself.

ica, led by Mexico City and Guanajuato, and many of them teemed with Blacks.

Prior to the abolition of Indian enslavement, Africans had commanded as much as ten times the price as native Mexicans. This large price differential was reflected in the ways in which members of the two groups were exploited for their labor. To be sure, neither population had it easy. But as Colin A. Palmer wrote about work on sugar plantations in *Slaves of the White God*: "While most Indians had a ten-hour work day (from eight to six), Black slaves often worked from three o'clock in the morning until eleven o'clock at night, a total of twenty hours." Unlike their Indian counterparts, Black slaves were also compelled to work in regimented shifts.

Scholars have paid precious little attention to the place of Mexico in the history of sugar in the early modern era, perhaps due to the fact that mining became so dominant, and because once it did, sugar cultivation quickly declined. But these Black brigades working in shifts bore a strong resemblance to gang-style plantation teams, a regime that would not emerge on Barbados until a full century later.

As the dying-off of the native population of Mexico accelerated, colonial authorities became seized with the importance of Black labor, which, although numerically small in comparison to the Indian workforce, "provided the foundation on which the entire structure of the labor force rested." This caused them to continually plea for increased numbers of Blacks. Two decades after the abolition of Indian slavery, the *cabildo*, or administrative council, of Mexico City, wrote to the crown, "[S]ince the personal services of the Indians have been taken away suddenly . . . there is a great need for labor in the haciendas, mines, sugar refineries, ranches and other businesses in the land, and the remedy cannot justly be other than to bring large numbers of negroes to this land." Brushing away intermittent papal concerns about the proliferating commerce in African slaves, the Spanish king Charles II commissioned a report on labor in the Spanish Americas which similarly concluded that, if there were no slave trade, "the landed properties, the main wealth of which consists chiefly of negro slaves, would be lost, and America would face absolute ruin."

The wealth of the Spanish Americas in this era implicated Blacks to a much greater extent than even their roles in mining, sugar production, and early textile manufacturing would suggest. About half the gold that Spain would obtain from the New World originated in the New Kingdom of Granada, as present-day Colombia, Panama, and Venezuela were then known, and this production was also largely brought about through the bound labor of Blacks. Spain's new colonial realm in the making also benefited from strong regional synergies, just like those we have observed between England, its sugar holdings in the West Indies, and the fledgling colonies of the North American mainland. Much as it had in Bolivia for Potosí, lowland agriculture powered by Blacks in Mexico, for example, provided the foodstuffs and ordinary trade goods that made extractive industry and even daily life possible in silver-mining areas such as Zacatecas and Guanajuato.

Some historians now argue that even a much belated widening of the frame like this inadequately reflects the fundamental nature of the African contribution to the establishment of a viable Spanish realm in the New World. A little recognized fact about early Spanish America, which the public imagines was populated by conquistadores and white settlers, is that unlike the English and even French colonies that would follow in its wake, very little use was made of European voluntary or indentured servants. During the first century or more of Spanish America's existence, in many parts of the Caribbean rim, Blacks and mixed-race people, or "mulattoes," outnumbered colonial Spaniards. This includes both important outposts like Cartagena, Havana, Veracruz, and Santo Domingo, and many broad stretches of rural territory, where people of African descent, including slaves, but also free Blacks, were the mainstay of all economic activity and occupied the land. There, they lived as "surrogate colonists" in the phrase of the historian of the early modern Iberian Atlantic David Wheat, effectively validating by their presence what would have otherwise been far more tenuous or possibly even unenforceable Spanish claims to sovereignty.

In 1598, this stark reality led Cartagena's governor to write, "In this land . . . Spaniards provide no services whatsoever, especially the lower occupations which no household can do without. Those who are employed are all blacks." This reality, as Wheat writes in his *Atlantic Africa and the Spanish Caribbean*, "complicated the very notion of European colonization of the Americas."

As Wheat and others have noted, Blacks also often contributed as advance men for Spanish explorers and conquistadores and, soon afterward, for militiamen in the defense of Spanish territories against the probing of English and other interlopers. These sorts of roles date to the very start of Castile's push into the New World. In 1502, Nicolás de Ovando, the newly appointed governor of Hispaniola, brought with him from Spain a number of Blacks, both as laborers and to help police the native population. Early in the conquest and settlement of Hispaniola, Spain designated some of its slaves *negros seguros*, or "safe Blacks," and armed them in order to help mount a defense against revolt by the Taino natives, a practice that was also employed by the Portuguese in Brazil as well as subsequent European colonizers in the New World.

During his conquest of Puerto Rico, in 1508, Ponce de Léon employed armed Africans. Fielding, as he said, "many black slaves," Diego Velázquez copied these tactics three years later during his conquest of Cuba. African slaves were heavily represented in Spain's 1526 expedition to the Carolinas, to Baja California in the 1530s, and Hernando de Soto's failed bid to gain control of Florida in 1539. Blacks helped establish the first European settlement on the American mainland, in Panama. With the assistance of thirty other slaves, Nuflo de Olano, an enslaved Black conquistador, helped Vasco Núñez de Balboa build a fleet of thirty ships on the Pacific coast of Panama. And in 1534, a contingent of two hundred Africans accompanied Pedro de Alvarado to Peru, which he discovered had already been conquered by Pizarro, who also employed numerous slaves.

The Englishman Sir Francis Drake famously allied himself

with Black *cimarrones* (maroons) and French Huguenot pirates to attack Nombre de Diós on the Caribbean coast of Spanish Panama in the early 1570s, capturing £40,000 in gold, silver, and pearls. But when he attempted to invade Tierra Firme, as the isthmus was then known, a second time, in 1596, one of his officers was shot by a loyal Spanish slave named Pedro Yalonga while trying to draw drinking water. Slaves and free Blacks this time, allied with the Spanish, fought against Drake's men and helped prevent them from capturing Panama City. Later, Yalonga, using his record of service, was able to successfully petition the local government for manumission.

The names of most of the Blacks involved in episodes like these are sadly lost to history. But one more story for which we fortunately have a name, that of Juan Garrido, however, stands out. Garrido, who was born in the Kingdom of Kongo sometime in the 1470s, made his way to Portugal as a young man, although whether as a slave or not is not known. Later, he traveled to Spain, where he was formally converted to Catholicism, and in 1502 he arrived as part of a Spanish expedition to Santo Domingo. From there, Garrido, whose adopted name means "handsome," took part in the invasions of Puerto Rico and Cuba, joining the forces of Hernán Cortés during that conquistador's takeover of Mexico.

Garrido lived as a free man among whites in Mexico City, where he married and fathered three children, and he is credited with being the person who introduced the cultivation of wheat, an Old World crop, to the Americas. In his 1538 petition for recognition of merit after three decades of service to the crown, he wrote:

> I, *Juan Garrido, black in color, resident of this city [Mexico], appear before Your Mercy and state that I am in need of providing evidence to the perpetuity of the king, a report on how I served Your Majesty in the conquest and pacification of this New Spain, from the time when the Marqués del Valle [Cortés] entered it; and without being given either salary or allotment of natives or anything else. As I am married and a resident of this city, where I have always lived; and also as I went to discover and pacify*

the islands of San Juan de Buriquén de Puerto Rico and also as
went on the pacification and conquest of the island of Cuba with
the adelantado Diego Velázquez; in all these ways for thirty years
I served and continue to serve Your Majesty—for these reasons
stated above do I petition Your Mercy. And also because I was the
first to have the inspiration to sow wheat here in New Spain and
to see if it took; I did this and experimented at my own expense.

This factual story provides a much better sense of the greatly underappreciated importance of the Black presence in Latin America, and indeed its centrality to the birth of an Atlantic world.

24

THE SLAVE RUSH

WHEN WE LAST SPOKE of the activities of the Dutch in West Africa, they had just seized Elmina from Portugal in 1637 after many years of trying, and from this stronghold they quickly established a new headquarters for the Dutch West India Company, along with a thriving trade in gold. In 1642, the Dutch would go on to evict the Portuguese from their last remaining outposts along this coast, much smaller forts at places like Axim. The Dutch had begun to capture more of the region's exports in gold than the Portuguese well before then, largely because of their superior trade goods. With their larger and better fleet, they could also deliver their merchandise at lower prices to local elites eager to snatch up exotic prestige items from afar. In its neatness, however, what this story misses is a messier contest that had started long before the determined assault on Elmina by the Dutch succeeded. For more than a century, the Gold Coast had been the target of fortune seekers from many other European nations, all poaching for a share of the trade in gold whose rights Portugal had claimed ever since the Treaty of Tordesillas in 1494. In 1542, for example, a French ship was able to purchase the considerable sum of a thousand ounces of gold on the nearby coast; little more than a decade later, English ships began to show up in the waters off the Gold Coast on what were essentially hit-and-run trading missions aimed at eluding Portuguese interception.

Dutch efforts to horn in on the Elmina trade had begun in earnest in 1593 after a Dutchman made his way home from imprisonment on São Tomé, where he had gained vital information about the sources of West African gold and quickly mounted a trading expedition of his own. In 1600, the first Dutch company with an explicit mission to trade for gold in Africa was formed in Amsterdam, and almost immediately requested protection from the Estates General for its voyages. Already before 1610, the Dutch were sending an average of twenty ships a year to trade on the Gold Coast, where they were able to acquire an annual yield of about two thousand pounds of gold, a major source of stimulus during the Dutch Golden Age. By the early seventeenth century, it has been estimated that gold from the Gold Coast accounted for a tenth of the world's supply. As the Dutch began to dominate this trade, their African windfall was so large as to account for nearly all the coinage of the United Provinces, as Holland was then known. Along the coast, the Dutch traders annually offered up in exchange "200,000 yards of linen, 40,000 pounds of copper basins, kettles, and other hardware, and 100,000 pounds of beads, as well as blankets and other goods." In the early sixteenth century, the Portuguese, by contrast, still based much of their trade for gold in this region on copper *manilhas*.

This new Dutch approach would be of great economic consequence, helping strengthen modernizing industries in that country, with textiles generating far more added value than did Portugal's commerce in simpler, scarcely transformed metal goods. By the 1640s, the trade in cloth with the Gold Coast had played an important role in the dramatic growth of the Dutch textile industry, which had been in crisis for much of the sixteenth century, its production having essentially fallen to zero by 1580.

The flood of Dutch cloth into the markets of the Gold Coast would also have equally profound and lasting consequences for the local African economy and society. As the quantities of mass-produced Dutch cloth rose and prices for it correspondingly fell, local textiles were largely squeezed out of the market, leaving the Gold Coast more and more dependent on the export of raw natural resources. This had originally meant gold, a globally accepted means of exchange. But beginning in the mid-seventeenth century, African societies increasingly started to use slaves, who had already proven their worth as the basis for production of valuable commodities in the New World, as a means to finance their external trade.

In each case, in exchange for their "goods," whether gold or human beings, the trading societies of the Gold Coast entered into a situation where they were accepting items of short-lived or diminishing value against an almost universal store of value like gold, or a slave, which meant a human being with considerable productive potential. The European trade goods included cloth and utilitarian metal items, like basins used for cooking, bathing, and storage, as well as cowries. To these, the outsiders soon began adding other consumables, things like rum and tobacco from the New World and guns.* In narrow commercial terms, African chiefs were often very astute traders, capable, as we will see, of using market intelligence and driving the hardest of bargains; however, as any modern economist can see, the very nature of these exchanges would steadily and fatefully shift the terms of trade against the continent over time.

With its takeover of Elmina, Holland appropriated Lisbon's broad claims of sovereignty over the Atlantic-fronting African world. This was both a matter of gaining access to rich sources of wealth—once again meaning gold, followed quickly by slaves—and attacking Portugal where it was most vulnerable, in order to avenge Spain's war against the Low Countries. But while Portugal's commercial and diplomatic sway over this region had endured for roughly a century and a half, Holland's would face stout challenges almost from the outset, especially from a rising England. By the standards of

---

* The persistence of patterns of economic life and commerce has shown remarkable endurance across the centuries. Modern Ghana not only remains almost entirely dependent on the export of raw materials, led by gold and cocoa, but a colorful, wax-printed style of cloth popularized in Africa by the Dutch early on remains a leading import for West African countries, where it still enjoys prestige value.

the Portuguese, and even the Dutch, England had been a hesitant and ineffectual comer to the West African gold scene, whose efforts mostly involved scattershot piracy without consistent state backing for most of the sixteenth century. This was due, in part, to the fact that England had been consumed by religious turmoil after Henry VIII's conversion to Protestantism in the 1530s, and was also still relatively poor compared with its main rivals, Spain and France. The country's early imperial energies had been largely focused on imposing control over Ireland. However, during the Elizabethan period, starting in 1558, London grew increasingly preoccupied with not being left behind in the era's search by European powers for new territories, new sources of wealth, and early empire. Queen Elizabeth and the aristocracy around her became obsessed with challenging Spain's dominance of Europe and the Americas, the pursuit of fortune, and confronting Catholicism. Her policies leaned on a blend of Protestantism, a pugnacious nationalism, and piracy; so much so that where one began and the other ended became difficult to distinguish. As one historian of the period has written, "It was the participation of the [Elizabethan] gentry that transformed the petty Channel roving of the earlier years into the oceanic ventures of the seventies and eighties, fusing into one diversified movement the ambitions of plunderers and traders." At its peak, during the eighteen years starting in 1585, the English pirated an estimated one thousand Spanish and Portuguese ships.

In 1583, Queen Elizabeth's principal secretary, Sir Francis Walsingham, dispatched Richard Hakluyt, a young Oxford cleric, as ambassador to Paris to research ways that the English crown could support colonies abroad. Hakluyt would go on to become one of the most important promoters of early English empire, starting with Virginia. This followed even earlier English interest in West Africa, where the queen began supporting voyages in 1561, lending royal ships to the effort, investing her personal finances, and partaking directly in the handsome profits. Most of these voyages were commanded by privateering adventurers like John Hawkins, who reached West Africa in 1562, and, according to Hakluyt's account, "got into his possession, partly by sworde, and partly by other meanes to the number of three hundred Negroes at the least." These he would sell on Spanish Hispaniola after crossing the Atlantic. There, Hawkins "made vent of the whole number of his Negroes: for which he received . . . by way of exchange such quantitie of merchandise, that hee did not onely lade his owne 3 Shippes with hides, ginger, sugars, and some qualntitie of pearles, but freighted also two other hulkes with hides and other like commodities." The writings of Hakluyt and accounts of the adventures of people like Hawkins and Sir Walter Raleigh were also grist for much popular literature in their era, which helped sell the idea of exploration, seafaring, conquest, emigration and settler colonialism to the broad public.

When the Company of Adventurers of London was chartered in England in 1631, it was inspired in large part out of a desire to compete with the increasingly prosperous Dutch, whose own chartered corporation, the Dutch West India Company, had already been up and running for a decade. But despite being granted a "monopoly" on trade with Africa between Cape Blanc and the Cape of Good Hope for a period of thirty years, the Company of Adventurers initially returned little gold compared with its Dutch competitors, eventually drawing criticism in Parliament for failing to locate the actual sources of the metal, which the English apparently hoped to seize control of.

In the 1660s, this initial English company was succeeded by the Company of Royal Adventurers into Africa, which was mentioned briefly in Part 3. The Company of Adventurers was optimistically granted a monopoly on England's Africa trade for a period of one thousand years, but its business was seriously perturbed by the Second Anglo-Dutch War of 1664–1665, and in 1672 it was succeeded by yet another entity with a similar charter, the Royal African Company. As it happens, the mid-seventeenth century was the precise moment of takeoff of the sugar plantation-complex in Barbados, which created a ferocious appetite in the English Caribbean for African slaves. In the first half of the century, 34,725 Africans were embarked on slave ships for sale in the English Caribbean, with

95 percent of them destined for Barbados. In that century's second half, more than ten times as many slaves took the same trip, with 55 percent of them going to Barbados. Early on, demand on the island was so high, in fact, that in 1698 the thousand-year monopoly of the Royal African Company was rescinded, and trade in slaves for the New World was opened to all comers—provided they pay a 10 percent tax intended to help cover England's costs in maintaining and defending its forts and trading posts in West Africa. A few years later, with demand and profits from the slave trade both still rising, in tandem with the booming Caribbean sugar industry, even this fee was dropped and the trade in slaves essentially became unrestricted at the twinned insistence of the West India Interest and a vigorous free trade lobby back in England. Driven by similar motives, France did much the same in 1701, eliminating the monopoly of slave trading enjoyed by its Guinea Company (and then by its successor, the Indies Company), in return for payment of a levy for each African sold by private traders.

The seventeenth century was a time of fevered jockeying among European states to build and operate trading forts along the coast of what is now modern-day Ghana; even nations that few today remember as having much history of involvement in West Africa got involved, including the Danish and the Brandenburg Prussians. The most important of these forts was the Cape Coast Castle, built by Sweden in 1653. It was seized by the English in 1664 and subsequently greatly expanded and fortified. That it sits at a distance of only seven miles from Elmina, which by that time had been held and operated at extraordinary profit by the Dutch for twenty-seven years, speaks clearly to England's desire to usurp Holland's dominant position in this region's trade. And the mid-seventeenth century saw persistent confrontation between these two powers in these parts. So much so that the tensions generated by their contest over the slaves and gold contributed to the outbreak of the Second Anglo-Dutch War of 1664–1665.

Somewhat less obviously, the English choice of Cape Coast as a rival site to Elmina was also a reflection of the strength of the African players along the coast relative to the Europeans. The political landscape on the coast was composed of petty kingdoms and chieftaincies, diminutive both in terms of population and territory, with few exceeding 1500 square kilometers, or 580 square miles. Often, they counted as few as three thousand to five thousand inhabitants. Despite their modest sizes, though, these African polities proved stubbornly unwilling to cede parcels of the seaboard to European powers so eager to trade on the coast, and they had the means to deny them. This was because any European advantage in technology in that day—i.e., guns and cannons—remained more apparent than real. The firing rate of their balky and inaccurate front-loaded muskets, in particular, was far too slow to halt a determined African onslaught, and Gold Coast armies often proved quite formidable.

Beyond questions of armaments and battle tactics, coastal kingdoms also deliberately constrained the outsiders to operating within close proximity of one another, reflecting an understanding that the skirmishing among the Europeans helped keep them in check. The historian David Eltis has observed, "Europeans would build forts only with the permission of the African ruler and even then, only if they had some assurance of preferential treatment from the African authorities in gaining access to gold or slaves. But promises of such treatment rarely meant much in practice." African agency was further enhanced by an active system of commercial intelligence practiced by indigenous groups along the coast, which often passed along information about exactly what sorts of goods arriving European ships were carrying and what prices they were seeking for their wares. This allowed locals to further pit Europeans against each other and to bargain from strength.

For the Dutch, gold, which it used to finance war against Spain, remained the primary motivation of trade on the Gold Coast. To be sure, slaves were also bought locally and shipped from Elmina, where they were sent to labor on the plantations that Holland had newly seized from Portugal (then conjoined in union with Spain) in northeastern Brazil in 1630 and would hold until 1654. For England, however, this equation was roughly reversed in the second half of the seventeenth century. The English, of course, by no means spurned gold, avidly trading for it whenever it could be bought. So much so, in fact, that between 1674 and 1714, the Royal African Company would mint 548,327 "guinea" coins using gold almost entirely drawn from these parts. Notwithstanding this boon, by 1660, England had become the clear volume leader in the North Atlantic slave trade, a position it would not relinquish until it abolished the trade in 1807.*

This, in fact, was the moment when the Gold Coast went from being predominantly prized as a gold mine to being regarded above all as a slave mine, whose Black labor had become highly prized in Jamaica and other parts of the English Caribbean. Between 1660 and 1713, an era of overall rapid growth in the trade in captive Africans, England far outstripped their Dutch rivals. England shipped an estimated 560,000 captives from Africa to the New World, compared with Holland's 205,000. This takeoff was particularly acute during what has been called the Slave Rush, the thirteen years between 1700 and 1713, when Gold Coast departures soared to quadruple the levels seen during the previous four decades, reaching 119,552 captives. England's headlong rush into slaving brought about a sharp and permanent vocational shift for the structures Europeans had been building along this stretch of coast, starting with Elmina. Gone were the fortified *comptoirs*, or outposts designed for a trade in gold. Henceforth, it would be the purpose-built slave dungeons that are now famous. And this was but one in a set of tightly interlocked milestones.

By 1700, the value of England's plantation-complex production—led by sugar, but also including rum, tobacco, ginger, indigo, and cotton—matched that of the rest of the European-controlled New World's production in all goods combined. By roughly this same time, historians also reckon that the value of trade in Africans had also surpassed the value of the trade in gold.

---

* British volume would not surpass the overall leader, Portugal, until the quarter century beginning 1726.

25

BARGAINS SHARP AND SINFUL

I F IT IS EASY TO UNDERSTAND, in practical terms, why a number of European nations threw themselves with growing abandon into the Scramble for Africans in the seventeenth century, coming to terms with the moral and ethical decisions involved must forever make people with human feelings uneasy. Standing alongside this most agonizing problem of Western civilization stands another troubling puzzle: Why did Africans so readily give themselves to a trade that at least from the standpoint of historical hindsight seems so clearly detrimental to the very regions where the slave trade was most intense or prolonged, as well as to the continent overall?

Although the details of the trade in humans varied significantly from region to region, some of the fundamentals involved in this puzzle are consistent. First among these was a prior and often long-lasting history of domestic or internal slavery in the affected African societies themselves. As was common in pre-modern times in societies across the world, slaves were seized in war in Africa from defeated rivals and treated as political prizes. The practice of capturing or purchasing slaves in order to put them to work for explicitly economic purposes has also been widely observed. This was the case in the sixteenth century both in imperial Songhai and in Kongo, for example, where slaves labored on large agricultural estates owned by the royal family and associated elites. It was the case as well on the Gold Coast, where slaves were used as porters along long-distance trade routes, hauling gold and ivory to the coast and imported goods inland. As we have seen, the prevalence of the tsetse fly in coastal West Africa, and the deadly trypanosome parasite it carried, deprived the denizens of this region of beasts of burden for portage.

As Europeans converged on the Gold Coast in search of the metal that gave the area its name, external demand for gold began to exceed the supply, which peaked no later than 1680 and then gradually declined. But by the time this change in export trend lines had occurred, local elites, the *abirempon,* had already long exhibited well-developed tastes for foreign fineries. These were the bases of both their wealth in trade and of much of their social standing.

As they strove to sustain their supplies of foreign cloths, Venetian beads and fine porcelain, silk, sundry manufactured goods, and guns in increasingly high volumes, Africans living along the coast had also gradually come to understand that what the Europeans prized most was Black bodies. And for the most part, as long as these captives came from rival neighboring states, leaders of the balkanized societies along the coast felt little moral compunction about selling them.

To understand this, it is important to consider that in an era when few Africans had yet made return voyages to Europe, and almost none had any picture of the purposes to which Africans were being put in the New World, little synthetic or unified sense of African identity existed. Because of this, there is no reason to assume any common sense of intra-African solidarity, certainly nothing akin to the shared identity that Africans and members of the African diaspora widely celebrate today.* On the Gold Coast, like in Upper Guinea, an organized slave trade that predated the transatlantic market had long-standing connections to Sudanic Africa and

---

* Much the same was true of members of Native American societies in their early encounters with Europeans.

to human traffic across the Sahara. But as we will see shortly, even in Central Africa, with its much more tenuous links to intercontinental and long-distance trade, preexisting practices of slavery and of the forms of commerce associated with it meant that when European demand strongly manifested itself in the sixteenth century, local markets quickly responded.

⌗

A NUMBER OF COMPETING INSIGHTS have been advanced to explain the prevalence of slavery in African societies, and the debate remains far from resolved. One view has long held that the pre-modern continent's very low population densities combined with its vast amounts of land made it hard for rulers to assemble large polities with strong central authority. This also notably hindered the collection of regular, appreciable taxation. How many people were under any ruler's command was a key traditional marker of monarchical wealth and power in Africa's human landscape. But under these circumstances, even put-upon or disgruntled members of an extended clan network could often simply opt to move away and reestablish themselves elsewhere. This made it difficult for rulers to exercise repressive measures over extended spaces to enforce their authority. Instead, they often sought ways to incorporate outsiders, including slaves, into their societies. Quick assimilation, therefore, became a common political strategy in much of West Africa. In practice, this often meant raiding for slaves from nearby societies, but then allowing full entry into their new culture via marriage, concubinage, or the equivalent of naturalization of children.

Another body of scholarship has long argued that it was the lack of a concept of private land ownership, or at least the common practice of it, in many African societies, that encouraged the trade in humans. People themselves thus became one of the most important forms of capital, both living and fungible. We have already seen how slaves were used as capital in trade with Europeans, a pattern whose spread may have been eased by preexistent notions of people as capital. The historian John Thornton writes:

Slavery was widespread in Atlantic Africa because slaves were the only form of private, revenue-producing property recognized in African law. By contrast, in European legal systems, land was the primary form of private, revenue-producing property, and slavery was relatively minor. Indeed, ownership of land was usually a precondition in Europe to making productive use of slaves, at least in agriculture. . . . Thus, it was the absence of landed private property—or, to be more precise, it was the corporate ownership of land—that made slavery so pervasive an aspect of African society.

Of course, deep-seated European notions that gave primacy to land-based wealth did nothing to prevent the European plantation societies in the New World from treating African slaves as fungible capital items themselves.

The documentary record of the details of slave practices and especially of slave trade volumes is unfortunately scant for the era preceding the arrival of the Portuguese and other Europeans for much of the African continent. Because of the intensity of European interest in the Gold Coast, however, a great deal is known about the commercial and political interactions between local elites and the outsiders. In order to build their fortified structures along the seafront and generate sufficient volumes of trade to justify their efforts, the Europeans were sucked into increasingly heated competition among themselves. This took the form of paying frequent fees for the rights to establish or operate their commercial outposts as well as offering what were called "dashes," a steady stream of putative gifts aimed at securing the elusive commercial loyalty of local leaders in a highly fragmented political environment. But this was not the end of the Europeans' troubles. Even after trade had been established, Europeans were faced with a scene of unremitting commercial competition among themselves, as African elites, logically enough, sought to maximize their own benefits from the trade.

During the peak era of the gold trade, as much as two-thirds of all the merchandise that European nations sold in Africa was traded along the 300-kilometer-long seaboard of the Gold Coast. This included no less than 85 percent of all the textiles shipped by the Royal African Company to West Africa. Demand for foreign goods was so stout that no single European power could remotely satisfy it entirely through its own production. As the historian David Eltis has observed, "As late as the 1680s—and into the nineteenth century for some items—the English obtained iron bars, spirits, a wide range of textiles, and hardware that they traded in Africa and the Americas from foreign suppliers, not from their own manufacturers." On the Gold Coast, to cite just one example, the European cloths in greatest demand were linen items known as *sletias*, which was a local corruption of Silesia, their source. The booming foci of the slave business along this stretch of the seaboard, in other words, had become important stimuli for circuits of exchange within Europe. This represented a deepening of a process we first saw with Portugal and its Africa trade beginning in the fifteenth century, where ties with the continent helped propel European integration. In the case of the Royal African Company, about one-half of the merchandise it traded with African societies in the pursuit of slaves before 1698 consisted of foreign goods, mostly sourced in Europe.

European visitors to the Gold Coast in the early 1600s were struck by the great cultural and linguistic diversity of the area. In 1623, Dierick Ruyters, a veteran Dutch trader in West Africa, remarked that every five or six miles one encountered a group that spoke a different language and had different customs. Well before the decline in the gold trade, Europeans, driven by a desire to minimize costs and maximize profits, had begun to seek ways to forge more lasting and exclusive alliances with polities on the Gold Coast—alliances that they must have realized would spur intra-African conflict. In 1612, for example, the Dutch received a Gold Coast delegation from the king of Asebu to discuss acquiring Dutch help against the Portuguese, and this was soon followed by the construction of a fort in Asebu by the Dutch Estates General.

In fact, as early as the first decades of the seventeenth century, some spoke openly of this divide-and-rule strategy and regarded the growth of a robust slave trade as a sort of dream outcome. A Portuguese trader wrote candidly, for example, that "there will soon be more war among them and that will make them have to trade more gold to finance their wars." It was only a small step from a thought like this to the notion that stoking violence among local populations would greatly boost the trade in slaves and, as many other accounts from the era show, that step was soon breached. The historian Toby Green observed, "The European factors along the coast noted that wars 'made gold scarce but negroes plenty,' and to encourage a continuous flow of slaves the sale of firearms was stepped up."

Following England's lead, the eighteenth century saw an explosion in the Europe gun business in slave-trading areas. Guns helped advance the outsiders' growing imperial objectives and were a lucrative source of profit. The gun trade, fueled in part by the trade in slaves, had at least one other notable effect. Just as Holland's ramping up of textile production and quality in response to demand on the Gold Coast had done wonders for that country's industry, the booming gun trade helped lay the foundation for English metallurgy, and subsequently for industrialization itself.

As the English and others sought ways to intensify the slave trade in West and Central Africa, guns came to be used (much as cloth had before it) as a form of money, or currency directly employed in commercial transactions. They also became used as a means of credit, with Europeans making firearms available to protagonists in African conflicts with the understanding that eventual payment would be provided in the form of slaves captured. Europeans had once been reluctant to sell guns to Africans, naturally enough fearing that they could be turned against them. Strategies for mitigating such a risk were not long in coming, though. The English and others took to selling low-quality or used or cosmetically refurbished firearms in African markets, guns of dubious reliability whose average life span may not have even exceeded one year. Not only did this limit their offensive potential for challenging outsiders in Africa, but as the historian of firearms Priya Satia has observed, "the enormous volume of the trade was driven partly by the need for frequent replacement."

Sure enough, here and there Africans began incorporating the use of European guns in their military tactics. In addition, they frequently traded for them by offering up slaves they had captured in localized conflicts, something seen as early as the latter fifteenth century in the Kingdom of Kongo, whose history lies just ahead. There are plentiful reasons to believe, meanwhile, that many Africans understood the chicanery involved in the high-volume sales of tricked-up goods, and were not overawed by European firearms technology until the emergence of more reliable, higher-power, and especially automatic weapons in the nineteenth century. In other words, many African societies continued to favor the use of swords, lances, and spears, along with the bow and arrow. And this they did quite rationally, even when guns were readily available for purchase or being employed by adversaries.

26

THE SPREAD OF THE WEST AFRICAN SLAVE TRADE

T O SPEAK MEANINGFULLY ABOUT the political development of Africa in the era when the American slave trade was intensifying one must take care in making generalizations. While the seaboard of the Gold Coast was made up of endlessly contending micro-states who waged short, often intense wars between themselves over everything from marriage alliances to trading rights with the Europeans, in the interior of what is now modern-day Ghana, the mid-seventeenth century saw the rise of one of Africa's most important empires, the Asante. This polity, made up of speakers of the Akan language from central Ghana, predated the Atlantic slave trade but had been a vassal of another local empire, the Denkyira. By uniting its clans and building other alliances, the Asante centralized under a king named Osei Tutu. A powerful and capable ruler, he went on to string together an impressive series of military victories against their previous overlords, the Denkyira, and then against almost every other group he fought against in the subregion. As a result of these victories, the Asante controlled virtually the entire gold trade in the Gold Coast by the 1750s and positioned themselves to play a dominant role in the slave trade as well.

The name Asante means "because of war," and over the first half of the eighteenth century, the victories this kingdom stitched together a territory roughly congruent with modern Ghana. During the nineteenth century the Asante waged a series of closely fought wars against Britain, too, as London pursued empire throughout Africa. The Asante were avid purchasers of European weaponry but also seem to have grasped the self-destructive economic paradox upon which much European-African trade was based: trading gold and human beings for cloth and other goods whose exchange value was certain to decline with usage. In their bid to escape a pattern of diminishing terms of exchange, during the global glut brought on by the discovery of vast amounts of gold in Brazil beginning in the 1690s, the Asante began hoarding their metal and eventually actually became net importers of gold. This, they saw as a means of steeling themselves against external challenges posed by the Europeans. What they never managed, however, was to lastingly sever the trade in slaves.

卐

THE SEABOARD TO THE EAST of the Gold Coast did not immediately attract great attention from Europeans seeking slaves to feed markets in the New World. There is considerable irony in this, in that by the late seventeenth century the region that runs from the Volta River in the west to the lagoon system of Lagos, in modern Nigeria, would come to be known as the Slave Coast, and living up to this label, it would eventually become one of the most prolific sources of New World slaves. The lukewarm initial interest in this region was partly due to its lack of natural harbors and the thunderous surf that crashes dangerously onto long stretches of its beaches. Until other means were devised, this meant that only small boats could safely approach the shore, limiting the ability to carry off slaves or trade in other goods. Another reason, perhaps equally important, was that the early demand of the Atlantic trade for slaves to be worked in São Tomé, in Iberia, and in Brazil and in the Spanish Americas, while it was still modest, could be readily met from existing sources.

This picture changed, however, as a result of important developments on both sides of the Atlantic. First, Benin, the large and sophisticated kingdom situated well to the east of the Gold Coast that had once been a promising source of slaves, decided to stop selling people into the European slave trade. Then, and more important, in 1630, the Dutch occupied Brazil's Pernambuco. Until that point the Dutch had displayed a near indifference toward the slave trade, shipping slaves in only eight of the 136 years between 1500 and 1636. But now, with an urgent need to supply labor for its new plantation holdings in the New World and thereby make its Great Design pay off, it threw itself into the traffic with gusto. Over the next hundred years, they shipped 326,757 slaves, or nearly 82,000 every quarter century. The Dutch held Pernambuco only until 1654 (and São Tomé from 1641 to 1648), but over time they would switch vocations from trying to be New World colonizers of the first rank to becoming profitable middlemen, eagerly purveying African captives to the French and English sugar islands of the West Indies, and then, from 1662, when they were granted an *asiento*, an imperial license, to their former enemies the Spanish as well.

With competition already stiff among Europeans on the Gold Coast, the outsiders then stepped up their prospecting efforts immediately to the east, turning trade in the region into a free-for-all. In the space of a few decades, beginning at the start of the eighteenth century, the Slave Coast rapidly went from new entrant to nearly dominant in this trade. The commerce in slaves in this region was driven not by tiny statelets, but by a series of powerful kingdoms. The first of these to make its mark was Allada, or Ardra, which was then followed and then joined in rivalry by a nearby coastal state, Whydah, before the two of them were eclipsed by a larger and even more successful kingdom based in the interior named Dahomey.

In the early 1990s, while I was living in Miami and covering the Caribbean for *The New York Times*, I flew with my family to West Africa, driving the 560 miles from Abidjan, Côte d'Ivoire, to Abomey, ancient Dahomey's capital, in the central region of the country known today as Benin. There, we visited a high adobe-walled imperial compound that was part of what was once one of the largest structures in all of West Africa. Only two of what had been twelve royal palatial wings, each built by a successive dynast, remained intact, however, because Dahomey's last autonomous ruler, a man named Béhazin, had ordered the complex destroyed to avoid its falling into the hands of advancing French armies.

After passing through an arched, clay entranceway, we toured temples and scrupulously whitewashed buildings along with a guide who lectured us about the kingdom's prolific martial history. Before each battle, he told us that the Dahomeans washed their weapons in the blood of their enemies; following each conquest, forty captives were ritually sacrificed, their blood mixed with palm oil and alcohol and poured into the earth to nourish the ancestors. In a letter sent in 1724 to the king of England as it set about conquering the smaller coastal kingdoms, Dahomey's monarch, a man named Agaja, said of himself, "I am gret admirer of fire armes, and have almost intirle left of the use of bows and arrows." In the same missive he claimed to have conquered no less than 209 "countries."

Even before the ascension of Dahomey, the rulers of Allada had given impressive demonstration of the martial and governance capabilities of the states that emerged in this area as the slave trade ramped up there in the late seventeenth century. This included confining the European powers to much more limited, and one might even say submissive, roles than they had enjoyed on the Gold Coast, something clearly due to their reading of the situation in those adjacent societies just to the west. As the historian Robin Law explains, "In 1670, when the French requested permission to construct their factory at Offra in the European fashion (presumably in brick or stone, rather than mud), the king of Allada refused, on the grounds that they might install cannon and turn it into a fortress which would make them masters of his kingdom as, he said, the Dutch had already done at Elmina on the Gold Coast." In Whydah, Europeans were squeezed even further, forced to respect the local religion—and the principal national cult, in particular, that of a python deity named Dangbe—or face the penalty of death. Law continues: "A French visitor called Du Casse in 1688 went further, and sought to ingratiate himself with the Whydah authorities by accompanying King Agbangla in the annual procession to the principal shrine of Dangbe, dressed in a leopard's skin." This act no doubt scandalized other Europeans resident in the kingdom but such abject currying of favor had surely been deemed worth it if it could secure better terms in one of Africa's most prolific slave markets. In a battle with Wydhah, four decades later, in 1727, Dahomey's armies captured about forty whites of various nationalities who had come to the coast in pursuit of slaves, including the governor of the British Royal African Company, marching them inland. There, in an audience with them, King Agaja told the whites "he was very sorry for what had happen'd, for he had given Orders to his Captains . . . to use the white Men well; but he hoped they would excuse what had befallen them, which was to be attributed to the Fate of War."

Stories like these help illustrate how much agency African rulers and elites sometimes came to exercise. They were sovereigns and not passive vessels. Very little in the traffic of captives to the Americas was generated by European slave hunters themselves, or by direct European military campaigns or even direct armed pressure on African kingdoms. Some historians, in fact, have estimated that at its peak, late in the 1720s, Agaja's professional army might have been one of the most formidable in the world. In any event, Europeans would have enjoyed nothing like overwhelming power or even a preponderance of force in most parts of the continent, such as they quickly came to enjoy in most of the New World until the nineteenth century, when the slave trade peaked and was then abolished. Modern repeating weapons were a major contributor to this belated military superiority, but considerable responsibility for this change in the balance of power was due to something far less obvious: the Europeans' development of a better understanding of the principles of disease and hygiene in the nineteenth century, without which whites suffered withering mortality rates.

If elite buy-in and in many cases even enthusiasm was necessary for the operation of a human traffic on this scale for such a long run of centuries, from the slave trade's modest beginnings in the 1400s to its sputtering end four hundred some years later, one must be careful not to construe the motives of African rulers like Dahomey's Agaja too narrowly. The trade in foreign goods that mostly consisted of prestige items, which few in the general population of these kingdoms ever saw or enjoyed, was a determinant of the willingness to sell fellow Africans into bonded shipment overseas, something that we know that some rulers intuited was economically and even politically harmful in the long run. But it was not the only factor. As the slave trade intensified greatly in the eighteenth century, it set into motion forces of heightened chaos and political destruction in West Africa that became almost impossible for most polities to escape. Under these circumstances, selling members of rival identity groups or defeated and captured enemies into the trade took on an element of rational, if to us nonetheless highly regrettable, statecraft. Often, short-term survival simply demanded it.

One sees the outlines of just such a situation in the history of Dahomey. Its precise motives in attacking the smaller slaving coastal kingdoms of Allada and Whydah may never be fully understood, but some historians have theorized that it took the offensive against its neighbors because their aggressive pursuit of slaves for sale to avid European buyers had become deeply destabilizing in the hinterland, Dahomey's own base of power. As Dahomey began to prevail over its smaller rivals, it, too, clearly participated in the slave trade, quickly becoming a major seller of captives. In fact, between 1720 and 1725, an estimated 400,000 Africans were shipped into bondage from the Slave Coast, more than any other region of the continent. Another prominent school of thought posits that Dahomey was motivated, in good measure, by a need to protect itself against another inland empire, the Oyo of present-day Nigeria, whose powerful, cavalry-based military—a new tactical development in the region—was advancing on it from the northeast. Seen in this light, the lucrative sale of slaves into the American trade, which was increasingly necessary to finance armament, can be understood as being as much about statecraft as it was about the greedy pursuit of luxury goods and commercial profits.

To this point, told of a rising tide of abolitionist sentiment in the north, the then ruler of Dahomey, King Agongolo is said to have replied to a European interlocutor, "You, Englishmen . . . I have been informed, are surrounded by the ocean, and, by this situation, seem intended to hold communication with the whole world, which you do by means of your ships; while we Dahomans, being placed on a large continent, and hemmed in amidst a variety of other people, of the same complexion, but speaking different languages, are obliged by the sharpness of our swords, to defend ourselves from their incursions, and punish the depredations they make on us. Such conduct is productive of incessant wars. Your countrymen, therefore, who allege that we go to war for the purpose of supplying your ships with slaves, are grossly mistaken. . . . In the name of my ancestors and myself I aver, that no Dahoman man ever embarked in war merely for the sake of procuring wherewithal to purchase your commodities."*

* The historian John Thornton has called into question the authenticity of this quote, which was reported by a slave trader and seems to defend the trade, but he adds, "Yet it is quite in character of the spirit of Dahomean discourse and the actual situation of the kingdom."

27

THE WAGES OF RESISTANCE

TWO MORE STOPS LIE ahead for us on this excursion eastward along the coast of western Africa, as we follow the Portuguese path of discovery during their historic navigational breakthroughs in the fifteenth century, and the spreading tentacles of the Atlantic slave trade. In retracing this route, our priority has been to convey the complexity and localized variety in patterns and practices in the commerce in human beings between Europeans and Africans, before turning our attention to its devastating consequences.

Like the other places we have spoken about in detail, the Bight of Biafra also became a high-volume source of slaves, and yet with characteristics that set it apart from the Slave and Gold Coasts. Some readers will recall Biafra from the name of the secessionist war from Nigeria in the late 1960s, one of the most terrible conflicts the continent saw in that era. This region, which stretches eastward from the Niger River delta in modern Nigeria to the thick forests of Gabon, situated to the south along the continent's long torso, would become one of the three leading sources of slaves sent across the Atlantic, accounting for roughly 1.6 million people in the three hundred years after 1550. The numbers of captives it generated would be especially high in the second half of the eighteenth century.

The Bight of Biafra merits close examination in part because it lacked a deep history of powerful state formation and of empire and yet still proved capable of generating large numbers of slaves into the Atlantic market. This was achieved in good measure as a result of warfare between a confederation known as the Aro and a proliferation of smaller groups in a politically fragmented landscape. This region delivered its initial burst of slaves to the European market in the 1640s, probably as a result of localized war, before slowing in the latter decades of that century. The trade then picked up dramatically in the 1740s as the Aro expanded throughout the ethnically Igbo hinterland, to the west and northwest. In doing so it created some of the busiest slave markets on the continent—places with surviving names like Bonny, New Calabar, and Old Calabar, all in southeast Nigeria.

The Bight of Biafra was remarkable for other reasons beyond its political makeup. Unlike the Slave Coast and the Gold Coast, at no time did Europeans attempt to establish forts or even permanent trading bases in this region. The region also supplied large numbers of captives into the trade despite the strongly negative views that European slavers unfairly held of its people, as explained below. This must be read as a reflection of the exploding demand in the Americas for bonded Africans in the eighteenth century. Finally, in a business that placed a big premium on males, this region also stood out for the unusually high ratio of female slaves it sold. As it packed off more and more women to the West Indies and Virginia, it surpassed the Gold Coast in volume and nearly approached the levels of exports of the Slave Coast.

Negative attitudes toward Biafra and its people were conditioned firstly by the very high mortality rates associated with the region, which applied both to the Europeans who came to these parts to buy slaves and to the people they purchased.* The latter died at a

---

* Virginia and Maryland became an important exception to these attitudes. According to the historian Michael A. Gomez, Igbos accounted "for nearly one-quarter of the total number of Africans imported into North America, placing [them] in a virtual first-place tie with West Central Africa[ns]." This heavy representation for people from this region of West Africa in

rate of over 18 percent, compared with the 10.8 percent who died after delivery to ship for Africa as a whole. Among traders and plantation owners, crudely racist stereotypes were developed about the purported ethnic characteristics of the residents of every region that produced large numbers of slaves. Bight of Biafra slaves were referred to disdainfully in Barbados in the seventeenth century as "supernumerary Negroes," which meant surplus, or bottom of the barrel. Whites who came to the area to traffic in humans attributed the high mortality rates, both for themselves and for the Africans in Biafra, to the supposed prevalence of bad air there, as well as to longer transit times to New World markets, which led to higher death rates for both ship crews and the slaves they trafficked. There was another factor involved, however, and that is rates of suicide that were unusually high by the standards of the trade.

The market prejudice that slavers and plantation owners sustained against Igbos, whether in the slave markets of the Biafran coast or those of the New World, held that they were short in height and as one account put it, "small, slender, weak, and tended towards a yellowish color." This counted against them at a time when Blackness in slaves was conventionally deemed a sign of strength and hardiness. Reflecting a strongly prevailing view, another account had it that Igbos were "suicidally despondent," especially Igbo men, who were reputed for refusing food aboard slave ships. Igbo females, meanwhile, were said to be unusually prone to running away, whether singly or in groups. One of our earliest surviving accounts of the reputed penchant for suicide comes from an Igbo captive himself, Olaudah Equiano, author of what is probably the best known of the written narratives left by former slaves. Equiano first describes his transit overland after being kidnapped in his home village in the mid-1750s at the age of eleven, traveling through territories inhabited by a diversity of "nations and people" in what is now southeast-

---

what became the United States was due to the receptivity shown toward Igbo slaves in the tobacco-growing Chesapeake region. It is worth recalling that the United States absorbed well under 4 percent of the overall population of slaves brought to the New World.

ern Nigeria. Then, shortly after being embarked upon a slave ship bound for Barbados, he wrote:

> One day, when we had a smooth sea and moderate wind, two of my wearied countrymen who were chained together (I was near them at the time), preferring death to such a life of misery, somehow made through the nettings and jumped into the sea: immediately another quite dejected fellow, who, on account of his illness was suffered to be out of irons, also followed their example, and I believe many more would very soon have done the same if they had not been prevented by the ship's crew, who were instantly alarmed.

Igbo slaves who disappeared, whether via suicide or escape, are thought to have contributed to a widespread belief in the New World in the idea that some slaves were able to magically fly back to Africa. In his classic book, *Exchanging Our Country Marks: The Transformation of African Identities in the Colonial and Antebellum South*, the historian Michael A. Gomez interprets these behaviors in connection with a deep Igbo religious belief in reincarnation. This, in turn, fueled a gruesome form of state terrorism, common from Barbados and Haiti to Louisiana, of decapitating recalcitrant slaves in order to disabuse the community of slaves from which they came of the idea of a return intact to their place of origin after death.

A discussion of high suicide rates among captives traded in the Bight of Biafra is important to a much larger point: understanding the broader impact of African resistance on the overall volume of the American slave trade. Europeans purchased Biafrans in vast numbers in the face of a deep and pervasive prejudice against them, and despite the high ratio of females to male. In the eighteenth century, when the sugar plantation boom was at its most intense, this was demonstration, as G. Ugo Nwokeji, a historian of the slave trade and early modern Africa, wrote, of "an ever-increasing need [that] left planters with no choice but to take captives from wherever they could be found." It may be tempting for some to see suicide as an act of surrender, or as mere self-destruction. Upon closer examination, though, it becomes clear that this worked as a vital form of defiant refusal. The reputation for high losses from suicide among captives from the Bight of Biafra was as discouraging to traffickers in its own way as was the equally pervasive reputation of slaves from the Senegambia region for revolt and rebellion, both on land and at sea.

Whether one speaks of suicide or rebellion, reputations like these force us to consider a counterfactual. Beneath the level of the local elites who profited from it, we must assume African resistance to enslavement to have been near universal, albeit taking different forms and exhibiting varying intensity from place to place. What course, then, would the American slave trade have taken without suicide, revolt, or other resistance? A leading historian of slavery, David Eltis, for one, has proposed an answer:

> Between 1700 and 1800, 5.5 million Africans were carried off from Africa. In the absence of resistance this figure would have been 9 percent greater. Thus, in the eighteenth century alone, resistance ensured that half a million Africans avoided the plantations of the Americas (and European consumers were forced to pay higher prices for plantation produce). In effect, Africans who died resisting the slave traders, as well as those who resisted unsuccessfully but survived to work on the plantations of the Americas, saved others from the middle passage.

Elsewhere in his writings, Eltis makes the additional point that beyond individual acts of rebellion and revolt, the slave trade was always strongly mediated by relations between European powers and their traders and African rulers and elites. All parties, at every instant, felt compelled to weigh a complex set of factors. These included the relative strength of the two sides on the ground, the prices offered for slaves, the quality and nature of the European trade goods available for exchange, and the needs of the African leaders themselves, in terms of local security, human resources, and strategic considerations vis-à-vis regional and extra-regional powers. On top of all of this, European traders usually had to curry favor with local African rulers in order to preserve their access to the market in slaves. The complexity of these interactions shines through powerfully in an anecdote recounted by the historian Christopher Brown.

In 1777 Captain Benjamin Hughes of Liverpool sold into slavery two freemen he had hired at Annamaboe [Gold Coast] to assist in navigating his ship to the West Indies. Several years earlier, the prince of Badagry on the Slave Coast had responded to a similar stunt by Captain James Johnson also of Liverpool by taking nine British hostages from a later ship in retaliation. To head off a similar conflict, the Company of Merchants Trading to Africa went to unusual lengths to assuage the injured parties at Annamaboe. First, they arranged passage to Jamaica for a kinsman, Cofee Aboan, so he could identify the surviving captive, Quamino Amissah. The committee then brought Aboan and Amissah back to England and, on Amissah's behalf, filed a suit against Captain Hughes. Considerable effort was made to return Amissah home in good health. Damages recovered in the suit were sent forward to Annamaboe in the hope of making restitution. Throughout the ordeal, the committee of merchants made a point of alerting Amissah's "Friends and Relations" to "the Pains the Committee have taken to see Justice done to him." The reason for these pains, they made explicit: "His safe Arrival in Africa, is of great importance to the trade of this Country."

28

SEIZED BY THE SPIRIT

I N 1995, AS A CORRESPONDENT for *The New York Times* I boarded a small propeller aircraft out of a country then known as Zaïre, to visit its smaller neighbor the Republic of the Congo. As reporters say, this was a breather of sorts, albeit an unusual one. During the preceding months, with little exaggeration, international media had taken to characterizing the devastating fighting under way in Zaïre, which I covered, as Africa's first world war. This was on the strength of the fact that neighbors had piled into Zaïre's civil war from every direction, supporting one side or another, as had Ukrainian mercenaries and other powerful patrons in both Europe and the United States.

My objective in heading to the Congo, though, was to find one of Africa's greatest writers, a novelist named Sony Labou Tansi. At that moment, in the era before effective treatments became available, it was said that he was dying of AIDS. Despite my sense of urgency, my search for him turned into a bit of a goose chase. I found the author's house in the capital, Brazzaville, easily enough, only to be told that he had repaired to a remote village in order to pursue traditional treatments after doctors in France told him they were powerless to save him. I found the village after driving for several hours and being ferried across a river in a narrow, precariously balanced dugout canoe. Safely on the other bank, it took me only a few minutes to confirm that no one there even knew who Tansi was. Having come this far, I was reluctant to give up, and drove back to the capital, where I was lucky to track down the novelist's son, who after a bit of coaxing agreed to accompany me to another village, where he assured me that both his father and mother were now living. Fortunately, the day had begun early, because this required another rough four-hour drive.

Arriving as far as a sandy path through a thick rain forest would take us, we climbed out of our jeep to hike the final leg of this journey. We knew we were drawing close when we saw wisps of smoke rising over a hilltop, and then heard the sound of drumming. Reaching a clearing, I inquired about Tansi to the first person we met, who immediately pointed into the near distance. There, the author was already striding in our direction, an enigmatic smile flickering across his face. His first words were "Mysteries still exist," explaining that he had been told by his traditional healer that same morning that a foreign stranger would be arriving to meet him that day.

That soothsaying healer herself soon arrived. She was dressed top to bottom in white, and she spoke in tongues, torrentially, while scribbling illegible things on a ream of computer paper to the boisterous accompaniment of drummers. When this scene finally quieted down, Tansi walked me to a nearby bamboo hut where his wife, Pierrette, lay, severely emaciated, dying. After sitting with her for a few minutes, I emerged to converse with Tansi. They would both be dead in a matter of days, but he was still convinced otherwise. Holding forth impassionedly, he told me his hopes had been revived through reimmersion in his own Kikongo culture. Its healing traditions held the secrets to his recovery, he said, but he didn't stop there. The key to resolving the problems of Africa's most violent and corrupt region, he insisted, lay in a return to tradition and to the reconstitution of polities that had been broken up hundreds of years earlier by European imperialism. Tansi went on to claim that his healer was the reincarnation of an important eighteenth-century prophetess, Dona Beatrice, who hailed from the most important and famous of these polities, the Kingdom of

Kongo, which provides the final stop of our long itinerary down the western coast of the continent.

As readers know from the stops we have previously made on this rock-skipping coastal itinerary, from Upper Guinea to the Bight of Biafra via the Gold Coast and Slave Coast, there is no African experience of the encounter with Europe that can be presented as entirely typical, none that can accurately serve as a surrogate for the history of the entire region. This is especially true for the first 250 years or so of the slave trade to the Americas, and the account given here, like others, is anything but exhaustive.

The history of the Kingdom of Kongo merits longer treatment than other chapters in this story, however, not just because of the great amplitude of the trade that would develop in a region that led all others, but because the particulars of the kingdom's extraordinary history stand out in so many ways. The story of Kongo is, firstly, an enormous tragedy, but it is also much more than that. It is also a window on the complex and unique struggles that African societies waged to forge their own paths toward modernity in this age—one that like modernity everywhere would incorporate powerful currents of influence from other, hitherto unfamiliar parts of the world. What is remarkable about the Kongo is how, from the very outset of contact with strange, importuning outsiders who suddenly appeared in their midst, it battled with persistence and real ingenuity to control its own destiny.

By the time of first European contact, with the arrival of the Portuguese explorer Diogo Cão, in 1483, the Kingdom of Kongo was already a sophisticated polity, one that had probably been founded in the late 1300s. As recently as the 1960s, the prevailing view among Western scholars had been that the portion of the continent commonly construed as "Black Africa" was incapable of complex state formation or of sophisticated government. Wherever signs of great achievement had been found, whether the sublime bronzes of Benin or the ruins of Nubia or of ancient Zimbabwe, they were deemed the work of mysterious invaders who were implicitly white, or of other superior but unknown outsiders. After the British sack of Benin, in

1897, that culture's bronzes were displayed in London for the first time, and one press report attributed them to a "wandering tribe of alien craftsmen." Even as the scholarship of the last few decades has completely overturned such racist ideas in the academy, views like these have persisted in the popular culture of the West. This is due to a failure to include Africa in the teaching of world history and to the entertainment industry's enduring penchant for trafficking in African primitivism.

The Kongo of the late Middle Ages was a centralized and expanding state that reigned over a sprawling territory that straddles present-day Angola and the Democratic Republic of the Congo (formerly Zaïre). During the years spanning from the mid-1500s to the middle of the next century, the height of its regional hegemony, Kongo ruled an area of nearly sixty thousand square miles. This made it 20 percent larger than England and almost twice as large as Portugal, which was soon to become its sometime partner, sometime adversary. Kongo had an unusual political system for a kingdom, selecting rulers not by simple direct inheritance, as is common, but rather via a more complex process involving electors drawn from the extended royal family and other elite clans. And it had a complicated spiritual life to match, involving both a supreme being as well as lesser sources of divine power seated in the ancestors.

The kingdom's early strengths and successes were built on an economic system that was based on trade and patronage networks which linked regions with highly varied geographies and equally diverse and specialized products. The king and his court occupied a central crossroads that permitted control over commerce and taxation. The most important of the kingdom's traded goods were copper; aquatic shells, *nzimbu*, which were used as an official currency; salt; and woven cloth, which the Portuguese explorer Duarte Pacheco Pereira judged to be "so beautiful that work like theirs is not done better in Italy."

Benin was another strong state with a diverse economy prior to European contact, but it had little use for European goods, or European religion. So little, in fact, that it shut down the trade in slaves with these newcomers soon after it had started. By contrast, for its own peculiar reasons, Christianity held a powerful, near instantaneous appeal to the rulers of Kongo. Part of this attraction can be explained by some of its own preexisting beliefs. By way of fateful coincidence, Kongo's cosmology held that a realm of higher being existed somewhere across the ocean, where white creatures dwelled. Although this is debated, the people of Kongo may have also already employed the cross as an important religious symbol; if so, they would have been bowled over when the sailing vessels of the Portuguese appeared on their shores prominently bearing a familiar form of religious iconography that Kongolese had thought innate to their own culture.

When Olaudah Equiano, whom we have recently met, was taken captive and sold into the slave trade as an Igbo youth along the coast of the Bight of Biafra, he described his terror at the thought of the plans he imagined his strange white captors held for him:

> *When I looked round the ship too, and saw a large furnace of copper boiling and a multitude of black people of every description, chained together, every one of their countenances expressing dejection and sorrow, I no longer doubted of my fate; and quite overpowered with horror and anguish, I fell motionless on the deck, and fainted. When I recovered a little, I found some black people about me, who I believed were some of those who brought me on board, and had been receiving their pay: they talked to me in order to cheer me, but all in vain. I asked them if we were not to be eaten by those white men with horrible looks, red faces, and long hair. They told me I was not.*

Images filled with terror like these must have been extremely common in many parts of the continental coast. Seeing smoke waft ominously from the Europeans' strange vessels, some Africans believed that their captors used human bones for fuel or boiled their flesh for oil. Some European ships bore large eyes painted on their prows, which were taken by some Africans along the continent's coast as a symbol of evil, and their towering sails, something hitherto unknown to them, might be taken as mysterious white wings or glinting knives, and hence as a cause for fear. As the historian James Sweet has reported, others imagined "the corpses of slaves were floated out into the Atlantic Ocean in order to serve as bait for collecting cowrie shells," which the whites possessed in enormous amounts as a trading currency. Even in the wake of established contact, many Africans believed that common products they associated with whites—things like red wine, or cheese—were made from the blood or brains of their fellow blacks, and that a deadly product used by whites, gunpowder, was concocted using their dried bones.

In distinct contrast to the parts of West Africa we have already discussed, Kongo had relatively little prior information about the outside world at the time of European contact. Trade links to other continents, whether via long-distance Muslim networks over heavily forested land or by sea, were far more tenuous than they were along the continent's western bulge—or, for that matter, along its long eastern coast. So when Diogo Cão's ships arrived in 1483, there was plenty of cause for bafflement.* During his first voyage to the Kongo region, Cão, the son of an elite northern Portuguese family who had been an associate of Henry the Navigator, landed on the southeast shores of an estuary of the Congo River, whose effluent was so broad and powerful that it could be detected at sea from a distance

---

* Fascinating parallels exist here between the Kongolese and the Inca of South America, one of the world's largest empires at the time of its first contact with Europeans in the early sixteenth century. The Inca also had a system of elected sovereigns that often led to tumultuous successions. They were in the midst of a civil war when Francisco Pizarro, at the head of a small Spanish expeditionary force, conquered its rulers. Historians have argued that the Inca had been cast into further confusion and self-doubt by a long-standing oracular prediction that the Twelfth Inca, their ruler at the time, would be the empire's last. The appearance of the Spanish was preceded by the devastation of a great epidemic, probably yellow fever, which was borne into the world of the Inca by the foreigners, even though it seemed to precede them, killing the reigning Inca emperor and setting off a struggle to succeed him. All of this may well have filled people with great doubt, perhaps leaving some to interpret the arrival of strange bearded men, whose houses moved upon the sea like wind and could "issue terrible thunder from their vessels" somewhat resignedly, as the prophesied harbingers of its doom.

of thirty leagues, or one hundred miles. There, he erected a stone *padrao*, the cross-shaped markers carried from home by the Portuguese sailors since the beginnings of the Henrican explorations of Africa. These were to be strung along the coast, like gems on a necklace, marking spots they deemed of special significance. From a place called Mpinda, which Cão quickly learned was part of an important kingdom located somewhere in the interior, he sent emissaries laden with gifts to the capital in order to initiate relations. As a precaution for their safety, it is said Cão took several members of the local elite hostage and then sailed to Elmina. Two years later, he returned from Portugal, again, laden with gifts for the leader of Kongo, but also with the hostages. In addition to serving as translators, they could now attest to life in a world hitherto unknown to Kongo just as the curtain was closing on the Middle Ages.

Much about Kongo's religious traditions is still debated, but one interpretation holds that albinos were considered water spirits who were able to traverse an important spiritual barrier between the world of everyday experience and an intangible realm of mystery, and were therefore worthy of veneration. Lest one leap too quickly to the view that this was a sign of peculiar African backwardness, something steeped in prelogical thinking, one must caution that the Portuguese (and other Europeans) of this era were more or less equally inclined toward religious superstition. As the historian David Northup has observed, "Iberian Christians fully accepted the existence of lesser spirits such as angels and devils, of spiritually powerful intercessors such as saints, and of the malevolent power of witchcraft, all of which had ready counterparts in African beliefs." Even a full century after the Portuguese initiated contact with Kongo, before they launched any military campaign, Portugal's imperial representatives in Central Africa performed elaborate religious exhortations, attending church as many as five times to spiritually arm themselves via Catholic ritual.

For the Kongolese at Mpinda, the strange sight of white men wearing the cross, a symbol widely employed in the art and ceremonies of their own religion, would have been an occasion not merely for dread, as it presumably was for some, but of attraction, spiritual awe, and perhaps even celebration. Cão's men had told the Kongolese that the whites were subjects of the king of Portugal, which we are told their hosts may have translated as *nzambi mpungu*, meaning of the highest spiritual authority. We should not assume, however, that they took this on faith.[*] In 1492, a Portuguese chronicler named Rui de Pina recorded the first encounter that Cão's men had with a local leader, the lord of Soyo, in 1483.

> *The Lord of this land, wherein they came to port on March 29, 1491, was a great Lord, uncle to the King [of Kongo], and his subject, who was called Manisoyo, a fifty-year-old man of good humanity and wisdom. He was two leagues from the port where he was given notice of the fleet, and was requested to send word to the king of the arrival. And the said Manisoyo, seeing the things of the King of Portugal, visibly and with signs of great joy, and of reverence [to the King of Portugal] touched both hands to the ground, and placed them on his face, which is the greatest sign of respect that can be paid to their Kings.*

The Manisoyo (Mwene Soyo), or lord of Soyo, the Kongo province where the Portuguese had made landfall, accepted initiation into the cult of the whites, which is to say he was baptized and reportedly agreed to the construction of a small church. After Cão's return from Portugal, the explorer was escorted to the capital, Mbanza Kongo, an overland journey of twenty-three days on which he was accompanied by two hundred of the kingdom's troops.

A densely populated city, Mbanza Kongo was situated atop a high plateau, with a distinctive, jutting promontory. Its immense, walled, mazelike quarter containing the king's residential compound was estimated to be a mile and a half in circumference. Some Portuguese visitors were so impressed by what they found there that they likened the Kongolese capital to a major city of their own, Évora. By

---

* The Portuguese interpreted *nzambi mpungu* to mean "lord of the world."

the time the first Portuguese saw it, couriers from Soyo would have already long notified the king of Kongo, Nzinga a Nkuwu, of their impending arrival.

> *On the day the Christians entered the Court, they were received by innumerable people, and with great commotion and were soon housed in some large and distinguished new houses, provided with everything to satisfy them. . . . [T]he King sent to the Captain and the friars many noble courtiers, made farcical in various ways, followed by countless Archers, and then Lancers, as well as others with other halberds of war, and also countless women divided into large groups, with many ivory trumpets and kettle drums, singing great praises to the King of Portugal and representing his greatness with much joy. And in this way they arrived before the King.*

There, amid great pomp, on May 3, 1491, fifteen months to the day before Columbus sailed westward from Spain on his first voyage to find the East Indies, and thereby, or at least as it is often asserted, launching the modern age, Nzinga a Nkuwu, the mani Kongo, king of the most substantial realm the Portuguese had encountered anywhere in tropical Africa, converted to Christianity. He adopted the reign name of João I, borrowed from the king of the same name who sat on the throne in Portugal. Six of João I's nobles were baptized at the same time, all adopting names from individuals in the Portuguese king's royal household. What is more, within a little more than a generation, the entire Kongo elite adopted Portugal's system of feudal titles, leaving the newly Christian kingdom full of dukes, counts, and the like.

The runaway momentum that Christianity acquired in these years is one of the most startling stories of the transition to the modern era anywhere, albeit one that is almost unknown outside of graduate-school African history courses. After his conversion, João I sent Kongo youth to Europe for literacy and education in matters of faith, setting in motion the adoption of the Portuguese language by the kingdom for official correspondence, diplomacy, and record keeping, which would have far-reaching consequences. Of most immediate importance is the fact that the creation of a literate elite allowed Kongo to become the first sub-Saharan state whose history was extensively documented and preserved in its own words and from its own perspective. It was not long before, in fact, João I of Kongo was himself exchanging letters with Manuel I (who had succeeded João II as king of Portugal) as "Brother." John Thornton, a historian of Kongo, estimates that the entire archive of documents left by the kingdom amounts to more than ten thousand items.

For all of its speed, however, it would be wrong to imagine from the tale of João I's conversion that Christianity was met with unanimous approval overnight in the kingdom. In the first years of this new era, some powerful members of the Kongo elite may have remained strongly skeptical and even resentful of the new faith. For some this may have been because they had not been chosen to be converted, alongside João, during his own baptism. For others, the outsiders' religion may have been perceived as a threat to personal and institutional stakes of their own in Kongo's native religion and social practices. Finally, there was the important matter of marriage. Christianity, as taught by the Portuguese who were sent to indoctrinate members of the elite in the new faith, imposed a strict requirement of monogamy in a cultural environment where polygamy reigned. Elite politics and succession rules in Kongo, moreover, were based on a complex organization of clans, or *mwissikongo*, whose structures were bound up in both polygamy and matrilineal succession rules.

According to one theory of the kingdom's politics, the selection of a new sovereign in Kongo revolved by design around shifting alliances between these clans, or *kanda*, with a resultant side effect being frequent violent conflict. If the unpredictable factional arrangements between rival lineages prevented the domination by a single royal line, as would seem intended, over time they would also prove to be a major source of debility, constituting the kingdom's

Achilles' heel. Upon the death of João in 1509,* the imported, but only partially adopted religion therefore became a new wild card in what was already a complicated machinery of succession.

In a move designed to deepen the roots of Christianity in his kingdom and ensure that it survived him, João had seen to the baptism of Mvemba a Nzinga, the first son by his principal wife. Upon João's death this son, who had been given the Christian name Afonso I, mounted a claim to the throne. According to the normal protocols of succession, as the historian Cécile Fromont has reported, "a group of qualified electors chose the new king from a pool of eligible candidates," a system of transition that "placed a high value on the ability of the chosen candidate to assert his rule and establish his legitimacy in political, military and supernatural terms." No definitive advantage accrued to the offspring of the king's principal wife or through the notion of primogeniture. Indeed, the rules all but barred direct inheritance of power through this line. As practiced and taught by the newcomers, however, both Portuguese tradition and the Christianity the outsiders practiced seemed to supply a compelling rationale for the inheritance of power in this alternative manner.

At the moment of his father's death, Afonso I was based outside of the capital, in the nearby province of Nsundi, where he held a governorship. Before he could reach Mbanza Kongo, a pagan half brother, Mpanzu a Nzinga, whose ambition to succeed his father enjoyed strong backing from other *mwissikongo*, claimed the throne and may even have been invested. Entering Mbanza Kongo secretly, possibly with the aid of his mother, Afonso I was able to raise a small force of about thirty-five men, which he led into battle against troops loyal to his half brother. The challengers may have included a few Portuguese. When the two sides clashed on the outskirts of the capital, Afonso, finding his men were badly outnumbered, cried out to St. James the Apostle (Santiago), whose reported sudden manifestation hoisting a cross, accompanied by one or more horsemen dressed

* Or perhaps 1506, according to the most recent scholarship.

in white, caused the enemy troops to suddenly break and flee. The pagans were then routed, and Mpanzu a Nzinga was captured and executed. This, at least, became the official legend of these events as left to history by the victorious Afonso.[*]

Whatever transpired in reality, the outcome shows that Afonso I had managed to successfully leverage the new alien faith in order to press his rules-bending claim for power. His next tasks were to win over the large pagan contingents of the elite and to consolidate his rule. To accomplish this, the new leader accelerated his kingdom's embrace of Christianity, which was made the state religion, and greatly deepened the reforms already begun by his father via deep engagement with the Portuguese. This, on the one hand, involved a broad attack on preexisting religious practices, such as the adoration of ancestors, which the new king may have played up in order to impress the Portuguese. Orders were given to destroy the idol figurines placed at elite gravesites throughout Mbanza Kongo. On the other hand, a religious infrastructure needed to be built up rapidly in order to institutionalize the new cult of Christianity. As a first step, an imposing new church was built on the grounds of the royal cemetery. It was dedicated to Our Lady of Victory, a conspicuous and quasi-permanent reminder to all of how Afonso had won power, through supposed divine intervention.

Not stopping there, Afonso either requested or was gifted a coat of arms for the kingdom commissioned by the king of Portugal and directly inspired by Portugal's own traditions of heraldry. It bore five swords representing the heavenly intervention of the fighters who won the day for him in battle; scallop shells, which are an attribute of St. James; and two broken idols, meant to symbolize the "supernatural endorsement of Afonso's support of the kingdom's conversion" and its defeat of paganism. In one of Afonso I's letters, he says of it proudly: "It seemed to us a very just thing, beyond the

---

[*] We have come across this cry at several occasions in our narrative, and it would be used yet again during the conquest of the Inca, who shared something like Kongo's system of royal succession that eschewed primogeniture, and succumbed to Spanish imperialism two decades later.

many graces and praises we had given to Our Lord for bestowing upon us such great mercy and clemency; and [that given] such a clear and evident miracle, and great victory, we honor this memory in our [coat of] arms, so the kings to come in the Kingdom and Lordship of the mani Kongo, will not forget at any time this great mercy and benefit, which was so marvelously done for their King, Kingdom and people."*

Another key aspect of Afonso's consolidation of power involved demonstrating complete mastery of the new faith. The extent to which his belief was wholehearted and unambiguous, or inspired more by tactical and political motives instead, however, is still debated by historians.

Similarly, even with the relatively abundant documentation that survives, it is impossible to establish a perfect hierarchy of priorities for the Portuguese in pursuing such deep relations with Kongo. From their earliest contacts, the newcomers were aware that the region abounded in high-quality copper deposits, which they surely coveted, along with various other minerals, particularly silver, whose unavailing pursuit there continued well into the eighteenth century. In the early history of Atlantic empire, where the motives of the Portuguese and Spanish were often bound up in the intense competition between them, some have been tempted to interpret Lisbon's obsession with silver in west Central Africa as a kind of echo that followed Spain's tremendous windfall discoveries of that metal at Potosí and in Mexico. In both of those places, silver mining experienced enormous booms in the second half of the sixteenth century.

To my own sense of things, this seems almost exactly backward. It was Spain, as I have argued, that was propelled in its discoveries and conquests in the Americas by its own covetous feelings toward Portugal following Lisbon's successes in West Africa, and in particular, the securing of an immensely profitable commerce in gold at Elmina. This trade took off roughly a half century before the begin-

---

* The sixteenth-century coat of arms is still used today by the city of Mbanza Kongo in Angola, where the ancient capital was located.

nings of the American silver bonanza and it fired Spain's determination to make discoveries of its own to match those of Portugal. By the 1490s, Lisbon was shipping nearly six hundred kilos of gold a year from Elmina.

Kongo and its immediate region, meanwhile, quickly became linked to Spanish silver extraction in the Americas, because Portugal by way of the Vatican-sanctioned Treaty of Tordesillas enjoyed exclusive rights to commerce in Africa, including the early Atlantic trade in slaves. Spain was therefore largely dependent upon Portuguese suppliers, via the *asiento*, for the Black labor that was indispensable to its development of mining and agriculture in its New World possessions. No later than 1629, slaves from Kongo and its vicinity were playing such an important role supporting Spanish silver mining in Bolivia, for example, that a catechism in Kimbundu, a major west Central Africa language, was published in Lima, and within a few decades, a Kimbundu-Spanish grammar was used in order to facilitate communication with the burgeoning numbers of Kongolese captives put to work in farming and other vital support roles around Potosí.

The slave traffic from Kongo, however, did not await Spain's big silver strikes on the other side of the Atlantic. Although Portugal's trade in human beings with this kingdom began quite small in scale, it commenced almost immediately. It also seems that at least since the establishment of commercial relations with the kingdom of Benin, to the northwest, the Portuguese were increasingly convinced that they were getting closer to unraveling the mystery behind the legendary African Christian monarch whom they called Prester John, believing that the Congo River might be the key to locating him. Alongside such motives, however, one must also cite the prestige and influence that Portugal stood to gain with Rome and in Europe through claims that its foundling imperialism was winning converts to the Catholic faith.

Whatever his own mixture of motives, what is certain is that the apparent earnestness of Afonso's conversion deeply impressed many of the European visitors to his realm. As one correspondent, Rui de Aguiar, wrote of Afonso to King Manuel of Portugal, in 1516:

> His [devotion to] Christianity is such that he seems to me not to be a man but rather an Angel that God has sent to this Kingdom so as to convert it . . . because I can relate to Your Highness that he himself knows more about the Prophets and the Gospel of Our Lord Jesus Christ, and of all of the lives of the Saints, and all the rites of the Holy Mother Church, than we do ourselves, and teaches us about them . . . he speaks so well and correctly, that it seems to me that it is always the Holy Spirit who speaks through him: because, my Lord, he does nothing other than study, and many times he falls asleep on top of his Books, and he often forgets to eat or drink because he is [lost in] speaking of the things of Our Lord.

Measures like these were just the beginning. Not only was Afonso, who would rule the Kingdom of Kongo for thirty-four years, a decisive and tactically astute leader, he was also far-seeing. Perhaps the best reflection of this is that he almost immediately undertook a vast expansion of efforts begun by his father to dispatch sons of the Kongo elite to Portugal, and eventually to other places in Europe, in order to undergo education in literacy, matters of faith, and the ways of sixteenth-century Europeans. These included as many as thirty-five of his own offspring and clan kinsmen, some of whom quickly distinguished themselves there for their capacity for learning.

For example, Henrique, one of Afonso's sons, was ordained in Portugal and in 1518 named bishop *in partibus infidelum*, meaning presiding at large over pagan territories in Africa. From the 1530s, and for a period stretching across the next century, Kongo frequently sent missions to the Vatican, reflecting the kingdom's keen understanding of the institutional power and political centrality of the Catholic Church in Europe. Although one early-seventeenth-century Kongolese ambassador to the Vatican, Antonio Manuel, was entirely educated in his own country, his fluency in Portuguese and

Latin and his mastery of scripture impressed his hosts so deeply that he was given last rites by Pope Paul V and later buried by the Vatican amid great ceremony. To this day, a portrait of Antonio Manuel remains in the baptistery of Santa Maria Maggiore in Rome. Although it was often frustrated, the kingdom's diplomacy steadfastly sought Rome's support as a counterweight to that of Portugal.

Despite this, for the space of a century or so, relations between Kongo and Portugal, two far-flung societies at the very start of a new era, are best understood as interpenetration and not one-sided domination—each side doing its best to advance its interests, but also to understand and even respect the other's unfamiliar social structure and remain thoroughly abreast of the events of the day. One among many signs of this interpenetration is the story of a Kongolese nobleman named Antonio Vereira, who occupied the important role of factor, or tax collector, in Portugal and married into that country's royal household in the mid-sixteenth century.

❖

HERE, ONE MUST PAUSE to contrast how different the contours of Kongo's story are from what was occurring at roughly the same time in the Spanish-held Americas, where major indigenous states such as the Aztec and Inca, to take two of the largest and most famous examples, were destroyed almost immediately following contact, the latter by a force of 170 men. Throughout Spanish America, Christianity was forcibly imposed and wielded as a tool of conquest, and if anything, the Portuguese in Brazil were even more scornful than the Spanish were of the indigenous cultures they encountered. Portugal disparaged its new colony's native population as having "neither god nor law," as it employed its religious orders to corral and indoctrinate the newly conquered.

Following the establishment of bilateral ties in the closing years of the fifteenth century, Kongo, by contrast, paid no tribute to Portugal, nor had Lisbon sought it. It is true that first João I, and then his son Afonso I, requested and received assistance of various kinds from Portugal, but such things were negotiated and scrupulously paid for. One military aid deal, for example, comprised six Portuguese ships manned by 180 sailors, 40 soldiers with firearms, two medium-caliber cannons, 1000 rounds of artillery, and 300 halberds, among other items. And from an early date, Afonso used the export of slaves to "sustain [his] diplomatic, material and cultural ties" with Portugal. In a missive sent to Lisbon in 1514, he noted that he had sent 50 slaves and 800 copper *manilhas* to Portugal to "buy us the said succor that we needed." Later, he referred to the export of five hundred slaves to cover the costs of hosting two of his nephews in Lisbon.

As it happened in fact, no African state of any size would be conquered by Europeans until the nineteenth century, not even in the face of the intense and sustained contact that drove the slave trade. For its part, Kongo enjoyed generally good relations with Portugal—relations that can only be understood as between functional peers—for more than a century and a half after Diogo Cão's discovery of the kingdom. This was due not only to any robustness inherent in the kingdom and its institutions at the time of contact between the two civilizations but also to the resourcefulness and intelligence of Kongo's statecraft and of some its leaders, such as Afonso I.

As the aid package just mentioned suggests, Afonso I had a clear vision of what he desired from the budding relationship with Portugal. He seems to have been especially attentive almost from the start to the need to protect his realm from political or ecclesiastical encroachment. Put more simply, he grasped early on that there was a fine line between pursuing close state-to-state relations and opening up Kongo to domination or destabilization from abroad. Dispatching students to Europe gave his elite a deep and nuanced understanding of the ways of the foreigners, and for a time this enhanced Kongo's efforts to safeguard its sovereignty. These included the creation of an independent local church, with parishes throughout the kingdom led not by Portuguese, but by indigenous lay teachers of the faith.

Literacy became another major tool of Kongolese statecraft, used both for the purposes of foreign relations with Portugal and Europe and for enhancing systems of taxation, the administration of justice, and even archival record keeping. This led to an emphasis on the creation of the kingdom's own education system. While it employed Portuguese instructors in that language and in Latin, as well as in some higher studies for select students, it insisted on careful control by the Kongo itself. Remarkably, by the mid-1520s, Afonso I had begun extending education to the rural population and had established schoolmasters in every part of the kingdom.

Although a full-blown crisis between Kongo and Portugal would not erupt until the seventeenth century, important points of tension and divergence started to crop up even during the first decades of the relationship. With its elite's rapid mastery of the Christian faith, Kongo began petitioning to be granted its own episcopal see less than two decades after adopting the new state religion. But Portugal, which saw value in controlling the Catholic Church as a means of maximizing its influence over Kongo and the surrounding region, lobbied Rome against this and prevailed. As a result, Lisbon's new colony of São Tomé, where Portuguese bishops would preside, became the administrative center for the church for the entire region. Kongo was similarly rebuffed in its request to be granted sovereignty over São Tomé, and it would suffer an additional snub in its pursuit of a seaworthy ship or ships of its own, which Afonso I sought to purchase from Lisbon. As São Tomé become the chief entrepôt for all Portuguese trade and communication in the region, it assiduously opposed anything that could increase Afonso I's autonomy, and even intercepted much of his official correspondence to prevent him from communicating with Lisbon. Meanwhile, King João III, who succeeded Manuel II on the Portuguese throne in 1521, saw little to be gained from supporting the interests of the African kingdom against those of his booming sugar colony off the coast.

29

DARK HEARTS

A MUCH MORE HISTORICALLY POWERFUL dynamic was coming into play, meanwhile, that would place the kingdoms of Kongo and Portugal on a fateful collision course with each other, even if it would take over a century for the crisis between them to fully ripen and play itself out. That dynamic was the momentous connections just then being forged between Old World and New. Lisbon's initial interest in trading for slaves with Kongo was fueled by rather prosaic needs. First among these were Portugal's own dismal demographics. The shortage of manpower at home, aggravated by the Black Death, badly crimped the kingdom's domestic economy while making it harder to compete with its far more populous neighbor, Spain, in the imperial sweepstakes getting under way. As we have seen, during the first quarter of the sixteenth century, more than twelve thousand slaves were shipped from West Africa to Europe, meaning mostly to Portugal, but also to Spain, where they were put to work in a wide range of roles.

Then came an even larger demand created by the need to feed fresh Black bodies into the plantation charnels of São Tomé, as it emerged as a sugar powerhouse early in the sixteenth century. Sugar was booming on the island by 1520, by which time the plantations that became prototypes for slave sugar production in the Americas had as many as three hundred Africans laboring at a time. The decision by Benin to shut down its slave markets must be recalled against this backdrop. It suddenly boosted Kongo's profile in Portugal as a conveniently located alternative source of labor. Benin had initially refused to sell males to the Portuguese and then shut down the trade in slaves with them altogether after Lisbon balked at the idea of selling it cannons unless and until this West African kingdom could prove its Christian bona fides. By contrast, Afonso I of Kongo seems, if anything, to have initially welcomed the opportunity to sell slaves. He soon began selling people into slavery to the Portuguese, reaching a level of four thousand annually by the middle of the century, according to a Kongolese inquest.

Although Kongo had long practiced domestic slavery, it had prohibited the sale of freeborn citizens into the trade. In a region where power had been traditionally defined, above all, in terms of demography—meaning in the number of people that a leader controlled or received customary loyalty and deference from—the institution of slavery may have resembled a form of dependent protective custody for the very weakest. As one historian wrote, "Slaves often originated in practice as humble outsiders, taken in circumstances that saved them from sheer starvation, from harm at the hands of pursuers, or from death by judicial condemnation."

This is not to prettify African bondage, or to assert that it was necessarily pleasant for those who were subjected to it, and historians take different views of this question. But what is certain is that the pathways that led out of slavery in environments like western Central Africa were comparatively abundant. They included marriage and absorption into the family lines of the owners, and did not typically involve transgenerational bondage, as under the chattel system. In Kongo, the children of slaves rose to be leaders of the state, as they did in other African societies in this era. After the death of its third leader, Askia the Great, in 1529, to take one example, the next six rulers of the Songhai Empire were the sons of concubines. In a mirror image of the rules that obtained in Benin, meanwhile, Kongo prohibited the sale of women into slavery. Beyond that, bondage was reserved for war captives and for those convicted of major crimes.

For a time, at least, Afonso found that without too much difficulty he could meet Portugal's growing demand for his fellow Africans. These he sold into slavery in exchange for services rendered by his new foreign partners to pay for their support as allies, as well as to procure swelling supplies of novelties and status goods. Kongo acquired many of these slaves it sold in trade with another kingdom, the Tio, who were located to the east. It was not long, however, before Lisbon's appetite for bound labor began to outstrip the readily available population of captives bought from the Tio, augmented by troublesome Kongo kinsmen who could easily enough be let go. In the meantime, the demand for exotic imports into the kingdom was acquiring a dangerous and uncontrollable momentum. Kongo first sought to supplement payment for its imports from Europe with copper and other local items, such as wax, ivory, and palm cloth, but by the 1560s, according to one estimate, captive human beings had essentially become the only "currency" that the Portuguese would readily accept in exchange for their coveted goods. This led to an escalating clash of values between a type of materialism centered on the power of money, just then strongly ascendant in Europe, and the common African pattern we have described, where power was based more on networks of human tribute than on trade. One of these systems was destined to prevail, and one of them, just as surely, had to gradually crumble.

When copper and wax proved of little utility in sustaining the prized trade in luxury goods with Portugal, Kongo launched a frontier war with its southern neighbor and claimed vassal, the Kingdom of Ndongo, in order to obtain captives whom it could, according to its own laws, sell legally into slavery. Although Kongo initially had the upper hand with its neighbor, its aggression helped spark a wider cycle of slaving wars that would gradually engulf the entire region.

An early harbinger of the crack-up to come is contained in two remarkable letters of complaint about the expanding slave trade addressed by Afonso I to his Portuguese counterpart, João III, in 1526. In the first of them, that July, the Kongolese sovereign wrote:

> *And this harm has come to us at such cost that the said merchants take our countrymen the sons of our land and the sons of our noblemen every day, as well as our vassals and parents, because the thieves and men of bad conscience captivate them with a desire to have the things and goods of this Kingdom of which they are greedy, they seize and sell them in such a way, Sir, that because of this corruption and licentiousness, our land is being all but depopulated, which would not be good to you nor to your service, Your Highness. And to avoid all of this in our Kingdom we don't need more priests [or] more people to teach in our schools, nor even more goods, except for wine and flour for the holy sacrament, because what we ask of Your Highness is to help and favor us in this matter by telling your factors to not bring merchants or goods here, because our will is that in this Kingdom there be no slave trade nor [any] outlet for it.*

And in the second letter, which followed in October, Afonso I, seemingly even more distressed, complained of what he called "a great inconvenience which is of little service to God." This "inconvenience" was the sale of his relatives, other noblemen, and common subjects alike "to the white men who are in our Kingdom."

In this historic communication one finds an accumulation of grievances. Afonso I was desperately requesting help in controlling a commerce in slaves that had begun spiraling out of control, but he was not demanding its cessation altogether. The Kongolese leader was also unhappy about the assistance that Lisbon had begun to provide its rival Ndongo, which Kongo claimed, and with which Portugal had also established a lively, separate trade. Afonso I was also disenchanted about the unscrupulous behavior of priests from Portugal who had begun trading on their own account for slaves in Kongo for shipment to São Tomé. In some cases, he alleged, the priests held young girls captive for their own sexual needs. He was also alarmed, finally, by the way São Tomé–based Portuguese traders had begun fanning out into the countryside of Ndongo, much as the Portuguese had done earlier in Upper Guinea. Establishing themselves in provincial capitals and towns, the foreigners exchanged European imports directly with regional leaders, badly undermining Afonso's control over the patrimonial networks that were a main pillar of his power. João III of Portugal, however, dismissed out of hand Afonso's entreaty to help rein in the slave business, replying that Kongo lacked anything of interest to Portugal other than its people for sale as slaves.

Although Afonso I lodged this famous first complaint about the slave trade in 1526, the demand for slaves from this region was just beginning to ramp up. Portugal discovered Brazil in 1501, but it wasn't until the 1530s that Lisbon committed to governing and exploiting that new territory as what we would recognize as a full-fledged colony. With that, Portugal began negotiating a strategic shift that would have the most far-reaching of consequences, elevating Brazil to the first rank of its priorities, even above India or the East. With the development of a more robust and steady supply of slaves—whose labor was required to fructify its new Brazilian colony—becoming a top priority, Kongo and the broader west Central African region gradually emerged as Portugal's main "solution." As a consequence, roughly 32,000 slaves were shipped to Brazil from this region (mostly Angola) during the last quarter of the sixteenth century. But that was only for starters. In each of the first two quarters of the seventeenth century the traffic was roughly five times higher than that, with 184,000 and 173,000 slaves, respectively, being borne off in chains to the Americas, half of them bound for Brazil alone. To achieve volumes like this meant flooding new markets in west Central Africa with goods, where they found avid buyers.

Putting aside for now the long-term political and economic consequences, as the slave business grew, the terms of trade appeared to dramatically improve for the African sellers, making the tide of new merchandise all that much harder to resist. Cloth acquired from Asia and from northern Europe came to play a particularly critical role.

As the late historian of slavery Joseph Miller wrote, "Wealthy princes bedecked themselves and their retainers in the finest and most stylish fabrics obtainable, with scarlet silks occupying a favored position, displayed their countenances beneath broad-brimmed hats, and had themselves transported from place to place in palanquins lined with fine taffetas." Chiefs and other lesser dignitaries swaddled themselves in copious amounts of cloth, which came in a mix of colors and patterns hitherto unknown. As markets expanded, "imported textiles [even] covered common folk with quantities of stuffs that only the wealthiest and powerful had once worn."

In a region that produced exquisite cloth of its own, albeit mostly for elite consumption, imported textiles became a potent founding item of local modernity, as the novelty and seemingly endless variety of new goods arriving from afar set in motion cycles of fashion and style unlike anything seen before. The power of attraction of these India goods, as they were known, as well as textiles from Europe, was such that cloth soon became the dominant medium of exchange as west Central Africa entered the Atlantic system. At the outset, in fact, when Afonso I (and later, other kings and rulers) still enjoyed relatively strong control over exchanges with Europeans, a bolt of imported material sufficiently long to amply clothe a member of the elite*—say five meters in length—became the most basic monetary unit for international trade. It was called, in fact, a "piece" of cloth, and early on it was traded one to one for a young and healthy male slave, who was also referred to and accounted for as a *peça da Índias*, meaning piece of the Indies, and often shortened simply to "piece."†

As the demand for slaves soared, though, inflation took hold, and once it did, it was not long before it took two "pieces" of cloth to acquire a single "piece," or captive, and on and on in a downward spiral. For the Europeans, this was, in reality, little more than a bookkeeper's loss, more than compensated for by what Miller described

---

* For most, body coverings were limited to the skins of domestic goats, the skin of cattle acquired via trade with regions to the south, pounded tree barks, and woven raffia cloth.

† The Portuguese eventually replaced the use of "piece" as an accounting term for slaves with *cabeça*, or head, perhaps in the late seventeenth century.

as the "returns in dependency" that imported cloth duly produced throughout the region as ever growing quantities of it washed in. Although cloth had no peer in terms of its market power during the slave trade, alcohol and firearms gradually also took hold as important commercial items. Western liquors were no substitute in volume for African drink, which had always existed. But they had enormous appeal as status items, not unlike fancy cloths. They helped set the chief or dignitary who entertained with them apart from others. Toward this end, a major political figure might sell four hundred or more slaves per year just to remain stocked in rum made in Brazil by slaves put to work there. According to one estimate, of the nearly 1.2 million captives embarked for slavery in the New World at Luanda, fully one-third were purchased through the importation of alcoholic drinks such as Brazilian cane brandy.

This was not the only dynamic to take hold, though. As the ready supply of legal candidates for sale into Atlantic slavery quickly dried up, war became the go-to means of acquiring new stocks of tradable human beings. All the while, the frontier of the slave trade was expanding in myriad other directions in this region, because each time the local supply of captives proved insufficient, mixed-race traders or Creoles known as *pombeiros* moved into new areas with plentiful goods and easy credit, offering to buy up human beings. In each newly exposed area, as the radius of the trade widened, a flood of foreign goods that still enjoyed maximum novelty value drove a succession of constantly renewed local market frenzies.

By 1540, Kongo itself appeared to have given up on the idea of resisting the expansion of the regional slave trade, which would only continue to accelerate in the decades ahead. In that year, Afonso I tragically wrote to his Portuguese counterpart to boast of his kingdom's unique ability to feed the insatiable market. "Put all the Guinea countries on one side and only Kongo on the other and you will find that Kongo renders more than all the others put together . . . no king in all these parts esteems Portuguese goods so much or treats the Portuguese so well as we do. We favor their trade, sustain it, open markets, roads and Mpumbu where the pieces [slaves] are traded."

卐

FROM THE MOMENT OF Afonso I's death, in 1542, it would take roughly another 120 years for Kongo's demise to fully play itself out, a period marked by frequent domestic instability but also by bold and imaginative diplomacy spanning three continents and by war waged both in alliance with and against some of the leading European nations of the day. First came two civil wars, marking the third consecutive time that succession in the kingdom had led to open conflict among the elite. In the midst of the second of these post-Afonso succession battles, Kongo suffered a devastating invasion by a mysterious group from the east known as the Jagas. Historians remain divided in their explanations of their origins and motives, with some viewing the Jagas as obscure factional participants in the civil war that brought to power a king named Alvaro I in 1568. Others, though, have portrayed the Jagas as residents of territories situated well to the east, beyond the frontiers of Kongo, who rose up violently either in response to the depredations of the slave trade that were sweeping their lands, or perhaps out of a desire to get in on the action themselves, including winning access to the lucrative commerce in foreign goods.

Whatever their precise motives, the Jagas were able to drive Alvaro and his court from the capital, Mbanza Kongo, leading for the first time to the widespread enslavement of freeborn people of Kongo. From his place of refuge, on an island located in the Congo River, Alvaro appealed to Portugal for assistance in mounting a counteroffensive and restoring royal authority in the capital. Portugal responded positively, but with demands of its own: it would deploy six hundred soldiers to help restore Kongolese authority, but in exchange it extracted tribute for the first time for a limited period, as well as Kongo's assent to the formation of a small Portuguese colony in a coastal area to the south long controlled by the African kingdom.

In 1571, King Sebastião of Portugal decreed this new colony into existence, naming as its leader the grandson of the explorer Bar-

tolomeu Dias, Paulo Dias de Novais, whom he empowered as governor for life and hereditary lord. When Paulo Dias arrived at Luanda
four years later, commanding an armada of nine ships that had borne
seven hundred men, along with plentiful artillery, he initiated the
creation of the first European fortified town built in sub-Saharan
Africa since Elmina nearly a century earlier. It would remain the
slaving headquarters for Portugal for an enormous stretch of western
Central Africa until the abolishment of the trade. Even as of this late
date, some in the Portuguese court still entertained dreams of discovering vast enough quantities of silver or gold to turn the Luanda
colony into a kind of "Potosí on the Kwanza," meaning the major
river of that name. But as Dias proceeded, he was most mindful of his
royal mandate to "subjugate and conquer the kingdom of Angola,"
which effectively meant Ndongo. No longer would the Portuguese
cultivate the goodwill of their hosts or rely on the power of trade
in novel goods, as they had for a century with neighboring Kongo.
Instead, they intended to "conquer and rule" Ndongo's inhabitants.
The megalomaniacal Dias was privately convinced that the new slave
markets within reach of his colony would generate enough wealth to
create a new, white-led civilization worthy of comparison with Rome,
a vision that was clearly fueled by the commercial nexus with slave
markets in the New World. Early on, Luanda's new governor pursued this agenda with the acquiescence of Kongo's king Alvaro, but
the alliance between Lisbon and the restored authority in Mbanza
Kongo soon foundered, in part over the issue of Portuguese support
to Kongo's sometime-vassal-sometime-rival Ndongo, which had led
to increasing slave raids on Kongo territories from the south.

  According to its own foundation story, the Kingdom of Ndongo
arose in the sixteenth century as an offshoot of the older and considerably larger Kongo to its north. Anxious to keep up with its neighbor, Ngongo had also dispatched a succession of envoys to Portugal
between 1518 and 1556, each of them petitioning Lisbon to establish relations, including missionary delegations, much as Portugal
had done more than a half century earlier with Kongo. In 1560, Lisbon finally acceded to this request, later entering into an explicit

alliance with Ndongo. However, this would not last and by 1579, the two sides were in open conflict. The Portuguese had assisted the Ndongo king, Kasenda, in his campaigns against disloyal provincial leaders, but as Dias's men established themselves more and more deeply throughout the kingdom, Kasenda came to believe, correctly, that their true aim was to overthrow him. In response, the Ndongo king ordered the arrest and execution of forty Portuguese living in his capital, Kabasa, prompting Dias to now openly pursue conquest. By 1582, Dias was boasting to King Sebastião that he had won over "seventy knights," whose power would enable him to defeat the "king of Ngola," whose armies began to suffer losses that mounted into the tens of thousands in individual campaigns. This, in turn, richly fed Portugal's traffic in slaves, which was a principal aim all along. According to contemporaneous Portuguese estimates, between 1575 and the 1590s, Lisbon shipped as many as fifty thousand slaves from Ndongo to Brazil.

In this period, according to John Thornton, Portugal succeeded in building "a wide-ranging network of settlements and trading communities" throughout the region, spanning the territories of both of these kingdoms and beyond for the purpose of continuing to ramp up its now fast-expanding Atlantic slave trade. By 1576, a Portuguese present in Luanda could boast of the new colony, "Here . . . one finds all the slaves which one could want and they cost practically nothing. Except for the chiefs, all the natives here are either born in slavery or can be reduced to that condition without the least pretext." By 1591, Portuguese officials were so enthusiastic about the prospects of their traffic in humans that one of them claimed to the crown that Luanda could supply slaves to Brazil "until the end of the world." But Portugal's mounting abominations eventually drove Kongo and Ndongo into tactical alliances with each other that on occasion enabled these rapidly globalizing Central African powers to inflict major defeats on the Portuguese. Meanwhile, each of them began casting about for foreign partners to help them defeat Lisbon.

In 1591, even before any such foreign help could be enlisted,

African armies nearly expelled the Portuguese from their new colony built around the bay of Luanda, which eventually came to be known as Angola. The resilient and determined Portuguese soon recovered, though, and by 1600 had extended their colony's reach to the north side of the Kwanza River, strongly encroaching on areas claimed by Kongo. This produced a sharp rupture between Kongo and Portugal and led Kongo's King Alvaro to lodge diplomatic complaints about Portuguese behavior with Lisbon, Madrid, and Rome. Portugal continued, meanwhile, to flex its muscles with Ndongo. Unable to defeat Ndongo's armies in that kingdom's core territories, however, in 1615 the Portuguese switched tactics, forging an alliance with a roving, ritually cannibalistic mercenary force in the region of mysterious origin known as the Imbangala, who may have themselves been victims of earlier depredations of the slave trade, or of drought. After a devastating two-year spree of murder, rape, and pillage, the Imbangala captured the Ndongo capital, forcing its king to flee.

Absorbing young, captured males irrespective of ethnic group as they went, these marauding warlord armies swelled enormously. By 1621, they had seized fifty thousand slaves, whom they sold to the Portuguese to feed the burgeoning Atlantic trade. The terror of the Imbangala campaigns was so total that the slave-trading fairs that the Portuguese had long operated to promote the trade were almost rendered obsolete. In their place came the mass enslavement of entire communities. For the first time, this included large numbers of young children, or *muleques*, breaking with the practice that prevailed in Atlantic Africa of prioritizing young adult male captives in their reproductive primes. The sudden prevalence of enslaved children was due in part to the Imbangala's own desire to conscript males of fighting age, but also to changes in Portuguese policy. Both via royal edict and taxation law, the rules of slave trading were amended to sanction child slavery and enhance its profitability. In parallel with the Imbangala terror, successive Portuguese pursued a strategy of fomenting near continuous war in order to turn local chiefs, or *sobas*, into vassals. The Europeans forced these chiefs to pay annual tribute in the form of captives, usually meaning children and women, adding to their slave commerce.

With success in executing Lisbon's original plan of taking control of Ndongo and using it as a seemingly inexhaustible source of slaves practically at hand, a new Portuguese governor, João Correia de Sousa, decided to direct Lisbon's alliance with the Imbangala against Kongo, in the hopes that like Ndongo, it, too, could be severely destabilized or destroyed outright. The pretext used by the Portuguese was one that would become a classic in the geopolitics of chattel slavery: they claimed that Kongo was furnishing asylum to runaway slaves from outlying territories. (American readers will of course recognize this as a familiar justification for the South's launching of the Civil War.) Kongo would indeed become a failed state in the face of the duplicity and aggression of Portugal (and Brazil), but that fate still lay decades into the future and would arrive only after it had played some of the most remarkable cards ever seen in the history of resistance to early European imperialism.

30

WAR FOR THE BLACK ATLANTIC

THE PORTUGUESE INVASION OF KONGO in alliance with the Imbangala, as it happens, was launched late in 1622, one year after the Dutch Estates General founded the West India Company. The Company was created with the unambiguous aim of depriving Spain of vital sources of revenue derived from the booming slave and sugar trades, both of which Portugal had hitherto dominated. The Kongolese and Dutch had been exploring relations with each other ever since Dutch seaborne missions began showing up in search of trade in the late sixteenth century. Readers will recall that Spain and Portugal had unified their crowns in 1580, and that for Holland, attacking the basis of rich new sources of Portuguese wealth derived from the exploitation of Africans was a potent means of weakening Spain's ability to finance its campaigns in the Thirty Years War.

In November 1622 a joint Portuguese-Imbangala force routed a Kongolese army in the south of the kingdom, producing accounts of cannibals eating a number of nobles. The attack also resulted in many other abductees being deported into the Atlantic slave trade. Kongo's armies soon rallied, though, and the following January, they roundly defeated their Portuguese-Imbangala enemies in a major encounter near the town of Mbanda Kasi. The Kongolese king Pedro II followed up this victory with a string of extraordinary diplomatic initiatives. In letters dispatched to the king of Spain and to the pope, he denounced the Portuguese aggression and the atrocities of the Imbangala and demanded the return of Kongo nobles and others who had been shipped to Brazil as slaves. Two years later, as a result of his protests, over a thousand of them were shipped back across the Atlantic and returned to their homes.

This was a remarkable turnabout, but Pedro did not stop there. That same year he and Count Manuel of Soyo, Kongo's powerful and semi-autonomous coastal province, each sent letters to the Dutch Estates General proposing a formal alliance in order to expel the Portuguese from Angola altogether. A Dutch merchant named Joris Pieterson carried these messages back home, informing the Estates General of Kongo's request "to provide them with four or five warships as well as five or six hundred soldiers for assistance on water as well as the land." Kongo, in return, offered to pay for "the ships and the monthly wages of the soldiers with gold, silver or ivory." Leaving no chance that the Dutch could overlook the strategic implications of Angola, Kongo offered to grant control over Luanda to its new Dutch allies, specifying that "more than twenty-four thousand blacks [were already being shipped] annually from there to Brazil the West-Indies and other places."

At the time this alliance offer was made, the Dutch were already busily casting about for ways of cutting the Spanish jugular to the New World wealth and to its prosperity so richly underpinned by African slavery. Among the ideas being contemplated by the newly born West India Company were the seizure of Havana and the takeover of the Canary Islands, which would have given the Dutch a decent base off the African continent from which to attack the transatlantic slave trade.

Angola represented a far bigger target than either of these objectives, though. By the 1620s, it was generating over half of all the slaves supplied to Brazil and the Spanish New World. Indeed, the "continual construction of Brazil," it was said, was so thoroughly based on the "constant destruction of Angola," that the two projects could not be disentangled. This made shutting down the human pipeline from western Central Africa the West India Company's best prospect for radically undermining the Atlantic complex of the Iberian powers.

An alliance offer like the one issued by Kongo could have come only from an African kingdom that was deeply informed about the state of politics in Europe. It must have been thoroughly *au fait* not only about the conflict between the Dutch and Spanish, and Portugal's union with Spain, but also probably about the recent creation of the West Indies Company. Such intelligence derived from Kongo's long-standing trade links to the Dutch, as well as its investments in maintaining robust diplomatic representation in Europe. But it was only the promise of support from a strong and determined African ally, one moreover that stood willing to subsidize the Dutch offensive, that made achieving such audacious aims seem workable.

What ensued was the largest interimperial conflict of the seventeenth century Atlantic, a complex, on-again, off-again naval and land war fought on opposite sides of the southern ocean, which played a major role in weakening Portugal and taxing Spain over the course of two decades and yet has been broadly ignored in histories of the Thirty Years War. And what seems clear is that without the strategic initiative of Kongo, no Dutch scheme of this era in the Atlantic would have ever been worthy of the name the Great Design.

In December 1623, the Dutch Estates General responded to Pedro II's letter of the previous year by dispatching a large fleet composed of twenty-six warships and 3300 combatants to Brazil. There they quickly captured Salvador, the capital of Bahia and, after Lisbon itself, the second most important city in the Portuguese imperial world. I am about as grizzled a traveler as one can find, having visited something like 120 countries, but few places have surprised me more than the old world extravagance of Pelourinho, Salvador's grand imperial center, which is lustily draped over a hill that offers gasp-worthy views of the broad and shielded Bay of All Saints. It is from the glittering blue beyond visible there that countless slaves arrived and into which the lucrative sugar of the Recôncavo, Bahia's richest plantation region, departed. Pelourinho is bedecked with extraordinary gilded churches and other architectural jewels dating

from the sixteenth through the eighteenth centuries, too numerous to count, many of them clustered around a grand square where
slaves were brought to be flogged in public. Here, Lisbon built
things to the finest standards of the age in Europe. Thanks to Black
labor, it could afford to, and the generalized opulence suggests the
Portuguese never imagined they would ever have to relinquish their
hold on the place. This also helps make obvious why once they did,
Portugal would pull out all the stops to oust the Dutch and restore
its control.

In August 1624, a fleet considerably smaller than twenty-six warships under the command of Piet Heyn, vice admiral of the Dutch
West India Company, set sail from Salvador, with the aim of capturing Luanda. Pedro II had requested between 500 and 600 soldiers,
but Heyn had just 420 men with him. He was confident nonetheless,
both because he carried with him a copy of the correspondence from
Pedro and also because he knew that ships under the command of
another Dutch officer, Phillips van Zuylen, were already present in
the area.

By the time Heyn arrived in the waters off western Central
Africa, though, matters had taken another abrupt turn. Pedro II had
died, eventually opening the way for yet another contested succession in Kongo. The kingdom was under attack, moreover, from both
the north and south, with the latter meaning from Portuguese and
their Imbangala allies. To his dismay, Heyn learned that his compatriot van Zuylen had already made a brief harrying attack on Luanda
before sailing off to the north. Heyn, undaunted, launched an assault
of his own on Luanda that began on October 30, 1624, but he abandoned the attack less than a week later under the defensive pressure
of strong bombardment by the Portuguese. Soon afterward, Heyn
sailed to the Kongo province of Soyo, where he found van Zuylen's
fleet at anchor. There, Heyn sought to persuade Count Manuel to
back his war on the Portuguese at Luanda, but this was refused on
the grounds that his Kongo correspondence might be forgeries, and
furthermore because the Dutch Lutherans were Protestant heretics,
whereas Kongo was staunchly Catholic. This remains hard to fully

comprehend insofar as Manuel, like King Pedro II, had previously petitioned the Dutch to ally with Kongo, but is perhaps explained in part by inducements or pressure on him brought to bear by the Portuguese.

Kongo would soon enter into a period of debilitating civil war, making it temporarily unfit for any kind of bold alliance or diplomacy. But events would soon take yet another dramatic twist, and they involved Heyn, who eventually sailed westward across the Atlantic again, where he pulled off an exploit that neither the English nor French had ever managed, despite their greater resources and persistent efforts. As we have seen, Heyn captured intact a major Spanish silver fleet off Cuba, in Matanzas Bay, in 1628. Flush with the booty from that triumph, the Dutch, who had in the meantime been expelled from Bahia, seized the adjacent Brazilian province of Pernambuco, which became the cornerstone of their empire. The desire to extract wealth from the booming sugar plantations of this region caused the Dutch to abandon their previous religious reservations about the Atlantic slave trade. This eventually led them back to Kongo, where they became major actors in this commerce in mid-seventeenth century.* The taint of slavery perhaps helps explain why New Amsterdam is by far the best-known and studied seventeenth-century Dutch colony in Holland today, and not the country's immeasurably more important Brazilian colony.

In 1635, after the Dutch found themselves overmatched in a naval confrontation off Angola, their retreating fleet anchored at Soyo, where a new count, named Paolo, invited them to restore commercial relations. By this time, the Dutch priority of purchasing slaves was clear, and Paolo allowed them to establish a "factory" for this purpose at Mpinda. This was the Soyo port where Diogo Cão had established Europe's first contact with Kongo a century and a half earlier. It was not until 1641, however, that Dutch-Kongolese ties would firm up into a solid alliance. This next phase in strategic

---

* The labor needs of Pernambuco also led to a shift of priorities at Elmina by the Dutch, from the commerce in gold to the traffic in human beings.

maneuvering came about only when the head of another Kongolese province, Garcia of Mbamba, wrote to the Dutch factor, "[I]f God Almighty makes me become king, as I hope he will soon, as I am the closest inheritor of the crown, I will look to attack the Portuguese, as here in Mbamba, I suffer great trouble from them."

On February 22, shortly after this correspondence was written, the governor of Mbamba was indeed installed king, under the name Garcia II. Less than six months later, the Dutch dispatched the single largest expedition in the history of the West India Company to Angola. It consisted of "twenty-two ships, two thousand soldiers from the Netherlands and elsewhere in Europe, and Native Americans from Brazil." The commander, Cornelis Cornelison Jol, was under orders to seize Luanda and "tie up an alliance with the King of Congo and with the Count of [Soyo] and the other neighboring kings and princes . . . [and] tighten with them a defensive and offensive alliance, in order to extend the power of our arms as far as possible." On their own, the Dutch enjoyed immediate success at Luanda, and then made contact with Kongo, which sent forces to help secure access to the coast, thus strongly complementing the West India Company's strategic plans. In March 1642, with the Portuguese under growing pressure, Garcia II signed a comprehensive alliance with the Dutch, granting them the right to trade for slaves in the area as well as to build forts. Characteristically jealous of his kingdom's sovereignty as a Kongolese monarch, though, Garcia II imposed two major restrictions: the Dutch would neither be granted the monopoly on trade they had hoped for, nor would they be allowed to promote the Protestant faith.

These limitations notwithstanding, the new allies inflicted a major defeat on the Portuguese in the south that September. Njinga, the powerful longtime queen of Ndongo, then entered into coordination with the Dutch as part of a loose pan–Central African alliance with Kongo. This, at last, seemed to offer a real prospect that Portugal could be completely driven from the region and evicted to "Brazil or Bengal," in Garcia II's phrasing. But unbeknownst to the combatants at the time, European politics had already radically realigned in ways that would profoundly reconfigure the situation in western Central Africa yet again. In December 1640, Portugal had risen up against Spanish rule and restored its own independence. The following year it made peace with the Netherlands. Weakening Spain had been the Dutch goal all along, so this eliminated the last compelling rationale for hostilities against Lisbon in Africa. Delayed word of the Dutch peace with Portugal reached Luanda only on September 21, 1642. King Garcia's armies were enjoying great success against the Portuguese at the time, but the shake-up in European politics pulled the rug out from under him. Ruthlessly cutting Garcia entirely out of the picture, the two European powers soon reached an agreement on commercial relations in and around Luanda. It included provisions that allowed the Jesuits to resume lucrative operations at more than fifty plantations they had created along the Bengo River to provision Luanda, as well as the resumption of its high-volume slave trade.*

Several more important shifts in this history lay just ahead, each of them helping underscore something vital to our understanding of the last four hundred years—something that is seldom taught: just how deeply the politics and economics of western Central Africa were connected with those of the broader Atlantic world. Kongo would go to war against Soyo, and each would dispatch diplomats or nobles across the Atlantic to Recife, the capital of Pernambuco, to try to win over the Dutch government there to their side. The Dutch would fight once again alongside Kongo in Central Africa, in part to prevent the collapse of Queen Njinga's armies in Angola. And Portugal would respond by sending a major fleet bearing troops from Brazil in 1648, including enslaved Blacks and Native Americans, to finally force their European rival's capitulation.

Later, Kongo fought on alone against Portugal, persisting even after Lisbon had reconquered Angola. Kongo was hobbled by terrible succession disputes again in the 1660s, and its armies were defeated in a major battle at Mbwila. As a result, Kongo's King

---

* As we have seen, the Jesuits were also operating large slave plantations to grow sugar for profit in Mexico around this same time.

Antonio was captured and beheaded by the Portuguese, producing a fierce civil war in the kingdom. Even in the face of this setback, Kongo continued to inflict major losses on Lisbon's forces. Portugal suffered what was perhaps its worst defeat during the entire history of its involvement in Angola in a battle at a place called Kitombo in 1670, where its entire force was annihilated. This, however, represented something of a last hurrah. Albeit at immense cost, Portugal gradually consolidated its control over Angola, which it would occupy, bleed, and then hold on to as a colony until 1975. Over the duration of the transatlantic slave trade, Luanda generated 1.3 million captives, making it the most prolific single source of slaves into the American trade.

Garcia II stands out as an unusually resourceful leader in a kingdom that produced a number of extraordinary statesmen, and this judgment is richly warranted even though by the end of his rule his kingdom was on its way to becoming a failed state. Garcia had understood the imperative of taking a gamble with the Dutch as a long-shot chance of ridding his land of the vampirish Portuguese. He had an equally nuanced sense of the complicated political matrix of his region's native kingdoms, and he maneuvered deftly to bring Ndongo, a rival state and sometime enemy, into the fold against their common antagonist, Lisbon. But he must also be seen as a deeply tragic figure. Only too late did he understand what the scourge of slavery would mean for Kongo—so late that he was unable to do anything about it.

In a 1643 letter to a Jesuit rector in Luanda, Garcia lamented how "in place of gold or silver or other things that serve as money in other places," slaves had become the currency of his entire region, adding that "in our simplicity we gave place to that from which grows all the evils of our country."

IF WE HAVE DWELLED for this long on two kingdoms in western Central Africa, Kongo and Ndongo, that are all but unknown to the general public, it is for more than the granular details of their histories, as astonishing and unsuspected as those are. As we have seen, they were both important and ambitious players in a momentous three-continent struggle over the South Atlantic, a crucial moment in the history of the early modern era, especially Kongo. The larger purpose is to assess the many deep and persistent ways that the Atlantic slave trade impacted Africa. And in doing so, to return to a topic that lies at this book's heart, the advent of modernity. Our task is to better understand Africa's path to its own deeply splintered version of that concept. One might well have used the rich histories of the Asante, in present-day Ghana, or Benin, the empire that rose up in what is now southern Nigeria, instead. The Asante spent most of the nineteenth century stoutly resisting the British in three major wars and numerous smaller conflicts, before finally being vanquished by the world's mightiest imperial power in 1900. Their defeat was assured only with the arrival of accurate, long-distance weapons like the Enfield and the Snider rifles, as well as modern artillery, which the British incorporated in the final third of the eighteenth century. Alas, Asante, too, partook heavily in the slave trade.

Kongo, though, offers the unique advantage of having left a rich documentary record of its own making, and together with Ndongo and a number of smaller, affiliated states in this region, takes a backseat to nowhere in the loss of life and of labor and its productive potential into American slavery. This political history, coupled with the demographic and human catastrophe of the Atlantic slave trade, leaves us with three categories of experience that can be usefully applied in considering the advent of modernity and later of modern state formation and independence to much of the rest of Africa south of the Sahara—albeit in different degrees.

If the Atlantic slave trade and the world-changing industries that it made possible (via sugar and then cotton) played vital roles in the ascension of Europe and, as we will show in Part V, the United States, our overriding purpose thus far has been to explore how they conditioned Africa's recent past and its entry into the present. Kongo's tragic history of relations with Europe and of massive enslavement provides a dramatic illustration of the much neglected political side of the early modern encounter between Africa and Europe. As one would expect, the political landscape of Africa was highly varied in the late Middle Ages, just as it was in Europe. Africa was filled with micro-states, most of them ephemeral, just as it was with many other societies that social scientists characterize as stateless. In Kongo, however, as in Ndongo to its south, and as in many other places, from coastal West Africa (Ghana, Senegambia, etc.) to the vast interior of that region, as well as areas encompassed by modern Mali and Nigeria, the late Middle Ages and the early modern era saw the formation of numerous complex, substantial, and impressively capable states.

This summons us to consider what would have happened to the political map of Africa over time had Europeans not arrived when they did, hell-bent on trading for gold and, later, for slaves? One can conceive of a multitude of possible alternative outcomes. Among them, it is not unreasonable to imagine that large parts of West and Central Africa would have followed their own gradual processes of political consolidation. These could have been based on a combination of peaceful alliances and gradual amalgamation, as well as on bloody conquest, much as happened in other parts of the world. Had Africa been afforded more time and space for its own relatively autonomous development, it might plausibly have been much better prepared for its subsequent integration into the global economy, and more capable of negotiating this crucial transition on terms substantially more favorable to itself. Under such a scenario, one can imagine an Africa that avoided the severe fragmentation that began at the Berlin Conference and continues to hang heavily over the continent today. The existence of fifty-four countries, many of them tiny, with haphazard borders drawn solely according to the whims of imperial Europe, constitutes a severe burden that the people of the continent now seem condemned to carry indefinitely into the future.

This holds especially true for the sixteen African countries, or nearly one-third of the entire continent, that are landlocked, with fourteen of them drawn up that way by Europeans. Landlocked countries are disproportionately represented among the world's least developed nations. On average, they trade 30 percent less than coastal countries. The costs of doing business in landlocked states are typically vastly higher than in their coastal counterparts. In Africa, this has led to few investments outside of extractive industries. The World Bank has estimated that the mere fact of being landlocked reduces annual national growth rates by an average of 1.5 percent. When one considers how such effects compound year after year, this constitutes a staggering ongoing penalty. Because they are surrounded on all sides by neighbors, landlocked countries are also much more susceptible to cross-border conflict, as well as to negative impacts from turmoil in neighboring states. As a result, landlocked countries generate a greatly disproportionate share of the region's refugees. To bring this all down to earth, one need look no farther than the Sahel region, which features so richly in the history of the late Middle Ages, and hence, our Atlantic world. Its landlocked states—Mali, Burkina Faso, Niger, and Chad—are among the poorest and least stable countries on the continent, and today the growing conflicts that fester in them are driving heavy migration within the region, to Europe, and even farther afield.

To be completely fair to our counterfactual, though, one must reach beyond the crippling legacy of borders imposed by outsiders and consider the even larger cost to Africa of having had its own sovereign political processes derailed under the twin pressures of the four-centuries-long Atlantic slave trade, and the brief hegemony on the cheap of colonialism that followed on its heels. Westerners in that latter era flattered themselves with the idea that they were fulfilling a so-called white man's burden by bestowing modern institutions and norms upon a hopelessly backward continent. The result was more often the destruction of indigenous institutions where they had once been strong, or the imposition of ersatz new arrangements based on a poor understanding of the complexities of local customs and identities under indirect rule to replace them, or simply the filling of a vacuum. According to the historian Sara Berry, colonial states were unable to "impose either [European] laws and institutions or their own version of 'traditional' African ones onto indigenous societies." Some scholars say this merely promoted instability in local structures of authority. Others, meanwhile, contend that the colonial invention of neotraditionalist institutions led to new African forms of authoritarianism, or a "decentralized despotism," in the phrase of the Ugandan scholar Mahmood Mamdani. Whatever the diagnosis, few are those today who see Europe as having placed Africa on a healthy or stable trajectory.

The transition from the era of the transatlantic slave trade to the advent of full-blown European colonies in Africa was a gradual and long-drawn-out affair, stretching from the late eighteenth until the late nineteenth century. Nowadays, the details of Europe's interactions with Africa during this period are scarcely recalled at all, but the details hold great interest for anyone who seeks to make sense of the questions we have posed about Africa's troubled path to modernity.

After the United States won its independence from Britain, that country begin to think seriously of empire in Africa for the first time. The continent had of course been vital to London as a source of slaves for its wealth-producing colonies in the Caribbean. By the end of the American War for Independence, however, France had become, by virtue of its colony of Saint Domingue, the greatest European beneficiary of the region's slave plantation-complex. Imperial Britain looked to Africa as a place where it could make rapid inroads as it now sought to develop a so-called empire of free trade. Here, two purposes were in play: to ease the psychological blow of its loss to the United States, and the securing of a tropical realm that could become an inexhaustible source of the kinds of agricultural products and raw materials that would be needed as the Industrial Revolution deepened. This became what was, in effect, the third incarnation of Africa as a European El Dorado, following the Iberian-led age of African gold and the long centuries of the slave trade. Unlike the others, this new age, which is all but forgotten now, would prove merely evanescent.

The idea of Africa as a potential source of astronomical growth grew out of a mythical belief in tropical exuberance. British and other European travelers to Africa (and Brazil and parts of tropical

Asia, for that matter) returned with wide-eyed tales about the magical productivity of lands so rich that one merely needed to sprinkle seeds about and maybe do a little occasional weeding to reap fantastic harvests. Among both abolitionists and industrialists alike, some began to argue the secret to obtaining such results lay not in slavery but in the British employment of African labor under the guidance of enlightened Western practices of agriculture, husbandry, and management. Africa's imagined potential in this light briefly drove a level of interest in the continent never before seen in the modern age, or indeed since. Britain may have been primed for a shift in attitudes toward Africa even before its loss of the United States. A strong hint of this can be found in the content of the prestigious British encyclopedia the *Universal History*, which was published between 1736 and 1765 in sixty-five octavo volumes. In a measure of Britain's growing imperial interests and equities, nearly half of the content was taken up by the history of the non-Western world, and remarkably, fully one-eighth of the total space allotted for modern history was devoted to Africa, or as much as East, Southeast, and South Asia combined.

Such enthusiasm for the continent foundered as quickly as it had arisen, though, for two reasons tightly bound up in matters of timing. As we have seen, in the late eighteenth century, when Britain began fantasizing about Africa as the next great platform for empire, Europeans still had little understanding of the role of hygiene in the control of disease and had not yet developed a modern theory of germs. As a result, those who arrived in West Africa totally lacking in resistance to many of the region's endemic tropical diseases perished at staggering rates. Mortality ranged between 25 and 75 percent for Europeans in their first year in coastal West Africa, which acquired a sinister moniker as the "white man's grave." Even those who survived a first year in this environment continued to die at an average annual rate of about 10 percent. Measured in European lives, this meant that the cost of doing business was much higher than in, say, India or the Caribbean.

British interest in South Asia, in fact, was booming at this very moment, in ways that would further contribute to nipping engagement with Africa in the bud. The British East India Company essentially took over the Indian subcontinent in the 1780s and 1790s. The Company's monopoly there would end in 1813, but by that time the India trade had become a far more developed and safer source of commerce than any conceivable African alternative, especially given the continent's fragmentation.

Once Britain abolished the slave trade in 1807 other European nations gradually banned it in turn over the next several decades. This came about, in part, through British interdiction efforts; financial inducements to other slaving countries also encouraged compliance with eradication. It is seldom remembered this way, but what followed the long slave-trade era was a remarkably short period of colonial rule, when a neat graft of Western laws and institutions onto Africa's bodies politic is sometimes imagined to have taken place. The reality was never so promising, however, not even from the outset. During this time, with few exceptions, the European powers committed precious few resources, whether budgetary or human, to developing or even administering Africa. I've written elsewhere about their extraordinarily light colonial footprint almost everywhere on the continent:

> By the late 1930s, France had a mere 385 colonial administrators commanding the destinies of 15 million African subjects. British Africa, with 43 million people, had a roughly comparable 1,200. By the late 1950s, the dawn of the independence era for the continent, out of a population of 200 million sub-Saharan Africans, European stewardship had produced only 8,000 secondary school graduates, half of whom were from just two colonies, Britain's Ghana and Nigeria. In France's territories only about a third of school-aged children received any primary education at all.

In India, according to the 1861 imperial census, the British population was 125,945. Although comprehensive statistics for Africa are hard to come by, there is little doubt that the British population on the continent was far lighter. Another powerful contrast can be drawn with Southeast Asia. According to one estimate, by the late 1930s, fully 10 percent of Vietnamese had attained literacy under French colonial rule. This is an order of magnitude greater than the educational performance of almost any colonial regime in Africa in the same era.

Europe's direct colonial tutelage neither began nor ended everywhere in Africa at the same time, but can be said to have roughly lasted from 1885 until the early 1960s. Outside of South Africa, it was not until after World War II, however, that infrastructure investments of any scale were finally undertaken. The few railways that were built were mostly small-gauge roads and focused on moving untransformed minerals from mine to port. One searches in vain for rail lines or highways connecting the colonies to one another. Seen in the light of the short duration and tenuous nature of European colonial commitments to Africa, it is little wonder that much of the continent has had a politically tumultuous and economically unfulfilling experience of post-independence development.

31

PEOPLE SCATTERED,
A CONTINENT DRAINED

W E WILL RETURN TO THE QUESTION of Africa's weak economic and institutional foundations as the continent entered the independence era. First, though, we must speak about another important dimension of the Atlantic slave trade: its stark effects on the continent's population.

According to the most widely accepted estimates, roughly 12.5 million Africans survived shipment across the Atlantic into the New World slave trade. Another 6 million Africans are thought to have left the continent by human trafficking via North Africa, the Red Sea, and the Indian Ocean. For good reason, the historian Paul Lovejoy has called this enormous outpouring of human beings a "radical break" in the history of the continent. For years, experts have sustained an intense debate over the demographic consequences of this drain on Africa's population. One sophisticated recent assessment of the continent's demographics has suggested that as a result of the slave trades of the modern era, by 1850, Africa's population had been reduced to roughly half of what it would have been had there been no mass trafficking in humans. Other studies have shown that Africa did not reach the population density that Europe enjoyed in 1500 until 1975.

As rigorous as this effort at modeling attempts to be, it nonetheless seriously underestimates the demographic impact of the slave trade by omitting any estimate of the loss of life on the ground in Africa occasioned during the act of trafficking itself. Establishing reliable numbers for the deaths that occurred during slaving-related warfare, capture, and especially the trek from the interior to the coast from slave-trading regions is probably an impossible task. Some historians have estimated, nonetheless, that as many Africans may have perished in these ways as survived the transatlantic passage. Taking into account the numbers of Africans who died aboard the floating tombs that ferried them across the Atlantic, perhaps as few as 42 percent of the people ensnared into the trade survived long enough to undergo sale in the New World. The historian Joseph Miller has estimated that on top of this horrendous toll, by the end of the three- to four-year "seasoning" period that slaves underwent after their arrival in Brazil (and in other plantation societies), perhaps only twenty-eight to thirty out of every hundred people taken captive in Africa were still alive.* Even though this represented an overall "wastage" rate of human life in the order of two-thirds, for decade after decade, the Portuguese and other major traders treated horrific losses like these as a morally unremarkable cost of "doing business."

If Miller's estimate that as many Africans died in captivity on the ground on their own continent as survived long enough to be boarded onto slave ships is even remotely accurate, this would have radical implications for overall estimates of slavery's demographic impact on Africa. Some experts believe that not only did population growth on the continent lag far below what it would have been had there been no slave trade, but that Africa's population actually declined in absolute terms during the four centuries of the Atlantic trade. But the question of how many people were lost to Africa matters for our story in ways that go well beyond the important search for accuracy. How many inhabitants the continent contained was one of the most important fundamentals shaping its path into modernity.

---

* Seasoning was a standard practice almost everywhere chattel slavery was developed in the New World. Death rates varied from place to place (as did the length of this acclimation process), but were substantial everywhere.

For most of its pre-modern history, Africa was seriously underpopulated in comparison with either Europe or Asia. This was due to the strong influence of exceptionally high disease burdens in tropical Africa in suppressing fertility and exacerbating infant mortality, and hence population growth.

By stripping away so many millions of people over a comparatively compact period of time, the Atlantic slave trade left Africa in a greatly weakened state for competition with other parts of the world at the very moment when human society was globalizing for the first time. Not incidentally, in this very same era the populations of Britain and many other parts of Europe were booming. Wherever it occurred in this age, robust population growth accelerated urbanization, which in turn drove all sorts of modernizing processes. Population growth led to bigger and more potent states, ones capable of organizing and fielding larger armies. This meant much larger markets, as well as the potential for greatly intensified trade. But the steady drain of slavery helped deprive Africa of all of these things, and it left the continent more vulnerable to outside competitors and aggressors, especially Europeans, who were not only growing fast themselves but, as we have seen, growing much richer through the appropriation of African labor, which by design consisted overwhelmingly of people in their productive primes.

Quite apart from the slave trade itself, moreover, Africa's population took a further important hit, as did its political institutions, during the period of widespread European conquest of the continent in the late nineteenth century. In fact, its population probably continued to decline even into the early colonial period, in the opening years of the twentieth century.

If the outflow of Africans that began in the late Middle Ages and peaked between the mid-eighteenth and mid-nineteenth centuries represented a radical break with the continent's past, the belated but dramatic rebound in African population growth that began during the interwar years of the twentieth century can be seen as another radical break—this time, though, not merely for Africa, but for all of humankind. The population of Africa, which in all of its history had never been known to undergo rapid sustained growth, increased by about 600 percent in the twentieth century, rising from perhaps 130 million people to 1 billion in one hundred years. Although this surpasses the pace of population growth ever previously seen on any continent in human history, most if not all of this growth should be understood as a kind of recovery or rebound from the depredations of the past. Africa's twentieth-century population boom, however, came too late to position it well for competition with Europe, North America, and other global centers of wealth and power. That is because the foundations of the ascension of these regions had already been laid a century or more earlier, as the world became tightly stitched together via maritime transport and trade, helping ensure the North Atlantic countries a much more favorable position in an era of highly globalized economies.

What many will find even more surprising is the fact that Africa's growth in the twenty-first century is on track to be even more prodigious than what it experienced in the record-breaking hundred years prior, and this will go a long way toward determining and defining our collective future as humans. From roughly 1.4 billion at this writing, according to projections by the highly regarded Population Division of the United Nations, Africa will have 2 billion people by midcentury, and could realistically attain 4 billion by the end of the twenty-first century. There is a bitter historic irony involved here. Africa's fastest population growth has come about not under the supposedly benign stewardship of the white man's burden, but rather in the wake of the independence era of the 1950s and 1960s. It was only then, and not during colonial rule, that important investments began to be made in public health, and especially in maternal and infant care.

The question that now looms heavily before the entire world is: What kind of life will the hundreds of millions of new Africans who will be joining the human race in the decades ahead be able to secure for themselves in the highly fragmented legacy states they are born into? The answer will affect life in every other corner of the world, no matter where you live or how remote Africa may seem to your concerns today. Humankind—and Europe, in particular—could face an immense bill for the extraction from Africa that it organized and profited richly from in the past. If things unfold badly for Africa throughout this century, this will take the form of unimaginably large waves of migration compared with levels seen today. We will see the spread of new emergent diseases, chronic warfare, and terrorism, all related to political instability and economic underdevelopment in Africa. And we will all suffer environmental degradation on a globally devastating scale, such as the destruction of the continent's vast surviving rain forests or the oceans it borders.

Alternatives to catastrophic outcomes like these will come only through working in a much more serious and concerted way to help dramatically improve Africa's present trajectory, in particular by boosting its economic development, including much greater industrialization. Employment and education, especially for girls, will be the keys both for this purpose and in order to decisively bend the demographic curve. Sadly, there is no sign yet that Europe, the West, or anyone else—including China, whose recent relations with the continent have drawn great attention—is really rising to this challenge. In fact, as the Harvard economist Dani Rodrik has pointed out, the rise of newly industrialized China over the last fifty years has made this subsequent industrialization on an important scale for anyone else far more difficult. This will especially hold true for most African countries, which were left saddled by the Berlin Conference with small markets and landlocked or marginally viable states.

A final consideration involving population concerns the enormous internal displacement within Africa that resulted from the slave trade. As the operating radius or catchment area of the business gradually expanded inward from the coastal areas, human chains of newly bound captives in groups ranging in size from twenty to a hundred were driven from place to place along their way to the coast. Joseph Miller has reported that "[a] ring around the right wrist of each individual bound her or him to the main chain and inhibited the use of the right hand to break the fetters. Individuals who resisted or fell found themselves dragged along the ground by the remainder of the group." With the surge in foreign demand to feed the plantations of the West Indies, and the dramatic increase in internal displacement in Africa that accompanied this development beginning in the eighteenth century, the continent experienced a paradoxical-seeming large increase in the practice of slavery among Africans themselves.

This occurred for a variety of reasons. For one thing, traditional value systems were radically transformed by the new forms of exchange, direct or indirect, with Europeans for imported goods. For another, order broke down in many places. Finally, many trafficked Africans were held in intermediate staging areas and never reached the coast. This severely destabilized their inadvertent "host" societies. Moreover, as coastal societies that had suffered population losses in the early phases of the trade became bigger players in this human traffic, many of them sought to absorb more recent victims of the trade who arrived from the interior. The newcomers helped replace some of their own missing populations, albeit as slaves, and to bulk up against rival neighbors. When the slave trade was finally brought to a halt in the first half of the nineteenth century, some West African kings and chiefs complained bitterly that not only were their livelihoods being destroyed, but that they were being left, in effect, holding the bag by having to feed and somehow integrate large numbers of newcomers brought in bondage from inland areas on the assumption that they would be sold onward. Inevitably, many of these people were made slaves in these new (to them) African environments.

This is a dynamic familiar to almost all cultures in coastal West Africa and one that remains uncomfortable to acknowledge or discuss. Whatever their ancestors' participation in the Atlantic trade, broad swaths of West Africa and western Central Africa were forced to absorb captives from elsewhere into their ethnic groups, and indeed into their families, via enslavement. This I know not just from studying the matter, but also from the traumatic experience of my own in-laws. In the midst of a family dispute some years ago, I learned that one branch of my wife's clan had been the slaves of another branch. This was long enough ago so that the two sides now regard each other as full-fledged cousins. The formerly enslaved are more prosperous than many among the former enslaving side of the family, however, and in an unguarded moment during a dispute, one of them pointedly let the other side know it, reopening a wound that all involved had thought long healed.

Other populations fled farther into the interior, often to places with hostile environments, meaning semideserts, rain forests, infertile zones, and even sheer cliffs. Decades ago, as a senior in college, I took the first of what would become many long overland trips on the continent from Abidjan, Côte d'Ivoire, to the middle belt of the Niger River in central Mali. There live a people known as the Dogon who sometime in the fifteenth century sought refuge from the slave trade that was sweeping their region by taking up residence in the sheer face of a mountain, where some of them still reside today.

These were some of the sorts of extreme measures that large numbers of Africans resorted to during the long centuries of the Atlantic commerce in Black bodies. In every part of the continent where the slave trade was intense, "shatter zones" filled with desperate and often heterogeneous mixtures of people fleeing the expanding radius of human trafficking.

TO CONCLUDE THE DISCUSSION of the question at the heart of Part IV of how the entanglement between Europe and Africa that began in the late Middle Ages affected Africa's place in the world over the long run, we must return to economic development and institution building. In earlier pages we described how Africa's severe balkanization and the creation of many landlocked states hobbled the continent's prosperity. Here we turn to other, perhaps more surprising possible causes for Africa's persistent economic and institutional debilities. The political scientist Nathan Nunn and his associate Leonard Wantchekon have shown a strong correlation between the intensity and duration of the slave trade in various parts of Africa and the lasting erosion of social trust. Work like theirs follows an accumulation of economic literature over recent decades emphasizing the importance of social trust to prosperity and economic development.

Nunn and Wantchekon bluntly assert that "the slave trade altered the cultural norms of the ethnic groups exposed to it, making them less trusting of others." Moreover, they continue, "areas with low levels of trust have developed weaker institutions, and [their] weaker institutions in turn have resulted in worse behavior and still lower levels of trust. These societies remain trapped in an equilibrium of uncooperative behavior, mistrust and inefficient institutions." Effects like these took hold, they argued, because under the pressure of the slave trade individuals sought to protect themselves from ensnarement by turning against others within their communities.

Sometimes this meant tricking the unsuspecting into slavery by luring them into households with offers of help or shelter. Other times it might mean selling them through formal legal processes, but ones that had been thoroughly corrupted by the slave business. One common tactic was what is nowadays called a honey trap: deliberately luring men (mostly) into attempts at adultery, which was strictly proscribed in many African societies, and then denouncing them either for an actual infraction or even the mere intention of committing a crime. Kings, chiefs, and headmen commonly had many wives, and sometimes deployed them in this endeavor of entrapment; this was followed by summary judgment and sale of the ensnared onward into the slave market. Local officials took advantage of their power, according to Joseph Miller, to convert "judicial institutions from courts of arbitration to tribunals condemning accused thieves, witches, and sorcerers from rural areas to sale and exile."

As a result of this perversion of judicial processes, Nunn and Wantchekon write that trust in institutions and in authority itself was badly undermined: "because chiefs often were slave traders, or were forced to sell their own people into slavery, the slave trade may have engendered mistrust of political figures, particularly local leaders."

We will eschew here the lengthy and detailed statistical arguments these authors develop in order to focus further, instead, on the supposed mechanisms by which this distrust spread, and upon the alleged consequences. Deploying a profusion of recent data (but unavoidably lacking data for precolonial Africa), Nunn and Wantchekon say that "in areas heavily exposed to the slave trade, norms of mistrust toward others [became] more beneficial than norms of trust, and therefore they would have become more prevalent over time."

This statistical work represents a valuable contribution to this field of study, and in recent years a wide variety of scholars have stressed the caustic and lasting effects of high-volume enslavement on social and political cohesion in Africa. For instance, the historian Walter Hawthorne has written, "The Atlantic trade was insidious because its effects penetrated deep into the social fabric . . . beyond the level of the state and to the level of the village and household. . . . Hence, in many areas, the slave trade pitted neighbor against neighbor." And over time, this began to seriously erode even the closest of social relationships.

A final consideration of the mechanisms through which African societies were profoundly and lastingly knocked off keel by the slave trade involves something admittedly more speculative, but scientifically inspired nonetheless. This is the theory that stresses of various types can be transmitted to one's offspring and from them down to further generations via what are called epigenetic channels. The observable traits of an organism (and in this case, we of course mean human beings), in other words, are affected not only by their genotype, but by their phenotype as well. According to the theory, this comes about as a result of interactions between the expression of their various genes and their environment and social conditions.

The examples above involving condemnation for adultery or witchcraft are one thing, but to understand how transgenerational epigenetic trauma might work one must imagine the constant background stress of having one's community preyed upon by slave traders. In an assessment based on the experience of people in western Central Africa, the region that was hardest hit by the Atlantic slave trade, Joseph Miller estimated that in any given year 0.25

to 0.5 percent of a total regional population of as much as twenty million people may have been marched westward from the interior toward slaving ports. Under these circumstances, he wrote, "[a] hypothetically average farming hamlet of one hundred people could thus expect to suffer the disappearance of one of its twenty or so young men once in the course of each agricultural cycle or two." The impact of such steady disappearance of people into the slave traffic like this, often stealthily and by surprise, injected an enormous dose of ambient environmental insecurity into people's lives, and this imposed social costs that went beyond the taxes on African manpower, production, and fertility that we have spoken of. It does not seem implausible to think that these may have included transgenerational epigenetic cost. As Miller wrote, "it became virtually inevitable that a close relative or friend would vanish without a trace during one's childhood." A transgenerational epigenetic theory may help us understand any social trust deficit in Africa in a deeper way. This is not only a matter of the trust that many in African societies lack toward institutions of government, toward the marketplace, or toward people outside of their ethnic groups or even in their immediate communities. It may also be something much deeper and even more insidious: the haunting echo of a wound that one carries down through the generations, a constant flinching as one lives in expectation of another grievous blow.

Antebellum United States and the
Caribbean basin

PART V

THE
BLACK ATLANTIC
AND A WORLD
MADE NEW

CHARLES
DESLONDES
LEADER

"Civilization is going to pieces," broke out Tom violently. "I've gotten to be a terrible pessimist about things. Have you read 'The Rise of the Coloured Empires' by this man Goddard?"

F. SCOTT FITZGERALD,
The Great Gatsby

32

THE SCENT OF FREEDOM

THE DETAILS OF THEIR LIAISONS were designed to be kept secret and they have remained that way; even the dates have been lost to time. But sometime in December 1810, a small group of slaves who worked the farmland along the final stretch of the lower Mississippi River Valley, a few dozen miles before the river spills its muddy waters into the Gulf of Mexico, met to plot the greatest slave uprising in the history of the United States, and the first one that required summoning forth the country's armed forces in order to put it down.

From all evidence, the plot was led by one Charles Deslondes, a mulatto slave on the plantation of Manuel Andry. Deslondes's trust, hard won from his owner, had lofted him to the favored position of driver. This conforms to a broad pattern of New World revolts led by slaves who enjoyed positions of relative confidence. Time after time they were coachmen, valets, and drivers. Deslondes, who was then about twenty-two years old, rang the bells every morning that summoned the slaves of the Andry plantation to begin their long days laboring in the sugarcane fields. He kept notes on their productivity that determined who would be punished by the lash, and who, more rarely, might receive some small favor. For Deslondes the rewards were rather greater. He was granted permission to leave the premises and travel along the River Road to another plantation, where his enslaved lover worked and lived, and that was to provide his window into history.

The River Road that strung the two plantations together cut through a fabulously rich part of the Orleans Territory known as the German Coast, due to a wave of immigration from that region in the early eighteenth century. Since then, with sugar plantations strung together densely along the Mississippi's east bank, in St. Charles Parish, it had risen to become one of the most spectacularly productive commodity-growing areas in the world. But that is not all. Via the great river that flowed through this territory traveled an enormous share of America's exports—so large a share in fact that by the early nineteenth century, the commerce that poured forth from the Great West via the Gulf of Mexico was as large as America's direct trade across the Atlantic. At the time of the revolt, the region's boom was so effervescent that it was powering a doubling of plantation property values year after year.

In 1803, Thomas Jefferson had pulled off a monumental coup to purchase the Louisiana Territory from France for the historical pittance of $15 million. With a single stroke this nearly doubled the size of the young United States, adding all or part of what became fifteen new states. All in all, these territories, which had belonged to and were still mostly under the control of Native Americans, amount to one-quarter of the country's present size. Upon sealing the deal with Napoleon's France, Robert Livingston, Jefferson's negotiator, proclaimed, "We have lived long, but this is the noblest work of our whole lives. The treaty we have just signed has not been obtained by art or dictated by force; equally advantageous to the two contracting parties, it will change vast solitudes into flourishing districts. From this day the United States take their place among powers of the first rank." Jefferson's purchase is often read as a farsighted bet on the future of what would become a continent-size nation, eventually stretching famously from sea to shining sea, but it was a breathtaking steal even in its time. That is because of the immense wealth the new region disgorged, almost all of which, of course, depended on slavery. A 1797 note to Congress spoke eloquently about how little the Louisiana Territory would have been worth under different circumstances. "Your Memorialists beg leave to represent that the great part of the labour in the Country is performed by slaves, as in the Southern States, and without which, in their present situation the farms in this District would be of little more value to the occupiers than an equal quantity of waste land."

Jefferson did not go into the Louisiana Purchase blind to the risks that inhered to a set of social relations fundamentally based on the intensive exploitation of chattel slaves. His famous ambition was to build what he called an "empire of freedom." By this he meant freedom for the white yeomen who would be lured from the East and beyond there, from Europe, to populate the new territories with the promise of prosperity built upon a reservoir of Black sweat. But at the time of the deal, Jefferson was already haunted by the risk of slave uprisings in his original Old South. One major appeal of his Louisiana project that is little emphasized in the traditional teaching of American history was to lessen that risk by using the Mississippi River Valley and the cotton plantations that began lining its banks as an escape valve for Virginia. His view was that a second great migration of slaves westward out of the Founder's state and out of places like the Carolinas, Maryland, and Georgia would lift the ratio of whites to Blacks there, and reduce the risk of Black revolutionary violence. And toward that very end, between 1820 and 1860, one million Blacks were duly "sold down the river," a euphemism for what was often a brutal trek. This was nothing short of a reprise of the deadly forced migration from Africa that had supplied America with slaves, only more than twice as large in volume. And it was engineered in the fulfillment of Jefferson's idea and in response to the booming demand for labor of cotton planters. This, incidentally, was driven by France's loss of Haiti, which had been a major supplier of cotton to the British textile industry.

Even making full use of this escape valve, Jefferson viewed Black revolt as only being a matter of time. The flood of slaves into New Orleans, he predicted, would inevitably turn that city and its region into a cauldron more explosive even than the one he feared in his own tobacco-growing region. "The first chapter of this history, which has begun in St. Domingo . . . will recount how all the whites were driven from all the other islands," Jefferson had written presciently. This was a reference to the plantation colony that was renamed Haiti in 1804, after the successful slave revolt there. "If something is not done and done soon, we will be the murderers of our own children. . . . The revolutionary storm that is now sweeping the globe will be upon us, and happy if we make timely provision to give it an easy passage over our land." Stopping the drive for freedom by the masses of enslaved Blacks in the New World was a bit like trying to control an epidemic once a respiratory virus has been widely loosed on a community: one struggles in vain to get ahead of it. Years earlier George Washington had had the same insight as Jefferson. In 1791, the year that the slave uprising in Saint Domingue was launched, he had written the French ambassador to his country to pledge his help: "I am happy in the opportunity of testifying how well disposed the United States are to render every aid in their power to our good friends and Allies the French to quell the alarming insurrection of Negroes in Hispaniola." "Alarming," not least because Washington himself was a large slave owner.

In 1811, New Orleans and its suburbs swelled with a population of 25,000, making it a medium-size city for its time, but a fast-growing one. Enslaved Blacks accounted for roughly 11,000 of this number, with free people of color tallying about 6,000. On the nearby German Coast, where sugar was king, and not the cotton that would soon come to so dominate wealth production in the Mississippi River Valley, more than 75 percent of the population was enslaved. Fully 90 percent of the white households in this area owned slaves.

When Charles Deslondes began making clandestine plans for his uprising in December 1810, he did so with a sense of timing as keen as one imagines his sense of history. His vision, in fact mirrored or even outdid Jefferson's in clarity and foresight. The end of the year was a time of decadent parties on the German Coast and in New Orleans. A further distraction to white preparedness lay in the fact that the United States army was at war with Spain in West

Florida, hoping to oust that fading European power from the American mainland. But there was more to Deslondes's daring than simple situational awareness. He and the small groups of slave confederates who planned the German Coast uprising together could practically smell the scent of freedom blowing in the wind, the air of history.

As many as 29,000 enslaved people had been imported to the Lower Mississippi Valley via New Orleans between 1770 and 1808, the year when the external trade in slaves was outlawed in the United States. Among these, considerable numbers had arrived from Saint Domingue, where the planter class had begun to flee after the start of the slave uprising in 1791. Whatever comforting myths whites managed to sustain about the rightfulness and even benevolence of slavery, all Blacks knew that freedom was both their natural right and just deserve. What the slaves who were imported from Haiti understood beyond this, though, was just as critical: for all of their wealth and apparent power, whites could be defeated through concerted and determined acts of bravery. Every bit as much as Jefferson was alarmed, slaves throughout the New World were buoyed by the news of the victory of Blacks in Haiti. There are many striking examples of this. Already by 1808, to take one, free Blacks in Philadelphia had taken to celebrating January 1, Haiti's independence day, as "the Day of Our Political Jubilee," in the words of one African American minister.

Some of the key participants in the German Coast revolt had themselves come from Haiti, where they would have had direct knowledge of the revolutionary events. Even those who didn't, however, were informed by what the historian Julius S. Scott called, in his seminal work of this name, the "common wind." This was an ability of slaves that sometimes seemed miraculous to the white master class to stay quickly abreast of developments throughout the Atlantic world that were of direct importance to their condition. Many of the information networks exploited by Blacks, both masterless and enslaved, radiated from port cities on the ocean's rim and especially in the Caribbean. There Blacks lived and worked in a wide variety of roles, including, as was the case with Olaudah Equiano, whom we've previously met, aboard ships. The most important nodes for the long-distance transmission of news and information were cities like Havana, Kingston, Cap François, Bridgetown, and Charleston, as well as New Orleans. Places like these were the New World descendants of Elmina in the sense that they had spawned vibrant new Creole cultures and networks of information, ideas, and fellowship that spanned land and sea.

There was more to it, though, than just this. Slave owners in Jamaica marveled that even enslaved people who worked in bondage on plantations on the island's hilly interior and far from ports somehow managed to receive news as fast or faster than their white masters. This forced some whites to concede that Blacks, despite their reputed lack of civilization, were nonetheless able to vexingly sustain an "unknown mode of conveying intelligence." As John Adams, the Founding Father and second American president, wrote bemusedly in his diary, "The negroes have a wonderful art of communicating intelligence among themselves. It will run several hundreds of miles in a week or fortnight."

As consequential as it was, the Haitian Revolution was not the only song of freedom wafting in the German Coast air on the eve of revolt there, lending resolve to those determined to fight for their own liberty. Here and there in the Black Atlantic, smaller fires were almost constantly being lit. And even though they were regularly extinguished, they helped keep alive an urgent current of liberation that passed from place to place. Wherever slaves resided, they could be assured of picking up some snippet of the news, however fragmentary, and often gained inspiration or learned lessons in preparation for the fire next time. As early American statesmen like Jefferson and Washington knew, a determined movement toward freedom had been building among slaves in the plantation economies of the Caribbean and along the Atlantic Rim throughout the eighteenth century. This included a major insurrection on the island of St. John, then a Danish colony, in 1733. It included the Stono Uprising in South Carolina in 1739, part of a vast and rolling contest over the spoils of the slave trade and rights to the continental Americas that stretched from Georgia to Cartagena. In the Stono revolt, slaves of English colonists rallied to the Spanish forces holding Florida because they seemed to promise freedom.

And it also included stout and recurrent insurrections waged by maroons in Jamaica pretty much throughout that same decade. Little remembered now, there were even uprisings in New York in 1712 and 1741. In the first of them, roughly thirty Blacks who were said to have been from the Gold Coast used guns, clubs, and knives to kill nine whites and wound seven others before the local militia put their revolt down. In 1749, slaves revolted in Caracas after a free Black named Juan de Cádiz had arrived from Spain and spread rumors that the king had ordered all enslaved people in the Indies be liberated. And something remarkably similar occurred in Martinique.

Here, one is skipping over many smaller revolts. But one cannot leave out an enormous 1760 insurrection in Jamaica that became known as Tacky's War—it shook the British Empire and sent its shock waves throughout the Americas. Virginia, for example, just then rapidly expanding its plantation-labor economy, sought to temporarily ban the importation of slaves from Jamaica for fear that they would become vectors of rebellion on the mainland. Although it became a colony-wide uprising, the aim of the so-called Coromantees, the slaves from the Gold Coast who led Tacky's revolt, was not so much to wage a conventional war against British troops as to bring the island's economy to a complete standstill. At the time, Jamaica was 90 percent Black, and undoubtedly the most profitable colony in the empire. It was also arguably the most politically influential colony, and putting down the revolt forced Britain to deploy its most powerful naval squadron in all the Americas.

Even beyond great uprisings like these among enslaved Blacks themselves, plantation workers brought across the Atlantic in chains were also aware of roiling ideological changes taking place among whites. The most important instances of these were in America and France. In Britain's American colonies, slave-owning whites themselves claimed to be victims of slavery to Britain because of their lack of political representation, and when push came to shove they fought a revolutionary war in order to secure what they called their "freedom." In 1779, hundreds of Blacks were brought from Haiti to fight on behalf of France and the American revolutionaries it supported to lift the British siege of Savannah in that war. That effort failed but nonetheless provided vital cover for American forces during their retreat. But rather than liberty for all, the American Revolution proved itself to be an affirmation of the right of whites to own Black slaves. In the words of the historian Christopher Tomlins, a foundational principle of the nascent republic, unstated but nonetheless present in its very DNA, held that "the elevated freedom of the free depended upon the resources generated by the enslavement of the slave."

Those from Saint Domingue who fought against the British and therefore for American independence at Savannah included Henri Christophe (the future king of Haiti, who was lightly wounded), André Rigaud, and Martial Besse—all names that would become vital entries in the who's who of the Haitian Revolution. Two other major revolutionary figures from French Saint Domingue, leaders named François Makandal and Dutty Boukmann, had freed themselves by escaping to that island from Jamaica, where they had been slaves.

We will turn to the Haitian Revolution shortly but for now limit ourselves to a telling anecdote about France's early effort to suppress it. Haiti's massive slave uprising began two years after the start of the French Revolution, which had powerfully shaped it. When Napoleon dispatched the Marquis de la Salle to put down the Haitian slave uprising in 1791, he ordered his troops to replace their slogan "Live Free or Die," a phrase directly inspired by the French Revolution, with something less subversive: "The Nation, the Law, the King." Otherwise, the marquis explained, "in a land where all property is based on the enslavement of Negroes, who, if they adopted this slogan themselves, would be driven to massacre their masters, and the army which is crossing the sea to bring peace and law to the colony."

France also sought to prevent the arrival in Saint Domingue of slaves from Europe who would have had direct knowledge of the revolution there, and there is little mystery as to why. Through the extraordinarily fast ramping-up of its slave population over a short few decades, France had turned the portion of Hispaniola that it controlled, the future Haiti, into the world's largest sugar and coffee producer. French ships bore more than 224,000 Africans across the Atlantic and into slavery in the decade before the Haitian Revolution alone, most of them bound for Saint Domingue. Roughly half of these enslaved Africans came from the region of Angola and Kongo. By the end of the 1780s, Saint Domingue produced more wealth than the rest of France's colonies combined. It alone generated a third of France's trade.

Perhaps the most consistent rule of this revolutionary age was that precautions taken to prevent the spread of information about human rights and freedom among Blacks were in vain. The common wind that circulated among people kept in bondage in the slave societies of the New World was far too penetrating for any regime of censorship to block. In 1802, in outlawing African Americans as mail carriers, Postmaster General Gideon Granger wrote to the chairman of the U.S. Senate oversight committee, warning that due to events on Hispaniola, American slaves "will learn that a man's rights do not depend on his color. . . . After the scenes which St. Domingo has exhibited to the world, we cannot be too cautious in attempting to prevent similar evils in the four Southern States, where there are, particularly in the eastern and old settled parts of them, so great a proportion of Blacks as to hazard the tranquility and happiness of the free citizens." By 1827, though, the first Black newspaper in the United States was openly inviting its readers to share knowledge about the spread of freedom. "What will be the case, when the slaves in the West Indies and the Spanish states, become all free citizens?" it asked.

Bringing our story back to the Lower Mississippi Valley, a conspiracy to mount what would later become seen as an important precursor to the German Coast uprising was undone at a place called Pointe Coupée in 1795. The plot unraveled when the Spanish, who then ruled the territory, discovered a copy of the 1789 French Declaration of the Rights of Man in a slave cabin. A few years before this, in 1791, a French planter in Martinique had anticipated the Declaration's impact, writing that there was "no one who does not shudder at the idea that a slave or even a free *homme de couleur* [man of color] might say, 'I am a man as well, so I also have rights, and those rights are equal for all.'"

⌗

WHEN CHARLES DESLONDES began to meet clandestinely with a few trusted co-conspirators, probably under the cover of his regular rendezvous with his lover, the participants were undertaking nothing less than a foundational act in what one might nowadays call Pan Africanism.

It is unlikely that he or any of his fellow rebel leaders explicitly thought of their actions in quite this way, but that needn't prevent us from doing so. Among its other qualities, Atlantic slavery was a kind of war waged by whites against the African race: "a war on brutes," or at least on people defined as such for the purposes of their total exploitation. On the African continent itself, a broad realization of the exclusive racial nature of this war—or indeed, a realization of the existence of a race of people called Africans—was slow in coming, even as Black otherness was being formally constructed and legally codified in the West. This, as we have seen, was mostly due to the highly atomized nature of the political landscape in Africa. Equally important was the fact that virtually no Africans had traveled to the New World to witness the epoch-changing project of chattel plantation slavery and returned home to explain its nature and the stakes involved for Black people in general.

In the brutal sugar colonies of the Caribbean, places like Jamaica, Martinique, and Barbados, the life expectancy of a slave hovered between five and seven years. In Saint Domingue, at the time of the revolution that would give birth to the free nation of Haiti, a large majority of the population was African born. Large-scale sugar plantations left little room for the family or for keeping relatives together across generations, and even less for old-timers. Given the low life expectancy, almost everyone who was Black remained to a considerable extent "African," at least culturally speaking. In the Mississippi Valley (and on the American mainland generally), however, a rather different situation obtained. Although sugar production dominated the German Coast, plantations growing cotton and other commodities were located nearby and expanding. The life expectancy of the enslaved in this world was substantially longer than on the sugar islands—so much so that there was in fact a "natural" population increase. The offspring of slaves more than replaced their parents in number, becoming known as Creoles, which in this context meant born on American soil.

Deslondes himself was in this category; he was mixed race to boot. His movement should be thought of as Pan African for the extent to which it drew people together around expanding ideas of shared Blackness. It drew in people who shared two features of his own background. These Creoles, or Blacks who were American born and raised, couldn't speak any African language. And there were almost certainly other people of mixed race, at least in small numbers.[*] There were slaves from a wide variety of African backgrounds. These included Gold Coast Coromantees, including two known co-leaders. As the historian Walter Johnson has written:

> Among their number were men named Charles, Cupidon, Telemacque, Janvier, Harry, Joseph, Kooch [or Kook], Quamana [or Quamena, or Kwamena] Mingo, Diaca, Omar, Al-Hassan. They were African- and American-born, French- and English-speaking, Christian, Muslim, Creole, Akan, and Congo, organized in companies that reflected their various origins. They represented all of the diversity of New World slavery dedicated to the single purpose of its overthrow.

In reference to Toussaint Louverture, Deslondes, and the latter's confederates, another scholar has observed that their creolizing

---

[*] In this, as in other slave revolts of the period, mixed-race people, slave and free, also sided with whites in helping put down revolts.

movement's ideology and tactical plans both evolved in "a lively and fertile milieu in which ideas and practices were exchanged between Europe and the Caribbean, as well as between Africa and the Caribbean."

In the case of slaves brought from both present-day Ghana and from western Central Africa, many would have recently been caught up in wars that had just then been roiling those two parts of the continent and that were driving the traffic in captives. Their experience of fighting may have enhanced the sophistication of the conspirators' planning and shaped the confrontation that was about to be played out. Many others had come from Haiti, where they had seen with their own eyes what Blacks were capable of in armed confrontation with whites, and indeed some would have been direct participants in Haiti's birth. In fact, the German Coast revolt fell a third of the way into what has been called "the period of the most active and carefully planned slave conspiring and rebelling in American history," the years between 1800 and 1831.

Notably, Deslondes and his fellow organizers also obtained support from maroon communities of escaped slaves; these groups lived in the swamps that stretched into the distance behind the German Coast plantations. In doing this, he was replicating a pattern of resistance first seen on São Tomé in the early sixteenth century, where slaves and maroons conspired together in defiance of efforts of whites to cut them off from each other. The coordination with the maroons may have boosted the numbers of Blacks participating in the uprising, but it also seems intended to have provided an escape route into the swamps and wild bayous in case the revolt failed.

There is little reason to doubt that Deslondes and his allies believed they could win their freedom by storming New Orleans after a thirty-six-mile march from their starting point. But they also must have known the odds were stacked against them. By its very design, win or lose, their uprising seemed motivated in part by the idea of transmitting a shock wave down through the ages, of keeping the scent of freedom in the air. They aimed to spill enough blood and make enough noise on behalf of the idea that Black people would do whatever it took to be free so that history would remember them.

Charles Deslondes initiated his uprising on the night of January 8, 1811, when he led a small group of slaves in an attack against Manuel Andry, the owner of the plantation where he worked. Andry had entrusted Deslondes, his slave driver, with the keys to the property, and the band that Deslondes led surprised the owner in his second-story sleeping quarters, killing his son and badly wounding Andry, but somehow failing to prevent his escape. The Andry plantation had been deemed an ideal first target because Andry was a leader of the local planters' militia and, as such, was believed to control a well-furnished stockade. In the event, though, the rebels found far fewer weapons than they had hoped for and had to content themselves with a handful of guns and a bunch of seized uniforms, which they wore, much as Haiti's rebels had.

As they proceeded southeast along the levee, slaves on other plantations rose up and joined them, quickly lifting their numbers from twenty-five or so at the outset to perhaps as many as two hundred men. Their ranks swelled even further when they attacked the plantation of a white settler named James Brown, where two Coromantee plotters, Kook and Kwamena, joined the uprising. As they advanced, the rebel army secured numerous muskets to supplement the farm tools and cutlasses that had been their main weapons. They also took possession of dozens of horses, which made it easier to cover greater distances and to scout the terrain ahead of them. By this time, the revolutionaries carried banners and marched to the beat of martial drumming and crying slogans like "On to New Orleans," and "Freedom or Death," which not only boosted their own morale but also sped word of their arrival far ahead of them. This rallied more and more slaves to their cause and sent whites throughout the German Coast, who had fresh memories of the slaughter of French planters and colonists in Haiti, fleeing toward the city. Manuel Andry, however, escaped to the western bank of the river and from there managed to raise a small army of heavily armed whites to head off the slaves.

The white response to the slave rebellion was halting and disorganized at first. Sentinels galloped into New Orleans early on the morning of January 9 warning of the events upriver, and within a few hours they were followed by a nine-mile-long train of whites, who trudged into the city under a driving rain seeking safety. By that afternoon the governor of the territory, William C. C. Clairborne, ordered the newly arrived commander of American forces in West Florida, Wade Hampton, to prepare a defense of the city. But with few men at his disposal, Hampton could muster only two companies of volunteers, stiffened by thirty regular troops.

As they set off in continuing heavy rain early that evening, Hampton's men were also joined by sailors from the fleet of the naval command at New Orleans, bringing their numbers to roughly one hundred. The slaves' plot seems to have anticipated this, but counted on the heavy majority of Blacks residing in New Orleans to attack the city's armory, where they hoped to seize a large supply of weapons and munitions. But when Hampton's forces set out to meet the revolting slaves, whom they dismissed as banditti, rioters, and brigands, they left behind just enough men to secure the armory, and a crucially important element of the uprising fizzled.

The first confrontation took place around four in the morning on January 10, at a sugar mill in a place fittingly called Cannes Brulées, about fifteen miles from New Orleans. The army of ex-slaves had wisely selected this spot to break their nighttime march: it offered them a fortified place of refuge among the solidly constructed buildings of the sugar works, replete with a picket fence. After extensive reconnoitering, the American forces advanced on horseback and quickly surrounded the rebels' camp. They were counting on the element of surprise as they launched a carefully conceived attack. But by the time the smoke from their heavy fusillade had cleared, all they found were a handful of unarmed Blacks; all of the others had successfully melted away well before the attack. The American army had no way of knowing it, but it had fallen victim to classic tactics from theaters of war in western Central Africa, whose armies were famous for scattering in the face of massed Portuguese attacks.

Drawn into confused pursuit, or simply reduced to exhaustion, the enemy could then be picked off singly or in small groups.

The rebels then aimed to confound Hampton's men by reversing course and streaming back to the northwest, away from the city, and harassing them along the way, but they were soon in for a surprise themselves; one far more lethal and decisive than this first encounter. Manuel Andry had managed to return across the Mississippi River as part of a militia force of about ninety men who were armed to the teeth, and whether through some piece of intelligence or sheer good luck, he did so within easy striking distance of the masterless Blacks.

A little after nine in the morning the two sides met in an open field. There, Andry's militia was joined by Hampton's small army and by another force of whites that had arrived from farther north. For the Blacks, this was now about more even than freedom. Down to the last man, they had to know that they would face extermination if defeated. In a demonstration of astonishing discipline, they formed themselves into a line of battle and steeled themselves for what was to come. Then, sure enough, the whites charged. Knowing that muskets lacked accuracy, Deslondes had given his men the order not to fire until the whites were all but upon them. Facing little limit to their ammunition, though, the whites fired furiously, commencing from afar and continuing without cease as they charged. Blacks began falling under the assault, first one by one, and then in bunches. Still, they held their line until their ammunition began to give out. What had begun as a real battle turned into a rout, and from rout into a massacre in which scores of rebellious Blacks were killed. A satisfied Miguel Andry later called it a "considerable slaughter."

Twenty-one of the rebels were taken to a nearby plantation. There they were tried by a jury that seethed with vengeful planters and condemned to death. These included the Coromantee ringleaders Kook and Kwamena. Kook proudly admitted to having killed the plantation owner François Trépagnier, the owner of Deslondes's female partner, with an axe, but he refused to give the planters information about any of the other participants. Kwamena was equally defiant: he acknowledged his guilt but "did not denounce anyone," according to the transcript. Charles Deslondes, for his part, had temporarily escaped the scene of the battle, fleeing into the nearby swamps, but he, too, was soon captured and executed in particularly gruesome fashion: his arms were chopped off, his legs were broken, and then he was shot. His killers were not satisfied with his mere death, though. In a final act of retribution, his limp and bloody body was finally put on a spit and roasted on public display.

Twenty-nine other survivors of the confrontation were taken to New Orleans, where they were given a more formal trial, albeit this time led by a white judge who had fled the Haitian Revolution. Later, the bloody heads of roughly one hundred of the participants in the uprising, including those who had been executed by the planters who killed Kwamena, were mounted on pikes. These were erected at regular intervals from the Place d'Armes in New Orleans all the way upriver along the levee to the German Coast "as a terrible example to all who would disturb the public tranquility in the future," in the words of the parish "court." While they rotted in the sultry air, feeding the birds that came to peck away at them, they provided cheer and reassurance to the planters, and warning, as if it were needed, to the surviving slaves.

Deslondes's rebellion was put down decisively but had a major impact on the political history of Louisiana, and thereby upon the entire Mississippi River Valley. Planter communities that had once looked upon the idea of integration into the United States with suspicion and hostility now quickly warmed to statehood. This was out of a shared belief that their local militias would never again be adequate to the task of enforcing the radical inequality and suffocating oppression that were the inescapable foundations of a slave society. Louisiana was admitted to the union in 1812, the boom resumed in New Orleans, and it even greatly accelerated. Cotton began its take-off throughout the region, powerfully hoisting the United States in its entirety and transforming the Atlantic world.

If Deslondes had intended for history to speak loudly of his movement, though, as I believe he did, little of that ambition was realized until recently. As the planters reestablished their grip on the region and as the economic takeoff and bid for statehood took hold, the rebellion was steadily and assiduously blotted from memory. As Daniel Rasmussen could write in a 2011 book, which began as an undergraduate thesis at Harvard, "Though the 1811 uprising was the largest slave revolt in American history, the longest published scholarly account runs a mere twenty-four pages." The least one can say is that this was not a matter of scholarly neglect alone. State politics turned to forgetfulness and erasure, a project that spanned generations and is nowadays in the hands of a lucrative plantation tourism industry.

While researching this book I spent time in the Mississippi River Valley, making my way from Memphis south through the cotton-growing Delta, into the German Coast and from there the short final drive on to New Orleans, hoping to find echoes of this history and mostly being disappointed. The search took me to some of the grandest surviving plantation homes, which now do a bustling business offering tours that have more to do with nostalgia for a strangely romanticized past and an oblivious kind of escapism for many who seem not to have given the past much thought at all. This includes weddings in period gowns and Belle Époque photo sessions. At the grand Evergreen Plantation in Louisiana's St. John the Baptist Parish, after I gave myself away as a "historian" interested in slavery in conversation with a white manager, I was politely warned in a hushed voice, "We don't really emphasize in great detail the experience of the slaves here." The main focus would be on architecture and the lifestyle of the whites, he said, as if these could be separated from the lifestyle of the Blacks they had owned. I paid and entered anyway, wanting to see the property that had helped provide one of the most vivid recent Hollywood depictions of the organized racial brutality of plantation life, Quentin Tarantino's *Django Unchained*.

A small crowd of paying visitors jostled that muggy spring day for photos on the lawn before the gleaming white big house's famous twin balustrades. We listened to explanations of the building's Greek Revival design, and when we went inside to tour some of the living quarters, we were treated to numerous little vignettes about the seasonal travails of the master and mistress of the house and about white life by the levee. Among other things, we learned that during the wet season, the River Road, which we could see from the long, second-story verandah, was reduced to a nearly impassible stretch of mud. The middle-aged white woman who guided us made no mention of who would have had to contend with that mud, freeing coach wheels from the muck and hauling provisions on behalf of white masters. Nor was a single word said about the great slave revolt that had occurred nearby.

When we had finished at the big house, most of the visitors peeled away for the exit but some of us elected for a follow-up tour of the slave quarters, which stretched toward the swamps out back. We piled into minivans, which we were told were obligatory, despite the short distance. This, it turned out, would be a chance to get to know a new guide, this time, Black. She was a thin woman in her fifties, who hammed things up with the passengers almost in a parody of a folksy Deep South style. After asking us where we were from, she peppered us with pop-quiz-like questions, which gave her a platform for bite-size history lessons peppered with names and dates.

We were let out of our chilled conveyance just shy of a magnificent lane that was luxuriantly shaded by gigantic live oak trees whose branches trailed gauzy webs of green moss. These were a feature of plantation homes I visited from Natchez to New Orleans, and I also remembered it instantly from the Tarantino film. Amid oohs and aahs, my fellow visitors took turns taking photos of one another before being nudged along gently by our guide. The slave cabins that had been best preserved lay just ahead, in the shaded far margins of the lanes, and how tidy they appeared, with their simple plank-wood construction and slight elevation off the ground in order to moderate seasonal temperature extremes. We were allowed to enter a couple of them and to imagine briefly how entire Black families would have had to live in single-room homes, with kitchens, living, and sleeping spaces all blended into one.

The visitors seemed taken aback by the obvious lack of comfort and privacy, although it was not quite clear to me what else they might have imagined. Visibly jarred by this, when we had reached the minivan again, they inquired about the hardships the slaves had been subjected to, and I suppressed the temptation to speak up. Our guide then explained, as it had almost certainly been explained to her, that the slaves in this region had been lucky, because the area had been colonized by the French, and the French, she said credulously, treated their slaves "best of all."

Fortunately, every place in the plantation tourism sector is not like this. Later that day I drove to another big house a short distance away. The Whitney Plantation was less grandiose but, if anything at first glance, even more commercialized. A fancy, air-conditioned visitors' center sat just inside its gated entrance, and it was full of ticket sellers, guides, and souvenir salespeople, preparing me to be disappointed. What ensued, though, was a totally different kind of experience that devoted more attention to the Black experience of slavery than to the white one of ownership or management. A group of about fifteen people listened quietly as our guide took us around the grounds, stopping before dark, granite steles inscribed with the names of slaves bought in New Orleans and brought here, or born on the plantation, along with the dates of their deaths. Some of them had kept African names, making it possible for me to guess at their origins across the Atlantic: present-day Ghana, Nigeria, Congo, and Guinea. Most had lived very short lives, but there were a few exceptions.

We walked alongside a stretch of swamp, in which we were told alligators still lived, as they had in the old days, constituting another form of danger, beyond the whip and the bloodhound, for any slave who entertained thoughts of escape. And then we rounded a corner, arriving at a ceremonial-looking space, and I came upon something that I had been unprepared for: three rows of realistic-looking Black heads, nineteen in all, in red or white bandannas covered in cowries, erected on pikes. In the artists' rendering, each of them had been given a distinctive face. There, out front in a row by himself, stood the head of Charles Deslondes, his mouth slightly agape as if caught in the act of speaking. The white marble plaque in front of it bore his name, together with a single-word legend: Leader.

33

THE BLACK JACOBINS

I N THE 1962 PREFACE TO HIS BOOK, *The Black Jacobins: Toussaint L'Ouverture and the San Domingo Revolution*, the Trinidadian historian of the Caribbean C. L. R. James summed up the Haitian Revolution in remarkably efficient and yet still majestic terms:

> *In August 1791, after two years of the French Revolution and its repercussions in San Domingo, the slaves revolted. The struggle lasted for 12 years. The slaves defeated in turn the local whites and the soldiers of the French monarchy, a Spanish invasion, a British expedition of some 60,000 men, and a French expedition of similar size under Bonaparte's brother-in-law. The defeat of Bonaparte's expedition in 1803 resulted in the establishment of the Negro state of Haiti, which has lasted to this day.*

James's opening take gives readers a quick foretaste of the monumental achievement of the sansculottes, the slave armies that fought "as naked as worms," in the words of Toussaint Louverture, to defeat wave after wave of Europeans who were determined to deny them their liberty. There is grist enough here alone to develop, as James did so well, one of the most remarkable stories of liberation that we have as a species: the largest slave revolt in human history, and the only one known to have produced a free state. Beyond that, he hints here and there over the course of the book at the linkages to other slave revolts in the New World that provided both precedent and encouragement to the Blacks who would lead the slaves of the French colony of Saint Domingue to freedom. But left largely outside of this already full scope is how the liberation of Haiti gave birth to continental power for the young United States, and changed world history to a degree matched by scant few other modern revolutions.

Like so many of the stories contained in these pages, outside of lineaments so bare boned that they would struggle to fill an almanac entry, the history of this revolution is scarcely known or appreciated even among highly educated Western readers. For at least two reasons, the invisibility of this self-liberation by slaves, most of them recently disembarked from Africa, is especially perverse and disturbing for Americans. That is because of the close physical proximity to America of Hispaniola, the island where Haiti is located, and the outsized impact of Haiti's revolution not just on the size and shape of the United States but on its very character as a nation and emergence as a world power.

In the same way the doomed uprising of Charles Deslondes was directly inspired by the news of the French Revolution, and by the uprising in Haiti that followed on its heels, the Haitian Revolution before it was inspired by similar precedents. Logically, the role of the French Revolution in Haitian events was even more direct and powerful than its influence on Louisiana, given that Saint Domingue was still a colony belonging to France. Less widely appreciated is the way that slaves brought to Haiti from Jamaica and other parts of the British Caribbean helped energize Black resistance in Saint Domingue and came to play many of the leading roles in the uprisings of the late eighteenth century there.

In remarkably little time, the French colony of Saint Domingue had become the richest piece of territory in the world. Just as remarkably, during an era when French foreign trade expanded fivefold overall, it became the source of one-third of all that external trade. What did it mean for the French-held third of Hispaniola to become the richest colony ever? It has been estimated that between

1716 and 1787, a period that covers France's greatest boom years in the eighteenth century, fully 15 percent of its economic growth derived from its Caribbean empire. No fewer than a million of the French king's subjects depended directly on the colonial trade for their livelihoods. Saint Domingue alone generated as much trade as the entire United States. The immense profits generated by the plantation societies Britain and France controlled in the West Indies helped power both their economies into the industrial era. "Never, for centuries had the western world known such economic progress," C. L. R. James wrote of this age. And in both countries, this strongly drove the creation of a new class of bourgeois, who helped usher in major social and political changes. Of France's leading Atlantic ports, James observed, "The fortunes created at Bordeaux, at Nantes, gave to the bourgeois that pride which needed liberty and contributed to human emancipation." James's list might be expanded to include Le Havre and Marseilles. Contemporary historians have begun to put his thought even more strongly, even directly claiming (as has Laurent Dubois, one of the most prominent contemporary historians of Haiti) that the new wealth generated by the slaves of Saint Domingue "helped lay the foundation for the French Revolution."

It is hard to overemphasize just how quickly this transformation built on the back of slave labor, this sugar miracle, came about. When Spain ceded Saint Domingue to France in 1697, the Europeans who lived there supported themselves through a mixture of piracy and cattle, which fed a trade in hides. By 1739, though, it was already the world's wealthiest slave colony, with the number of sugar mills reaching 450, up from just 35 at the turn of the century. As we have seen through plentiful examples, the very phrase "slave colony" meant an utter dependence on Black bodies for the creation and sustenance of wealth. What made Saint Domingue different from others was mostly a matter of the rate at which it consumed African bodies, which increased rapidly throughout the century to attain monstrous heights on the eve of revolution there. The French thirst for new wealth from sugar, indigo, cotton, and coffee was such that in the decade prior to the uprising the volume of slaves brought to Saint Domingue tripled compared with the level of the previous decade. Many years during that decade, the number of slaves brought to the island exceeded 30,000, by themselves surpassing the number of whites living in the colony. Fittingly, slave imports reached their peak in 1790, the year before the revolt began. In all, roughly 685,000 slaves were shipped in chains to this charnel house during the eighteenth century, with a significant concentration of them coming from the general region of the Kongo. Although white planters seem not to have fully appreciated it, the inclination and willingness to put up with their exploitation of a population of slaves dominated by people brought to the island directly from Africa may have been low compared to Creoles raised in bondage. The African newcomers had a fresh, lived experience of freedom and many of them, like the Kongolese, would have already tasted the arts of resistance and of war. As would happen decades later in the American South, Saint Domingue's planter class lulled itself into a false sense of security by somehow imagining their slaves, who were suffering the most extreme forms of duress and suffering ungodly mortality rates, to be content with their lot. "Let an intelligent and educated man compare the deplorable state of these men in Africa with the pleasant and easy life which they enjoy in the colonies," one of them wrote. "Sheltered by all the necessities of life."

It may seem perverse to say so, but in many ways, Saint Domingue can be understood as a victim of its own success, or at least of the grotesque levels of greed that prevailed there. France, whose navy and merchant marine strength paled in comparison with Britain's, struggled to meet the unquenchable demand for more bound labor through its transatlantic trade, and this fatefully led white settlers to trade for slaves with the far more mature English slave colonies nearby. Here, "more mature" refers to the fact that the British colonies had considerably earlier starts in building large plantation-complexes, but it also means places where both slave rebellion and maroon culture had much deeper roots. Principal among these was Jamaica, an island with large and long established maroon communities and numerous instances of organized slave resistance in the first half of the eighteenth century. As we have seen, this resistance reached a crescendo in Jamaica in 1760, during the Seven Years War, with Tacky's War, which killed over five hundred people and seriously threatened colonial rule. This Jamaican rebellion has been called "the most severe wartime challenge before the twentieth century to British rule by internal as opposed to external enemies."

Tacky's War coincided with the most important rebellion in Saint Domingue prior to the uprising that created the free state of Haiti, a revolt led by a former slave, Maroon, and a religious leader named François Makandal. This man's broad influence in the north of the island depended in part on the fact that Makandal employed Catholic iconography and language that was readily adaptable to many African faiths. Furthermore, although the open practice of African religions was officially proscribed, the island's white settlers had little appreciation of the fact that Catholicism had been practiced in Kongo already for nearly two centuries by that time. In Saint Domingue, religious leaders were very often recent survivors of the slave trade who had led traditional religious practices in their African homelands, in places like Kongo or Dahomey. The widespread conflict and political instability that swept these places made them highly fluid in matters of language and faith. Far from condemning them to "social death" in the famous phrase of Orlando Patterson, the Middle Passage into enslavement positioned trafficked Africans to use their mastery of religious customs to forge powerful new identities and alliances, as well as to quickly integrate the esoteric vocabulary and rituals of Catholicism in the New World. This would prove true not only in Saint Domingue, but everywhere where revolts became common, from Brazil to New Orleans.

Makandal was eventually caught, accused of sorcery, and burned at the stake in 1758, after roughly five thousand people had died during the resistance movement he led, many from apparent poisoning. Makandal was blamed for the wave of mysterious deaths, but historians have recently pointed out that a great many of the victims were Black and likely perished due to coincidental and unrelated contamination of flour with mold-derived mycotoxins that had flourished in poor storage conditions. Makandal had arrived in Saint Domingue from Jamaica, after escaping from that island. So, too, had a slave named Dutty Boukmann, who was also a clandestine religious leader and is widely seen as an initiator of the 1791 Haitian slave uprising, which was launched in a secret, nighttime Vodou ceremony in the north of the colony. Another important revolutionary leader in Saint Domingue, Henri Christophe, was born as a slave on the British plantation island of St. Kitts.

On the eve of this revolution there were roughly 460,000 enslaved Blacks in Saint Domingue, compared with a mere 31,000 whites. Positioned between these two populations, enslavers and enslaved with interests that were irreconcilably opposed, there existed a third group, so-called free coloreds, who were almost equal in number to the whites. This is a simplification of an enormously complicated sociological setting. Free coloreds are often imagined as light-skinned, mixed-race people, but in fact they came in all kinds of complexions. The operative word in the term was "free," as these were people of African descent who lived unbound. Many divisions also existed among whites, for example, on the basis of wealth, class, and whether they owned plantations and slaves; similar divisions existed among free coloreds. Put in its simplest form, though, life in the colony that prodigiously laid golden eggs for France was permanently afflicted by a vicious race triangle, and had become "pathologically stratified" on the basis of skin color.

White resentment toward metropolitan France surged almost immediately after the colony's economic takeoff in the 1720s, with pushback by restive planters against taxation without representation that strongly anticipated a dominant theme of the American Revolution. Planters also chafed over the restrictions of French mercantilism, which gave the state a monopoly over the supply of slaves, always judged inadequate by those seeking their fortunes in sugar. French policies also mandated that colonials could sell their goods only back to the motherland, and according to terms that it alone decided. Resentment intensified once again in the 1780s, after France began introducing modest reforms to the set of rules regulating the exploitation of slaves, the Code Noir. One of the reforms gave slaves Saturday afternoons off, in addition to the traditional Sunday break, and also mandated small improvements in food and clothing. One white official in the colony denounced the new rules as an attack on the "sacred right of property." In 1785, another asked, "How can we make a lot of sugar when we work only 16 hours a day?" Here, "we" meant slaves. He answered his own question, saying that the wealth of the colony's plantation economy was ineluctably linked to the rate of "consuming men and animals." As one thinker put it, "All laws, however just and humane they may be in favor of Negroes will always be a violation of the rights of property if they are not sponsored by the colonists. . . . All laws on property are just only if they are supported by the opinion of those who are interested in them as proprietors." By the eighteenth century, the objection about inviolable rights of property owners had become a nearly universal theme in white-dominated slave societies.

Contradictions between the three broad racial categories of Saint Domingue society sharpened steadily over the course of the century until, finally, the 1789 French Revolution forced a definitive reckoning. By midcentury, whites had resolved that they needed to enlist free coloreds to help them suppress maroon rebellions that were spreading through the colony, much as they had in nearby Jamaica. Coloreds could own property, exercise professions, and even own slaves, but they had been barred from participation in the colonial assembly, and thus deprived of political representation. Whites' dependence on them as military allies, however, prompted coloreds to make the same claims to representation that whites had demanded. Ratcheting tensions even further, as their dependence on the colored for their own security grew, white notions about race hardened into an ever more sharply delineated separation of people according to their color. Believing that their own privileged position atop the island's social pyramid could only be maintained by ever stricter racial discrimination, whites worked at codifying imagined differences between human beings of different ancestry. In 1767, for example, one ministerial decree aimed at the aspirations toward equality of the free coloreds stated, "[T]he stain of slavery of people with African ancestry cannot be erased with the gift of freedom."

Too little did either France or its settlers in its most lucrative possession sense that Saint Domingue's vicious racial triangle had placed it on a path of devastation. In the words of the Comte de Mirabeau, the island was "sleeping at the foot of Vesuvius." Although revolution in Saint Domingue was very much an unintended consequence, the announcement of the volcano's inevitable eruption came with the launch of the French Revolution. The very first article of the Declaration of the Rights of Man, adopted by the National Assembly a few weeks after the fall of the Bastille, was earthshaking: it announced, "Men are born and remain equal in rights." Not only were coloreds, predictably enough, emboldened by language like this, in 1789, slaves rose up in French Martinique, too. They interpreted the news borne by the common wind to mean that the king had decided to grant their freedom, only to be blocked by greedy planters who were suppressing the decree.

Meanwhile, with the launch of the French Revolution, ferment increased among Saint Domingue's free coloreds, who were well apprised of the political developments in the métropole. Some whites responded in early 1791, saying that the only solution to the racial tensions on the island was a purge of the coloreds, who they said should be slaughtered. This notion was part of a larger scheme to cast off domination by metropolitan France by inviting Britain to take a role in protecting the colony. Meanwhile, calls were made for slaveholders throughout the Americas to band together to suppress their Black subjects, reject the early stirrings of reformism in Europe, and stop the "contagion of liberty," in order to ensure the survival and perpetuation of the plantation-society model. Here, readers will recall the George Washington letter pledging solidarity in slave ownership to the French ambassador to his country. With France largely preoccupied with its own revolutionary struggles, open armed conflict broke out in Saint Domingue between whites and coloreds, and would continue off and on over the next two years. On occasion, each side opportunistically sought to enlist slaves.

A decade earlier, even before the French Revolution, Abbé Raynal, the French chronicler and encyclopedist of colonialism, had written presciently about the inevitability of Black liberation in Saint Domingue. Raynal argued that slaves had no need of advice about the desirability or even the practicality of freedom as a goal. They didn't need examples, either, for ready ones existed in maroon societies in places like Jamaica and Suriname, which were the product of successful revolts. In Saint Domingue, all they needed was the right opportunity to revolt and the right leaders. "All that the negroes lack is a man courageous enough to carry them to vengeance and carnage . . . Where is he, this great man, that nature owes to its vexed, oppressed, tormented children? Where is he? He will appear, do not doubt it."* The intensifying conflict between whites and coloreds in Saint Domingue, as well as the pushback against France by the colony's planters, provided the opportunity for revolt. And in the person of Toussaint Louverture, a former plantation coachman, the island's unfree population found their extraordinary leader. In fact, Toussaint—who was born in slavery, and freed only in his midforties, by which time he had become not only literate but a student of Machiavelli, Montesquieu, and Rousseau—was said to have been especially captivated by the words of Raynal, which he had read over and over, adopting as his own personal call to arms.

---

* Some historians have recently theorized that these words were those of the French philosopher Denis Diderot, and adopted by Raynal, uncredited, in his edited volume.

34

GILDED NEGROES

W HAT BECAME THE HAITIAN REVOLUTION commenced where the plantation complex was centered, in the far north of the colony, around 10:00 p.m. on August 22, 1791. It helps to understand it if we resist the admittedly powerful temptations of teleology. According to long-standing historiographic tradition, things began with a nighttime uprising by slaves launched at a place called Bois-Caïman (Crocodile forest) amid an African-style religious ceremony. Leaders gathered there are said to have a sacrificed a pig and quaffed its blood, swearing oaths of loyalty and shared determination as they poured libations. Amid heavy, rhythmic drumbeat resounding loudly through the night, enslaved people from nearby plantations began joining in the revolt. As they did so, the sky turned a bright red, as the cane fields, plantation works, and mansions of their masters were all lit ablaze. By the time of the revolution's conclusion in 1804, with the birth of a new Black-ruled republic, only the second independent state and government of its kind in the hemisphere, these events had yielded what one historian has aptly called "the most radical declaration of human rights the world had ever known." In at least one sense, in fact, what occurred in Haiti was indisputably more radical than the far more glorified American Revolution that preceded it by two decades. The new Haitian republic banished slavery and race discrimination from the land, steps that the United States would take only haltingly over the next century and a half.

Toussaint Louverture did not live to see the republic, but more than anyone else he had defined its revolutionary purpose. This meant living up to the unfulfilled ideals of the French Revolution, of universal freedom and true *fraternité*, things that could never be realized as long as slavery endured. In stating his aim, the military leader once declared: "Whatever their color, only one distinction must exist between men, that of good and evil. When Blacks, men of color, and whites rule under the same laws, they must be equally protected and they must be equally repressed when they deviate from them." As one historian has noted, "no other leader anywhere would even give lip service to such an ideal for many decades to come." One must contrast sentiments like these with the thoughts of leading contemporaries in Enlightenment-era Britain and America. In 1805, Talleyrand wrote, "The existence of a negro people in arms, occupying a country which it has soiled by the most criminal acts, is a horrible spectacle for all white nations." Similarly, the commanding British general dispatched to Hispaniola to defeat Toussaint had defined London's aim as preventing the contagious spread from Saint Domingue to Britain's own rich West Indian slave colonies of "the wild and pernicious Doctrines of Liberty and Equality."

As the slave uprising spread in the northern part of the French colony, terrified whites coursed into Cap François, then the biggest city in Saint Domingue and one of the largest in the hemisphere; they formed long, chaotic streams of refugees and created scenes of panic that prefigured New Orleans in 1811. Haiti's slave revolt may have appeared to be spontaneous to these whites, but it was anything but. In its earliest phase, the uprising was led in part by the religious leader named Boukman, whom we have met previously. Boukman was born in Senegambia and had previously lived in Jamaica, where he was employed as a slave driver. This final detail meant that he would have had special privileges during the run-up to the revolt, including the ability to travel off plantation on his weekly day of rest—and this was key to plotting revolutionary action. At the Bois-

Caïman ceremony that set northern Saint Domingue afire, Boukman spoke in starkly messianic terms, urging the slaves who were willing to join him in revolt to revere the cultures and religions of their ancestors. "Throw away the image of the god of the whites who thirsts for our tears," he said, "and listen to the voice of liberty that speaks in the hearts of all of us."

One proximate spark for the events in Saint Domingue appears to have been a rumor that spread in Hispaniola claiming that an order by French king Louis XVI abolishing use of the whip and mandating that slaves be granted three days' rest each week had been set aside by local authorities. The 1789 slave revolt in Martinique that was mentioned earlier had been ignited over similar causes. It was a familiar pattern that would play itself out over and over in this era, only this time with a different ending. An even more important spur to the slaves, however, was the French Revolution itself, which many had interpreted to mean that whites in France had freed themselves of enslavement by others of their own kind. If them, why not us, flowed the thinking among Saint Domingue's enslaved, with the result that by late September 1791, plantations in a broad swath of the north surrounding Cap François had been destroyed by tens of thousands of slaves in revolt. Before long, most of the colony was at war.

Haiti's revolution did not begin with Toussaint Louverture visible at the forefront, nor would it end with him at its helm. Its early stages played out, instead, under a somewhat diffuse leadership. In early November, with violence spreading and more than a thousand plantations reduced to ashes, Dutty Boukman, one of the most prominent figures thus far, was captured and killed. Hoping to restore order by winning their allegiance, revolutionary France responded to the unrest with a decree granting equal rights to the colony's free colored population. This happened as discussions were already building in the métropole over the future of the institution of slavery. Both these developments enraged the whites of Saint Domingue, with one planter saying, "There can be no cultivation in Saint Domingue without slavery; we did not go to find and purchase five hundred thousand savage slaves on the African coast in order to introduce them into the colony as French citizens. Their existence as free people is physically incompatible with the existence of our European brethren." Few could have yet imagined it, but within a year that is precisely what they would become, at least on paper.

That October, the powers of Louis XVI were suspended, leading to the birth of the French Republic, and that same month, the second son of an Allada king, stepped to the fore, more or less pronouncing himself the leader of the revolting slaves. "I want Liberty and Equality to reign in Saint-Domingue," he declared. "Unite to us and fight with us for the same cause." His name, of course, was Toussaint, and C. L. R. James wrote that the most important secret of his genius for leadership was his ability to convey to people so utterly dehumanized by enslavement "there was no need to be ashamed of being Black." The revolution that he took over leadership of gave the newly freed a sense of "the possibility of achievement, confidence and pride." Of Toussaint, who soon adopted the name L'Ouverture (later simplified to Louverture), which has been interpreted as someone who somehow always finds a way, or creates an opening, James added: "With the exception always of Bonaparte, no single figure in the whole period of the French Revolution had traveled so fast and so far."

Saint Domingue's racial triangle was never as neat as it might sound. As the revolt gained steam, divisions quickly emerged between poor and rich whites, between planters and workers, and between royalists (most of the wealthy and entitled remained) and republicans. The island's planters appealed for help from whites in nearby British colonies—especially Jamaica, which was less than a day's sail distant—employing the highly plausible theory that a successful slave revolt in the biggest plantation society in the West Indies would quickly spread to other places. With that fear in mind, Britain intervened by launching a full-blown invasion, which commenced with the landing of redcoats on the island in September 1793. Britain hoped to preserve both the economic model and institutions of plantation slavery in the hemisphere. Wherever invading British forces conquered territory in Saint Domingue, they were instructed to restore slavery and restart the production of sugar and other cash crops. London's aim was not just to prevent a contagion of liberty, however. At the same time, it was bidding to profit from the anarchy that reigned on the island by snatching away the richest colony of its biggest rival. And this amounted to a major escalation of the global war that had pitted France and Britain against each other throughout much of the eighteenth century.

It is not possible here to fully render the Haitian Revolution, a world-historical event of the highest magnitude, in all of its immense complexity, horror, and grandeur. With no pretension of being exhaustive, our purpose is to focus mainly on the effects the revolution generated, in Europe, in ending transatlantic slavery, and in launching anticolonialism globally, as well as its formative impact on the young United States. These are precisely the sorts of things that have traditionally been left out of standard history curricula of the birth of modernity and the rise of the West.

The arriving British troops saw their first resistance from free colored armies. But bigger troubles were already brewing for them. By the time of their intervention, Toussaint was already well on his way to building a formidable fighting force composed mostly of freed slaves but supplemented by defecting white French colonists. Soon, he also allied himself with Spain, which controlled the eastern two-thirds of Hispaniola, and for a time his army fought against both Britain and France. "Here were white men offering them guns and ammunition and supplies, recognizing them as soldiers, treating them as equals and asking them to shoot other whites," James wrote of Toussaint's tactical shift toward the Spanish. The vicious struggle that emerged among Europe's leading imperial powers, Britain, France and Spain, had odd resonances with the savage racial triangle that prevailed during this period among white settlers, free colored, and slaves, with the Europeans, alone or in coalitions, backing one or another of the island's racial groups in its conflict with the others. And the United States would soon come into play, replacing Spain as the third leg in this triangle.

Among Toussaint's greatest qualities was his gift as a tactician. Once the French Republic decreed the end of slavery, he soon switched his allegiance back to France. Using battle strategies possibly inspired by the recent arrival of huge numbers of slaves who had been combatants in the wars roiling Kongo and Angola, Toussaint's troops repeatedly defied British attempts at engaging them in conventional massed formations. His men timed their attacks to coincide with violent thunderstorms to sow fear and confusion among the British, and they melted away into the hills or brush, picking off the enemy opportunistically and harrying them as they traveled the island's roads. Toussaint also put Hispaniola's tropical disease environment to his advantage. The British, despite nearly a century and a half of experience in the Caribbean, still displayed little understanding of such matters. The invaders obstinately marched in heavy flannel uniforms. They treated fevers with mercury, cayenne pepper, or that longtime standby blood-letting; furthermore, not understanding germ theory (particularly, the mosquito-borne origins of the diseases that killed the largest numbers of their men, yellow fever and malaria), they built their largest hospital adjacent to a swamp in the capital, Port-au-Prince. Toussaint may not have known of the existence of viruses and parasites, but he had observed that the foreign troops were at their weakest and most susceptible during the wet seasons, and therefore planned many of his biggest operations for then.

With its original invasion force withered by the combination of Toussaint's generalship, his disciplined armies, and a murderous disease environment, Britain tried to salvage the situation by launching a second expedition late in 1795. At the time, it was the largest this nation had ever sent into war. London even supplemented its own fighters by buying slaves straight off of ships carrying them to the West Indies from Africa and training them hastily for war with the promise that if they survived, they would eventually be given freedom. This renewed offensive opened an era, between 1795 and 1807, when the British military became the biggest slaveholder in the empire, purchasing roughly one in ten slaves sold in the Caribbean. All of this, however, was for naught, and by 1798 Parliament, alarmed at the cost of Britain's adventurism in Saint Domingue, and with no obvious prospect of success, was determined to pull the plug. Edmund Burke famously complained that trying to take over the French colony had been "like fighting to conquer a cemetery." What he and other supporters of empire didn't seem to grasp was the radically different incentive structure that motivated the ex-slaves. "We are fighting that liberty—that most precious of all earthly possessions—may not perish," Toussaint told his men.

In October 1798, five years after the launching of their invasion of Saint Domingue, the British lowered the Union Jack for a final time, stowed it away, and withdrew. With three-fifths of the twenty thousand men they had deployed dead, no other choice made sense. Toussaint Louverture, who was raised as a slave, was now celebrated as the island's liberator, and his victory had come at the expense of the greatest empire there was. Like so much of the history presented here, few are taught much, if any, of this outside of advanced history courses. More British soldiers fought and died in the failed attempt to take over Saint Domingue than at the hands of America's revolutionary army two decades earlier. And yet the Black colony's name has never appeared on a regimental banner in remembrance of a major campaign or sacrifice, marking yet another act of historical silencing in this symphony of erasure.

IN MARCH 1802, nearly two and a half years after Napoleon Bonaparte seized power in France, adopting for himself the revolutionary title of First Consul, Britain signed a peace treaty at Amiens with its perennial rival. Freed of war in Europe and at sea with the English, Bonaparte quickly set out to reestablish France's control over its colonies as a means of generating more revenue and regaining its status as a leading European power. Logically, the reassertion of French control over the riches of Saint Domingue became a top priority. The French dictator's expansive scheme foresaw not only the restoration of great profits from sugar and coffee grown by slaves but also the diplomatic recovery from Spain of the vast Louisiana territory. France saw these lands as an indispensable breadbasket and source of raw materials needed to keep France's island plantation societies in the Caribbean humming. This cannot be said to have been an altogether original thought. We have already seen how from the time of colonial America, places like New England played the same role for London's slave societies, from Barbados to Jamaica. As John Adams put it just prior to the American Revolution, the so-called West India trade served as "an essential link in a vast chain, which has made New England what it is, the southern provinces what they are, [and] the West India islands what they are." As with so many things with the First Consul, though, what distinguished Napoleon's vision of integrating domains with different economic vocations was its immensity and grandeur of scale.

At the very same time France was returning its imperial gaze to the West Indies, Toussaint Louverture, the former livery coachman now festooned general, was openly assuming the mantle of outright leader of the colony. For now, he officially remained a loyal officer in the French army, but on the soil of Saint Domingue Toussaint began to exercise power increasingly in the mold of a dictator, even adopting the position of governor-general for life. As many have remarked, he and Napoleon resembled each other in numerous respects, from their diminutive stature and their military genius to their desire for unchallenged authority—and all of this helped place them on a collision course.

In a new constitution promulgated in 1800, Napoleon had decreed that "because of the difference in the 'nature of things and the climate' the colonies were to be governed by special laws," and would henceforth be denied representation in the French assembly. Although he had taken care to specify "the sacred principle of the liberty and equality of the blacks will never suffer, among you, any attack or modification," historians have often read this as the beginning of a series of moves to restore slavery in the Caribbean, which is in fact what France would attempt more openly, less than two years hence. Sensing what was coming, a wary Toussaint told the Consulate's representative, "We are free today because we are the strongest. [Bonaparte] maintains slavery in Martinique and the Île Bourbon [Réunion]; we will also be enslaved when he becomes the strongest."

Without France's permission or indeed any prior consultation, Toussaint followed Napoleon's decree with a decree of his own, and it took the form of a local constitution. Saint Domingue was to remain part of France, but "it is not a circumstantial liberty conceded only to us that we want . . . it is the absolute acceptance of the principle that no man, whether born red, black or white can be the property of another," a defiant Toussaint wrote. Henceforth, in Saint Domingue, he vowed, "slaves cannot exist; servitude is permanently abolished. . . . All men within it are born, live and die free and French."

Toussaint took frequent pains to praise France and to flatter its leader, hoping in this way to reassure the colonial power that Saint Domingue was not seeking an outright rupture, but Napoleon was livid nonetheless. He said that Toussaint's statement had "included many good things," but also "some that are contrary to the dignity and sovereignty of the French people." Perhaps worst of all from Napoleon's perspective was the ex-slave's temerity to address him as an equal, "from the first of blacks to the first of whites," as Toussaint put it in one letter. In fact, the French emperor had already given orders for an expeditionary force to be deployed to the Caribbean before he had seen Toussaint's constitution; once it arrived in his hands, confirming his fears, he merely increased the size of the deployment.

The flotilla Napoleon assembled became not only the largest ever launched to attack Saint Domingue, but one of the largest overseas deployments by any European nation up to that time. Its unequivocal mission was to defeat the Black generals there and bring the colony back into the fold. All in all, the convoy of fifty ships carried 35,000 French soldiers and sailors, including many of the best generals of a nation that was just then near the peak of its powers. Among these was the overall commander of the mission, Napoleon's brother-in-law, Charles-Victor-Emmanuel Leclerc, who had married Paulina Bonaparte. In France, Napoleon presented his offensive as "a crusade of civilized people of the West against the black barbarian that was on the rise in America," offering that "the Spanish, the English, and the Americans also are dismayed by the existence of this black Republic." Meanwhile, Napoleon ordered General Leclerc to eliminate from the colony any Blacks who held the rank of captain or higher, employing the famous phrase "Rid us of these gilded negroes and we shall have nothing more to wish."

However, James Stephen, an English abolitionist lawyer and later member of Parliament, who was an especially astute student of affairs in the Caribbean, could see the disaster in the making. It would be as impossible to submit the people of Saint Domingue to slavery, he wrote, as it was "to renew in a philosopher the superstitions of the nursery, so that he should again believe in giants and magicians; or to frighten a man of mature age with the rod of his schoolmaster."

For his part, seeing the enormous number of ships gathering off the coast, in a rare defeatist moment, Toussaint exclaimed, "We must perish. All France has come to Saint-Domingue." His habitual defiance returned soon enough, though, and the order was given to burn the newly rebuilt Cap François and to give no quarter in the vicious fighting that ensued with Leclerc's troops. Toussaint later declared, "I took up arms for the freedom of my color, which France alone proclaimed, but which she has no right to nullify. Our liberty is no longer in her hands: it is in our own. We will defend it or perish."

The ex-slaves of Saint Domingue waged such a spirited resistance that Leclerc's frustration burst into the open even as his army advanced. "Victors everywhere, we possessed nothing but our rifles. The enemy held nowhere, and yet never ceased to be master of the country," the French commander wrote. This was further testament to not only the inspired generalship of the Blacks but also the wartime experience and above all battlefield tactics that recently freed slaves had brought with them from Africa. The French troops soon began to gain the upper hand, nonetheless, gradually winning whites, free coloreds, and finally, albeit only temporarily, two of Toussaint's ablest allies, Jean-Jacques Dessalines and Henri Christophe, to their side. In the face of these setbacks, Toussaint himself was eventually lured into negotiations with the French and finally tricked into a meeting that resulted in his arrest and deportation. His last recorded words before he departed the island could hardly have been more prophetic: "In overthrowing me you have cut down in Saint-Domingue only the trunk of the tree of liberty; it will spring up again from the roots, for they are numerous and they are deep." Taken to prison in France's Jura Mountains, Toussaint died on April 7, 1803.

The decapitation of the colony's main Black leadership seemed like it might be a decisive turn in France's favor. But this change in luck was illusory and would not hold. Black resistance waned but never completely died down. Indeed, new leadership sprung up under revolutionary leaders like Macaya and Jean Baptiste Sans Souci, who had been fighting since the beginning of the rebellion and commanded forces of so-called *bossales*, men who, like themselves, were born in Africa, where they had acquired experience fighting in Kongo's civil wars. Soon, however, events in triumphant France kicked the rebellion into a new phase that would be more intense than ever before. In May 1802, the National Assembly voted 211 to 60 in favor of the restoration of slavery on Martinique, Réunion, and other French islands. That July word of the restoration leaked back to Saint Domingue, carried by slaves from Guadeloupe who jumped ship while anchored in harbor in Cap François. General Leclerc immediately sensed the risks this posed of fueling rebellion on Saint Domingue and sent a message to Napoleon to urge caution. "Do not think of establishing slavery here for some time," he urged. Later, Dessalines, who would become the first leader of independent Haiti, issued his own warning, to Leclerc, telling him, "There will be an earthquake!" The French emperor was not to be dissuaded, though. The return of slavery to France's richest colony would indeed be proclaimed late that year.

This book has offered several opportunities to contemplate fascinating historical counterfactuals, and in Napoleon's about-face on slavery we find one of the most compelling of all. Had France upheld Saint Domingue's autonomy and stood by its earlier prohibition of slavery, Toussaint and his successors might have become powerful allies against Britain in the West Indies. At a minimum this might have destabilized Jamaica, or others among its rival's holdings by its very example. Toussaint might conceivably have helped liberate them at the head of an invasion force. More than mere fantasies, none other than Charles-Maurice Talleyrand, then the French foreign minister, envisioned scenarios like these at the time. For his part, Napoleon justified his decisions in the starkest of racial terms, and ones that strike the ear as oddly contemporary: "I am for the whites because I am white; I have no other reason, and that one is good. How could one grant freedom to Africans, to men who have no civilization, who don't even know what a colony is, what France is?"

Knowing what we know about the ensuing history of the Atlantic world, there is no reason to restrict this speculative exercise to the Caribbean. The freeing of slaves in Saint Domingue would have also likely rocked the slave plantation-complex in the United States at the very moment of its explosive growth in the Deep South and in the Mississippi Valley, where we will soon turn. We have already seen how the example of Haiti's successful liberation had spurred revolt in Louisiana. How much more powerful might its effects have been had France stolen a march on Britain in its opposition to the slave trade? And how might this have affected calculations about acceptable civilized norms in the young American republic, where Francophilia was strong? Alas, this was not to be. What transpired in the first decade of the nineteenth century instead was that Britain became the global leader in suppressing the slave trade. Not only that, it leveraged the moral dividends that accrued from this initiative both to help it defeat Napoleon in Europe and to strengthen its own empire. This the British notably accomplished, while doing nothing to liberate the 600,000 slaves whose labor they still profited from in the West Indies.

Not long before Toussaint died in Jura, Leclerc began to sense that the tide in the conflict was turning irrevocably against the French. The ex-slaves, and especially the *bossales*, seemed to him fanatical in their determination to remain free, even in the face of his army's terrorist tactics, and he complained about their indifference toward death. Despairing that Blacks who had already tasted freedom and known battle against France could ever be forced to submit, he told Napoleon that the only solution was a "war of extermination" and restocking the colony with Africans who knew nothing of the last decade of struggle, slaves who were brought fresh from the continent. In October 1802 Leclerc wrote warning Napoleon of his dire need of reinforcements, given the accumulating setbacks, including the terrible toll that yellow fever had taken on his men, just as it had with the British. That same month, Dessalines and Christophe defected, returning to the command of the armies of resistance. "Send 12,000 replacements immediately, and 10 million francs in cash, or Saint-Domingue is lost forever," he wrote. It was his last letter. Leclerc himself succumbed to yellow fever on the night of November 2.

Leclerc's replacement, Vicomte de Rochambeau, responded to France's desperate situation on the island with a degree of fanaticism that surpassed anything yet seen in a conflict already filled with horror. Described as an "expert in atrocity" by one historian, Rochambeau took to heart the idea of extermination, suffocating Blacks by loading them into the holds of ships where sulfur was then burned, in one of the first known examples of modern chemical warfare. He imported large dogs from Cuba, which he trained to attack Blacks. But Rochambeau's extreme violence merely had the effect of uniting Blacks and coloreds; it also inspired Black troops, especially those under the command of Dessalines, to carry out mass executions of whites in reprisal. Saint Domingue was bound to be free, and Rochambeau, who spent the final days of his command living in drunken debauchery, knew it, finally surrendering to Dessalines, who took command of the colony and declared it independent. The triumphant Blacks renamed the land Haiti, said to have been used by the island's original inhabitants, the Taino. "It is not enough to have expelled the barbarians who have bloodied our land for two centuries," their declaration of independence read. "We must, with one last act of national authority, forever assure the empire of liberty in the country of our birth."

Napoleon, whose reputation as a military genius is matched by few in the modern era, is equally famous for his defeat in his Russian campaign of 1812. It is seen not only as a monumental miscalculation but as a textbook example of hubris. Believing that Black people—who had already won their liberty once, and successfully defended it against the other two greatest empires in Europe, Britain and Spain—could be brutalized and bullied back into slavery by a power situated on the far side of the Atlantic, though, was a folly of similar order as marching an army to Moscow to fight in the winter. And the price that the French emperor paid for it was enormous. More than 50,000 French died trying to set the clock back on freedom, including eighteen generals. As one historian wrote, "Napoleon suffered more casualties in St. Domingue than he would at Waterloo."

Much like Britain's defeat at the hands of Toussaint's armies, little of this is taught in schools across the United States. But as momentous as victory on Hispaniola was for the Blacks brought to Haiti as slaves from Africa, or on Napoleon and his French armies, it was what these events soon yielded on the North American mainland that still resonates most deeply for the world today.

35

BLUES AND THE AMERICAN TRUTH

O N THE LONG DRIVE while researching this book that bore me south in parallel with the Mississippi River, to the area where Charles Deslondes had led the German Coast revolt and then onward to New Orleans, I stopped for a few days in the little town of Clarksdale. I had been there once before, thirty years earlier, driving through the Mississippi Delta hypnotized by its utterly flat landscapes of black soil that stretched to the horizons. That time we had come up from Miami during a summer vacation with my wife, Avouka, and our two small sons, William and Henry Nelson. Our main purpose was to cover key sites in the American civil rights struggle of the 1950s and '60s, places like the Edmund Pettus Bridge in Selma, Alabama, where my parents had participated in the historic march to Birmingham.

At the time, I was the bureau chief for *The New York Times* covering the Caribbean and Central America. I was already deeply curious then about the history of slavery, and about the array of deep cultural connections that linked Black Americans to West Africa. Looking back across decades, though, I cannot help but remark how far I was still from fully connecting many of the dots that are explored here. That summer, as we wandered the narrow, alluvial plain of the Delta, which measures two hundred miles south to north, from Vicksburg to Memphis, and from the Mississippi River in the west to the loess bluffs of the Yazoo region in the east, two things struck us most powerfully. It may seem like a cliché, but one of them was the pervasive feeling of anachronism, of throwback timelessness to the texture of things: here, life seemed to ooze more than flow. The other was a generalized poverty, albeit one unmistakably skewed against the area's Black population, as it always had been. We ate dinners of fried catfish, mashed potatoes, and coleslaw on linoleum tabletops in small cafeterias with squeaky ceiling fans that looked like they were extruded from 1950s postcards. The Black waitresses were dressed in almost institutional-looking white uniforms, and we were often surrounded by starchy white patrons whose looks of wariness and disbelief at seeing a family of Black diners of widely varying hues who switched seamlessly between the French that Avouka grew up speaking in Côte d'Ivoire and English, clearly marking us as certain outsiders in their midst. Their confused stares reminded me of a puzzled exclamation attributed to Woodrow Wilson's secretary of state, William Jennings Bryan, while dealing with a crisis in Haiti. "Think of it!" the top American diplomat is said to have uttered. "Niggers speaking French."

We happily spent hot afternoons on that trip, in the early 1990s, getting lost on back roads. We watched in wonderment as slow-moving crop dusters circled and looped lazily over fields planted with cotton before releasing their poisons in long, streaming white clouds, and with horror we took in the sight of all-Black work crews hacking away at the high grass along state roads with machetes in a practice reminiscent of the chain gangs of old. Those, in turn, descended from the "coffles," or human chains of slaves force-marched to this region from the Old South.

We stopped back then to talk with people, especially elderly Black folk, whom we found in barbershops or sitting on creaky porches savoring a cooling breeze. We visited the famous Riverside Hotel in Clarksdale, which had been the favored lodging of generations of Black musicians during Jim Crow. It had even entered into the realm of mythic, because this was the place that Bessie Smith,

Empress of the Blues, was taken in 1937, after a nighttime crash on the highway from Memphis, back when the brick building was still an African American hospital. Because it seemed poetically plausible, a legendary but untrue version of that event quickly took hold that she had perished after being turned away from the town's white hospital. Finally, we toured Clarksdale's Delta Blues Museum, our main destination, which was then housed on the second floor of the town's stout Carnegie Public Library. Like hundreds of others, the library was built with a $10,000 grant from the steel magnate Andrew Carnegie; it opened in 1914.

In the heyday of big cotton, the Delta was three-quarters Black, not so far from the kind of ratio common in the Caribbean. One would never know that, though, by visiting the sleepy downtown, a tidy grid of scarcely more than a dozen blocks, where white people predominated. The Black Clarksdale that survived was mostly hidden away, located on the east side of town, literally across the railroad tracks, along narrower, ill-paved streets that radiated from the banks of the sluggish, cypress-lined Sunflower River. Avouka and I snuck out to visit the African American town at night, when it came alive, after seeing to it that our children were sound asleep, guiltily wagering that they wouldn't wake up during our hurried forays. There, we visited dive bars and smoky juke joints that featured loudly amplified blues and pool games that drew bettors who threw down ten- and twenty-dollar bills. These contests sometimes grew so raucous and fevered that they emptied the dance floor as crowds formed around the fluorescent-lit tables.

I had a developed a deep fondness for Delta blues in high school, an interest that was a bit unusual for the son of a middle-class African American family living in the Northeast. By then, this sound was considered retrograde and for some maybe even a little embarrassing. But my tastes had always been eclectic, and this choice had been tipped by a strong attachment to the music of Jimi Hendrix, and then, more indirectly, by the wave of interest blossoming among white schoolmates, who had been turned on by the open emulation of the blues by chart-topping but plainly derivative white rock acts like the Rolling Stones. In 1961, Keith Richards and Mick Jagger had bonded musically while listening to Muddy Waters records. And the Stones' biggest hit, "(I Can't Get No) Satisfaction," was directly inspired by this experience. This all had even older roots, of course. Elvis Presley, well before the Stones, had blazed a trail of enormous stardom and fortune via straight-up appropriation of Black artists.

Since those days, I had come to understand that the importance of the Delta ran a lot deeper than the familiar narrative that surrounded it as merely the birthplace of a narrow and particular style of gritty and sometimes apocalyptic Black country music. Its foundational performers were pioneers like Son House, Charley Patton, Arthur "Big Boy" Crudup, and, most famously among early practitioners, Robert Johnson. Its reputation as a proximate birthplace for the style had latterly become Clarksdale's calling card. It catered to white tourists from afar who flock there to hear "authentic" blues and to see its sights, like the intersection of Highway 61 and Route 49, where Johnson was said to have traded his soul to the devil for his musical gifts.

There is no gainsaying the Delta was a major fount of one of the two broadest and most powerful artistic currents (the other being jazz) that have contributed to what generally makes American music most distinctive, most American. The styles that emerged from here were part of what the art historian Robert Farris Thompson once called the "flash of the spirit of a certain people specially armed with improvisatory drive and brilliance." This was a reference to the mélange of African traditions (and especially those of Yoruba, Dahomey, Kongo, and Mande) that melded with European influences in the cultural cauldron of the New World that was the Black Atlantic. Cross-fertilizations on the western edges of this ocean had given birth not just to jazz and the blues, but to rock, reggae, samba, bossa nova, and mambo as well.

The feature most particular to the Delta blues was that it had grown out of the experience of generations of slaves who picked cotton, and of the multitudes of sharecroppers who had toiled in their wake through the same furrowed paths. Theirs was a life of hands left bleeding and callused from the thorns concealed in every puffy boll, of backs left aching by the filling of the long, heavy bags of cotton that Black laborers had to lift and trail behind them. Like all of these styles, the music had older roots, murky but unmistakable, that linked back to the transit across the Atlantic of millions of Africans in chains and to the determined efforts of these people both to mourn together and to survive, not just physically, but culturally and spiritually. Going back even further, the music of the Mississippi Delta seemed to link to another great river and its true delta, the Niger, with its kingdoms and empires that date back a thousand years. And it linked back just as surely to the Bight of Benin. Places like these employed instruments that anticipated the high-hat cymbal and the guitar and banjo styles that emerged from the cotton fields, a fact attested to by the natural- and unforced-sounding collaborations of contemporary Niger Delta musicians, like Ali Farka Touré, and Mississippi Delta ones.

"Blues is the parent of all legitimate jazz," the cultural critic LeRoi Jones (Amiri Baraka) once wrote, of that other absolutely foundational American product. Jazz's exact origins are somewhat more obscure, though. Beyond some roots in the blues and in the African American experience of slavery, its effective birth is usually traced to Black urbanism in the South. Of special importance to jazz was the emergence of a diverse Creole society and culture in New Orleans, which drew on Haitian and African influences as well as Spanish, French, and early American ones. All stewed up together, these elements produced something utterly new and sublime.

Not incidentally, New Orleans was the specific point, 336 miles to the south of Clarksdale, where the treasured, billowy white product of the cotton fields of the Delta was loaded onto ships for Liverpool. There, from the late eighteenth to the middle of the nineteenth century, this fiber drove an industrialization in Britain that was both stronger and more precocious than similar economic transitions seen anywhere else in the world. As one historian of the era has written, "It was Britain's success in becoming the first industrial nation, combined with its corresponding success in becoming the world's pre-eminent financial nation, which propelled it to . . . global hegemony by the middle of the nineteenth century." In the thousand years before 1800, there had never been a remotely comparable leap in economic growth anywhere in the world, and it was cotton and the plantation slavery, above all in the Delta, that had made it possible.

Without the blues and jazz, each in its own separate way original fruits of the cotton plant, it is hard to imagine much else in American popular culture, and certainly not in its music, that was so fully distinguishable from the traditions of Europe or that so powerfully stamped its style upon the world. W. E. B. Du Bois spoke of these unique musical traditions as one might of the sap that oozes from an aromatic tree; they flowed, he said, from the American slave experience as an "anointing chrism," and constituted "the only gift of pure art in America." The music critic Ted Gioia put this thought in a different way. "The influence of the Delta on the sound of our musical lives is so pervasive today that it is almost impossible to take full measure of its impact. One might as well try to imagine cooking without herbs and spices, or medicine before the arrival of penicillin."

For all of my love of the blues, what brought me back to the Delta on this second visit, recently, was cotton, but even there, it was the music that had pointed the way. As a young man, one of my favorite artists had been McKinley Morganfield, a performer mainly known by his stage name, Muddy Waters. Waters was raised from infancy by a grandmother who had labored as a sharecropper on the Stovall farm, a cotton plantation started by a family of that name before the Civil War. As a child he had picked cotton, then pulled corn, and finally drove a tractor, before finding his way out of farm work through this music. The Stovalls' 4500-acre plantation sits just six miles west of the Clarksdale town center. When I visited there for the first time, in the early 1990s, the small, dilapidated shack where the bluesman spent his youth still sat within view of a lazy bend of a two-lane asphalt highway. It was a typical sharecropper dwelling: a ramshackle home to the landless upon the land, a place without electricity or plumbing, whose sole heat was provided by a wood-burning stove. By that time, the front porch was long gone, having slowly rotted away before being struck by a tornado that finished it off. It was on that porch that during his twenties, Muddy had regularly held forth during Saturday night "jukes" and fish fries—parties enlivened by blindingly powerful bootleg whiskey drunk straight from the bottle, by dancing and gambling, and often enough by flashes of violence. It was in this environment that Muddy was forged. It was a milieu that rejected the respectability politics of a modest and fragile Black middle class that preached self-improvement through education "and especially by conducting oneself with extreme politeness and decorum," in the 1950s characterization of the Black sociologist Charles S. Johnson. It was there that a creative ferment took hold of him.

"I wouldn't say I was supporting myself exactly, but I worked," Waters said much later, describing those early years. "I didn't get much in the way of schooling. The schools weren't too good, and No. 1 I didn't really have time, I thought, in those days, to be bothered with it." The blues artists of this generation, like the cotton sharecroppers who had predeceased them of course, knew that theirs was a region, with its fifty-foot-deep topsoil laid down over the ages by what T. S. Eliot memorably called the "strong brown god" of the Mississippi River, that generated unbelievable wealth. Equally sure was their knowledge that this was a wealth strictly reserved for others, especially in faraway places like New York and London. They also knew that for most of those who lived and labored here, seemingly unbreakable poverty and segregation would remain their lot. Finally, they knew that none of this was an accident; things had clearly been designed this way. In the words of the great, late African American novelist and critic Albert Murray, the blues were about stating the low-down facts of life, "a device for making the best of a bad situation. Not by rendering capitulation tolerable . . . but in its orientation to continuity and adversity."

Clarksdale didn't build its first high school for Blacks until the 1950s, and the few, poor elementary schools that did exist bent their calendars so far to the needs of the cotton planters that it was said that classes met only on days so rainy that the fields were too muddy to work. James K. Vardaman, a former governor of the state who was one of its U.S. senators when Muddy Waters was born, explained this by saying that educating the Black man "simply renders him unfit for the work which the white man has prescribed, and which he will be forced to perform . . . the only effect is to spoil a good field hand and make an insolent cook." Later, the state university, Ole Miss, named a hall after Vardaman. It was in this environment that Muddy Waters honed his slide-guitar skills, while also developing his powerful and distinctive baritone. It was a sound that contained pain and anger, yes, but it was also filled with insolent defiance and a mystical, almost preternatural belief in his brilliant destiny. Muddy boasted it had all been prophesied before his birth by a gypsy woman, and the confidence he seemed to draw from this got him off the farm and to Chicago and from there out into the world—unimaginably far from the cotton-bounded realm of his ancestors, which he would sing about often but never return to.

The Stovalls, too, got away, after a fashion. Wealth derived from their plantation helped launch a Chicago-based industrial real estate firm that went public in 1993 and was sold in 2006 for $3.5 billion. In a story like this, one glimpses the crystallized reflection of an entire region's history. Clarksdale was named after an English architect, John Clark, who had settled in Coahoma County in 1882. "The Europeans made the county the Golden Buckle on the Cotton Belt, retaining the wealth they drained from the soil and the slaves, now invested in machines and chemicals rather than in Black muscle and sweat. The slaves' descendants still struggle to survive," wrote Françoise N. Hamlin in *Crossroads at Clarksdale: The Black Freedom Struggle in the Mississippi Delta After World War II.*

The shack Waters inhabited during what he called his "mannish" boyhood is now housed in a new Delta Blues Museum, which honors him along with a host of other musicians who contributed to building the distinctive Delta blues sound. Theirs is a catalog that swells with names like John Lee Hooker, Howlin' Wolf, Elmore James, and many more. Between wanderings on the nearby levee and long walks through tiny, riverside ghost towns, I located the spot where that shack had once sat. It was at the margins of an enormous field that had just been prepared for planting—not with cotton, but nowadays with corn and soy. Still, there was no way to suppress my feelings of awe over thoughts of the crop that replaced sugar at the turn of the nineteenth century as the dominant source of agriculturally generated wealth in the Western world, and by the sweat and blood that had produced it.

By 1836, the year the land I surveyed entered into the hands of the Stovall family, cotton was the most valuable product in the most powerfully emergent economy of the era, and yet cotton-derived wealth, which really meant slave-derived wealth, was still more than two decades shy of its apogee in the United States. During the first half of the nineteenth century, America's surging cotton output had also become the one central and truly indispensable input in the rising industrialization of England. Without it, there could be no mass-produced and mass-marketed textiles. Nationwide, in Britain, a decade before the close of the eighteenth century, cotton textiles, although already handsomely profitable, had accounted for a mere 2.6 percent of the marginal increase in value gained from the processing or transformation of goods, or what economists call the value added. By 1801, they accounted for 17 percent, and by 1831, this number had risen yet further, reaching 22.4 percent. By that time, one in six British workers were employed in textile production, and, as the historian Sven Beckert has noted, the rise of the cloth and garment industries had also become principal driver behind the early development of Britain's railroad networks, its iron foundries, and many other emerging types of economic activity.

There is no way to be too clear in saying that none of this would have been possible without the violent takeover of Native American lands throughout the Mississippi Valley. Plans for just such an outcome began to come together a mere five years after completing the Louisiana Purchase from France in 1803, when a U.S. government agent advised the secretary of war that "there will never be quietness on any of these frontiers until the Indians are removed over the Mississippi." In May 1808, when a group of Cherokees went to Washington to plead for their rights, President Jefferson himself urged them to "settle on our [*sic*] lands beyond the Mississippi."

What ensued was a prolonged campaign of forced dispossession, unstoppable by the 1830s, a decade that began with ratification of the Indian Removal Act. Employing genocidal means, that campaign killed, dispersed, or drove west members of the Creek and the Choctaw, as well as large elements of the Chickasaw and Seminole nations. In a letter to Congress written the very same year that the Stovalls acquired their land, John Ross, a chief from another affected nation, the Cherokee, wrote: "Our property may be plundered before our eyes; violence may be committed on our persons; even our lives may be taken away, and there is none to regard our complaints. We are denationalized; we are disenfranchised. We are deprived of membership in the human family." The eventual rejoinder took many forms, most of them violent, but their spirit was best captured in 1825 by Henry Clay, the senator and statesman from Kentucky, whose comments in a cabinet meeting exchange about the native population with John Quincy Adams were recorded thusly: "He believed they were destined to extinction, and, although he would never use or countenance inhumanity towards them, he did not think them, as a race, worth preserving. He considered them essentially inferior to the Anglo-Saxon race, which were now taking their place on this continent. They were not an improvable breed, and their disappearance from the human family would be no great loss to the world." The result of the Indian removal and subsequent settlement by whites was so absolute that the violent history of the Mississippi River Valley in this era would inspire white settler movements promoted by European governments elsewhere well into the next century. These included places in southern Africa and Kenya, as well as French-dominated Algeria. As Claudio Saunt wrote in *Unworthy Republic*, "Notoriously, during the Nazi conquest of Eastern Europe, Hitler equated 'indigenous inhabitants' with 'Indians' and declared "the Volga must be our Mississippi."

36

THE GIFTS OF BLACK FOLK

WHEN WE THINK ABOUT New World slavery, we tend to think of it as only a matter of the planting and harvesting of crops. From tobacco and rice to cotton, the early American economic model was so thoroughly built on the proliferation of plantations that this is perhaps inevitable. But while not altogether wrong, the picture we sustain of the creation of prosperity in mainland North America is woefully incomplete. Before it was taken over by ethnically European settlers, the Mississippi River Valley that native peoples once treasured as their home consisted in large parts of heavily forested wilderness, full of immense cypress, gum, and ash trees, replete with cougars and bears, and of extensive swamplands and incredibly dense vines, all of which needed to be cleared before this conquered earth could be put to any Western-style productive use. Although nowadays largely forgotten, this, too, was the work of Black slaves. Traveling with slave drivers in flatboats, sometimes in chains and carrying their own crude tools, they had to fell enormous expanses of woodlands, drain wetlands, saw wood, construct houses, build fences, and dress fields. Without all of this labor, in which many tens of thousands of slaves were worked to exhaustion and early death, the farming itself would have scarcely been possible.

Today, everyone knows the outcome, even as we commit

memories of the process to oblivion, but it was essential work like this that laid the foundations of a new, continent-size nation that would become rich beyond measure. As *American Cotton Planter* magazine said, speaking of the Delta in 1853, this was brought about because the South boasted a combination of nearly endless amounts of land and "the cheapest and most available labor in the world [and] produce[s] almost exclusively a staple, which, next to food, is the most necessary comfort of the human race, and enters most largely into its consumption." By 1830, the very decade when the Stovalls acquired the Clarksdale farmland upon which Muddy Waters's grandmother would toil, while a sixth of all Britons were employed in textile production, a million people, or one in thirteen Americans—overwhelmingly slaves—worked in cotton farming.

In the written Chinese language, the character for house is an ideogram composed of two elements. One of them is a roof, and the other, a pig. Here we find a starkly simple representation of what it took in ancient times to constitute (or at least begin to build) a household: a shelter and the favored domesticated animal of the time. With the era of Big Cotton dawning in the Mississippi River Valley, as it was opened up to white men pouring in from the East, three elements were considered essential to their social legitimacy and personal wealth: a Caucasian woman for a wife, a parcel of land, and slaves. The ownership of Blacks who could be put to work for planters did far more than simply make production possible, though. It was a grand multiplier that facilitated the acquisition of new land, whether one's first holdings or the expansion of a big estate; in addition, the wealth derived from this formula, of soil and Black sweat, steadily drew in white women who were willing to marry for life on the cotton frontier.

It was slaves, and slaves alone, who made this world go round, and the obsession of whites in the Mississippi Valley—both established planters and Thomas Jefferson's idealized "yeomen," the fortune seekers constantly streaming into the new cotton El Dorado alike—was with how to obtain them. As Joseph Ingraham, an author of the era, remarked, "To sell cotton in order to buy negroes—to make more cotton to buy more negroes, 'ad infinitum,' is the aim and direct tendency of all the operations of the thorough-going cotton planter; his whole soul is wrapped up in the pursuit." The cotton farmers of the valley may not have known the deep history behind this idea, but readers will remember that its pedigree traces all the way back to the early sugar boom in Barbados in the 1640s. The Delta was the last part of the lower Mississippi River Valley to be opened up to plantation production, but it quickly proved to be the best place of all to grow cotton, and therefore it soon absorbed more slaves than any other. Washington County, in the heart of the Delta, provides a fairly typical example. By 1840, just four years after the Stovalls acquired their plantation nearby, for every white resident there were ten slaves. Just ten years later, white families in the county possessed more than eighty slaves on average.

America's legal importation of slaves from abroad may have ended in 1807, but this did nothing to interrupt the supply of slaves to places like Mississippi, Alabama, and Louisiana, the heartland of cotton, where the crop was just then taking off. Indeed, slaves continued to arrive in dizzying numbers, and it was entirely legal. Most of the Blacks who were sucked into the vortex that supplied them were first uprooted from the Upper South, the states of Virginia and Maryland, which had been the heartland of American slavery during the eighteenth century. Already, these unfree Black people, or many of their immediate forebears, had survived the Middle Passage. They had survived the terrible seasoning period, with its frighteningly high mortality rates. And they had survived the brutal work regimes and meager rations of plantation life in the Chesapeake region. But now they were suddenly being dispatched in large numbers, with their families, unrecognized under the law, typically broken up and scattered to the four winds.

Under this domestic, or internal slave trade, small-time businessmen and speculators bought up Blacks from the Upper South, often a handful to a dozen at a time, and had them walked to the new cotton-growing areas like cattle on the hoof, albeit in chains and under armed guard. As they proceeded through the South, through Georgia and all the way to Louisiana, they were sold off to avid planters as they went. Between 1790 and 1810, the first two decades of the cotton boom that gripped the nation, nearly 100,000 slaves left Virginia and Maryland in this manner for points south and southwest, but this was only the start. In the 1830s, Mississippi alone imported 130,000 slaves, who were forcibly moved from older slaveholding states. Eventually, in the fifty years before the Civil War, roughly a million slaves would be marched or shipped out of the Upper South by sea, roughly twice the number of Blacks who had been landed in British North America from Africa. We are talking here about a migration—or, more accurately, a mass deportation—that ensnared more Black people than the number of whites who undertook the wagon train settlement of the American West, the fodder of so much Hollywood legend in the twentieth century. It was bigger, too, than the emigration of Jews from Russia and eastern Europe in the nineteenth century. And yet who learns about this in any detail today in school? The historian Walter Johnson has observed:

> As it became clear that there was a great deal of money to be made in buying, transporting, and reselling slaves, a set of highly organized firms sprung up to compete with the footloose speculators. Companies like these often maintained offices complete with high-walled jails that could house as many as a hundred slaves at a time, large yards where the human property could be exercised, and showrooms where interested buyers could question and examine the people they hoped to purchase, at both ends of the trade.

And as this lucrative trade flourished, regular auctions came to be held in major towns at both ends of the trade, places like Charleston and New Orleans, often on the front steps of the local courthouse.

In 1859, just a few years before its culmination with the South's defeat in the Civil War, this "negro fever," and the exodus it produced, reached its apex with the single largest slave auction ever recorded.

It took place in Savannah, Georgia, organized at the behest of a man named Pierce Mease Butler, the scion of a rich planter family, who liquidated his holding in slaves in order to cover his debts. Butler had gambled away much of his fortune on the stock market and lost yet more through an expensive divorce. Newspapers that year had announced the event with headlines that trumpeted things like:

FOR SALE
LONG COTTON AND RICE NEGROES!
A GANG OF 440

Accustomed to the culture of Rice and Provisions, among them are a no of good mechanics and house servants
Will be sold on 2nd and 3rd day of March at Savannah by
J Bryan (the agent)

Just before the sale, Butler's slaves were assembled in a pen in the center of the city, at a site adjacent to the spot where Savannah's oldest Black church, the First African Baptist Church, would eventually be built. As the date of the sale drew close, they were then taken to a race track that was long a favorite gathering spot of the city's white elite. The historian Anne Bailey describes the scene: "The buyers paraded them and made them dance. They opened their clothing to check for wounds; they pinched their limbs and flexed their muscles. They searched earnestly for scars, since scars were said to be evidence of a rebellious nature." And later, over drinks, the Negro buyers, as the white agents were known, exchanged tips among themselves about the "best methods to control a 'refractory nigger.'"

By the time the Stovalls had acquired their plantation, the toil of slaves supplied through methods like these had already made the deep topsoil of the Delta the most valuable farmland on earth. Such rich, black earth had produced a torrent of wealth that vastly exceeded even the enormous fortunes created for France by Saint Domingue, and it had more millionaires per capita than anywhere else in the United States to show for it. The numbers, however true, still strain credulity. In 1790, American cotton production hovered somewhere around 1.5 million pounds. By 1800, it had risen to 36.5 million pounds. In 1820, annual production stood at 167.5 million pounds. And by the eve of the American Civil War, the output of cotton, expanding geographically but still concentrated in the Mississippi River Valley, was nearing an astounding 2 billion pounds annually. In the comparison of the historian Sven Beckert, cotton became to the nineteenth-century United States what oil was to Saudi Arabia in the twentieth, making it the richest and most successful slave society in history. As American output soared, it established itself firmly as the world's most valuable commodity. On a per capita basis, this made residents of the South wealthier than the people of any European country other than England.

Throughout much of this period, cotton was essentially the only item that the rest of the world coveted in large and regular quantities from the United States. By one estimate, the South accounted for two-thirds of American exports, but only one-tenth of its imports, a testament to the extreme inequality and deprivation that was the very essence of chattel slavery. As a newspaper editorial from Natchez, Mississippi, put it in the 1840s, the large planters of the region "sell their cotton in Liverpool, buy their wines in London or Havre; their negro clothing in Boston; their plantation implements and supplies in Cincinnati; and their groceries and fancy articles in New Orleans."

A design feature of plantation slavery that readers first encountered in São Tomé in the early 1500s, and which remained roughly consistent in different geographies and across different crops, involved imposing just above bare subsistence levels of consumption on most unfree Blacks. Thus, the economics of slaves' metabolisms was viewed with the same eye toward profit margins as was their output in the field. This held as true for the slaves who labored on George Washington's Mount Vernon, who numbered 124 at the time of his death, as it did for those in Mississippi and Alabama. The enslaved were fed meat only infrequently, and every other component of their diet, from broken rice to salt fish, was tightly rationed.

Limits like these were a matter of return on investment, to be sure, but they also had a clear psychological purpose. They were part of a deliberate strategy of social domination and dehumanization, one that constantly sought ways of reinforcing differentiation between the races by demeaning the one and elevating the other. In this way, chattel slavery must be seen as a foundational element in America's "ascriptive hierarchies," a system that has long worked to assign different stations in life to people of different origins or descriptions. The flip side of this, of course, is that chattel slavery played a central role in the development and reinforcement of whiteness itself as a racial identity, one of modernity's most impactful by-products. As the novelist Toni Morrison wrote: "Nothing highlighted freedom [for whites]—if it did not in fact create it—like slavery."

I saw the relics of this system during tours of the Greenwood Greathouse, a moldering grand plantation that survives on the north coast of Jamaica. There even the most privileged slaves, those said to be of the "house," were forced to tread a path between kitchen and table that was designed to keep them under constant surveillance while serving food to their masters. Otherwise, a knowing Black guide informed me, they might steal a morsel for their own consumption, and thereby enjoy delicacies reserved solely for the racial overclass.

THIS PICTURE OF ALIMENTATION as a basic and important feature of the economics of slavery opens a window for us to consider chattel slavery in the United States much more broadly, as not only a means of generating vast quantities of commodities, but also as a seriously underrated element in America's ingenious and innovative, if morally depraved, early capitalism. In addition to serving as agents of production, of equal importance, the enslaved became critical units of capital and stores of value. As such, they were intensively deployed as collateral in order to secure loans, whether to buy new land and equipment or to purchase more slaves. This financial feature of slavery came into play at least as early as Barbados, when big English banks helped finance sugar growers, who commonly used the value stored in slaves to secure their loans. But in the Mississippi Valley, this practice both broadened and intensified. The action was not limited to important international financiers like Barings and the Rothschilds, or even to large American banks, all of which avidly partook in this business and profited hugely from it. Small local banks, too, proliferated in order to take advantage of the opportunities for profit that abounded in slave finance. Indeed, in recent years some studies have estimated that the value of slaves in antebellum America was greater than the value of all of the other industrial and transportation assets (railroads, roads, ports, etc.) combined, and equivalent to the value of between one and two times the entire national income.

As the historian Bonnie Martin has shown, the practice of issuing mortgages collateralized through the value stored up in slaves can be traced back as far as the 1730s, when it was current both in French Louisiana and in English Virginia. But as she noted, "it was ordinary southerners, not international bankers, who made the most of this fiscal strategy." This they accomplished through neighbor-to-neighbor financing arrangements secured by slaves. By mortgaging property in human lives in this way, slave owners were able to continue profiting from their chattel's work, as well as from any appreciation in their value, if they were children. Because of one of the cruelest conventions of New World slavery, they also profited from the birth of new offspring, who in turn automatically became slaveholders' property. By the time the Mississippi River Valley came under widespread cotton production, Martin estimates that the value of capital raised in this manner could vary in a given year between 20 percent to 175 percent or more of the value of the staples that planters produced.

In developing some of these arguments, I have drawn heavily upon the work of recent generation of historians—some of them quoted or cited here, and many others who are not. Taken together, their research has offered new clarity and depth about the ways in which the rise of the United States was predicated directly on slavery and especially on the wealth generated by the cotton-growing South. This ongoing revolution in historiography has helped overturn a number of long held notions, some of which border on a denial of slavery's fundamental economic importance to America. Among other things, these arguments have asserted that slavery was in the main only an affair of the South, with the North developing along a separate, economically independent, and putatively ethically superior path. Others have contended that slavery, as practiced in the American South, wasn't truly capitalist at all. They have argued, furthermore, that the South was fundamentally backward compared with the North and that slavery was no boon; if anything, in fact, according to this formerly prevalent view, it was a drag on the country's development. For these reasons and others, it has sometimes been argued that slavery all along was doomed to failure.

In fact, Indian removal, the relocation of Black slaves from the Old South, and the establishment of new plantations in the cotton-lands of the Mississippi Valley and nearby regions were all avidly financed by Wall Street and other northeastern financiers, who earned enormous profits in the process, making them "the North's equivalent of the southern planters." This lucrative underwriting of plantation production by faraway financial centers where slavery was already in general disrepute, moreover, was supplemented by even wider investment networks stretching across the ocean to London, making the continuing exploitation of Black bodies the very opposite of a parochial Southern affair; it was a broad and economically vital pan-Atlantic enterprise.

Of course, much of this recent research has powerful antecedents in the work of Black intellectuals who have been challenging conventional, mainstream accounts of slavery's role in the history of the Atlantic and of the United States for a century. Earlier, we discussed the ideas of the Trinidadian historian and statesman Eric Williams in this light. In the United States, the African American scholar W. E. B. Du Bois was even further ahead of his time, leaving an enormous intellectual output that exploded many of the notions raised just above. For example, in 1924, in his *The Gift of Black Folk: The Negroes in the Making of America*, Du Bois wrote, "It was black labor that established the modern world commerce which began first as a commerce in the bodies of the slaves themselves and was the primary cause of the prosperity of the first great commercial cities of our day." In his masterpiece, *Black Reconstruction in America: An Essay Toward a History of the Part Which Black Folk Played in the Attempt to Reconstruct Democracy in America*, which was published a decade later, Du Bois proclaimed, with ample justification, that Black labor "became the foundation stone not only of the Southern social structure, but of Northern manufacture and commerce, of the English factory system, of European commerce, of buying and selling on a worldwide scale."

The image of slaves taken from Africa as the very fulcrum of modernity is, of course, the central and unifying idea that runs throughout this entire volume. Du Bois's ideas were disparaged by establishment historians of his time. They were also dismissed by the mainstream press, which on topics like these has so often worked to enforce historical conformity while performing erasure of the foundational Black contribution to America and to the larger Atlantic world. *Time* magazine, then one of the country's most powerful shapers of public opinion, for example, called Du Bois an "ax-grinder," and said that American history as recounted in his *Black Reconstruction* was a "wonderland in which all familiar scenes and landmarks have been changed or swept away."

I believe that the sooner denial about the large and foundational role that slavery played in creating American power and prosperity is put to definitive rest, the better Americans as a people will come to understand both themselves and their country's true place in world history. What is abundantly clear, even at a glance, is that during the decade or two that followed the American Revolution, the United States in its infancy remained a relatively minor player in the economy of the greater Atlantic; it was a country with considerable potential, to be sure, and yet anything but a predestined powerhouse or the economic dynamo that it later became. In the space of a short few decades, though, meaning by the middle of the nineteenth century, it had ridden plantation slavery—based on one crop above all, cotton—to become a rapidly industrializing nation and an incipient world power. Indeed, as one historian has written, "The cotton trade was the economy's only 'major expansive force.'"

37

HOW THE WEST WAS MADE
AND "WON"

L ET US CONSIDER THE two rival theories for how this situation developed and unfolded. Of this pair, the first, which is the prevailing view, is heavily technological; the other, seldom explored or emphasized in most curricula even now, is centered on American politics and the ways they were conditioned by the history of the broader Atlantic world. Rival perspectives exist, but most are essentially mythology based and focus on the courage, initiative, and ultimately the ingenuity of white men who set out from the East Coast, after arriving there from Europe, to "tame" and thus bring into production the vast American wilderness that lay to the west and southwest of the Appalachian Mountains. This is a story we have all been taught, if no longer so much formally in the classroom, passively, as it washes over us via television and film and in our political discourse.

The technologically driven account of the country's rise to industrialization and greatness is remarkably centered on the invention of a single, transformative device, the cotton gin, and on its inventor, Eli Whitney. It is a story that almost all Americans learn in school, one whose simplest moral is of the indomitable native ingenuity of their countrymen in the face of technical obstacles to economic progress. Whitney's cotton gin was introduced in 1793, at a time when American cotton production amounted to little more than nine thousand bales annually. All by itself, we are taught, the invention lifted two enormous bottlenecks, allowing America to meet the surging demand from industrializing Britain. The processing of cotton, once picked, was unusually slow and laborious, often requiring a whole, tedious hour of manual labor per slave to separate the seeds from a mere pound of white cotton balls. What is more, the amount of land that could be put under this valuable crop was sharply limited, because the prized, "long-staple" Sea Island variety, which grew along the coasts of Georgia and South Carolina, where most early American cotton was produced, fared poorly in the vast interior. In one stroke, this story goes, Whitney's gin changed all of that by making it possible to process, or deseed "short-staple" cotton. This variety absolutely thrived inland, in the so-called upcountry. The triumphant narrative that surrounds this breakthrough, which had already begun to form in the early nineteenth century, is perhaps best captured in the title of a 1956 book by Constance McLaughlin Green and Oscar Handlin: *Eli Whitney and the Birth of American Technology*.

The point here is not to thoroughly gainsay Whitney or the utility of his invention, even though a lively debate persists over the man's exact role. Cotton gins had already existed in India for nearly fifteen hundred years, although those devices employed a somewhat different technology. Many historians have also objected to the way that the standard narrative of the Whitney gin's invention long promoted a view of the South as a world of indolent slaves and backward whites. The region's denizens were presented as having been powerless to fundamentally change the economics of the region—that is, until fortune brought them Whitney, a Yale-educated northerner who quickly solved the riddle bedeviling the production of a crop that he had no prior exposure to.* Recounted almost as a miracle, this traditional story line also neglects the sense of urgency felt in the United States in

* The best account of Whitney's role in cotton gin innovation and of the historiographical debates surrounding his device is Angela Lakwete's 2003 book *Inventing the Cotton Gin: Machine and Myth in Antebellum America*.

the 1780s to find alternatives to tobacco, hitherto the overwhelming mainstay of the American economy, amid a sharp decline in prices.

It is beyond dispute that cotton production took off in the 1790s in the American South, and that the Whitney gin played a not inconsiderable role. By one estimate, prime land used to grow cotton quickly tripled in value after its adoption. What else, then, is missing from this story? Processing technology was not the only bottleneck restricting cotton production in this era, nor was it even the most important one. As we have seen, cotton output grew massively over the next decade or so, reaching 36 million pounds by the turn of the nineteenth century. More than the new gin, to which most of the credit is attributed, the increase in cotton production was due to a series of developments involving slaves. First came surging imports in human beings from Africa. And once that trade was permanently banned, in 1807, the massive redeployment of slaves out of the Upper South into new cotton-growing regions accelerated. But this is more than a classical story of how an increase in capital goods, i.e., slaves, resulted in a big boost in production. Almost entirely overlooked in traditional accounts of the rise of American cotton, was the concomitant massive increase in slave productivity on the plantation, which the historian Edward Baptist has estimated at 400 percent in the period from 1800 to 1860. This, he argues, was procured through a systematic increase in violent methods of supervision and punishment, combined with ever more far-reaching record keeping:

> *In 1801, 28 pounds per day, per picker, was the average from several South Carolina labor camps. By 1818, enslaved people on James Magruder's Mississippi labor camp picked between 50 and 80 pounds per day. A decade later, in Alabama, the totals on one plantation ranged up to 132 pounds, and by the 1840s, on a Mississippi labor camp, the hands averaged 341 pounds each on a good day—"the largest that I have ever heard of," the overseer wrote. In the next decade, averages climbed higher still.*

Whether the production increases were obtained through new technologies or by the ever more severe abuse of slaves, though, at a certain point cotton output was bound to run into limitations more formidable even than those once posed by the costs of onerous hand processing: a lack of new, frost-free lands suitable for the growing of the crop. This bottleneck was not relieved via any of the more comfortable and familiar story lines of American history—things like homespun ingenuity, sacrifice, and perseverance—or even solely through the new forms of inhumanity inflicted upon slaves, such as those documented by Baptist. It was lifted, instead, as the ironic result of the unquenchable desire of Blacks on Saint Domingue to live in freedom.

That is because the looming loss of Saint Domingue forced Napoleon to largely abandon his visions of empire on the American mainland. In January 1803, Thomas Jefferson nominated James Monroe to join Robert Livingston in Paris to discuss the purchase of New Orleans from France. Their aim was to secure an outlet to the sea for American goods produced between the Ohio and Mississippi River Valleys and thereby ensure the economic viability of the expanding frontier. Two months later, Jefferson's representatives were stunned by the French counteroffer: that the Americans purchase imperial rights to the entire 828,000 square miles of Native American lands that constituted the Louisiana Territory instead. Never having dreamed of such a windfall, they promptly agreed to a price of $15 million, or about three cents per acre (not including the considerable cost of many subsequent "compensation" settlements forced upon the native populations).

PRIOR TO THE TERRITORY'S SALE to the United States, French colonization of Louisiana had been tenuous bordering on theoretical. It was an imperial project that made sense for France only as a kind of colonial back office or supply platform to provision the country's cornerstone overseas possession, its extraordinarily lucrative colony of Saint Domingue. This strategic vision had already taken shape by 1789, when France's minister, or ambassador, to the United States, had written a report urging Paris to move quickly to recover Louisiana from Spain, saying that it "could become a center for the northern fur trade, a customer of the mother country, a depot of supplies for the Antilles, and the theater of a vast trade with the United States." This was nothing more, in effect, than an updating of the old European dream of achieving immense slaving synergies via imperial integration that we first encountered in the Dutch Great Design. Napoleon later adopted this concept as his own, believing that once the slave revolt in Saint Domingue was put down and the plantation system there restored, wealth from the island would, in the words of historian Robert Paquette, "drive France's other American possessions and probably France itself into an interdependent and, above all, self-contained prosperity."

The defection from the French side of Jean-Jacques Dessalines and Alexandre Pétion, a free person of color and cofounder of Haiti, in Saint Domingue in October 1802, and the death of General Leclerc there the following month, along with the renewal of war with Britain, finally brought Napoleon to see the writing on the wall for his doomed colony. "Damn sugar, damn coffee, damn colonies," the French emperor is said to have exclaimed, as he was forced to cut the gigantic financial losses he had incurred in Saint Domingue in order to salvage his hopes of dominating Europe. And this abandonment by Napoleon of his dreams of Atlantic empire centered on Saint Domingue was the key to two of the greatest events of the nineteenth century. For Britain, France's defeat in the Caribbean removed that country as a competitive threat in the plantation-centered world of the Atlantic, psychologically freeing the British to slowly work their way toward abolition. This was achieved not with the end of British slave trading, in 1808, but only thirty-five years later. Resolute in their desire for freedom, the Haitians were equally instrumental in placing America on the path to great powerhood in the nineteenth century. More than any other single event that has happened in the country's entire history, in fact, Saint Domingue's self-liberating slaves formed and shaped the continent-size America we know on the map today.

Generation after generation of American writers and educators have contributed to the downplaying of these facts, but American traditions of historiography are not alone in their tendency to mutely glide past details that run so contrary to convenient myths. "One would expect such 'facts,' none of which is controversial, to generate a chain of mentions, even if negative," lamented my late friend Michel-Rolph Trouillot, in his landmark work, *Silencing the Past: Power and the Production of History*, speaking of the links between the Haitian Revolution and the Louisiana Purchase. "Yet a perusal of French historical writings reveals multiple layers of silence."* And much the same is true with Britain and the heroic way it imagines itself as having almost single-handedly ended Atlantic slavery.

卐

ACQUISITION OF PROPERTY on a scale so vast as the Louisiana Purchase allowed Jefferson and others in the Virginia elite to pursue a long held aim: the partial divestment of their state of slaves, whose concentrated presence in their midst had all along been considered a potentially mortal danger. With the example of the Haitian Revolution fresh in people's minds, this took on fresh urgency. By the early nineteenth century, the half million Blacks enslaved at the time of the American Revolution had grown to a million, and although no white statesman could have known this with any precision, the slave population was on its way to the four million it would reach by 1865. Jefferson's move must also be seen as part of an older and indeed deeper project to catalyze American whites on the basis of both expansion and exclusion; this project implicated other major figures including Franklin, Adams, and Washington. From the very start, the twin menaces of Indian resistance and Black revolt, con-

---

* The Haitian Revolution is not even mentioned in France's general *lycée* curriculum. British education does little better, not requiring the study of history after the age of fourteen.

joined with the promise of an expanding white frontier, were strategic essential ingredients in the mortar used to bind the young nation together.

Jefferson had long understood the events leading up to the creation of a Haitian state in terms of the threat they posed to the power and safety of American whites. Black freedom equaled menace. As much as this should appall us today, it nonetheless obeys a clear and obvious logic. After all, as the historian Annette Gordon-Reed has written, "[t]he colonists knew exactly what it [had taken] to bring these people to their shores, into their fields, and into their homes. Theirs was a society built on and sustained by violence, actual and threatened." This is the reality that caused Alexis de Tocqueville to write that the specter of race "constantly haunts the imagination of [all] Americans like a nightmare."

For his generation, Alexander Hamilton was rare in his open recognition of the gift of Louisiana that Haiti's liberation had made possible, saying, "[T]o the courage and obstinate resistance made by its Black inhabitants are we indebted for the obstacles which delayed the colonization of Louisiana." But gratitude to a slave revolution for America's enormous geopolitical good fortune was well beyond Jefferson, for whom Toussaint Louverture was a mere "cannibal." "Never was so deep a tragedy presented to the feelings of man," Jefferson wrote of the revolution in Haiti, continuing, "I become daily more convinced that all the West India islands will remain in the hands of the people of colour, and a total expulsion of the whites sooner or later take place. It is high time we should foresee the bloody scenes which our children certainly and possibly ourselves (south of the Potomac) will have to wade through and try to avert them."

In Virginia, the wealthiest and arguably most politically important of the American colonies, the days of getting-rich-quick from tobacco farming had already ended by the mid-seventeenth century, and diversification away from that crop into wheat and corn was well under way by the mid-eighteenth. George Washington, a leading planter himself, cut back on tobacco farming in 1763 and three years later stopped growing the plant altogether. Tobacco farming was not nearly as arduous as that of Caribbean sugar, but it kept slaves busy on the land for nine months of the year. As tobacco prices declined, however, far less labor-intensive crops like corn reduced demand for slave labor among Virginia's big planters. The peak years for slave imports into the colony came in the 1730s, when newly arrived Africans made up between 34 and 44 percent of the population. As the historian Alan Taylor writes, "By the 1760s, Virginia's leaders worried that they had more than enough slaves for the economy and too many for their own security from revolt." The banning of the transatlantic trade in the United States in 1808 then sparked a rush to capitalize on the booming demand for slaves and the high prices they fetched in the newly acquired territories, creating the thriving internal trade mentioned above.

The Louisiana Purchase allowed Jefferson to pursue his long held dream of creating an expansive "empire of liberty," as he famously called it, without intended irony (despite the phrase's being in the Haitian declaration of human rights), using the newly acquired territories to the west to help establish a new class of white, yeoman farmers. These were mostly English, Irish, and Germans, whom he believed would best incarnate and perpetuate the young democracy's republican values. For Jefferson, exporting Blacks from the slave-congested East was like killing multiple birds with one stone, and that is not even counting the fact that the "new" lands in question were the habitat of native communities who were being violently driven farther west. This was indeed all one enormous and coordinated enterprise. Many of the routes and trails that Indians employed in their forced exile out of the eastern United States were the precise pathways that chained Black slaves would tread. Enslaved Blacks were hoovered up from the Virginia countryside and elsewhere in the Old South by freelancing headhunters; these traders, working on commission, offered irresistible prices to white farmers who were having trouble making profits in tobacco, rice, and wheat. The resold Blacks were then strung together in "coffles" usually of thirty to forty people at a time, but sometimes in groups that ran into the hundreds. Under the vigilance of whites riding in wagons, the captives were marched—with their wrists handcuffed, and all linked together by an enormous length of chain—across the Southeast to booming slave markets in places like Natchez, and especially New Orleans. In the latter city, perhaps a half million Blacks were sold at public auctions, which rivaled the French Opera House and the Théâtre d'Orléans as a source of white entertainment. Despite this, according to one historian of this thriving internal commerce in enslaved Black people, New Orleans had only one public historic marker as of 2015 commemorating this trade. However well-intentioned, the sign, placed on a wall outside of a restaurant called Maspero's, unfortunately misidentifies the location of a slave market known as Maspero's Exchange.

Virginia alone served up nearly 450,000 Blacks to the booming Mississippi region in this way between 1810 and 1860. For the single year of 1857, the officially recorded revenue of this human traffic in Richmond amounted to $4 million, or the equivalent of roughly $440 million today. Not only would the evacuation of Blacks from the Old South lessen the dangers they were perceived as posing to whites in the heartland of Jefferson's beloved Virginia, as well as make good money both for Virginian slave owners and, via taxation, for the state, but the slaves sold to the southwest would work for those yeoman whites, furnishing Jefferson's grand imperial vision with a practical foundation: forced Black labor. And from Jefferson's perspective, this was just in the normal order of things. The decongestion of the Old Dominion and other slave-dense areas of the Old South also forestalled the emergence of a feared potential alliance between Blacks and the worst off of the whites, many of whom had recently been indentured servants. As Gordon-Reed observes, "Instead, poor whites, encouraged by the policies of the elites, took refuge in their whiteness and the dream that one day they, too, could become slave owners" in the western parts of the country that were just opening up.

Naturally, every course of action that a statesman takes forecloses other possibilities, and it is no different with Jefferson's approach to the Mississippi River Valley and to the American West generally. Historians have recently argued that Jefferson could have conceivably used monies raised from the sale of western lands to purchase the freedom of Blacks from the slavery that he sometimes professed to loathe. If heavy concentrations of Blacks living in the midst of whites were simply deemed intolerable, though, he might also have set aside portions of the enormous western territories for the resettlement of freed slaves.* Embedded in an idea like this is a criticism of the teleology that saturates so much of our thinking about this era—i.e., that what happened in the past was simply inevitable, what the French historian François Furet called the second illusion of truth. In his book *The Forgotten Fifth*, the historian Gary Nash notes that pro-slavery sentiment had not yet taken firm hold of the young country, making bold scenarios like these far less outlandish seeming than they might appear from the perspective of today.

But America's early southern-dominated political leadership soon found other motivations for a slave-powered expansion westward and especially into the Mississippi River Valley, even beyond Jefferson's original considerations. In the War of 1812, Britain actively encouraged the desertion of Blacks from southern plantations, eventually giving freedom to thirty-four hundred slaves who escaped their masters in the Chesapeake region. This revived terrors among whites in all the big slaveholding states of an unholy alliance between the English and the two big groups of peoples of color in the colonies: Native Americans and Blacks. Thomas M. Bayly, a colonel in the Virginia militia, and later a congressman, said, "In addition to the danger to be apprehended from foreign enemies, we have in the bosom of our Country an enemy more dangerous than any we can expect from the other side of the Atlantick." This race panic fundamentally misunderstood reality. Britain had not sought to destroy its colony as it fought to put down what became the American Revolution, nor had it sought to field large numbers of armed

---

* An idea like this would have done nothing, of course, to relieve the moral catastrophe inflicted on native peoples, referred to as "savages" in the Declaration of Independence, as America pursued it expansion westward.

Blacks in hopes of turning the War of 1812 into a race war. In fact, in their desperation, it was Virginians themselves who had armed five hundred slaves to fight the English during the Revolution, but thereafter this was denied and largely stricken from historical memory. Both of these actions to arm the enslaved, British and American, echoed prior events in the American War of Independence, although few Americans learn about these facts in school nowadays, either. As it happened, fear of a British-Black axis was so real that just as the British assault on Washington, D.C., during the War of 1812 commenced, unfounded rumors of a slave revolt caused members of the American militia to flee the capital and surrounding counties in Maryland and Virginia. This opened the way for British troops to take the undefended city, scarcely firing a shot. The Americans, of course, eventually turned the tide in the war in the battle for Baltimore, which produced the Francis Scott Key song that would become the national anthem. Those singing "The Star-Spangled Banner" daily in stadiums and ballparks are rarely aware of the taunting line in the third stanza that celebrates the suppression of this imagined revolt: "No refuge could save the hireling and slave."

In addition to the various motivations just cited, expanding the settlement of whites and of slavery westward to the Mississippi Valley and beyond thus also became a means of enhancing national security against the twinned threats of attacks by the British and of a revolt by slaves. Just how seriously Jefferson and his Virginia peers took this idea can be discerned through both words and deeds. Patrick Henry, the planter-politician immortalized by his phrase "Give me liberty, or give me death," also wrote, albeit less famously, "Our country will be peopled. The question is, shall it be with Europeans or with Africans? . . . Is there a man so degenerate as to wish to see his country the gloomy retreat of slaves? No; while we may, let us people our lands with men who secure our internal peace, and make us respectable abroad." Jefferson, for his part, warned ominously about the impossibility of whites and Blacks ever being able to coexist in freedom: "Deep rooted prejudices entertained by the whites; ten thousand recollections, by the Blacks, of the injuries they have sustained;

new provocations; the real distinctions which nature has made; and many other circumstances, will divide us into parties and produce convulsions, which will probably never end but in the extermination of the one or the other race." Of the supposed "real distinctions" between the races, Jefferson added in a lengthy passage denigrating the intelligence of Blacks that "one could scarcely be found capable of tracing and comprehending the investigations of Euclid; and that in imagination they are dull, tasteless, and anomalous."

Prejudices like these caused Jefferson and other prominent members of the Virginia establishment to multiply their efforts to limit or reduce the Black population of the state. When in 1806 Virginia passed a new manumission law governing the terms under which the tiny numbers of Blacks who were freed by their masters could be liberated, for example, it specified that these ex-slaves would be required to leave the state within a year. Patrick Henry, it should be noted, never freed any slaves, and Jefferson, America's third president, only two during his life, neither of whom were the direct offspring he produced via the enslaved woman named Sally Hemings whom he controlled sexually. In his 1785 *Notes on the State of Virginia*, Jefferson, by that time already the father of Black children, wrote that Blacks must be "removed beyond the reach of mixture."*

As large as they were, Virginia's sales of Blacks to the Deep South were deemed inadequate to the challenge of reducing the threat of slave revolts in the state, and this led Jefferson and others, including James Madison and James Monroe, Virginians who were respectively the fourth and fifth presidents of the United States, to explore the idea of resettling large numbers of slaves to Africa. Worried, as others were, about the prohibitive cost of deporting males in their prime (who commanded the highest market values) Jefferson, for a time, promoted the idea of buying up infants and girls as a cheaper way of winding down the slave population. In the words of Alan Taylor, Jefferson "dismissed the suffering that losing children

---

* At Jefferson's death in 1826, all but five of his slaves were sold at auction, in order to pay off his creditors.

would cause to black families as inconsequential compared to the good of the republic and the superior 'happiness' of their children once free in Africa." Propositions like these involving the deportation of African Americans were discussed between Washington and Lafayette, and would continue to fascinate American political leaders as an attractive solution to the country's "race problem," leading to the creation of an outfit called the American Colonization Society (ACS), which was dedicated to sending American Blacks "back" to Africa. The idea survived all the way to the presidency of Abraham Lincoln, who openly considered shipping slaves off to freedom in Africa prior to and during the Civil War, as well as sending Blacks to live in Central America and the Caribbean.* Lincoln urged northern Blacks to get behind this idea, telling them, "[T]here is an unwillingness on the part of our people, harsh as it may be for you colored people to remain with us." At the time, it is worth emphasizing, the proportion of Blacks who were born in the United States was much higher than that of whites.

The ACS was privately founded in 1816 and gathered strong backing in the decade that followed from both pro-slavery politicians and abolitionists. They were tactically united in the belief that "there was no future for an interracial democracy in the United States." This came in the wake of signs of substantial interest among African Americans in the idea of leaving the United States for friendlier shores—someplace where they would be free not only of slavery, but of racial violence of all kinds and of the pervasive discrimination that existed throughout American society. In the 1810s, for example, a movement was launched by northeastern Blacks brought together by a man named Paul Cuffe to emigrate to somewhere in Africa. Toward the end of the decade, however, the objective shifted to Haiti, for the prestige it enjoyed among educated Blacks for winning independence, and over the next several years as many as thirteen

---

* In December 1862, Lincoln signed a contract with a shady businessman for the settlement of five thousand Blacks on the Haitian island Île à Vache. Four hundred of them actually made it there, but those who survived returned the United States in 1864.

thousand African Americans settled on the island, although many later returned.

The ACS, which parroted some of the language of Black groups urging emigration, might itself have even captured widespread Black adhesion, except for two obvious facts: the stark paternalism of its promoters, who allowed no place for Black representation among its leadership, and the ACS's own rhetoric. Its language was filled with racist characterizations of Black people, as a "special subordinate, more bestial caste within the human species," which were used to justify the idea of deporting them. This drove Black suspicion and, ultimately, strong rejection of the scheme in the 1820s, at the precise time when it was gathering momentum among prominent whites. Beyond the question of dubious white motives, by this time many Blacks had rightfully come to believe deeply that America was their country at least as much as anyone else's, and to reject altogether this idea that the solution to America's crisis of race was for them to find another home. One Black abolitionist, David Walker, whose urgent 1829 publication, *Appeal to the Colored Citizens of the World*, has been compared with Thomas Paine's *Common Sense*, spoke of African Americans as the "chosen people" through whose struggles alone could America's ideals be fully realized.

In point of fact, as early as the late eighteenth century, most enslaved people in the United States were the product of natural population increase among the unfree in America, meaning through their own reproduction on American soil as opposed to via importation from Africa. Few people in bondage would have had any direct knowledge of the continent of their ancestors, and indeed none would have this once the transatlantic trade was banned. Furthermore, no consideration was ever given to the idea of returning slaves to the specific shores where their ancestors came from, only to a generic homeland in Africa. This did nothing to stop the ACS from sending "volunteers," beginning in 1822, to the so-called Pepper Coast of West Africa for resettlement there. Resettled slaves in the Pepper Coast declared independence in 1846, becoming Africa's first republic, Liberia, which would go unrecognized by the United States until

1862. By 1867, an estimated thirteen thousand Blacks had been sent there by the United States, many dying from tropical diseases and poor hygiene in one of the rainiest stretches of the West African coast.

⁜

BY THE 1820s, the business of American expansion had become the primary focus of the United States government. In 1828, Andrew Jackson, a southern slaveholder, was swept into the White House as America's seventh president, in good part on the basis of his reputation as a general who had made his spurs in a number of murderous anti-Indian campaigns. Most famous was the Battle of Horseshoe Bend at the end of the U.S.-Creek War, in which his men slaughtered between eight and nine hundred natives. As president, in his first annual message to Congress, in December 1829, Jackson called for the "voluntary" departure of Native Americans to lands in the western territories beyond the Mississippi. This, of course, was for the settling of the Mississippi region itself by whites. Putting it under the plow to continue priming the extraordinary boom made possible by Blacks enslaved under the cotton kingdom had become an all-consuming endeavor. Surveyors put to work by President Jackson to map and subdivide hundreds of millions of acres of land and plan new towns entirely from scratch struggled to keep up with the demand. Jackson had to hire a full-time clerk to sign stacks of new deeds for eager buyers. Most popular of all were the standard-size 160-acre rectangular plots that stretched with numbing geometric regularity lengthwise inland from the riverfront, from which cotton could be easily brought to port.

This commodification of the land proceeded hand in hand with the steadily intensified commoditization of slave labor as it was marched to the new cotton kingdom from Virginia and other points east. So long as one cared nothing for human life, it was an incredible combination, arguably unbeatable in history. During the years between 1820 and 1860, the slave population in the lower Mississippi Valley increased sevenfold, while cotton production exploded by a factor of forty. A rise this steep was fueled not just by more hands working more land but, as we have seen, by radically increased slave productivity, acquired in large part by the lash. Until recently, slavery has been almost entirely absent from the history of business management. But new scholarship has shown that the "peculiar institution" played a pioneering role as a source of innovation in management, an avatar of modernity if there ever was one; indeed, this occurred well before the railroads were given credit for this by the famed Harvard scholar Alfred Chandler, who called them the initiator of the "managerial revolution."

With cotton, in particular, slaveholders "sought to determine how much labor their slaves could perform in a given amount of time, and they pushed them to achieve that maximum," as Caitlin Rosenthal wrote in *Accounting for Slavery*. In fact, this was a story that went back to the obsession with bookkeeping in order to master the devilish intricacies of sugar production of the Draxes in Barbados. But it gained accelerated momentum in the American South, where Big Cotton, much simpler to produce than sugar, sought to ever more systematically quantify every input and variable that could be measured in the pursuit of higher yields and bigger profits. This included data on the birth, death, purchase, and purported ethnicity of slaves. One of the most detailed accounts of American slavery we have is that of Solomon Northup, a free Black man who was kidnapped in Washington and trafficked to Louisiana. His memoir, *Twelve Years a Slave*, published soon after he was freed, memorably explained how terror and the extreme focus on productivity were joined as one on a cotton plantation.

No matter how fatigued and weary he may be—no matter how much he longs for sleep and rest—a slave never approaches the gin-house with his basket of cotton but with fear. If it falls short in weight—if he has not performed the full task appointed him, he knows that he must suffer. And if he has exceeded it by ten or twenty pounds, in all probability his master will measure the next day's task accordingly. So, whether he has too little or too much, his approach to the gin-house is always with, fear and trembling.

38

TOWARD A NEW VISION
OF OUR ORIGINS

SOLOMON NORTHRUP OBTAINED HIS freedom in 1854, only after extraordinary legal challenges were launched in New York, where he was from. This in an era where the wealth of America's biggest city had never seemed so dependent on southern slavery and cotton, from its banks to its commodity brokers and insurance companies. Very few other kidnapped free Blacks would be so fortunate. Only the American Civil War, which came seven years later, halted the rush toward plantation-derived wealth, along with the atrocious practice of abduction, one of its derivatives. Then and now, people in the North have obtained tremendous moral satisfaction for their region's role in fighting and dying to end slavery. But like Britain, where ending slavery has been woven into the very core of the national legend, conveniently overshadowing the fact that that nation was the superpower of Atlantic slavery for two centuries, the moral story of the American experience is a largely mythologized one. To anyone who has cared to really look, there is no escaping the fact that Black bondage benefited the North as much as the South, albeit in very different ways. When the rupture between the country's two "sections" finally came, W. E. B. Du Bois explained the conflict in these terms:

The South was fighting to take slavery out of the Union, and the North fighting to keep it in the Union; the South fighting to get it beyond the limits of the United States Constitution, and the North fighting for the old guarantees;—both despising the Negro, both insulting the Negro.

Words like these can still jar contemporary readers who have been raised on the idea that the war all along was about slavery, with the North heroically mobilizing to wipe out this cruel institution. Few are taught Lincoln's clarifying words:

If there be those who would not save the Union unless they could at the same time save slavery, I do not agree with them. If there be those who would not save the Union unless they could at the same time destroy slavery, I do not agree with them. My paramount object in this struggle is to save the Union and is not either to save or to destroy slavery. . . . [I]f I could save it by freeing all the slaves, I would also do it. . . . . What I do about slavery, and the colored race, I do because I believe it would help to save the Union.

In the end, it was descendants of people from Africa, men and women, who rose to the challenge of liberating themselves by undermining the southern economy and its war effort. This came first through slowdowns, spying, and many other nonconfrontational means, including throwing down their tools and simply walking off of hundreds of plantations to get behind northern lines, as many thousands did. In an echo of the "common wind" effect we saw in slave societies in the Caribbean, many escaped slaves arrived in Union camps reciting the exact provisions of emancipation acts that provided for their freedom. Later, they were permitted to fight for the Union, and by war's end, 180,000 Blacks had worn Union colors, or over a fifth of the nation's adult male Black population under the age of forty-five. Blacks had fought in many of the crucial battles in Virginia late in the war, and, as the historian Ira Berlin has noted, "[n]othing more clearly marked the transformation of the war for union into a war for freedom than the appearance of Black men in blue uniform."

It takes little away from Lincoln to say that he predicated Emancipation, in part, on Black participation in the war as a military strategy. No one knew better how heavily northern whites had been bled in battle and just how weary and resentful of the war they had become. The July 1863 riots against the draft in New York City, the nation's business and financial capital, were, in the historian Eric Foner's words, "the largest civil insurrection in American history apart from the South's rebellion itself," and required troops fresh from the Battle of Gettysburg to suppress. What tipped the balance was allowing Blacks to join the war effort, and when Emancipation came, General Ulysses S. Grant exulted, "The problem is solved. The Negro is a man, a soldier, a hero." As Grant acknowledged, Blacks heartily occupied the vanguard in the fight for their own liberation. But that is not all: the Black struggle for freedom was inseparable from the very emergence of the United States as a nation, as well as from the fulfillment of its most famous promise, about self-evident truths. This had begun not in 1862, when Blacks were allowed to enlist, but at the very inception of the country, when Blacks, free and slave, fought on both sides during the revolution, especially following the proclamation by the British governor of Virginia, John Murray, Earl of Dunmore, of November 7, 1775, offering freedom to slaves who fought for Britain. This was an idea that originated with runaway slaves themselves.

For obvious reasons, given that many of the American founders were enslavers, a hugely disproportionate number of slaves fought for the loyalist side, a fact that is almost treated like a dark secret in standard school curricula. But at least five thousand also fought in the Continental Army and Navy. Black and native militiamen were present at the foot of the "rude bridge" in Concord, Massachusetts, in April 1775, when the shot was fired that was "heard round the world." Two months later, 150 Blacks fought in the Battle of Bunker Hill—about 5 percent of the patriots present, and double the proportion of their number in the population. And the following year Blacks helped pull down King George's statue in Manhattan's Bowling Green park. Black companies fought under the command of George Washington in the Battle of Yorktown, where Britain surrendered, in 1781.

Washington had originally sought to exclude slaves from enlisting in the War of Independence, but as the historian Manisha Sinha has written, the "desperation at Valley Forge" brought a change of heart. Historically speaking, none of this was unusual: chattel societies have almost always resorted to arming slaves to defend against external threats. But these facts were steadfastly effaced from accounts of how the country was born because the main business of the men who became its founders was binding together white colonists to form a nation. Toward that end, the emphasis in "patriot" news coverage and in revolutionary propaganda resolutely stuck to narratives about "domestic insurrectionists" and "merciless savages." By the same token, it was important that "good" Blacks and Indians—who, as the historian Robert Parkinson observes, "were not eligible for any of the benefits of American independence" in any event—go unheralded.

Britain's aim in harboring tens of thousands of runaways, meanwhile, including those it armed, was not the destruction of slavery in America or indeed anywhere. Neither side in the War of Independence ever regarded slavery or its abolition as a goal of the conflict. But that didn't prevent Blacks from seeing it as a war for their own freedom, especially slaves in the South. Indeed, with slaves streaming behind British lines in all thirteen colonies, the historian Gary Nash has called the American Revolution the largest slave revolt in the country's history, albeit one that has never been recognized as such: "For African Americans, a revolution within a revolution had occurred, and they rightfully considered their 'glorious cause' to be the purest form of the 'spirit of '76.'"

As this history summons us to remember, Blacks have played a leading role in supplying energy, creativity, and moral urgency to the American project from the very outset. It has been their struggle, more than any other, that has cemented the association of the idea that Americans sustain of themselves—and of their country—with the fundamental value of universal freedom.

卐

THESE IDEAS WERE BEING REAFFIRMED even as I completed this book, as cheering crowds watched statue after statue of Confederate war "heroes" being hauled down throughout the South, much as King George was toppled in New York nearly 250 years earlier, and as Americans all over the country questioned anew the lives of even the most revered Founders and other towering figures like Lincoln over the moral compromises they made with regard to Black lives. The southern icons once thought immovable included a statue of John C. Calhoun, vice president to John Quincy Adams and Andrew Jackson and staunch defender of slavery, in Charleston, where the Civil War began in April 1861, and Robert E. Lee, in Richmond, the Confederate capitol whose capture in early April 1865 brought the war to an end a few days later.

The history of the Civil War and, much more so still, the broader history of American slavery, are, of course, immense and almost bottomless topics, ones that easily fill entire volumes and, well beyond that, row after row of library shelves. As with all of the principal themes of this book, on these subjects, one makes no pretense of exhaustiveness. That would be impossible in spanning five centuries and the four continents covered here. The main thought I would like to leave readers with is that of the crucial participation of Black people in their own liberation and in the preservation of the young American union. This was the second extraordinary act of the African diaspora in making the New World safe for democracy, coming sixty-one years after the Haitian Revolution. A central task of this volume is to challenge us to ask why such things have not been accorded far more prominence in the ways they are taught and remembered. And in doing so, to highlight the immense work that lies ahead for the United States if it is to understand itself more fully.

In every section of this text, through stories of African gold and slavery and sugar and cotton, each bigger economically and more transformative than the last, I have endeavored not only to place Africans and people of African descent in the New World at the center of the history of modernity and of its advent, but to depict them as prime movers in every stage of that history. The great English historian Eric Hobsbawm once described industrialization as the greatest event in the history of humankind. The story of slavery, of plantations, and of the Black labor that generated the most important product of that era, cotton, is by any reasonable standard a core element in this immense human change. But that is not all: the economic activity that surrounded cotton also lifted banking and insurance and drove globalized commerce on scales never seen before. It profoundly reshaped the political maps of continents. It positioned the United States to become the world's largest and most dynamic economic power already by the late nineteenth century. And it helped propel the new American colossus to swiftly attain twice the size of Britain's economy by 1914.

In some ways, though, it is what happened after the formal end of slavery that best helps us to comprehend the vital role played by stolen and expropriated Black labor. Here, we may be reminded of how determinedly Britain, France, and Spain invested their blood and treasure throughout the eighteenth century and into the nineteenth in order to gain or hold on to any advantage in controlling slave plantation real estate in the Caribbean, even though most conventional histories expend little ink in emphasizing the importance of sugar slavery in Europe's rise. Their willingness to sacrifice entire fleets and armies to this effort—and not on behalf of some abstract notion like glory, as some still insist—tells us what we need to know about how they perceived the economic stakes that attached to these properties. Similarly, with American slavery, the best sense available to us of its worth to the South, and indeed to the nation, are the extraordinary lengths to which society went to restore a facsimile of slavery just a few years after it was abolished. In 1865, the Civil War barely ended, a newspaper in Georgia, the *Macon Telegraph*, stated unabashedly: "the great question now before our people is how to appropriate all the African labor of the country"; indeed, that is what a new system, built upon the ashes of antebellum slavery, immediately set out to do.

That system came to be known as sharecropping and its bedfellow, Jim Crow. It would dominate economic life in the plantation South, continuing to supply Black labor and the agricultural output that it produced at steeply discounted rates for the next eighty years, from 1865 to 1945. The rise of the sharecropper system began even before the total defeat of Dixie, when white planters who were desperate for Black workers began offering them wage and crop share agreements in order to keep them in the field and prevent "defection" to the Union. A mortal blow was dealt to sharecropping by the commercialization of a new machine that has received far less attention than Whitney's cotton gin, but which arguably represented a more dramatic advance: the mechanical cotton picker, whose first demonstration of a production-ready model came in, of all places, Clarksdale, Mississippi, on October 2, 1944. A single machine could do the work of fifty sharecropping Blacks, a fact not long lost on the white planters of the Delta.

Before the advent of this mechanical invention, myriad social and legal innovations were required to keep Blacks locked in peonage, working on farms under arrangements designed to rob them of the fruits of their own labor and to prevent them from ever accumulating any wealth, education, or hope. This is the world that the grandmother of Muddy Waters was born into and the system she would have labored under. The institution of sharecropping relied on the isolation of the region, on political domination of the Deep South by neorestorationist whites in the Democratic Party, and on a reign of violence, of which lynching was merely the most infamous tactic. But for most of this era, the idea of escape to the North offered no magic solution, either: the public in most of the North was starkly hostile to the idea of Black migration, and industrial jobs were reserved for whites by the existence of a firm color line.

Of this starkly enclosed region ruled by terror, a cousin of mine, Simeon Booker, wrote in the early 1960s, "Mississippi could easily rank with South Africa, Angola or Nazi Germany for brutality and hatred." As a reporter for *Jet* magazine, Booker spent years investigating Black life in the South, personally obtaining the photograph of Emmett Till's mutilated body in his casket. In large part because of that image, Till's murder near Money, Mississippi, a mere forty-eight miles by car from Clarksdale, brought international attention—assuredly unwelcome in Washington—to the plight of Blacks in the South, and propelled civil rights activism in the Delta. Cousin Simeon, who was close to my parents' age and therefore called uncle, also covered the Freedom Rides and the violent advent of political rights for African Americans in the region. In May 1961, as a Trailways bus he was riding in limped into Birmingham, Alabama, after having been attacked at previous stops, he somehow managed to slip away from the station as Freedom Riders were being savagely beaten by a white mob, taking a cab to the home of a local Black church leader, Fred Shuttlesworth, where Booker called a senior official in the Kennedy administration's Justice Department to demand federal protection. This was a time, Booker later wrote, when outsiders were treated with uniform suspicion by whites as troublemakers, when few Blacks dared look a white man in the eyes, and when those who spoke up often later died in "freak accidents."

It was more than violence in deed, though, that kept this evil system going. It was also violence written into the law through a proliferation of new "Black Codes" that weaponized the concept of vagrancy to mean whatever white people wanted it to. Mississippi and South Carolina were the first to introduce Black Codes, in late 1865, but they quickly spread throughout the South. These new laws did things like require all Blacks to provide written proof of employment every January. Vague notions that included things like being idle, neglecting one's supposed calling, or even misspending one's own money were placed under the capacious and now criminalized rubric of vagrancy. Anything deemed insulting to whites, including "malicious mischief," was outlawed, and this category even encompassed preaching the Gospel without a license. As Eric Foner wrote, it became illegal to offer higher wages to lure away Black workers who were already under contract, and illegal for Blacks to refuse to work for anything but "the usual and common wages given to other laborers." Other restrictions prevented Blacks from hunting, fishing, or grazing cattle on public land, lest they be able to provide for themselves off the plantation.

In order to shut down another possible escape route, Blacks were forbidden to rent land in urban areas. Things got far worse after the collapse of Reconstruction, during the so-called Redemption era, when the open and absolute restoration of the racial subordination of Blacks became the central purpose of government. The means employed toward this end are simply too numerous to describe exhaustively here. State government spending was slashed on public services of all kinds, lest Blacks benefit. Boards of education were eliminated, harsh sentences were imposed for petty crimes, including life imprisonment for burglary, and Black convicts were impressed into work on farms, much like slaves. "The whole South—every state in the South [has] gotten into the hands of the very men that held us as slaves," lamented Black Louisianan Henry Adams.

A tentative shift in white priorities began only when the cotton-picking machine was commercialized right after World War II. Then, planters and indeed many other whites began to feel like Jefferson-era white Virginians: in their minds, so many Blacks in their midst now posed a big threat. By this time, things were already far removed from the era when anyone could have seriously floated a proposal to deport Black people en masse to Africa, bruted openly the last time during the white Redemption years. Southern Blacks now openly yearned for a freer life elsewhere, for a few even including in Africa, but that was a transitory sentiment. "We are not Africans now, but colored Americans, and are entitled to American citizenship," a correspondent wrote in 1887 to Blanche K. Bruce, who was born as a slave in Virginia and became the first African American to serve a full term in the Senate, where he represented Mississippi as a Republican from 1875 to 1881.

The escape valve that may have prevented a broad uprising in the South—or, indeed, an explosion—turned out to be Black migration to other parts of the country, especially to the region we call the Rust Belt, and to the mid-Atlantic and West. In 1948, Fielding L. Wright, the governor of Mississippi, and that year's vice presidential candidate under Strom Thurmond, on the States' Rights Democratic Party, announced the hostile new tune on state-wide radio "advising" Black people in Mississippi to go elsewhere if they contemplated eventual social equality. Black people were in no need of such tips and had already begun flowing out of the region; Chicago became their most famous focal point, especially after the Illinois Central Railroad bought out older rail systems in the Delta in 1892 and began integrating them into its own network. This pierced the isolation of the Delta like nothing else had done before, and Black migration soared, with half a million people leaving the South by 1920.

As the numbers show, Blacks were by no means merely resigned to their fates or waiting fatalistically to be liberated by a new technology. They poured forth out of the South in what has been called the greatest internal migration of modern times. "Many black parents who left the South got the one thing they wanted just by leaving. Their children would have a chance to grow up free of Jim Crow and to be their fuller selves," Isabel Wilkerson wrote in her masterly account of the Great Migration. By the time a cotton-picking machine became a reality, talk of deportation to Africa was passé. As a perceptive Black man named Aaron Henry put it, about the attitudes of whites toward people of his kind, "Chicago was close enough," and this was borne out by data. The number of Blacks in Chicago grew roughly fivefold between 1910 and 1930, when it reached 234,000.

The history of this great migration must be stitched together with the saga that our story commenced with, of the great history-altering movement of peoples out of Africa, across the Atlantic and into the Caribbean, Brazil, and Mexico and then into what became the continental United States—all in chains. This must be woven together, in turn, with the internal slave trade that brutally seeded the expanding South with a burgeoning Black population, only to step into freedom from the harsh peonage that followed outright bondage to transform their nation yet again. The resulting tapestry is so grand that we must take a step or two backward to fully apprehend it. As Wilkerson notes, it was this final exodus that gave this country its first wave of Black municipal leaders, mayors like Harold Washington of Chicago, Tom Bradley of Los Angeles, and David Dinkins of New York. By the same token, children of this outpouring produced some of its greatest writers, people like Toni Morrison, James Baldwin, and August Wilson. It generated the music that perhaps more than any other marked the twentieth century, from Thelonious Monk and Miles Davis to John Coltrane in jazz, to Aretha Franklin and Jimi Hendrix, to rhythm and blues, the Motown sound, and Michael Jackson in pop. In sports it produced Joe Louis and Jesse Owens, Jim Brown and Willie Mays, and Venus and Serena Williams, and others more numerous than one can count.

Muddy Waters, that object of cultural and artistic fascination of mine from my early twenties, also made his way out of the Delta on a May day in 1943, aboard the 4:00 p.m. out of Clarskdale. Like so many others, he was bound for Chicago, not with his parents, but as a Whitmanesque character, young, confident, and self-inventive, and he was as determined as anyone had been to make a new life for himself in the big, brawny city to the north. It wasn't so much the rail he had ridden on that May afternoon, though, as his dreams, borne by a voice that was distinctively low, assertive, and comfortable in its own idiom. In his first recording, done for the Library of Congress on a chance encounter with a researcher named Alan Lomax in January 1941, he had all but foretold this in a song called "I Be's Troubled." Later, it would be slightly rewritten and renamed, "I Can't Be Satisfied."

> *Well, if I feel tomorrow like I feel today*
> *I'm going to pack my suitcase*
> *And make my getaway.*

AFTERWORD

I N THE EARLY SECTIONS OF THIS BOOK, from time to time I had occasion to speak of my wife's family, which has its roots in a place in western Ghana called Bonyere, which is located in the headlands quite near where the trade in gold was initiated in the fifteenth century between African kingdoms of the surrounding area and questing Portuguese who began arriving from afar by sea.

Here in ending this book, I would like to briefly open a discussion of my own family, whose history on my mother's side we can trace back to the late stages of American slavery, meaning a half century before that institution was brought to an end by the Civil War. It is a story situated in Virginia, the starting point and center of another trade, not of gold, but of Africans sold into chattel servitude in British North America, a state that at the turn of the nineteenth century still held more Blacks in bondage than any other.

Some of the happiest times of my life were summers spent as a child in Virginia on land painstakingly pieced together and passed down to us by our enslaved ancestors. To tell something of their story, I must begin with a personal recollection. It involves my mother, Carolyn, who took history seriously and wanted her children to do so, too. In the summers, when we would gather at our ancestral home, a place called Brownland, on more than one occasion we made the thirty-minute drive to Charlottesville to visit Monticello, the hilltop mansion and working slave plantation that Thomas Jefferson designed.

My mother made sly sport of our tours there; later, as her eight children grew up, we sustained this as a family tradition. The game began during group tours of the Jefferson estate, where the guides would center their commentaries on the signs of Jefferson's genius that survive there on his mountaintop: the unusual octagonal room in his columned mansion; his remarkable library; the fancy bed in which he read sitting upright by night; the clever devices, advanced for their day, for keeping track of the time and weather; the mounted specimens of wildlife collected by this Renaissance man whose insatiable curiosity had also made him a naturalist and amateur biologist. Politely but insistently, my mother would disrupt the intended flow of the proceedings by asking pointed questions about the enslaved workers whose labors had made all of this grandeur possible. The appreciative oohs and aahs of the tourists stopped and the consternation on the faces of the guides showed, but my mother was just getting started. What about the slaves who were Jefferson's actual offspring? Only then came the pièce de resistance, when she would inquire by name about Sally Hemings, the enslaved half-sister of his wife, with whom Jefferson produced six children. Stories like these were just rumors, the staff would insist back then, fuming. As professionals, they said, their job was to limit themselves to the proven record. The story of Jefferson and Hemings, widely rumored even while the Founder was alive, was detailed in its fullness by the groundbreaking work of the African American historian Annette Gordon-Reed, in 1997. Still the guides persisted. However dubious, they maintained this stance until the following year, when DNA testing on Hemings's descendants definitively confirmed Jefferson's paternity.

This story had particular resonance for my mother because our family line can be traced to the purchase of an enslaved woman named Priscilla in 1812 by one James Barbour. This is no matter of conjecture. We possess a copy of the bill of sale. During his long public career, James Barbour, a scion of one of the First Families of Virginia, served as secretary of war under John Quincy Adams and as a U.S. senator, among other positions. His younger brother, Philippe Pendleton Barbour, was a Speaker of the House of Representatives and Supreme Court associate justice, appointed by Andrew Jackson in 1835, the same year that Roger Taney was named the court's chief justice. Taney is infamous for the Dred Scott decision of 1857, which formally condemned American Blacks to second-class status, "perpetual and impassible," and in making this ruling, Taney leaned on arguments advanced earlier by Barbour. At the time of Priscilla's purchase, though, James Barbour was the newly installed governor of Virginia, and the first to reside in the governor's mansion.

Although we have not yet benefited from the DNA analysis of the kind that tied Jefferson to Hemings, our family tradition passed down the generations has always held that with Priscilla, whom he was known to favor, Barbour sired Winifred in 1835, my grandfather's grandmother. Winifred later married J. Albert Newman, who had been a slave on the adjoining Burlington plantation, which was owned by a cousin of the Barbours by the name of Newman. J. Albert was also the product of Jefferson-style miscegenation. Family tradition has also long held that he was promised land in the will of his white father, who died in the 1850s. But in the aftermath of the Dred Scott decision, made possible, in part, by the very brother of the slave owner next door, Newman's white offspring succeeded in ensuring that their Black half sibling got none of it.

After Emancipation, J. Albert, a cobbler, and his brother Edgar, a blacksmith, rejected their slave name and adopted the family name Brown (one assumes for their color). Together, in small allotments, the two set about purchasing what eventually became one hundred acres of land. That is our Brownland.

The determined struggle of the Browns was nothing less than a quest for full citizenship in the country they had helped build. Indeed, this has been the common quest of all African American families who came to this land by way of slavery, even those in the North for whom citizens' rights were kept vague and attenuated, even in places where slavery itself was banned. And it remains so today.

In a meditation on this history addressed to the place of worship of my Brown ancestors, the Blue Run Baptist Church, in Barboursville, Virginia, written for Black History Month in 2009, my mother, Carolyn, spoke of the travails of many generations of our family in this struggle, through slavery and dispossession, Reconstruction, and the Red Summer of 1919. Of my generation, as one of eight siblings, all raised to remember, she wrote: "The foundation of their upbringing is built upon the faith, hopes and dreams of their ancestors." As much as anything else, the story of my ancestors put me on the path to study the broader history of the Atlantic world contained within these covers. Ending the invisibility of Africa in the construction of what we all know and experience as the modern lies at the heart of that struggle.

ACKNOWLEDGMENTS

Unusual, perhaps, for a work of history, this book grows, in the first instance, out of personal experience, both of life and of work. By the former, I mean the lessons I had already begun learning, as an African American child, of the many ways—running the gamut from subtle to violent—in which my society worked to marginalize people whose ancestry traces back to Africa.

The most vivid early experience of this was being forced out of a public swimming pool with my siblings on a sweltering summer day in small-town Virginia not long after we had turned up there. Jim Crow in its most explicit form was already dead or fast-dying by the mid-1960s, when this incident occurred, so the managers temporarily closed the pool to everyone, white and Black, to send me, an elementary-school child, and my siblings away and thereby enforce de facto segregation.

My first thanks go to my late parents, Carolyn and David, who helped prepare me for the many obstacles that America's history of race metes out to people who descend from Africa. Thanks also to my seven sisters and brothers, who shared with me in education and struggle, and who have always taught and supported me with their love.

A new source of learning came when I began traveling to Africa as a young man, and then soon thereafter, moved to the continent, making me more and more aware of the depth of the erasure that Africa suffers from. For friends from my school years in America, I might as well have joined a colony on Mars, so strange and unfamiliar a choice like this seemed to them. Later, making my way into a career as a journalist, the lesson of Africa's marginality to the concerns of the people who shape the public's sense of the world was constantly reinforced to me, to the point where I came to appreciate that associating oneself deeply with Africa was a liability. Yes, the continent could serve as a springboard—something the history in this book now renders ironic for me—but little else.

As I have explained elsewhere here, accidents of professional biography sent me over and over to report from parts of the world that became vital to this book. These include years of roaming the West Indies, the Caribbean-fronting regions of Latin America, as well as a return to West and Central Africa as a bureau chief for *The New York Times*. Questions about Africa's role in the making of the modern world took further shape in my mind throughout all of these experiences. In a way that may not be immediately obvious, though, the more than a decade I spent afterward living and working as a journalist in East Asia serviced this reflection, too. There, the question of why the West had so long been ascendant was never far from the surface, and this state of affairs was never taken as inevitable or permanent. Thank you to my loving family—Avouka, William, and Henry—for accompanying me, supporting me even when things were difficult, and finding ways to grow together during these shared adventures.

This book, of course, is by no means primarily a work of journalism, reportage, or memoir. It is the product of years of reading about the Atlantic world, and of an effort to stitch Africa and Africans back into the human narrative of the last six centuries, not as the marginalia or ghostly apparitions that they have been traditionally confined to, but rather, into the heart of the matter, where they, in fact, belong. Throughout this process, I have benefited enormously from the encouragement, counsel, and criticism of any number of academic historians; people whose life's work is the stuff of my narratives. This book is an homage to them: people whose ideas I have wrestled with seriously and without whose groundbreaking efforts I could never have progressed very far.

As I embarked on this project, one of my earliest conversations came over dinner with Linda M. Heywood and John K. Thornton, prodigious scholars of Central Africa and of the Atlantic world at Boston University. Since then, John has been unstintingly generous both with his thoughts and reading suggestions. Another early conversation, this time with my colleague at Columbia University, Christopher L. Brown, a deep thinker about slavery, abolition, and the construction of an Atlantic world, was equally instrumental to my work. Frederick Cooper, an emeritus historian of Africa at New York University also kindly agreed to have lunch with the stranger that I was to him at an early and still formative date, greatly helping shape my thoughts. At all stages of this project, Toby Green, of King's College London, has been remarkably generous, sharing thoughts, offering suggestions, and making criticisms that have helped me improve this book in many ways. Robert Garfield of DePaul University helped guide me on São Tomé, introducing me to people on that island and schooling me on its history. Laurent Dubois, of the University of Virginia, was extremely generous with his ideas and criticisms on the subject of Haiti, as was Randy M. Browne, of Xavier University, about the Caribbean more broadly. Another Columbia University colleague, Jelani Cobb, provided thoughtful and clearheaded suggestions on American history, in particular, that also helped strengthen this work.

All of the scholars named here read portions of this book, and in one case, the entire manuscript, and although their generosity in this regard helped me improve things immeasurably, this is the proper place to say that the responsibility for any errors of commission or omission is mine alone.

My efforts in writing this book were also boosted in crucial ways by the assistance I received from a two-member research team. Reynolds Richter, a talented, young historian of Africa, read an early draft, and provided comprehensive criticisms and suggestions. Rafaela Yoneshigue Bassili came aboard to help me locate and then translate Portuguese documents from the late-medieval and early modern eras, but quickly demonstrated much broader gifts as a researcher. Beyond her enormous work product, her unflagging enthusiasm helped keep me going. Rafaela joins me in thanking the New York Public Library, and the libraries of Columbia University for helping quickly obtain otherwise seemingly unfindable items.

Alisa LaGamma, the Ceil and Michael E. Pulitzer Curator of the arts of Africa, Oceania, and the Americas, of the Metropolitan Museum in New York, has been a wonderful intellectual companion for a decade now. I am indebted to her and her team for their help in researching and securing permissions for images used in this book. Many thanks also to Wang Boxia, who designed this book's maps, and to Narukawa Hajime, of Keio University, for his kind permission to use the cartographic projection of the Atlantic World that appears as frontispiece. Judah Grunstein, the editor-in-chief at *World Politics Review*, where I write a regular column, also kindly read through the manuscript in its late stages.

I would also like to extend my sincere thanks to Patrick Gaspard, formerly director of the Open Societies Foundations. Patrick expressed belief in this project from the very first mention, and OSF helped fund the work that went into it, both travel and research. Thanks go, too, to Leonard Benardo of OSF, who helped expedite this vital assistance.

My publisher, W. W. Norton/Liveright, has also been strongly and consistently supportive. Our relationship began quite by accident at a big industry lunch, where I was seated next to Drake McFeely, who was then president. Drake and I quickly connected over our shared love of history, and he would soon become instrumental in acquiring *Born in Blackness*. Robert Weil, publishing director and editor-in-chief of Liveright, then took the project under his wing as editor, and with his perceptiveness, his sure hand, and his unflagging enthusiasm, he helped carry me to the finish line in things both big and small. Through his focus and care, Trent Duffy, who also helped edit the book, improved my work in countless ways. Rebecca Homiski also took an active and encouraging role in overseeing things. Finally, the peerless Haley Bracken served as over all orchestra master and reliable and gracious source of answers to every manner of question.

An extra-special thank you goes to my agent, Gloria Loomis, who has worked with me since my first book. I am indebted to her for her early belief and her constant support. With reason, I sign my messages to her with love.

My gratitude also goes to Selase Kove-Seyram, a wonderful former student who accompanied me during my research in Ghana, showing impressive resourcefulness and fantastic humor at all times. And renewed thanks and love, finally, to my second son, Henry, who also accompanied me on that and other trips and was a warm and eager intellectual companion throughout my work on this book.

NOTES

INTRODUCTION

2 "he had been a medieval man": Marie Arana, *Silver, Sword, and Stone: Three Crucibles in the Latin American Story* (New York: Simon & Schuster, 2019), 48.

4 the dawning of this kind of consciousness: Mahmood Mamdani, *Neither Settler nor Native: The Making and Unmaking of Permanent Minorities* (Cambridge, Mass.: Belknap/Harvard University Press, 2020), 2.

5 "we can look at the difference": Charles Taylor, "Two Theories of Modernity," *Public Culture* 11, no. 1 (Jan. 1999): 153.

5 "I do not know in this Kingdom": João de Barros, *Décadas da Ásia* (Lisbon: 1778), vol. 1., bk. 3, ch. 12, pp. 264–65 (author's translation).

6 "No African trade, no negroes; no negroes, no sugars": Peter Earle, *The World of Defoe* (New York, 1977), 131.

8 an extreme mental and psychological test: Randy M. Browne, *Surviving Slavery in the British Caribbean* (Philadelphia: University of Pennsylvania Press, 2017), 3.

9 By 1846, the average Mississippi cotton picker: Edward E. Baptist, *The Half Has Never Been Told: Slavery and the Making of American Capitalism* (New York: Basic Books, 2016), 126.

1. THE CRACKLING SURFACE

18 In its early phases of growth, the city counted: Roderick J. McIntosh and Susan Keech McIntosh, "The Inland Niger Delta Before the Empire of Mali: Evidence from Jenne-Jeno," *The Journal of African History* 22, no. 1 (Jan. 1981): 1–22.

18 Another thirty thousand: Michael A. Gomez, *African Dominion: A New History of Empire in Early and Medieval West Africa* (Princeton, N.J.: Princeton University Press, 2018), 18.

19 The problematic idea of something called Black Africa: Ousman Oumar Kane, *Beyond Timbuktu: An Intellectual History of Muslim West Africa* (Cambridge, Mass.: Harvard University Press, 2016), 17.

20 the desert-hardy camel: Timothy F. Garrard, "Myth and Metrology: The Early Trans-Saharan Gold Trade," *The Journal of African History* 23, no. 4 (1982): 449.

20 Ghana's wealth and prestige: Toyin Falola and Kevin D. Roberts, eds., *The Atlantic World, 1450–2000* (Bloomington: Indiana University Press, 2008), 12.

20 Ancient Ghana maintained twin capitals: Nehemia Levtzion, *Ancient Ghana and Mali* (New York: Africana Publishing, 1980), 23.

21 "I saw at Awdaghust a warrant": Ghislaine Lydon, *On Trans-Saharan Trails: Islamic Law, Trade Networks, and Cross-Cultural Exchange in Nineteenth-Century Western Africa* (Cambridge: Cambridge University Press, 2009), 62.

21 two-thirds of the supply of the metal: Levtzion, *Ancient Ghana and Mali*, 132.

22 "The ruler who preceded me": Gomez, *African Dominion*, 100.

25 In the initial phase of empire, it shared key features: See Rudolph T. Ware III, *The Walking Qur'an* (Chapel Hill: University of North Carolina Press, 2014), 86.

25 With equal alacrity it had also begun: See Levtzion, *Ancient Ghana and Mali*, 20.

25 The clan at the center of Malian power, the Keïtas: Gomez, *African Dominion*, 70.

25 "The people come out, dressed in their white": Levtzion, *Ancient Ghana and Mali*, 92.

26 the embrace of Islam by Malinke traders: Lydon, *On Trans-Saharan Trails*, 9.

26 The supple form that the religion took: Ware, *The Walking Qur'an*, 89.

26 secured Islam's hitherto vulnerable presence in Europe: David Levering Lewis, *God's Crucible: Islam and the Making of Europe, 570 to 1215* (New York: W. W. Norton, 2008), 360.

2. BLACK KING, GOLDEN SCEPTER

28 a cover story for an abrupt shift: François-Xavier Fauvelle-Aymar, *The Golden Rhinoceros: Histories of the African Middle Ages* (Princeton, N.J.: Princeton University Press, 2018), 165.

28 The combined population: Michael A. Gomez, *African Dominion: A New History of Empire in Early and Medieval West Africa* (Princeton, N.J.: Princeton University Press, 2018), 123.

29 Mali also began to extend: See Nehemia Levtzion, *Ancient Ghana and Mali* (New York: Africana Publishing, 1980).

29 "The emperor could ensure his cut": Frederick Cooper, *Africa in the World: Capitalism, Empire, and Nation-State* (Cambridge, Mass.: Harvard University Press, 2014), 44.

30 "under very large banners or flags": Gomez, *African Dominion*, 115.

30 Ināri Kunāte: Levtzion, *Ancient Ghana and Mali*, 211.

31 Mūsā commanded more devotion: Felipe Fernández-Armesto, *Before Columbus: Exploration and Colonisation from the Mediterranean to the Atlantic, 1229–1492* (Houndmills, Eng.: Macmillan Education, 1987), 147.

31 161,000 tons of gold: Brook Larmer, "The Real Price of Gold," *National Geographic*, June 2009, 49.

32 "When I went out to meet him": Gomez, *African Dominion*, 116.

32 "Insofar as the Mamluk ruler": Ibid., 117.

33 "these people became amazed at the ampleness": Ibid., 119.

33 an inexhaustible source of Black bondsmen: Cooper, *Africa in the World*, 45.

33 approximately 3 million Black slaves: Pier Larson, "African Slave Trades in Global Perspective," *The Oxford Handbook of Modern African History*, October 1, 2013, https://doi.org/10.1093/oxfordhb/9780199572472.013.0003.

33 sent to the Americas: Paul E. Lovejoy, *Transformations in Slavery: A History of Slavery in Africa* (Cambridge: Cambridge University Press, 1983), 70.

34 Mali as an integral part of the Islamic world: Gomez, *African Dominion*, 122.

35 the great Inca Empire: John Hemming, *The Conquest of the Incas* (London: Macmillan, 1970), 55.

3. RETHINKING EXPLORATION

38 Zheng He's biggest vessels: Howard W. French, *Everything Under the Heavens: How the Past Helps Shape China's Push for Global Power* (New York: Alfred A. Knopf, 2017), 96.

38 DNA analysis has recently revealed: Alexander G. Ioannidis et al., "Native American Gene Flow into Polynesia Predating Easter Island Settlement," *Nature* 583, no. 7817 (July 2020): 572–77.

38 native populations in the Amazon: Helen Thompson, "A DNA Search for the First Americans Links Amazon Groups to Indigenous Australians," *Smithsonian Magazine*, https://www.smithsonianmag.com/science-nature/dna-search-first-americans-links-amazon-indigenous-australians-180955976/, accessed December 20, 2020; Vitorino Magalhães Godhinho, *A expansão quatrocentista* (Lisbon: Dom Quixote, 2008).

40 the Portuguese king of the time, João II: Bailey W. Diffie and George D. Winius, *Foundations of the Portuguese Empire, 1415–1580*, vol. 1 of *Europe and the World in the Age of Expansion* (Minneapolis: University of Minnesota Press, 1977), 162.

40 "inching down the coast of Africa": Peter Gordon and Juan José Morales, *The Silver Way: China, Spanish America and the Birth of Globalization* (Melbourne: Penguin Books, 2017), 24. See also Diffie and Winius, *Foundations of the Portuguese Empire*, ch. 2, "The Search for a Way Around Africa to the East" (to their credit, these authors do mention African gold, but place little emphasis on it).

40 "In just over thirty years": William D. Phillips Jr. and Carla Rahn Phillips, *The Worlds of Christopher Columbus* (Cambridge: Cambridge University Press, 1992), 1.

41 "Europeans of the fifteenth century": Ibid., 36.

41 "a fit of absence of mind": John Robert Seeley, *The Expansion of England: Two Courses of Lectures* (Boston: Roberts Brothers, 1883).

42   the historical determinism of a Western ascendancy: Michael A. Gomez, *Reversing Sail: A History of the African Diaspora*, 2nd ed. (Cambridge: Cambridge University Press, 2020), 47.

43   a gold-rich empire called Mali: Felipe Fernández-Armesto, *Before Columbus: Exploration and Colonisation from the Mediterranean to the Atlantic, 1229–1492* (Houndmills, Eng.: Macmillan Education, 1987), 147.

43   a surviving 1339 map: Alisa LaGamma, ed., *Sahel: Art and Empires on the Shores of the Sahara* (New York: Metropolitan Museum of Art, 2020), 149.

43   "the road to the land of the Negroes": Paolo F. De Moraes Farias, "Islam in the West African Sahel," in ibid., 127.

44   Catalan Atlas of 1375: Tony Campbell, review of *Mapamundi: The Catalan Atlas of the Year 1375*, by Georges Grosjean, *Imago Mundi* 33 (1981): 115–16.

44   Asia appears as an entire continent: Clara Estow, "Mapping Central Europe: The Catalan Atlas and the European Imagination," *Mediterranean Studies* 13 (2004): 6.

45   New maps like these: Felipe Fernández-Armesto, "The Origins of the European Atlantic," *Itinerario* 24, no. 1 (Mar. 2000): 121.

45   "sovereign of the land": Fernández-Armesto, *Before Columbus*, 147.

45   the map of Ali al-Masudi: Diffie and Winius, *Foundations of the Portuguese Empire*, 9.

46   "Through this place pass the merchants": Marq de Villiers and Sheila Hirtle, *Timbuktu: The Sahara's Fabled City of Gold* (New York: Walker, 2007), 77. See also cresqueproject.net/Catalan-atlas-legends/panel-iii.

4. ENTER THE AVIZ

48   Abraham Cresques: Clara Estow, "Mapping Central Europe: The Catalan Atlas and the European Imagination," *Mediterranean Studies* 13 (2004): 2.

49   "From 1247, Jaime I": Felipe Fernández-Armesto, *Before Columbus: Exploration and Colonisation from the Mediterranean to the Atlantic, 1229–1492* (Houndmills, Eng.: Macmillan Education, 1987), 135–36.

49   dwell in Islamic North Africa: Ibid., 136.

49   Jews, possibly accompanied by Genoese: A. H. de Oliveira Marques and J. Serrão, *A Nova história de expansão portuguesa* (Lisbon: Editorial Estampa, 1998), 2:33–34.

49   "Antonio Malfante, a Genoese": M. D. D. Newitt, *A History of Portuguese Overseas Expansion, 1400–1668* (London: Routledge, 2005), 5.

49   clothing woven by their coreligionists: Toby Green, *The Rise of the Trans-Atlantic Slave Trade in Western Africa, 1300–1589* (New York: Cambridge University Press, 2012), 42. See also Labelle Prussin, "Judaic Threads in West African Tapestry: No More Forever?," *The Art Bulletin* 88, no. 2 (2006): 333, 344–45.

49   "paper economy of faith": Ghislaine Lydon, *On Trans-Saharan Trails: Islamic Law, Trade Networks, and Cross-Cultural Exchange in Nineteenth-Century Western Africa* (Cambridge: Cambridge University Press, 2009), 3.

51   chronic shortage of specie: Fernand Braudel, "Monnaies et civilisations: De
      l'or du Soudan à l'argent d'Amérique," *Annales* 1, no. 1 (1946): 9–22; John Day,
      "The Great Bullion Famine of the Fifteenth Century," *Past & Present* 79, no. 1
      (May 1978): 3–54.

51   "Since the thirteenth century, the Maghreb": Braudel, "Monnaies et civilisa-
      tions," 12 (author's translation).

51   vast quantities of African gold: Day, "The Great Bullion Famine," 37.

51   "The problem of money predominates": Aeneas Syvius Piccolomini (Pope
      Pius II) to the Council at Siena, 1436, in *Reject Aeneas, Accept Pius: Selected
      Letters of Aeneas Sylvius Piccolomin*, ed. and trans. Thomas M. Izbicki, Ger-
      ald Christianson, and Philip Krey (Washington, D.C.: Catholic University of
      America Press, 2006), 95.

52   the new crown desperately needed to find: Newitt, *A History of Portuguese
      Overseas Expansion*, 10.

53   "shut in by the sea": Académie des Inscriptions et Belles-Lettres, ed., *Recueil
      des historiens des Croisades: Historiens occidentaux* (Paris: Imprimerie
      Royale, 1844), 728.

53   Prince Henry, then all of twenty-one: P. E. Russell, *Prince Henry "the Navi-
      gator"* (New Haven: Yale University Press, 2000), 51.

5. ISLANDS IN THE OFFING

56   "easy to conquer . . . and at small cost": Bailey W. Diffie and George D. Win-
      ius, *Foundations of the Portuguese Empire, 1415–1580* (Minneapolis: Univer-
      sity of Minnesota Press, 1977), 43.

56   "We saw naked people": Jill Lepore, *These Truths: A History of the United
      States* (New York: W. W. Norton, 2018), 4.

56   "with 50 men all of them could be held": Ibid., 18.

57   "with enough force to knock": John K. Thornton, *A Cultural History of
      the Atlantic World, 1250–1820* (Cambridge: Cambridge University Press,
      2012), 26.

57   "They leap from rock to rock": G. R. Crone et al., *The Voyages of Cadamosto
      and Other Documents on Western Africa in the Second Half of the Fifteenth
      Century*, 2nd ser., no. 80 (London: Hakluyt Society, 1937), 14.

57   the islanders prevailed using wooden swords: John Mercer, *The Canary
      Islands: Their Prehistory, Conquest, and Survival* (London: Collins, 1980),
      186.

60   "They have no faith": Crone, *The Voyages of Cadamosto*, 88.

61   "find Christian princes, in whom the good nature": Gomes Eanes de Zur-
      ara, *Chronica do descobrimento e conquisita da Guiné* (Paris: J.P. Aillaud,
      1841), 47 (author's translation).

61   "The 'India' that Henrican documents have in mind": P. E. Russell, *Prince
      Henry "the Navigator"* (New Haven: Yale University Press, 2000), 121.

63   "the plantation production of sugar": Wendy Warren, *New England Bound:
      Slavery and Colonization in Early America* (New York: Liveright, 2016), 52.

63   those rapidly depopulating islands: John Reader, *Africa: A Biography of the Continent* (New York: Alfred A. Knopf, 1998), 353.

63   the Imraugen, a tribe of fishermen: Russell, *Prince Henry "the Navigator,"* 97.

63   Yet another expedition, in 1436: Duarte Pacheco Pereira and Raphael Eduardo de Azevedo Basto, *Esmeraldo de Situ Orbis* (Lisbon: Imprensa Nacional, 1892), bk. 1, ch. 23, p. 42.

63   "for in the first years, seeing the big fleets": Eanes de Zurara, *Chronica do descobrimento e conquisita da Guiné*, 103–4 (author's translation).

65   Henry would go down as another: Ibid., 106.

65   Ferdinand and Isabella, Spain's monarchs: Felipe Fernández-Armesto, *Ferdinand and Isabella* (New York: Taplinger, 1975).

6. THE AFRICAN MAIN

66   the bishop of Algarve: Hugh Thomas, *The Slave Trade: The Story of the Atlantic Slave Trade, 1440–1870* (New York: Simon & Schuster, 1997), 57.

67   this woman of unknown name: Herman L. Bennett, *African Kings and Black Slaves: Sovereignty and Dispossession in the Early Modern Atlantic* (Philadelphia: University of Pennsylvania Press, 2019) 62.

67   the governor of the Portuguese town of Tomar: Duarte Pacheco Pereira, *Esmeraldo de Situ Orbis*, edited by George H. T. Kimble (London: Hakluyt Society, 1927), 74–75.

68   "upon a powerful horse": Gomes Eanes de Zurara, *Chronica do descobrimento e conquisita da Guiné* (Paris: J.P. Aillaud, 1841), 135 (author's translation).

68   "I pray to you that my tears": Ibid., 135 (author's translation).

68   "Who could finish that apportionment without great struggle": Ibid. (author's translation).

69   "For among them there were some": Ibid., 91 (author's translation).

69   "the salvation of those souls": Ibid., 133 (author's translation).

70   "savage to slave": Bennett, *African Kings and Black Slaves*, 37.

71   mutual recognition of sovereignty: Ibid., 85.

71   the capitalization of Iberian economies: Newitt, *A History of Portuguese Overseas Expansion*, 30.

71   referred to as the "New World": P. E. Russell, *Prince Henry "the Navigator"* (New Haven: Yale University Press, 2000), 12.

72   swift dugout canoes: Robert Smith, "The Canoe in West African History," *The Journal of African History* 11, no. 4 (1970): 515–33.

72   "their dangerous way of fighting": Eanes de Zurara, *Chronica do descobrimento e conquisita da Guiné*, 416 (author's translation).

72   Africans wielding poisonous arrows: Ibid., 402.

73   Portugal's fortune seekers: Toby Green, *The Rise of the Trans-Atlantic Slave Trade in Western Africa, 1300–1589* (New York: Cambridge University Press, 2012), 74.

74   "all the eloquence of a Greek prince": David Northrup, *Africa's Discovery of Europe, 1450–1850*, 3rd ed. (Oxford: Oxford University Press, 2014), 27.

74 the Jolof went on to become: Green, *Rise of the Trans-Atlantic Slave Trade*, 84.

76 cottons (still a rarity in Europe) from India: Prasannan Parthasarathi, "Why Europe Grew Rich and Asia Did Not: Global Economic Divergence, 1600–1850," EBook Comprehensive Academic Collection—North America, 2011, 23–26; https://doi.org/10.1017/CBO9780511993398.

76 Europeans could scarcely trade for slaves: Colleen E. Kriger, *Cloth in West African History* (Lanham, Md.: AltaMira Press, 2006), 142; David Richardson, "West African Consumption Patterns and Their Influence on the Eighteenth Century English Slave Trade," in *The Uncommon Market: Essays in the Economic History of the Atlantic Slave Trade*, ed. Henry A. Gemery, Jan S. Hogendorn, and Mathematical Social Science Board (New York: Academic Press, 1979), 319.

76 Afonso's licensing terms: Newitt, *A History of Portuguese Overseas Expansion*, 35.

77 "some tall red cliffs": Duarte Pacheco Pereira and Raphael Eduardo de Azevedo Basto, *Esmeraldo de Situ Orbis* (Lisbon: Imprensa Nacional, 1892), bk. 2, ch. 3, p. 64 (author's translation).

77 reached a village called Shama: Ibid., bk. 2, ch. 4, p. 68.

78 the Gold Coast: K. Y. Daaku, *Trade and Politics on the Gold Coast, 1600–1720: A Study of the African Reaction to European Trade* (London: Clarendon Press, 1970), xviii.

79 a wreck hundreds of miles to the west: Pereira and Basto, *Esmeraldo de Situ Orbis*, bk. 2, ch. 3, p. 64.

80 Isabella, who had not been raised: Felipe Fernández-Armesto, *Ferdinand and Isabella* (New York: Taplinger, 1975).

80 "gather an invasion army": John Vogt, *Portuguese Rule on the Gold Coast, 1469–1682* (Athens: University of Georgia Press, 1979), 10.

81 "under penalty of death and loss of all your goods": Bailey W. Diffie and George D. Winius, *Foundations of the Portuguese Empire, 1415–1580* (Minneapolis: University of Minnesota Press, 1977), 149.

81 The haul in gold alone: John W. Blake, *Europeans in West Africa, 1450–1560* (London: Hakluyt Society, 1942), 1:236.

81 "all the islands already discovered": Diffie and Winius, *Foundations of the Portuguese Empire*, 152.

82 Portugal was obtaining 8000 ounces: Ivor Wilks, "Wangara, Akan and Portuguese in the Fifteenth and Sixteenth Centuries. II. The Struggle for Trade," *The Journal of African History* 23, no. 4 (Oct. 1982): 463–72.

82 the many references to the search for gold: Felipe Fernández-Armesto, *Before Columbus: Exploration and Colonisation from the Mediterranean to the Atlantic, 1229–1492* (Houndmills, Eng.: Macmillan Education, 1987), 205.

82 in Columbus's journals: *Journals and Other Documents on the Life and Voyages of Christopher Columbus*, ed. and trans. Samuel Eliot Morison (New York: Heritage Press, 1963), 70–72.

82 his project of crossing the Atlantic: Alan Mikhail, *God's Shadow: Sultan Selim, His Ottoman Empire, and the Making of the Modern World* (New York: Liveright, 2020), 109.

82 "Christopher Columbus landed first": C. L. R. James, *The Black Jacobins: Toussaint L'Ouverture and the San Domingo Revolution*, 2nd ed. (New York: Vintage, 1989), 3.

83 Ships that set sail from the Azores: Fernández-Armesto, *Before Columbus*, 207.

83 It was in the wake of his maritime victory: Ibid., 194.

83 "disremember" some of the traditional accounting: Lisa Lowe, *The Intimacies of Four Continents* (Durham, N.C.: Duke University Press, 2015), 3–4.

7. THE MINE

88 The plot was discovered: A. R. Disney, *A History of Portugal and the Portuguese Empire: From Beginnings to 1807* (Cambridge: Cambridge University Press, 2009), 135.

89 Dias, by contrast, was granted: Bailey W. Diffie and George D. Winius, *Foundations of the Portuguese Empire, 1415–1580* (Minneapolis: University of Minnesota Press, 1977), 161.

89 "I was in the castle": William D. Phillips Jr. and Carla Rahn Phillips, *The Worlds of Christopher Columbus* (Cambridge: Cambridge University Press, 1992), 106.

90 cannons and plentiful ammunition: John Vogt, *Portuguese Rule on the Gold Coast, 1469–1682* (Athens: University of Georgia Press, 1979), 21.

90 an unauthorized Portuguese trader: Ibid., 22.

91 thirty cannons they had arrived with: Ibid., 31.

91 "a jerkin of brocade": Ibid., 23.

92 the inhabitants were anything but surprised: Ivor Wilks, "Wangara, Akan and Portuguese in the Fifteenth and Sixteenth Centuries. II. The Struggle for Trade," *The Journal of African History* 23, no. 4 (Oct. 1982): 463–72.

93 "more deafening than pleasing to the ear": Vogt, *Portuguese Rule on the Gold Coast*, 23.

93 "In general, they were all armed": João de Barros, António Baião, and Luís F. Lindley Cintra, *Asia de João de Barros: Dos feitos que os Portugueses fizeram no descobrimento e conquista dos mares e terras do oriente* (Lisbon: Imprensa Nacional—Casa da Moeda, 1988), bk. 3, ch. 1, pp. 158–60 (author's translation).

93 "touch his fingers and then snap": Herman L. Bennett, *African Kings and Black Slaves: Sovereignty and Dispossession in the Early Modern Atlantic* (Philadelphia: University of Pennsylvania Press, 2019), 33.

93 a "brother" and ally: Disney, *A History of Portugal and the Portuguese Empire*, 58.

94 "The Christians who have come": Toby Green, *The Rise of the Trans-Atlantic Slave Trade in Western Africa, 1300–1589* (New York: Cambridge University Press, 2012), 113.

94 "Friends who met occasionally": Vogt. *Portuguese Rule on the Gold Coast*, 24.

95 masons built the inner walls: Ibid., 26.

8. ASIA SUSPENDED

96 between 46 and 57 kilograms: John Vogt, *Portuguese Rule on the Gold Coast, 1469–1682* (Athens: University of Georgia Press, 1979), 38.

96 By 1506, with the tentacles: Ibid., 89, 91.

97 about 680 kilograms of gold per year: K. Y. Daaku, *Trade and Politics on the Gold Coast, 1600–1720: A Study of the African Reaction to European Trade* (London: Clarendon Press, 1970), 8.

97 it propelled complex economic integration: Vogt, *Portuguese Rule on the Gold Coast*, 74.

97 swathed in material luxury: A. R. Disney, *A History of Portugal and the Portuguese Empire: From Beginnings to 1807* (Cambridge: Cambridge University Press, 2009), 59.

97 a growing cabotage trade: Vogt, *Portuguese Rule on the Gold Coast*, 9.

98 Senegambia to Timbuktu: M. D. D. Newitt, *A History of Portuguese Overseas Expansion, 1400–1668* (London: Routledge, 2005), 49.

98 Kongo was a vastly larger: Ibid., 52.

98 a minor court figure, Vasco da Gama: Ibid., 54.

99 "And he told the most serene king": P. E. Russell, *Prince Henry "the Navigator"* (New Haven: Yale University Press, 2000), 128.

99 "Then the king, understanding clearly": William D. Phillips Jr. and Carla Rahn Phillips, *The Worlds of Christopher Columbus* (Cambridge: Cambridge University Press, 1992), 181.

100 twice the amount in real returns: Robin Blackburn, *The Making of New World Slavery: From the Baroque to the Modern, 1492–1800* (London: Verso, 1997), 107–8.

100 "an aside in the formation of the West": Herman L. Bennett, *African Kings and Black Slaves: Sovereignty and Dispossession in the Early Modern Atlantic* (Philadelphia: University of Pennsylvania Press, 2019), 40.

100 drill in deep waters offshore: Felipe Fernández-Armesto, "The Origins of the European Atlantic," *Itinerario* 24, no. 1 (Mar. 2000): 124.

9. WEALTH IN PEOPLE VERSUS WEALTH IN THINGS

102 "at least a minor aspect of economic life": Philp D. Curtin, *The Rise and Fall of the Plantation Complex: Essays in Atlantic History* (Cambridge: Cambridge University Press, 1990), 8.

102 "There is nothing notably peculiar": Orlando Patterson, *Slavery and Social Death: A Comparative Study* (Cambridge, Mass.: Harvard University Press, 1982), vii.

103 The Akan, who controlled the richest sources: J. Bato'ora Ballong-Wen-Mewuda, *São Jorge Da Mina (1482–1637): La vie d'un comptoir portugais en*

Afrique Occidentale (Lisbon: Fondation Calouste Gulkenkian / Paris: Centre Culturel Portugais, 1993), 232.

103 **"have only trifles [bagatelles] for their trade"**: Robin Law, *The Slave Coast of West Africa 1550–1750: The Impact of the Atlantic Slave Trade on an African Society* (Oxford: Clarendon/Oxford University Press, 1991), 135.

103 **sinking mine shafts**: Toby Green, *A Fistful of Shells: West Africa from the Rise of the Slave Trade to the Age of Revolution* (Chicago: University of Chicago Press, 2019), 53.

104 **the primary measures of wealth and power**: On this concept see, for example, Jane I. Guyer, "Wealth in People, Wealth in Things—Introduction," *The Journal of African History* 36, no. 1 (Mar. 1995): 83–90.

105 **In the chronicle he wrote:** J. Bato'ora Ballong-Wen-Mewuda, *São Jorge Da Mina*, 324.

106 **Archaeological surveys**: Fred Pearce, "The African Queen," *New Scientist*, September 11, 1999, https://www.newscientist.com/article/mg16322035-100-the-african-queen/.

106 **a highly centralized government**: Elizabeth M. McClelland, *The Kingdom of Benin in the Sixteenth Century* (London: Oxford University Press, 1971), 46.

106 **The Benin monarchy**: Andrea Felber Seligman, "Ambassadors, Explorers and Allies: A Study of the African-European Relationships, 1400–1600," *Undergraduate Humanities Forum 2006-7: Travel*, April 1, 2006, 18; https://repository.upenn.edu/uhf_2007/13.

106 **"a man of good speech"**: David Northrup, *Africa's Discovery of Europe, 1450–1850*, 3rd ed. (Oxford: Oxford University Press, 2014), 31.

106 **"Great feasts were held"**: Ibid., 32.

107 **the elaborate so-called lost wax technique**: "Sculpture: The Bronzes of Benin," *Time*, Aug. 6, 1965.

107 **between twelve and fifteen** *manilhas*: Robert Garfield, *A History of Sao Tome Island, 1470–1655: The Key to Guinea* (San Francisco: Mellen Research University Press, 1992), 46.

108 **"transformation in subjectivities"**: José Lingna Nafafé, *Colonial Encounters: Issues of Culture, Hybridity and Creolisation; Portuguese Mercantile Settlers in West Africa* (New York: Peter Lang International Academic Publishers, 2007).

108 **adverse prevailing eastward ocean currents**: John L. Vogt, "The Early Sao Tome-Principe Slave Trade with Mina, 1500–1540," *The International Journal of African Historical Studies* 6, no. 3 (1973): 464.

108 **the men who ran Elmina were clamoring**: Ivor Wilks, "Wangara, Akan and Portuguese in the Fifteenth and Sixteenth Centuries. II. The Struggle for Trade," *The Journal of African History* 23, no. 4 (Oct. 1982): 463–72.

108 **15 percent of their profits**: Vogt, "The Early Sao Tome-Principe Slave Trade" 454.

109 **the oba sequestered:** Northrup, *Africa's Discovery of Europe*, 33.
109 **adding people in this way:** Curtin, *The Rise and Fall of the Plantation Complex*, 41.
109 **Deprived of a supply of slave labor:** Saidiya V. Hartman, *Lose Your Mother: A Journey Along the Atlantic Slave Route* (New York: Farrar, Straus and Giroux, 2007), 111.
110 **successive obas may have imagined:** Andrea Felber Seligman, "Ambassadors, Explorers and Allies: A Study of the African-European Relationships, 1400–1600," *Undergraduate Humanities Forum 2006–7: Travel*, April 1, 2006, 19; https://repository.upenn.edu/uhf_2007/13.
110 **Lisbon's attentions were shifting:** David Eltis, *The Rise of African Slavery in the Americas* (Cambridge: Cambridge University Press, 2000), 139.

10. CIRCUITS OLD AND NEW

113 **an estimated 100,000 Jews:** David Brion Davis, "The Slave Trade and the Jews," *New York Review of Books*, Dec. 22, 1994.
113 **Jewish newcomers perished soon after their arrival:** Robert Garfield, *A History of Sao Tome Island, 1470–1655: The Key to Guinea* (San Francisco: Mellen Research University Press, 1992), 30.
114 **an important role in São Tomé's early innovations:** Arlindo Manuel Caldeira, "Learning the Ropes in the Tropics: Slavery and the Plantation System on the Island of São Tomé," *African Economic History* 39 (2011): 48.
115 **In 1504, 900 slaves:** Garfield, *A History of Sao Tome Island*, 28; John L. Vogt, "The Early Sao Tome–Principe Slave Trade with Mina, 1500–1540," *The International Journal of African Historical Studies* 6, no. 3 (1973): 466.
116 **home to far larger plantations:** Philip D. Curtin, *The Rise and Fall of the Plantation Complex: Essays in Atlantic History* (Cambridge: Cambridge University Press, 1990), 12.
116 **the highly regimented nature:** Sidney Wilfred Mintz, *Sweetness and Power: The Place of Sugar in Modern History* (New York: Viking, 1985), 51.
116 **the indispensable killer apparatus of modernity:** Caldeira, "Learning the Ropes in the Tropics," 51.
117 **sharpest ascent that any food crop:** Mintz, *Sweetness and Power*, 142.
117 **four times more Africans:** Philip Misevich, Daniel Domingues, David Eltis, Nafees M. Khan, and Nicholas Radburn, "A Digital Archive of Slave Voyages Details the Largest Forced Migration in History," *Smithsonian*, May 1, 2017, https://www.smithsonianmag.com/history/digital-archive-slave-voyages-details-largest-forced-migration-history-180963093/.

11. UNTO THE END OF THE WORLD

119 **the seminal role the Catholic Church:** Herman L. Bennett, *African Kings and Black Slaves: Sovereignty and Dispossession in the Early Modern Atlan-*

tic (Philadelphia: University of Pennsylvania Press, 2019), 64; Hugh Thomas, *The Slave Trade: The Story of the Atlantic Slave Trade, 1440–1870* (New York: Simon & Schuster, 1997), 57.

120   the verb *descobrir*: Thomas, *The Slave Trade*, 73.

122   300,000 arrobas: Robert Garfield, *A History of Sao Tome Island, 1470–1655: The Key to Guinea* (San Francisco: Mellen Research University Press, 1992), 64.

122   between sixty and eighty mills: Ibid., 72.

122   the small community of whites: Ibid.. 73.

123   Potosí, the Bolivian mine: Marie Arana, *Silver, Sword, and Stone: Three Crucibles in the Latin American Story* (New York: Simon & Schuster, 2019), 99, 104.

124   carving out plantation lands: Philip D. Curtin, *The Image of Africa: British Ideas and Action, 1780–1850* (Madison: University of Wisconsin Press, 1964), 451.

124   the total population of Native Americans: Alexander Koch et al., "Earth System Impacts of the European Arrival and Great Dying in the Americas After 1492," *Quaternary Science Reviews* 207 (Mar. 2019): 13–36.

124   death rates of 10 percent per annum: Curtin, *The Image of Africa*, 71.

124   2.5 million Africans were shipped: Herbert Klein, *The Atlantic Slave Trade*, 2nd ed. (Cambridge: Cambridge University Press, 2010), 67.

125   long lines of resupply: John Thornton, "Early Kongo-Portuguese Relations: A New Interpretation," *History in Africa* 8 (1981): 186; https://doi.org/10.2307/3171515.

125   literacy, especially in the Sahel: Curtin, *The Image of Africa*, 31.

125   literacy rate of enslaved Muslim Africans: Sylviane A. Diouf, *Servants of Allah: African Muslims Enslaved in the Americas* (New York: New York University Press, 1998), 160.

126   "second-best alternative": David Eltis, *The Rise of African Slavery in the Americas* (Cambridge: Cambridge University Press, 2000), 149.

126   "On plantations, escape was easy": Eric Eustace Williams, *Capitalism and Slavery* (Chapel Hill: University of North Carolina Press, 1994), 19.

12. PATHWAYS OF RESISTANCE

129   190 slaves: John L. Vogt, "The Early Sao Tome-Principe Slave Trade with Mina, 1500–1540," *The International Journal of African Historical Studies* 6, no. 3 (1973): 461.

131   became known as *mocambos*: Arlindo Manuel Caldeira, "Learning the Ropes in the Tropics: Slavery and the Plantation System on the Island of São Tomé," *African Economic History* 39 (2011): 61.

133   active rebellions took place: Michael Craton, *Testing the Chains: Resistance to Slavery in the British West Indies* (Ithaca, N.Y.: Cornell University Press, 1982), 24.

133   Sierra Leone River: Lorenzo J. Greene, "Mutiny on the Slave Ships," in

Freedom's Odyssey: African American History Essays from Phylon, ed. Alexa Menson Henderson and Janice Sumler-Edmond (Atlanta: Clark Atlanta University Press, 1999), 350.

134 sugar's migratory spread: Craton, *Testing the Chains*, 33.

134 places like Palmares: Robert Nelson Anderson, "The Quilombo of Palmares: A New Overview of a Maroon State in Seventeenth-Century Brazil," *Journal of Latin American Studies* 28, no. 3 (1996): 545–66.

134 nowhere did Washington even mention: Philip D. Morgan, "'To Get Quit of Negroes': George Washington and Slavery," *Journal of American Studies* 39, no. 3 (2005): 408.

134 rotting heads of rebellious slaves: Matthew Parker, *The Sugar Barons: Family, Corruption, Empire and War* (London: Hutchinson, 2011), 267.

134 "It is the innocence": James Baldwin, "The Fire Next Time," in *Collected Essays* (New York: Library of America, 1998), 292.

135 crept into French as well: Sylviane A. Diouf, "Slavery's Exiles: The Story of the American Maroons," EBook Comprehensive Academic Collection—North America, 2014, 81.

135 "coined to describe domesticated cattle": Joseph Kelly, "The Masterless People: Pirates, Maroons, and the Struggle to Live Free," *Longreads* (blog), October 30, 2018, https://longreads.com/2018/10/30/the-masterless-people -pirates-maroons-and-the-struggle-to-live-free/.

135 brought to Hispaniola in 1501: Richard Price, *Maroon Societies: Rebel Slave Communities in the Americas*, 3rd ed. (Baltimore: Johns Hopkins University Press, 1996), 1.

135 first to settle a part of what: Kelly, "The Masterless People."

136 a team spearheaded: The 1619 Project, *The New York Times*, August 14, 2019, https://www.nytimes.com/interactive/2019/08/14/magazine/1619-america -slavery.html.

136 *Homo* merited subdivision: Philip D. Curtin, *The Image of Africa: British Ideas and Action, 1780–1850* (Madison: University of Wisconsin Press, 1964), 44.

136 "Let an intelligent and educated man": C. L. R. James, *The Black Jacobins: Toussaint L'Ouverture and the San Domingo Revolution*, 2nd ed. (New York: Vintage, 1989), 112.

137 "I once passed a colored woman": Frederick Douglass, *The American Anti-Slavery Almanac*, April 28, 1848, 45.

137 "Though most slaves were whipped": Daniel J. Boorstin, Brooks Mather Kelley, and Ruth F. Boorstin, *A History of the United States* (Needham, Mass.: Prentice Hall, 1989), 229.

13. BECOMING CREOLE

138 fifteen to twenty thousand residents: Ira Berlin, *Generations of Captivity: A History of African-American Slaves* (Cambridge, Mass.: Harvard University Press, 2004), 25.

138 "at African sufferance": Ira Berlin, "From Creole to African: Atlantic Creoles and the Origins of African-American Society in Mainland North America," *The William and Mary Quarterly* 53, no. 2 (1996): 259.

139 These Luso-Africans provide perhaps: Toby Green, *A Fistful of Shells: West Africa from the Rise of the Slave Trade to the Age of Revolution* (Chicago: University of Chicago Press, 2019), 120. See also José da Silva Horta, "Evidence for a Luso-African Identity in 'Portuguese' Accounts on 'Guinea of Cape Verde' (Sixteenth–Seventeenth Centuries)," *History in Africa* 27 (2000): 99–130; https://doi.org/10.2307/3172109.

139 The experience of French trader-explorers: In their 2007 book, the historians Linda Heywood and John Thornton have made a persuasive case that western Central Africans, speakers of the Kikongo and Kimbundu languages, were overwhelmingly the most important source group of these early Atlantic Creoles. See Linda M. Heywood and John K. Thornton, *Central Africans, Atlantic Creoles, and the Foundation of the Americas, 1585–1660* (New York: Cambridge University Press, 2007), 238.

139 at the behest of the sovereigns: Barry Hatton, *Queen of the Sea: A History of Lisbon* (London: C. Hurst, 2018), 98.

140 generations of culturally polyvalent operators: Berlin, *Generations of Captivity*, 274.

141 "charter generation": Ibid., 30.

141 first settlers of the Chesapeake region: Ibid., 268.

141 roughly 30 percent of the population in 1640: Wendy Warren, *New England Bound: Slavery and Colonization in Early America* (New York: Liveright, 2016), 177.

141 "There were people who came": K. Y. Daaku, *Trade and Politics on the Gold Coast, 1600–1720: A Study of the African Reaction to European Trade* (London: Clarendon Press, 1970), 96.

142 "a new group of people": Ibid.

142 the importance of west Central Africa: Mariana Candido, *An African Slaving Port and the Atlantic World: Benguela and its Hinterland* (Cambridge: Cambridge University Press, 2015), 1–10; Christina Frances Mobley, "The Kongolese Atlantic: Central African Slavery and Culture from Mayombe to Haiti," (Ph.D. diss., Duke University, 2015), v.

142 "Black life in mainland North America": Berlin, "From Creole to African," 254.

143 "Blacks were steady": "Toni Morrison: The Pieces I Am," *American Masters*, PBS, June 23, 2020, https://www.pbs.org/wnet/americanmasters/toni-morrison-the-pieces-i-am-about/12366/.

14. FOR A FEW ACRES OF SNOW

148 something he called the "Western Design": Michael Guasco, *Slaves and Englishmen: Human Bondage in the Early Modern Atlantic World* (Philadelphia: University of Pennsylvania Press, 2014), 176.

149   As such, it was a rough copy: Carla Gardina Pestana, *The English Conquest of Jamaica: Oliver Cromwell's Bid for Empire* (Cambridge: Belknap Press, 2017), 8.

149   a Dutch blueprint for conquest: John K. Thornton, "The Kingdom of Kongo and the Thirty Years' War," *Journal of World History* 27, no. 2 (2016): 189.

149   by 1660 England emerged: David Eltis, *The Rise of African Slavery in the Americas* (Cambridge: Cambridge University Press, 2000), 12.

149   rising value of its exports: David Richardson, "West African Consumption Patterns and Their Influence on the Eighteenth Century English Slave Trade," in *The Uncommon Market: Essays in the Economic History of the Atlantic Slave Trade*, ed. Henry A. Gemery, Jan S. Hogendorn, and Mathematical Social Science Board (New York: Academic Press, 1979), 305.

150   holding on to tiny Guadeloupe: Matthew Mulcahy, *Hubs of Empire: The Southeastern Lowcountry and British Caribbean* (Baltimore: Johns Hopkins University Press, 2014), 202.

151   shipping and trade: Daniel A. Baugh, *The Global Seven Years War, 1754–1763: Britain and France in a Great Power Contest* (Harlow, Eng.: Longman, 2011), 3.

151   the performance of Saint Domingue: Eltis, *Rise of African Slavery*, 266.

151   "if the British in North America": Baugh, *The Global Seven Years War*, 575.

152   British healthy enough for combat: Trevor G. Burnard and John Garrigus, *The Plantation Machine: Atlantic Capitalism in French Saint-Domingue and British Jamaica* (Philadelphia: University of Pennsylvania Press, 2016), 88.

152   a takeover of Martinique: Michel-Rolph Trouillot, *Silencing the Past: Power and the Production of History* (Boston: Beacon Press, 1995), 17.

152   "in 1761 it led the British Empire": Burnard and Garrigus, *Plantation Machine*, 89. See also Laurent Dubois and Richard Lee Turits, *Freedom Roots: Histories from the Caribbean* (Chapel Hill: University of North Carolina Press, 2019), 73.

153   15 percent of France's overall economic growth: Burnard and Garrigus, *Plantation Machine*, 21–22.

154   "place the Caribbean at the center": Selwyn H. H. Carrington, "Capitalism and Slavery and Caribbean Historiography: An Evaluation," *The Journal of African American History* 88, no. 3 (2003): 304.

154   "It is no exaggeration": Zadie Smith, "What Do We Want History to Do to Us?," *New York Review of Books*, Feb. 27, 2020.

154   "the development of the Caribbean colonies ": Carrington, "Capitalism and Slavery," 304.

154   "Dozens of British political and economic historians": Scott Reynolds Nelson, "Who Put Their Capitalism in My Slavery?," *Journal of the Civil War Era* 5, no. 2 (2015): 290.

154   the British antislavery movement: David Brion Davis, *Inhuman Bondage:*

The Rise and Fall of Slavery in the New World (New York: Oxford University Press, 2006), 248.

155   "The rise of Liverpool": Ibid.

156   "The whole world now became a British colony": Eric Eustace Williams, *Capitalism and Slavery* (Chapel Hill: University of North Carolina Press, 1994), 142.

156   Reformist Islam movements then sweeping West Africa: Bronwen Everill, *Not Made by Slaves: Ethical Capitalism in the Age of Abolition* (Cambridge, Mass.: Harvard University Press, 2020), 45–46.

156   The peak years of the transatlantic: Eltis, *Rise of African Slavery*, 12.

157   "part of a universal battle": Michael Taylor, *The Interest: How the British Establishment Resisted the Abolition of Slavery* (London: Bodley Head, 2020), 18.

157   "Support for slavery": Christopher Leslie Brown, *Moral Capital: Foundations of British Abolitionism* (Chapel Hill: University of North Carolina Press, 2006), 27.

158   "as a by-product of preparations for war": Charles Tilly, *Coercion, Capital, and European States, AD 990–1992* (Cambridge, Mass.: Blackwell, 1993), 75.

158   "as did the claims": Ibid., 83.

158   "Empire was making the British state": Frederick Cooper, *Africa in the World: Capitalism, Empire, Nation-State* (Cambridge, Mass.: Harvard University Press, 2014), 12.

15. FIGHTING FOR AFRICANS

161   What caused the Portuguese: John Vogt, *Portuguese Rule on the Gold Coast, 1469–1682* (Athens: University of Georgia Press, 1979), 191.

161   five tons of gold per year: Ibid., 185.

162   "The World Is Not Enough": Hugh Thomas, *World Without End: The Global Empire of Philip II* (London: Allen Lane, 2014), 275.

162   Philip banned Dutch shipping: Vogt. *Portuguese Rule on the Gold Coast*, 145.

162   rich supplies of salt at Punta de Araya: Philip D. Curtin, *The Rise and Fall of the Plantation Complex: Essays in Atlantic History* (Cambridge: Cambridge University Press, 1990), 90.

162   "West India can become the Netherlands' great source": Jan de Vries, "The Atlantic Economy During the Seventeenth and Eighteenth Centuries," in *The Atlantic Economy During the Seventeenth and Eighteenth Centuries: Organization, Operation, Practice, and Personnel*, ed. Peter A. Coclanis (Columbia: University of South Carolina Press, 2005), 1; https://doi.org/10.2307/j.ctv1169bdh.

163   "divert the king of Spain's arms": John K. Thornton, "The Kingdom of Kongo and the Thirty Years' War," *Journal of World History* 27, no. 2 (2016): 191.

164   seized a large Spanish silver fleet: De Vries, "The Atlantic Economy," 4.

164   "Its domestic supply of men": Tilly, *Coercion, Capital, and European States*, 92.

165   Luanda had been supplying: Joseph Calder Miller, *Way of Death: Merchant*

Capitalism and the Angolan Slave Trade, 1730–1830 (Madison: University of Wisconsin Press, 1988), 232. In the 1780s, this Luanda traffic would peak at roughly 40,000 slaves per year.

165 **"Without Angola no slaves":** Natalie Arsenault and Christopher Rose, "Africa Enslaved: A Curriculum Unit on Comparative Slave Systems for Grades 9–12," https://liberalarts.utexas.edu/hemispheres/_files/pdf/slavery/Slavery_in_Brazil.pdf.

165 **"One can say we found nothing of profit":** Hugh Cagle, *Assembling the Tropics: Science and Medicine in Portugal's Empire, 1450–1700* (Cambridge: Cambridge University Press, 2018), 171.

165 **"scarce, ignoble, and bad":** Ibid.

165 **the greatest spice of all:** Sidney Wilfred Mintz, *Sweetness and Power: The Place of Sugar in Modern History* (New York: Viking, 1985), 44.

166 **Portuguese absolutism depended for its lifeblood:** Robin Blackburn, *The Making of New World Slavery: From the Baroque to the Modern, 1492–1800* (London: Verso, 1997), 163.

167 **Brazil's output of the commodity:** Curtin, *Rise and Fall of the Plantation Complex*, 26.

167 **the predominant source of sugar:** Mintz, *Sweetness and Power*, 38.

16. ENDLESS DEATH IN LANDS WITH NO END

168 **"The planters owned the land":** Philip D. Curtin, *The Rise and Fall of the Plantation Complex: Essays in Atlantic History* (Cambridge: Cambridge University Press, 1990), 53–54.

170 **a soil found in parts of the Brazilian northeast:** Lilia Moritz Schwarcz and Heloisa Maria Murgel Starling, *Brazil: A Biography* (London: Allen Lane, 2018), 43.

171 **"The population that was in these parts":** Stuart B. Schwartz, *Sugar Plantations in the Formation of Brazilian Society: Bahia, 1550–1835* (Cambridge: Cambridge University Press, 1985), 44.

171 **Even the common cold:** Nathan Nunn and Nancy Qian, "The Columbian Exchange: A History of Disease, Food, and Ideas," *Journal of Economic Perspectives* 24, no. 2 (June 2010): 165.

172 **"Stricter, more thorough Catholic instruction":** Hugh Cagle, *Assembling the Tropics: Science and Medicine in Portugal's Empire, 1450–1700* (Cambridge: Cambridge University Press, 2018), 189.

172 **"gold scarce but negroes plenty":** K. Y. Daaku, *Trade and Politics on the Gold Coast, 1600–1720: A Study of the African Reaction to European Trade* (London: Clarendon Press, 1970), 30.

173 **"Felling a single four-foot tree":** Charles C. Mann, *1491: New Revelations of the Americas Before Columbus* (New York: Alfred A. Knopf, 2005), 339.

174 **incorporated runaway Blacks:** Schwarcz and Murgel Starling, *Brazil*, 41.

174 **"weapon of the weak":** James C. Scott, *Weapons of the Weak: Everyday Forms of Peasant Resistance* (New Haven: Yale University Press, 1985).

174   Without its hold on a New World: Felipe Fernández-Armesto, *Pathfinders: A Global History of Exploration* (New York: W. W. Norton, 2006), 142, 157.

175   the largest mortality event: Alexander Koch et al., "Earth System Impacts of the European Arrival and Great Dying in the Americas After 1492," *Quaternary Science Reviews* 207 (Mar. 2019): 13–36.

175   "material deprivation and starvation": Jeffrey Ostler, *Surviving Genocide: Native Nations and the United States from the American Revolution to Bleeding Kansas* (New Haven: Yale University Press, 2019), 5.

175   plummeted to a mere 730,000: Mann, *1491*, 146.

17. THE PERPETUAL OVEN

177   manservants and as skilled workers: Alberto Vieira, "Sugar Islands: The Sugar Economy of Madeira and the Canaries, 1450–1650," in *Tropical Babylons: Sugar and the Making of the Atlantic World, 1450–1680*, ed. Stuart B. Schwartz (Chapel Hill: University of North Carolina Press, 2004), 68.

178   "Only in the mid-nineteenth century": Caitlin Rosenthal, *Accounting for Slavery: Masters and Management* (Cambridge, Mass.: Harvard University Press, 2018), 14.

178   lower slave mortality rates: Philip D. Curtin, *The Rise and Fall of the Plantation Complex: Essays in Atlantic History* (Cambridge: Cambridge University Press, 1990), 53.

179   700,000 arrobas: Robin Blackburn, *The Making of New World Slavery: From the Baroque to the Modern, 1492–1800* (London: Verso, 1997), 172.

180   "The most excellent fruit": Stuart B. Schwartz, "A Commonwealth Within Itself: The Early Brazilian Sugar Industry, 1550–1670," in *Tropical Babylons*, ed. Schwartz, 161.

180   Portuguese income from Brazil: Ibid.

180   "Whoever sees those tremendous ovens": Sermon XIV from 1633, "Impression of Slave Labor on Brazilian Sugar Plantations," http://www.dominiopublico. gov.br/pesquisa/DetalheObraForm.do?select_action=&co_obra=16412.

181   Stiff European demand for these goods: Vitorino Magalhães Godinho, *Os descobrimentos e a economia mundial* (Lisbon: Editôra Arcádia, 1963), 1:432–65.

181   silver in Ming markets: Peter Gordon and Juan José Morales, *The Silver Way: China, Spanish America and the Birth of Globalization* (Melbourne: Penguin Books, 2017), 54.

181   "the highest stage of feudalism": Robin Blackburn, *The Making of New World Slavery: From the Baroque to the Modern, 1492–1800* (London: Verso, 1997), 129.

182   "easier to keep track": Ibid.

182   "Unlike the Dutch, the English, and the Venetians": Charles Tilly, *Coercion, Capital, and European States, AD 990–1992* (Cambridge, Mass.: Blackwell, 1993), 92.

182   the Council of the Indies: Blackburn, *The Making of New World Slavery*, 131.

183 "almost all of our gold": Adam Smith, *The Wealth of Nations* (New York: Collier, 1902), pt. 2, pp. 283–86.

183 "It should be emphasized": Stuart B. Schwartz, *Sugar Plantations in the Formation of Brazilian Society: Bahia, 1550–1835* (Cambridge: Cambridge University Press, 1985), 241.

184 key ports in the spice trade: Hugh Cagle, *Assembling the Tropics: Science and Medicine in Portugal's Empire, 1450–1700* (Cambridge: Cambridge University Press, 2018), 258.

18. THE COCKPIT OF EUROPE

185 And for the English: Matthew Mulcahy, *Hubs of Empire: The Southeastern Lowcountry and British Caribbean* (Baltimore: Johns Hopkins University Press, 2014), 3.

186 "the cockpit of Europe": Eric Eustace Williams, *From Columbus to Castro: The History of the Caribbean, 1492–1969* (New York: Harper & Row, 1971), 71.

187 "one of the most influential": Russell R. Menard, *Sweet Negotiations: Sugar, Slavery, and Plantation Agriculture in Early Barbados* (Charlottesville: University of Virginia Press, 2006), 111.

187 "unknown in other parts of colonial America": Mulcahy, *Hubs of Empire*, 57.

187 its "cultural hearth": Menard, *Sweet Negotiations*, 112.

188 high-concept plans for an integrated empire: Wim Klooster, *The Dutch Moment: War, Trade, and Settlement in the Seventeenth-Century Atlantic World* (Ithaca, N.Y.: Cornell University Press, 2016), 3.

188 the Dutch East India Company: Jan de Vries, "The Atlantic Economy During the Seventeenth and Eighteenth Centuries," in *The Atlantic Economy During the Seventeenth and Eighteenth Centuries: Organization, Operation, Practice, and Personnel*, ed. Peter A. Coclanis (Columbia: University of South Carolina Press, 2005), 2; https://doi.org/10.2307/j.ctv1169bdh.

188 "The 'Atlantic Reality' never came near": Ibid., 1.

188 31,533 Africans: Ibid., 4.

189 "[M]en are so intent": Mulcahy, *Hubs of Empire*, 51.

189 "[B]y the 1680s, more than half": Wendy Warren, *New England Bound: Slavery and Colonization in Early America* (New York: Liveright, 2016), 11.

190 "The labors of the colonists": Adam Hochschild, *Bury the Chains: Prophets and Rebels in the Fight to Free an Empire's Slaves* (Boston: Houghton Mifflin, 2005), 54.

190 "It is by means of": Trevor G. Burnard and John Garrigus, *The Plantation Machine: Atlantic Capitalism in French Saint-Domingue and British Jamaica* (Philadelphia: University of Pennsylvania Press, 2016), 95.

191 Henry Winthrop: Mulcahy, *Hubs of Empire*, 35.

191 armed with £300 and a dream: Menard, *Sweet Negotiations*, 26.

191 kingpins of the sugar industry: Matthew Parker, *The Sugar Barons: Family, Corruption, Empire and War* (London: Hutchinson, 2011), 15.

191   the *William and John* encountered a Portuguese vessel: For the best account of this, see Stephanie E. Smallwood, *Saltwater Slavery: A Middle Passage from Africa to American Diaspora* (Cambridge, Mass.: Harvard University Press, 2007).

192   the words of Richard Ligon: Menard, *Sweet Negotiations*, 17.

192   slaves brought from Madeira: Stuart B. Schwartz, "A Commonwealth Within Itself: The Early Brazilian Sugar Industry, 1550–1670," in *Tropical Babylons: Sugar and the Making of the Atlantic World, 1450–1680*, ed. Stuart B. Schwartz (Chapel Hill: University of North Carolina Press, 2004), 159.

194   "an incorporated band of robbers": Christopher Leslie Brown, *Moral Capital: Foundations of British Abolitionism* (Chapel Hill: University of North Carolina Press, 2006), 140.

195   "conquered the Cape Verde Islands": Hugh Thomas, *The Slave Trade: The Story of the Atlantic Slave Trade, 1440–1870* (New York: Simon & Schuster, 1997), 199.

195   "took on the character": Brown, *Moral Capital*, 263.

195   "supply slaves to Barbados": Hilary McD. Beckles and Andrew Downes, "The Economics of Transition to the Black Labor System in Barbados, 1630–1680," *The Journal of Interdisciplinary History* 18, no. 2 (1987): 243.

195   An estimated 32,496 Africans: Mulcahy, *Hubs of Empire*, 55.

195   fallen by 35 percent from the highs of the 1640s: Beckles and Downes, "The Economics of Transition to the Black Labor System in Barbados," 243.

195   more men, women, and children: William A. Pettigrew, *Freedom's Debt: The Royal African Company and the Politics of the Atlantic Slave Trade, 1672–1752* (Chapel Hill: University of North Carolina Press, 2013), 1.

196   "empire of credit": H. V. Bowen, "Elites, Enterprise and the Making of British Overseas Empire," in *Britain's Oceanic Empire: Atlantic and Indian Ocean Worlds, c. 1550–1850*, ed. H. V. Bowen, Elizabeth Mancke, and John G. Reid (Cambridge: Cambridge University Press, 2012), 92.

19. DUNG FOR EVERY HOLE

197   "[S]ome people in power in Britain": Sidney Wilfred Mintz, *Sweetness and Power: The Place of Sugar in Modern History* (New York: Viking, 1985), 61.

197   "[o]ne thousand pounds spent by a planter": James Edward Gillespie, *The Influence of Oversea Expansion on England to 1700* (New York: Columbia University Press, 1920), 13.

197   New commercial outfits: Charles Davenant, *Reflections on the Constitution and Management of the Trade to Africa* (London: 1709), 33.

198   a system of rival political parties: William A. Pettigrew, *Freedom's Debt: The Royal African Company and the Politics of the Atlantic Slave Trade, 1672–1752* (Chapel Hill: University of North Carolina Press, 2013), 4.

198   "controlled laboratories . . . from monarchical lead": Joseph C. Miller, review of *The Making of New World Slavery*, by Robin Blackburn, *The American Historical Review* 104, no. 5 (December 1999): 1635–36.

198 Drax's mill made for "quite a sight": Peter Thompson, "Henry Drax's Instructions on the Management of a Seventeenth-Century Barbadian Sugar Plantation," *The William and Mary Quarterly* 66, no. 3 (2009): 569.

198 "was not only cheaper": Hilary McD. Beckles and Andrew Downes, "The Economics of Transition to the Black Labor System in Barbados, 1630–1680," *The Journal of Interdisciplinary History* 18, no. 2 (1987): 247.

198 "the worst poor man's country": Russell R. Menard, *Sweet Negotiations: Sugar, Slavery, and Plantation Agriculture in Early Barbados* (Charlottesville: University of Virginia Press, 2006), 45.

199 fifty thousand political prisoners: Ibid., 38.

199 95 percent of the workforce: Beckles and Downes, "Economics of Transition to the Black Labor System," 227.

199 the first governor of the colony, Sir John Yeamans, founder of Charleston: William James River, *A Sketch of the History of South Carolina: To the Close of the Proprietary Government by the Revolution of 1719* (N.p.: 1856), 107–9. See also Hugh Thomas, *The Slave Trade: The Story of the Atlantic Slave Trade, 1440–1870* (New York: Simon & Schuster, 1997), 203.

200 relentless tinkerers: See Justin Roberts, *Slavery and the Enlightenment in the British Atlantic, 1750–1807* (Cambridge: Cambridge University Press, 2018).

200 "accomplished capitalists of their time": Trevor G. Burnard and John Garrigus, *The Plantation Machine: Atlantic Capitalism in French Saint-Domingue and British Jamaica* (Philadelphia: University of Pennsylvania Press, 2016), 37.

200 much "like a horse or a cow": Dunn, *Sugar and Slaves*, 73.

200 assign women to some of the harshest of tasks: See Jennifer L. Morgan, *Laboring Women: Reproduction and Gender in New World Slavery* (Philadelphia: University of Pennsylvania Press, 2004).

200 they planted, weeded, and harvested: David Eltis, *The Rise of African Slavery in the Americas* (Cambridge: Cambridge University Press, 2000), 100.

201 people of European stock: Menard, *Sweet Negotiations*, 71.

201 "The nature of labor": Thompson, "Henry Drax's Instructions," 574.

201 "the strong sense of honor": Orlando Patterson, *Slavery and Social Death: A Comparative Study* (Cambridge, Mass.: Harvard University Press, 1982), 11.

201 "Theire is No producing good Canes": Simon P. Newman, *A New World of Labor: The Development of Plantation Slavery in the British Atlantic* (Philadelphia, University of Pennsylvania Press, 2013), 208.

201 this produced soaring disease rates: Ibid., 209.

201 "The only break in the work week": Mintz, *Sweetness and Power*, 49.

202 These sugar-mill labor practices: Menard, *Sweet Negotiations*, 15.

202 a death rate of 3 to 5 percent: Thompson, "Henry Drax's Instructions," 575.

202 the average life expectancy: Robin Blackburn, *The Making of New World Slavery: From the Baroque to the Modern, 1492–1800* (London: Verso, 1997), 339.

202 "In Brazil the senhor de engenho": Dunn, *Sugar and Slaves*, 64.

203 "The English planter combined": Ibid., 65.

203 "cheaper to work slaves to the utmost": Menard, *Sweet Negotiations*, 84.

203 gain from reproduction "cannot be great": Ibid.

203 "the fundamental prop and support": Jack P. Greene, *Evaluating Empire and Confronting Colonialism in Eighteenth-Century Britain* (Cambridge: Cambridge University Press, 2013), 27.

204 95,572 African lives: Menard, *Sweet Negotiations*, 47.

204 By 1810, the toll for Barbados: Mintz, *Sweetness and Power*, 53.

204 "the total British Caribbean slave population": Randy M. Browne, *Surviving Slavery in the British Caribbean* (Philadelphia: University of Pennsylvania Press, 2017), 3.

204 "only 665,000 slaves were still alive": Ibid.

205 "prevent idleness and make the Negroes": Thompson, "Henry Drax's Instructions," 578.

205 Drax made a practice: Blackburn, *The Making of New World Slavery*, 344.

205 "[a] first gang slave": Newman, "A New World of Labor," 207.

205 "It has often occurred to me": Ibid., 208.

206 "Slaves fed the cane": Ibid., 211.

207 "No industrial advances": Marie Arana, *Silver, Sword, and Stone: Three Crucibles in the Latin American Story* (New York: Simon & Schuster, 2019), 100.

207 "The devil was in the Englishman": Neil Oatsvall and Vaughn Scribner, "'The Devil Was in the Englishman That He Makes Everything Work': Implementing the Concept of 'Work' to Reevaluate Sugar Production and Consumption in the Early Modern British Atlantic World," *Agricultural History* 92, no. 4 (2018): 461–90; https://doi.org/10.3098/ah.2018.092.4.461.

207 "[I]t is inconceivable that any societies": Eltis, *The Rise of African Slavery in the Americas*, 7.

20. CAPITALISM'S BIG JOLT

208 "not only swam against the stream": Robin Blackburn, *The Making of New World Slavery: From the Baroque to the Modern, 1492–1800* (London: Verso, 1997), 377.

208 importing about 1.2 million kidnapped Africans: Statistic from SlaveVoyages, https://slavevoyages.org/estimates/pVr7i5. See also Tom Zoellner, *Island on Fire: The Revolt That Ended Slavery in the British Empire* (Cambridge, Mass.: Harvard University Press, 2020), 7.

209 French slave shipments doubled again: For figures for France and other imperial powers in this period, see "Trans-Atlantic Slave Trade—Estimates," SlaveVoyages, https://slavevoyages.org/estimates/E1PNmWdH.

209 By the 1620s, Brazil's combined trade: Blackburn, *The Making of New World Slavery*, 173.

209 by 1700, Barbados alone: Russell R. Menard, *Sweet Negotiations: Sugar, Slavery, and Plantation Agriculture in Early Barbados* (Charlottesville: University of Virginia Press, 2006), 18; Richard S. Dunn, *Sugar and Slaves:*

The Rise of the Planter Class in the English West Indies, 1624–1713 (New York: W. W. Norton, 1973), 48.

209 exports of all of Spain's New World colonies: Menard, *Sweet Negotiations*, 18.

209 sugar consumption in Britain would increase 2500 percent: Sidney Wilfred Mintz, *Sweetness and Power: The Place of Sugar in Modern History* (New York: Viking, 1985), 73.

209 the market value of sugar would consistently exceed: Ibid., 44.

209 the number of refineries shot up: Menard, *Sweet Negotiations*, 80.

210 from guns to ships: David Brion Davis, *Inhuman Bondage: The Rise and Fall of Slavery in the New World* (New York: Oxford University Press, 2006), 81.

210 the English found especially important new markets: Blackburn, *The Making of New World Slavery*, 375.

210 "[g]old and silver are fictitious riches": John Smith Athelstone Carnota, *Memoirs of the Marquis of Pombal: With Extracts from His Writings, and from Despatches in the State Papers Office, Never Before Published* (London: Longman, Brown, Green, and Longmans, 1843), 125.

211 "In 1770 the continental colonies": Eric Eustace Williams, *Capitalism and Slavery* (Chapel Hill: University of North Carolina Press, 1994), 108.

211 one historian has estimated: Matthew Mulcahy, *Hubs of Empire: The Southeastern Lowcountry and British Caribbean* (Baltimore: Johns Hopkins University Press, 2014), 81.

212 a further 6.1 million: Blackburn, *The Making of New World Slavery*, 377.

212 "the key of the Indies": Wendy Warren, *New England Bound: Slavery and Colonization in Early America* (New York: Liveright, 2016), 42.

212 "of colonial shipping trading": Stephen J. Hornsby, "Geographies of the British Atlantic World," in *Britain's Oceanic Empire: Atlantic and Indian Ocean Worlds, c. 1550–1850*, ed. H. V. Bowen, Elizabeth Mancke, and John G. Reid (Cambridge: Cambridge University Press, 2012), 31–32.

213 "the fruits of overseas coercion": Kenneth Pomeranz, *The Great Divergence: China, Europe, and the Making of the Modern World Economy* (Princeton, N.J.: Princeton University Press, 2000), 4.

213 2.5 billion hours of labor: Blackburn, *The Making of New World Slavery*, 581.

214 number had risen to 14 percent: Sidney Wilfred Mintz, *Sweetness and Power: The Place of Sugar in Modern History* (New York: Viking, 1985), 133.

214 "Per capita consumption of sugar": Mulcahy, *Hubs of Empire*, 46.

215 the first coffee shop: Mitchell Stephens, *A History of News*, 3rd ed. (New York: Oxford University Press, 2007), 34.

215 "the first time in history": Michael Schudson, "News," in *The International Encyclopedia of Journalism Studies*, ed. Tim P. Vos and Folker Hanusch (Hoboken, N.J.: Wiley-Blackwell, 2019), https://doi.org/10.1002/9781118841570.

215 "The numerous coffeehouses": Brian William Cowan, *The Social Life of Coffee: The Emergence of the British Coffeehouse* (New Haven: Yale University Press, 2005), 171–73.

215 "Dinner over, to Tom's": Stephens, *A History of News*, 34.

216 "[A]n acre of tropical sugar land": Pomeranz, *The Great Divergence*, 275.

216 "By 1815, Britain imported 100,000,000 pounds": Ibid., 27.

217 English manufactures found their way: Knick Hartley, "Commodity Frontiers, Spatial Economy, and Technological Innovation in the Caribbean Sugar Industry, 1783-1878," in *The Caribbean and the Atlantic World Economy: Circuits of trade, money and knowledge, 1650-1914*, ed. Adrian Leonard and David Pretel (Houndmills, Eng.: Palgrave Macmillan, 2015), 165-66.

218 This triangular boom: J. E. Inikori, *Africans and the Industrial Revolution in England: A Study in International Trade and Economic Development* (New York: Cambridge University Press, 2002), 91-92.

218 What clearly emerges through their data: Daron Acemoglu, Simon Johnson, and James Robinson, "The Rise of Europe: Atlantic Trade, Institutional Change, and Economic Growth," *The American Economic Review* 95, no. 3 (2005): 546.

220 "the legitimacy of the English state": William A. Pettigrew, *Freedom's Debt: The Royal African Company and the Politics of the Atlantic Slave Trade, 1672-1752* (Chapel Hill: University of North Carolina Press, 2013), 2.

220 "not the relics of a traditional": Ibid., 5.

220 the West India Interest: Michael Taylor, *The Interest: How the British Establishment Resisted the Abolition of Slavery* (London: Bodley Head, 2020), 14.

221 "The evidence weighs against": Acemoglu, Johnson, and Robinson, "The Rise of Europe," 562.

221 "the rise of Europe": Ibid., 562-63.

222 the fiscal-military state: Charles Tilly, *Coercion, Capital, and European States, AD 990-1992* (Cambridge, Mass.: Blackwell, 1993), 83.

222 an economic divergence compared to other regions: Valentina Romei and John Reed, "The Asian Century Is Set to Begin," *Financial Times*, March 26, 2019, https://www.ft.com/content/520cb6f6-2958-11e9-a5ab-ff8ef2b976c7.

223 £20 million in compensation from their government: Matthew Brown, "Fact Check: United Kingdom Finished Paying Off Debts to Slave-Owning Families in 2015," *USA Today*, June 30, 2020, https://www.usatoday.com/story/news/factcheck/2020/06/30/fact-check-u-k-paid-off-debts-slave-owning-families-2015/3283908001/.

223 "Some deny that coercion": Pomeranz, *The Great Divergence*, 186.

21. MASTERS OF SLAVES, MASTERS OF THE SEA

225 "No other part of the world": David Geggus, "The Caribbean in the Age of Revolution," in *The Age of Revolutions in Global Context, c. 1760-1840*, ed. David Armitage and Sanjay Subrahmanyam (Houndmills, Eng.: Palgrave Macmillan, 2010), 83.

225 Some have wrongly preferred theories: Lawrence James, *Empires in the Sun: The Struggle for the Mastery of Africa: 1830-1990* (London: Weidenfeld & Nicolson, 2016), 40.

226 "The commercial and naval strategies": Robin Blackburn, *The Making of New World Slavery: From the Baroque to the Modern, 1492–1800* (London: Verso, 1997), 378.

226 "All turns on mastery of the sea": N. A. M. Rodger, *The Command of the Ocean: A Naval History of Britain, 1649–1815* (London: Allen Lane, 2004), 151.

226 "The great fleets of which everyone": Ibid.

227 British admiral Edward Vernon: John Robert McNeill, *Mosquito Empires: Ecology and War in the Greater Caribbean, 1620–1914* (New York: Cambridge University Press, 2010), 2.

227 In six weeks of active fighting: Elena A. Schneider, *The Occupation of Havana: War, Trade, and Slavery in the Atlantic World* (Chapel Hill: University of North Carolina Press, 2018), 12.

228 "the worst catastrophe ever to befall": Laurent Dubois, *Avengers of the New World: The Story of the Haitian Revolution* (Cambridge, Mass.: Belknap/Harvard University Press, 2004), 3.

228 "In 1789 the French West Indian colony": C. L. R. James, *The Black Jacobins: Toussaint L'Ouverture and the San Domingo Revolution*, 2nd ed. (New York: Vintage, 1989), ix.

229 "territories cleared of native peoples": Blackburn, *The Making of New World Slavery*, 383.

22. SHATTER ZONES

234 archaeologists scraped away: Saidiya V. Hartman, *Lose Your Mother: A Journey Along the Atlantic Slave Route* (New York: Farrar, Straus and Giroux, 2007), 114.

234 "the first leg of their journey from humanity to cattle": Zora Neale Hurston, *Barracoon: The Story of the Last "Black Cargo,"* ed. Deborah G. Plant (New York: Amistad/HarperCollins, 2018), 5–6.

236 the true birthing ground: Toby Green, *The Rise of the Trans-Atlantic Slave Trade in Western Africa, 1300–1589* (New York: Cambridge University Press, 2012), 69.

236 its first slaving charter: Ibid., 99.

236 Lisbon's population of about 100,000: Barry Hatton, *Queen of the Sea: A History of Lisbon* (London: C. Hurst, 2018), 97.

236 "In Evora, it was as if": Nicolas Clénard, *Correspondance de Nicolas Clénard*, ed. A. Roersch (Brussels: 1940), 3:36 (author's translation).

236 a 1565 census of the city of Seville: Michael Guasco, *Slaves and Englishmen: Human Bondage in the Early Modern Atlantic World* (Philadelphia: University of Pennsylvania Press, 2014), 91.

237 "because sir, [the slaves] constitute": António Brásio, *Monumenta missionaria africana: Africa ocidental*, 2nd ser. (Lisbon: Agência Geral do Ultramar, Divisão de Publicações e Biblioteca, 1958), 1:453–54.

237 "no person, irrespective of rank": Walter Rodney, *A History of the Upper Guinea Coast, 1545–1800* (New York: Monthly Review Press, 1970), 75.
237 3500 slaves were being purchased: Brasio, *Monumenta missionaria africana*, 1:658.
237 "in these past days when I went": Ibid., 107.
237 "mêlée of peoples": Rodney, *A History of the Upper Guinea Coast*, 103.
238 "Indeed, the whole": Ibid.

23. *NEGROS SEGUROS*

239 Alonso Prieto: Colin A. Palmer, *Slaves of the White God: Blacks in Mexico, 1570–1650* (Cambridge, Mass.: Harvard University Press, 1976), 7.
239 By 1501, the enslavement of Africans: Richard Price, *Maroon Societies: Rebel Slave Communities in the Americas*, 3d ed. (Baltimore: Johns Hopkins University Press, 1996), 1.
239 approximately 277,000 Africans: "Trans-Atlantic Slave Trade—Estimates," SlaveVoyages, https://www.slavevoyages.org/assessment/estimates.
240 2.07 million people: Alex Borucki, David Eltis, and David Wheat, "Atlantic History and the Slave Trade to Spanish America," *The American Historical Review* 120, no. 2 (2015): 445.
240 indispensable to making Hispanic Latin America viable: Ibid., 434.
240 "Not a single monograph": Ibid., 460.
241 two plantations in the archbishopric: Palmer, *Slaves of the White God*, 73.
241 his personal sugar works near Oaxaca: Ibid., 67; Hugh Thomas, *The Slave Trade: The Story of the Atlantic Slave Trade, 1440–1870* (New York: Simon & Schuster, 1997), 116.
241 Vázquez de Espinosa: Palmer, *Slaves of the White God*, 46.
241 a population nearly as large: Marie Arana, *Silver, Sword, and Stone: Three Crucibles in the Latin American Story* (New York: Simon & Schuster, 2019), 97.
241 half a dozen cities: Borucki, Eltis, and Wheat, "Atlantic History and the Slave Trade," 455.
241 second largest corporate owner: Borucki, Eltis, and Wheat, "Atlantic History and the Slave Trade," 455.
242 Africans had commanded as much: Palmer, *Slaves of the White God*, 35.
242 "While most Indians had a ten-hour work day": Ibid., 69.
242 "provided the foundation": Ibid., 73.
242 "[S]ince the personal services of the Indians": Ibid., 77.
242 "the landed properties, the main wealth": Elizabeth Donnan, *Documents Illustrative of the Slave Trade to America* (New York: Octagon Books, 1965), 1:350.
243 the New Kingdom of Granada: Borucki, Eltis, and Wheat, "Atlantic History and the Slave Trade," 454.

243 "surrogate colonists": David Wheat, *Atlantic Africa and the Spanish Caribbean, 1570–1640* (Chapel Hill: University of North Carolina Press, 2016), 14.

244 "Spaniards provide no services whatsoever": Ibid., 5.

244 "complicated the very notion": Ibid., 8.

244 subsequent European colonizers: John K. Thornton, *Africa and Africans in the Making of the Atlantic World, 1400–1800*, 2nd ed. (New York: Cambridge University Press, 1998), 141.

244 "many black slaves": Matthew Restall, "Black Conquistadors: Armed Africans in Early Spanish America," *The Americas* 57, no. 2 (2000): 176.

244 African slaves were heavily represented: Ibid., 182.

244 Nuflo de Olano: Ibid., 183.

244 accompanied Pedro de Alvarado: Ibid., 183, 185.

244 Sir Francis Drake: Kris E. Lane, *Pillaging the Empire: Piracy in the Americas 1500–1750* (Armonk, N.Y.: M. E. Sharpe, 1998), 42; Matthew Mulcahy, *Hubs of Empire: The Southeastern Lowcountry and British Caribbean* (Baltimore: Johns Hopkins University Press, 2014), 28.

245 using his record of service: Wheat, *Atlantic Africa and the Spanish Caribbean*, 2.

245 invasions of Puerto Rico and Cuba: Peter Gerhard, "A Black Conquistador in Mexico," *The Hispanic American Historical Review* 58, no. 3 (1978): 451–59.

245 "I, Juan Garrido": Restall, "Black Conquistadors," 171.

24. THE SLAVE RUSH

248 a Dutchman made his way home: Robert Garfield, *A History of Sao Tome Island, 1470–1655: The Key to Guinea* (San Francisco: Mellen Research University Press, 1992), 265.

248 an average of twenty ships a year: K. Y. Daaku, *Trade and Politics on the Gold Coast, 1600–1720: A Study of the African Reaction to European Trade* (London: Clarendon Press, 1970), 11.

248 a tenth of the world's supply: Ibid., 8.

248 coinage of the United Provinces: Ibid., 11.

248 "200,000 yards of linen": Ibid.

248 the Dutch textile industry: Toby Green, *A Fistful of Shells: West Africa from the Rise of the Slave Trade to the Age of Revolution* (Chicago: University of Chicago Press, 2019), 144.

249 Spain's war against the Low Countries: John K. Thornton, "The Kingdom of Kongo and the Thirty Years' War," *Journal of World History* 27, no. 2 (2016): 190.

250 "It was the participation": Kenneth R. Andrews, *Elizabethan Privateering: English Privateering During the Spanish War, 1585–1603* (Cambridge: Cambridge University Press, 1964), 16.

250   the English pirated: Alan Gallay, *Walter Raleigh: Architect of Empire* (New York: Basic Books, 2019), 170.

250   dispatched Richard Hakluyt: Michael Guasco, *Slaves and Englishmen: Human Bondage in the Early Modern Atlantic World* (Philadelphia: University of Pennsylvania Press, 2014), 11.

250   earlier English interest in West Africa: George Frederick Zook, *The Company of Royal Adventurers Trading into Africa* (Lancaster, Pa.: Press of the New Era, 1919), 4.

251   "got into his possession": Richard Hakluyt, *The Principal Navigations: Voiages, Traffiques and Discoveries of the English Nation, Made by Sea or Over-Land, to the Remote and Farthest Distant Quarters of the Earth, at Any Time Within the Compasse of These 1500 Yeeres, Devided into Three Severall Volumes, According to the Positions of the Regions, Whereunto They Were Directed*, ed. George Bishop et al. (London: G. Bishop, R. Newberie and R. Barker, 1598), 10:8.

251   grist for much popular literature: Gallay, *Walter Raleigh*, 172.

252   the thousand-year monopoly: Anne Ruderman, "Intra-European Trade in Atlantic Africa and the African Atlantic," *The William and Mary Quarterly* 77, no. 2 (2020): 229.

252   this fee was dropped: K. Y. Daaku, *Trade and Politics on the Gold Coast, 1600–1720: A Study of the African Reaction to European Trade* (London: Clarendon Press, 1970), 10; William A. Pettigrew, "*Freedom's Debt: The Royal African Company and the Politics of the Atlantic Slave Trade, 1672–1752* (Chapel Hill: University of North Carolina Press, 2013), 10–11.

252   the outbreak of the Second Anglo-Dutch War: Daaku, *Trade and Politics on the Gold Coast*, 16–17.

253   five thousand inhabitants: John K. Thornton, *Africa and Africans in the Making of the Atlantic World, 1400–1800*, 2nd ed. (New York: Cambridge University Press, 1998), 105.

253   The firing rate: Green, *A Fistful of Shells*, 114.

253   "Europeans would build forts": David Eltis, *The Rise of African Slavery in the Americas* (Cambridge: Cambridge University Press, 2000), 132.

254   548,327 "guinea" coins: Green, *A Fistful of Shells*, 117.

254   the clear volume leader: See "Trans-Atlantic Slave Trade—Estimates," Slave-Voyages, https://www.slavevoyages.org/assessment/estimates.

254   the Slave Rush: Eltis, *The Rise of African Slavery in the Americas*, 177; "Trans-Atlantic Slave Trade—Estimates"; Daaku, *Trade and Politics on the Gold Coast*, 15.

254   By 1700, the value: Eltis, *The Rise of African Slavery in the Americas*, 39.

254   trade in Africans had also surpassed: Ibid., 150–51.

25. BARGAINS SHARP AND SINFUL

255   in imperial Songhai and in Kongo: Nehemia Levtzion, *Ancient Ghana and Mali* (New York: Africana Publishing, 1980), 117; Anne Hilton, *The Kingdom of Kongo* (Oxford: Oxford University Press, 1985), 78.

256   external demand for gold: David Eltis, *The Rise of African Slavery in the Americas* (Cambridge: Cambridge University Press, 2000), 253.

256   much of their social standing: Toby Green, *A Fistful of Shells: West Africa from the Rise of the Slave Trade to the Age of Revolution* (Chicago: University of Chicago Press, 2019), 122.

256   intra-African solidarity: Frederick Cooper, *Africa in the World: Capitalism, Empire, Nation-State* (Cambridge, Mass.: Harvard University Press, 2014), 17.

257   its much more tenuous links: John K. Thornton, *Africa and Africans in the Making of the Atlantic World, 1400–1800*, 2nd ed. (New York: Cambridge University Press, 1998), 13.

257   simply opt to move away: See, for example, Jeffrey Herbst, "War and the State in Africa," *International Security* 14, no. 4 (1990): 117–39.

257   Quick assimilation: Cooper, *Africa in the World*, 14.

257   the most important forms of capital: K. Y. Daaku, *Trade and Politics on the Gold Coast, 1600–1720: A Study of the African Reaction to European Trade* (London: Clarendon Press, 1970), 49.

258   "Slavery was widespread in Atlantic Africa": Thornton, *Africa and Africans in the Making of the Atlantic World*, 74.

259   85 percent of all the textiles: Eltis, *The Rise of African Slavery in the Americas*, 173.

259   "As late as the 1680s": Ibid., 41.

259   linen items known as *sletias*: Colleen E. Kriger, *Cloth in West African History* (Lanham, Md.: AltaMira Press, 2006), 142.

259   about one-half of the merchandise: David Richardson, "West African Consumption Patterns and Their Influence on the Eighteenth Century English Slave Trade," in *The Uncommon Market: Essays in the Economic History of the Atlantic Slave Trade*, ed. Henry A. Gemery, Jan S. Hogendorn, and Mathematical Social Science Board (New York: Academic Press, 1979), 307.

259   In 1623, Dierick Ruyters: Green, *A Fistful of Shells*, 123.

259   the king of Asebu: Daaku, *Trade and Politics on the Gold Coast*, 12.

260   "there will soon be more war": Green, *A Fistful of Shells*, 140.

260   "The European factors along the coast": Ibid., 120.

260   Guns helped advance: Priya Satia, *Empire of Guns: The Violent Making of the Industrial Revolution* (New York: Penguin Press, 2018), 1.

260   the foundation for English metallurgy: Ibid., 6.

260   a means of credit: Daaku, *Trade and Politics on the Gold Coast*, 30.

260   "the enormous volume of the trade": Satia, *Empire of Guns*, 9.

261   incorporating the use of European guns: Hilton, *The Kingdom of Kongo*, 69.

26. THE SPREAD OF THE WEST AFRICAN SLAVE TRADE

262   the Asante controlled: Toby Green, *A Fistful of Shells: West Africa from the Rise of the Slave Trade to the Age of Revolution* (Chicago: University of Chicago Press, 2019), 300.

263   the Asante began hoarding: Ibid., 440.

263   one of the most prolific sources of New World slaves: See "Trans-Atlantic Slave Trade—Estimates," SlaveVoyages, https://www.slavevoyages.org/assessment/estimates.

264   they shipped 326,757 slaves: Ibid.

264   they would switch vocations: Robin Law, *The Slave Coast of West Africa 1550–1750: The Impact of the Atlantic Slave Trade on an African Society* (Oxford: Clarendon/Oxford University Press, 1991), 121.

265   "I am gret admirer": John K. Thornton, *A Cultural History of the Atlantic World, 1250–1820* (Cambridge: Cambridge University Press, 2012), 92.

265   "In 1670, when the French requested": Law, *The Slave Coast of West Africa*, 150.

265   "A French visitor called Du Casse": Ibid., 155.

266   "he was very sorry": James H. Sweet, *Domingos Álvares, African Healing, and the Intellectual History of the Atlantic World* (Chapel Hill: University of North Carolina Press, 2011), 9.

266   Agaja's professional army: Ibid., 26.

266   the principles of disease and hygiene: Philip D. Curtin, *The Image of Africa: British Ideas and Action, 1780–1850* (Madison: University of Wisconsin Press, 1964), 346.

267   an estimated 400,000 Africans: Sweet, *Domingos Álvares*, 14.

267   being as much about statecraft: Thornton. *A Cultural History of the Atlantic World*, 93.

268   "You, Englishmen . . . I have been informed": Archibald Dalzel, *The History of Dahomy: An Inland Kingdom of Africa; Compiled from Authentic Memoirs by Archibald Dalzel* (London: Cass, 1967), 217.

268   "Yet it is quite in character": Thornton. *A Cultural History of the Atlantic World*, 94.

27. THE WAGES OF RESISTANCE

269   1.6 million people in the three hundred years: See "Trans-Atlantic Slave Trade—Estimates," SlaveVoyages, https://www.slavevoyages.org/assessment/estimates.

270   Bonny, New Calabar, and Old Calabar: G. Ugo Nwokeji, *The Slave Trade and Culture in the Bight of Biafra: An African Society in the Atlantic World* (New York: Cambridge University Press, 2010), 34.

270   unusually high ratio of female slaves: Ibid., 22.

270   surpassed the Gold Coast in volume: Ibid., 42.

270 "for nearly one-quarter": Michael A. Gomez, *Exchanging Our Country Marks: The Transformation of African Identities in the Colonial and Antebellum South* (Chapel Hill: University of North Carolina Press, 1998), 90.

271 18 percent, compared with the 10.8 percent: Nwokeji, *The Slave Trade and Culture in the Bight of Biafra*, 22.

271 "supernumerary Negroes": Edwin Stede and Stephen Gascoigne, "Petition of Edwin Stede and Stephen Gascoigne, Agents to the Royal African Company, to Sir Jonathan Atkins, Governor of the Caribbee Islands" (1679), *The Calendar of State Papers, Colonial: North America and the West Indies 1574–1739* (London: n.d.), 9: 515.

272 "One day, when we had a smooth sea": Henry Louis Gates, ed., *The Classic Slave Narratives* (New York: Signet Classics, 2012), 61.

272 decapitating recalcitrant slaves: Gomez, *Exchanging Our Country Marks*, 90–100.

272 "an ever-increasing need": Nwokeji, *The Slave Trade and Culture in the Bight of Biafra*, 43.

273 "Between 1700 and 1800": David Eltis, *The Rise of African Slavery in the Americas* (Cambridge: Cambridge University Press, 2000), 160. See also David Richardson, "Shipboard Revolts, African Authority, and the Atlantic Slave Trade," *The William and Mary Quarterly* 58, no. 1 (2001): 75.

274 "In 1777 Captain Benjamin Hughes": Christopher Leslie Brown, *Moral Capital: Foundations of British Abolitionism* (Chapel Hill: University of North Carolina Press, 2006), 306.

28. SEIZED BY THE SPIRIT

277 the Kingdom of Kongo was already a sophisticated polity: Cécile Fromont, *The Art of Conversion: Christian Visual Culture in the Kingdom of Kongo* (Chapel Hill: University of North Carolina Press, 2014), 2.

277 Wherever signs of great achievement: Wyatt MacGaffrey, "A Central African Kingdom: Kongo in 1480," in *The Kongo Kingdom: The Origins, Dynamics and Cosmopolitan Culture of an African Polity*, ed. Koen A. G. Bostoen and Inge Brinkman (Cambridge: Cambridge University Press, 2018), 43.

278 "wandering tribe of alien craftsmen": Barnaby Phillips, *Loot: Britain and the Benin Bronzes* (London: Oneworld, 2021), 123.

278 the height of its regional hegemony: Koen Bostoen and Inge Brinkman, "Introduction: Cross-Disciplinary Approaches to Kongo History," in *The Kongo Kingdom*, ed. Bostoen and Brinkman, 3.

278 "so beautiful that work": Duarte Pacheco Pereira and Raphael Eduardo de Azevedo Basto, *Esmeraldo de Situ Orbis* (Lisbon: Imprensa Nacional, 1892), 84 (author's translation).

279 "When I looked round the ship": Henry Louis Gates, ed., *The Classic Slave Narratives* (New York: Signet Classics, 2012), 57.

279   human bones for fuel: Toby Green, *A Fistful of Shells: West Africa from the Rise of the Slave Trade to the Age of Revolution* (Chicago: University of Chicago Press, 2019), 220.

280   "the corpses of slaves": James H. Sweet, *Domingos Álvares, African Healing, and the Intellectual History of the Atlantic World* (Chapel Hill: University of North Carolina Press, 2011), 28.

280   common products they associated with whites: Joseph Calder Miller, *Way of Death: Merchant Capitalism and the Angolan Slave Trade, 1730–1830* (Madison: University of Wisconsin Press, 1988), 5.

280   landed on the southeast shores: Hugh Thomas, *The Slave Trade: The Story of the Atlantic Slave Trade, 1440–1870* (New York: Simon & Schuster, 1997), 81.

280   "issue terrible thunder": Marie Arana, *Silver, Sword, and Stone: Three Crucibles in the Latin American Story* (New York: Simon & Schuster, 2019), 34.

281   "Iberian Christians fully accepted": David Northrup, *Africa's Discovery of Europe, 1450–1850*, 3rd ed. (Oxford: Oxford University Press, 2014), 31.

281   elaborate religious exhortations: Linda M. Heywood, *Njinga of Angola: Africa's Warrior Queen* (Cambridge, Mass.: Harvard University Press, 2017), 30.

282   "The Lord of this land": Rui de Pina and Alberto Martins de Carvalho, *Crónica de el-rey D. João II* (Lisbon: 1950), 158.

282   escorted to the capital: Green, *A Fistful of Shells*, 207.

282   Mbanza Kongo was situated: Hilton, *The Kingdom of Kongo*, 44.

282   *nzambi mpungu*: Anne Hilton, *The Kingdom of Kongo* (Oxford: Oxford University Press, 1985), 50.

283   "On the day the Christians": António Brásio, *Monumenta missionaria africana: Africa ocidental*, 2nd ser. (Lisbon: Agência Geral do Ultramar, Divisão de Publicações e Biblioteca, 1958), 1:113 (author's translation).

283   Six of João I's nobles were baptized: Hilton, *The Kingdom of Kongo*, 51.

284   exchanging letters with Manuel I: John Thornton, "Early Kongo-Portuguese Relations: A New Interpretation," *History in Africa* 8 (1981): 183; https://doi.org/10.2307/3171515.

284   ten thousand items: John K. Thornton, "The Kingdom of Kongo," in *Kongo: Power and Majesty*, ed. Alisa LaGamma (New York: Metropolitan Museum of Art, 2015), 87.

285   "a group of qualified electors": Fromont, *The Art of Conversion*, 2.

285   a pagan half brother: Hilton, *The Kingdom of Kongo*, 53; Thornton, "The Kingdom of Kongo," 91.

285   Or perhaps 1506: John K. Thornton, *A History of West Central Africa to 1850* (Cambridge: Cambridge University Press, 2020), 33.

286   the official legend: Ibid. (both).

286   destroy the idol figurines: Hilton, *The Kingdom of Kongo*, 62.

286   "supernatural endorsement of Afonso's support": Fromont, *The Art of Conversion*, 4.

286 "It seemed to us": Brásio, *Monumenta Missionaria Africana*, 1:268–69 (author's translation).
287 coat of arms is still used today: Thornton, "The Kingdom of Kongo," 92.
288 nearly six hundred kilos of gold: Thomas, *The Slave Trade*, 109.
288 largely dependent upon Portuguese suppliers: Miller, *Way of Death*, 484.
288 a catechism in Kimbundu: Discussion with John Thornton. See also Thomas, *The Slave Trade*, 169.
288 Portugal's trade in human beings: Linda M. Heywood, "Slavery and Its Transformation in the Kingdom of Kongo: 1491–1800," *The Journal of African History* 50, no. 1 (2009): 4.
289 "His [devotion to] Christianity": Fromont, *The Art of Conversion*, 38.
289 thirty-five of his own offspring: Hilton, *The Kingdom of Kongo*, 64.
289 ordained in Portugal: Thornton. "The Kingdom of Kongo," 95.
290 portrait of Antonio Manuel: Ibid., 98.
290 each side doing its best: Thornton, "Early Kongo-Portuguese Relations," 191.
290 the latter by a force of 170 men: John Hemming, *The Conquest of the Incas* (London: Macmillan, 1970), 47.
290 "neither god nor law": C. R. Boxer, *The Golden Age of Brazil, 1695–1750: Growing Pains of a Colonial Society* (Berkeley: University of California Press, 1962), 34.
290 paid no tribute to Portugal: John K. Thornton, *A Cultural History of the Atlantic World, 1250–1820* (Cambridge: Cambridge University Press, 2012), 183.
291 One military aid deal: Louis Jadin and Mireille Dicorato, eds., *Correspondance de Dom Afonso; Roi du Congo, 1506–1543* (Bruxelles: Académie Royale des Sciences d'Outre-mer, 1974), 18–19.
291 "sustain [his] diplomatic, material and cultural ties": Heywood, "Slavery and Its Transformation," 3.
291 "buy us the said succor": Brásio, *Monumenta missionaria africana*, 1:294–323.
292 extending education to the rural population: Thornton, "The Kingdom of Kongo," 94.
292 saw little to be gained: Robert Garfield, *A History of Sao Tome Island, 1470–1655: The Key to Guinea* (San Francisco: Mellen Research University Press, 1992), 53.

29. DARK HEARTS
293 twelve thousand slaves shipped from West Africa: See "Trans-Atlantic Slave Trade—Estimates," SlaveVoyages, https://www.slavevoyages.org/assessment/estimates.
293 as many as three hundred Africans laboring: Philip D. Curtin, *The Atlantic Slave Trade: A Census* (Madison: University of Wisconsin Press, 1969), 99–101.

294   Benin had initially refused to sell males: A. F. C. Ryder, *Benin and the Europeans, 1485–1897* (Harlow, Eng.: Longmans, 1969), 52.

294   four thousand annually: Discussion with John Thornton.

294   "Slaves often originated": Joseph C. Miller, *Way of Death: Merchant Capitalism and the Angolan Slave Trade, 1730–1830* (Madison: University of Wisconsin Press, 1988), 51.

294   Askia the Great: Michael A. Gomez, *Reversing Sail: A History of the African Diaspora*, 2nd ed. (Cambridge: Cambridge University Press, 2020), 40.

295   bondage was reserved for war captives: Linda M. Heywood, "Slavery and Its Transformation in the Kingdom of Kongo: 1491–1800," *The Journal of African History* 50, no. 1 (2009): 6.

295   the only "currency" that the Portuguese: Ibid., 9.

296   "And this harm has come": Afonso's letter from July 6, 1526, in Visconde de Paiva-Manso, *História do Congo* (Lisbon: 1877), 53–54 (author's translation). See also John Reader, *Africa: A Biography of the Continent* (New York: Alfred A. Knopf, 1998), 375.

296   complained of what he called "a great inconvenience": Levy Maria Jordão, *Historia do Congo* (Lisbon: Typ. da Academia, 1877), 56–58.

296   to provide its rival Ndongo: John Thornton, "Early Kongo-Portuguese Relations: A New Interpretation," *History in Africa* 8 (1981): 193; https://doi.org/10.2307/3171515.

296   the unscrupulous behavior of priests: Heywood, "Slavery and Its Transformation in the Kingdom of Kongo," 6.

297   undermining Afonso's control: Anne Hilton, *The Kingdom of Kongo* (Oxford: Oxford University Press, 1985), 115.

297   184,000 and 173,000 slaves, respectively, being borne off: "Trans-Atlantic Slave Trade—Estimates"; Curtin, *The Atlantic Slave Trade*, 106–7. See also Thomas, *The Slave Trade*, 185.

298   "Wealthy princes bedecked themselves": Miller, *Way of Death*, 80.

298   "imported textiles [even] covered common folk": Ibid., 80–81.

298   For most, body coverings were limited: Miller, *Way of Death*, 80.

298   replaced the use of "piece": Ibid., 68.

299   "returns in dependency": Ibid., 70.

299   to remain stocked in rum: Ibid., 84.

299   1.2 million captives embarked: José C. Curto, *Enslaving Spirits: The Portuguese-Brazilian Alcohol Trade at Luanda and Its Hinterland, c. 1550–1830*, vol. 2 of *The Atlantic World* (Leiden: Brill, 2004), 185.

299   "Put all the Guinea countries": Anne Hilton, *The Kingdom of Kongo* (Oxford: Oxford University Press, 1985), 61.

300   obscure factional participants in the civil war: John K. Thornton, "The Kingdom of Kongo and the Thirty Years' War," *Journal of World History* 27, no. 2 (2016): 195.

300   residents of territories situated well to the east: See, for example, Joseph

C. Miller, "Requiem for the 'Jaga' (Requiem pour les 'Jaga')," *Cahiers d'Études Africaines* 13, no. 49 (1973): 121–49; John K. Thornton, "A Resurrection for the Jaga (La Résurrection des Jaga)," *Cahiers d'Études Africaines* 18, no. 69/70 (1978): 223–27; Anne Hilton, "The Jaga Reconsidered," *The Journal of African History* 22, no. 2 (1981): 191–202.

300 the Jagas were able to drive Alvaro: Heywood, "Slavery and Its Transformation in the Kingdom of Kongo," 7.

300 it extracted tribute: John K. Thornton, *A Cultural History of the Atlantic World, 1250–1820* (Cambridge: Cambridge University Press, 2012), 183.

301 Paulo Dias de Novāis: Hilton, *The Kingdom of Kongo*, 105.

301 the slaving headquarters for Portugal: Linda M. Heywood, *Njinga of Angola: Africa's Warrior Queen* (Cambridge, Mass.: Harvard University Press, 2017), 25.

301 vast enough quantities: Miller, *Way of Death*, 110.

301 "subjugate and conquer the kingdom of Angola": Heywood, *Njinga of Angola*, 35.

301 "conquer and rule" Ndongo's inhabitants: David Wheat, *Atlantic Africa and the Spanish Caribbean, 1570–1640* (Chapel Hill: University of North Carolina Press, 2016), 70.

301 The megalomaniacal Dias: David Birmingham, *Trade and Conflict in Angola: The Mbundu and their Neighbours Under Portuguese Influence, 1483–1790* (Oxford: Clarendon Press, 1966), 38.

301 an explicit alliance with Ndongo: Thornton, "The Kingdom of Kongo and the Thirty Years' War," 195.

302 "seventy knights": Heywood, *Njinga of Angola*, 25, 26.

302 shipped as many as fifty thousand slaves: Ibid. 27.

302 "a wide-ranging network": Thornton, *A Cultural History of the Atlantic World*, 185.

302 "Here . . . one finds all the slaves": Fr Dieudonée Rinchon, *La Traite et l'esclavage des congolais par les européens* (Brussels: 1929) (author's translation).

302 "until the end of the world": Domingos de Abreu e Brito, *Um inquérito à vida administrativa e econômica de Angola e do Brasil em fins do século XVI* (Coimbra: 1931), 35 (author's translation).

303 Absorbing young, captured males: Thornton, "The Kingdom of Kongo and the Thirty Years' War," 196.

303 the rules of slave trading were amended: Wheat, *Atlantic Africa and the Spanish Caribbean*, 72, 100.

30. WAR FOR THE BLACK ATLANTIC

306 shipped back across the Atlantic: John K. Thornton, "The Kingdom of Kongo and the Thirty Years' War," *Journal of World History* 27, no. 2 (2016): 198.

306 "to provide them": Ibid., 199.

306 "the ships and the monthly wages": Ibid.

306 "more than twenty-four thousand blacks": Ibid., 199.

306 takeover of the Canary Islands: Ibid., 192.

306 a far bigger target: Ibid., 200.

306 "continual construction of Brazil": David Wheat, *Atlantic Africa and the Spanish Caribbean, 1570–1640* (Chapel Hill: University of North Carolina Press, 2016), 71.

307 the largest interimperial conflict: Wim Klooster, *The Dutch Moment: War, Trade, and Settlement in the Seventeenth-Century Atlantic World* (Ithaca, N.Y.: Cornell University Press, 2016), 3.

308 a copy of the correspondence from Pedro: Thornton, "The Kingdom of Kongo and the Thirty Years' War," 201.

308 persuade Count Manuel: Ibid., 203.

309 The taint of slavery: Klooster, *The Dutch Moment*, 7.

310 "[I]f God Almighty makes me become king": Thornton, "The Kingdom of Kongo and the Thirty Years' War," 206.

310 "twenty-two ships": Linda M. Heywood, *Njinga of Angola: Africa's Warrior Queen* (Cambridge, Mass.: Harvard University Press, 2017), 133.

310 "tie up an alliance": Thornton, "The Kingdom of Kongo and the Thirty Years' War," 207.

310 "Brazil or Bengal": John K. Thornton, "The Kingdom of Kongo," in *Kongo: Power and Majesty*, ed. Alisa LaGamma (New York: Metropolitan Museum of Art, 2015), 98.

311 King Garcia's armies: Thornton, "The Kingdom of Kongo and the Thirty Years' War," 210.

311 resume lucrative operations: Toby Green, *A Fistful of Shells: West Africa from the Rise of the Slave Trade to the Age of Revolution* (Chicago: University of Chicago Press, 2019), 213.

311 sending a major fleet: Thornton, "The Kingdom of Kongo and the Thirty Years' War," 212.

312 a place called Kitombo: Thornton, "The Kingdom of Kongo," 103.

312 Luanda generated 1.3 million captives: Wheat, *Atlantic Africa and the Spanish Caribbean*, 73.

312 "in place of gold or silver": Linda M. Heywood, "Slavery and Its Transformation in the Kingdom of Kongo: 1491–1800," *The Journal of African History* 50, no. 1 (2009): 11.

313 Their defeat was assured: Robert B. Edgerton, *The Fall of the Asante Empire: The Hundred-Year War for Africa's Gold Coast* (New York: Free Press, 1995), 67.

314 better prepared for its subsequent integration: Howard W. French, *A Continent for the Taking: The Tragedy and Hope of Africa* (New York: Vintage, 2005), 16.

315 reduces annual national growth rates: Jean-François Arvis, Gaël Raballand,

and Jean-François Marteau, "The Cost of Being Landlocked: Logistics, Costs, and Supply Chain Reliability," Policy Research Working Paper no. 4258 (Washington, D.C.: World Bank, 2007), https://openknowledge.world bank.org/handle/10986/7420.

315 "impose either [European] laws and institutions": Sara Berry, *No Condition Is Permanent: The Social Dynamics of Agrarian Change in Sub-Saharan Africa* (Madison: University of Wisconsin Press, 1993), 24.

315 this merely promoted instability: Ibid.

316 "decentralized despotism": Mahmood Mamdani, *Citizen and Subject: Contemporary Africa and the Legacy of Late Colonialism* (Princeton, N.J.: Princeton University Press, 2018), 37.

316 an inexhaustible source: Philip D. Curtin, *The Image of Africa: British Ideas and Action, 1780–1850* (Madison: University of Wisconsin Press, 1964), 13, 89.

317 enlightened Western practices: Ibid., 451.

317 one-eighth of the total space allotted for modern history: Ibid., 13.

317 British interest in South Asia: William Dalrymple and Olivia Fraser, *The Anarchy: The Relentless Rise of the East India Company* (New York: Bloomsbury, 2019), 39.

318 "By the late 1930s": Howard W. French, "A History of Denial," *New York Review of Books*, April 19, 2018, https://www.nybooks.com/articles/2018/04/19/africa-history-of-denial/.

319 10 percent of Vietnamese had attained literacy: Benedict R. O'G Anderson, *Imagined Communities: Reflections on the Origin and Spread of Nationalism*, rev. ed (London: Verso, 2006), 128.

319 infrastructure investments of any scale: Frederick Cooper, *Africa in the World: Capitalism, Empire, Nation-State* (Cambridge, Mass.: Harvard University Press, 2014), 22.

31. PEOPLE SCATTERED, A CONTINENT DRAINED

320 roughly 12.5 million Africans survived shipment: See "Trans-Atlantic Slave Trade—Estimates," SlaveVoyages, https://www.slavevoyages.org/assessment/estimates.

320 a "radical break" in the history: Paul E. Lovejoy, "The Impact of the Atlantic Slave Trade on Africa: A Review of the Literature," *The Journal of African History* 30, no. 3 (1989): 365.

320 reduced to roughly half: Nathan Nunn, "The Long-Term Effects of Africa's Slave Trades," *The Quarterly Journal of Economics* 123, no. 1 (2008): 142.

320 Other studies have shown: Francis Fukuyama, *The Origins of Political Order: From Prehuman Times to the French Revolution* (New York: Farrar, Straus and Giroux, 2011, 90.

321 as many Africans may have perished in these ways: Joseph Calder Miller, *Way of Death: Merchant Capitalism and the Angolan Slave Trade, 1730–1830* (Madison: University of Wisconsin Press, 1988), 153.

321   as few as 42 percent of the people ensnared: Shane Doyle, "Demography and Disease," in *The Oxford Handbook of Modern African History*, ed. John Parker and Richard J. Reid (New York: Oxford University Press, 2013), 3.

321   three- to four-year "seasoning" period: Miller, *Way of Death*, 440.

321   Africa's population actually declined: Lovejoy, "The Impact of the Atlantic Slave Trade on Africa," 394.

322   seriously underpopulated in comparison with: Doyle, "Demography and Disease," 1.

322   exceptionally high disease burdens: Ibid., 2. For a compact, recent summary of the historiographical debate over the demographic impacts on Africa of the trade, see Ana Lucia Araujo, *Public Memory of Slavery: Victims and Perpetrators in the South Atlantic*, (Amherst, N.Y.: Cambria Press, 2010), ch. 1.

322   its population probably continued to decline: Doyle, "Demography and Disease," 1.

323   600 percent in the twentieth century: Ibid., 4.

323   investments began to be made in public health: Ibid., 9.

324   this subsequent industrialization: Dani Rodrik, "Premature Deindustrialisation in the Developing World," *Frontiers of Economics in China* 12, no. 1 (Apr. 2017): 1–6.

324   "[a] ring around the right wrist of each individual": Miller, *Way of Death*, 194.

325   some West African kings and chiefs complained bitterly: Toby Green, *A Fistful of Shells: West Africa from the Rise of the Slave Trade to the Age of Revolution* (Chicago: University of Chicago Press, 2019), 507–8.

326   taking up residence in the sheer face of a mountain: Howard W. French, "Treasures of the Sahel," *New York Review of Books*. May 14, 2020, https://www.nybooks.com/articles/2020/05/14/art-treasures-sahel/.

326   "shatter zones": James C. Scott, *The Art of Not Being Governed: An Anarchist History of Upland Southeast Asia* (New Haven: Yale University Press, 2009), x.

327   "the slave trade altered the cultural norms": Nathan Nunn and Leonard Wantchekon, "The Slave Trade and the Origins of Mistrust in Africa," *The American Economic Review* 101, no. 7 (Dec. 2011): 3223.

327   "judicial institutions from courts of arbitration": Miller, *Way of Death*, 123.

327   "because chiefs often were slave traders": Nunn and Wantchekon, "The Slave Trade and the Origins of Mistrust in Africa," 3226.

328   "in areas heavily exposed": Ibid., 3222.

328   "The Atlantic trade was insidious": Walter Hawthorne, *Planting Rice and Harvesting Slaves: Transformations Along the Guinea-Bissau Coast, 1400–1900* (Portsmouth, N.H.: Heinemann, 2003), 106–7.

328   epigenetic channels: M. I. Lind and F. Spagopoulou, "Evolutionary Consequences of Epigenetic Inheritance," *Heredity* 121 (2018): 205; https://doi.org/10.1038/s41437-018-0113-y.

329   "[a] hypothetically average farming hamlet": Miller, *Way of Death*, 154.

329   "it became virtually inevitable": Ibid.

32. THE SCENT OF FREEDOM

334   the commerce that poured forth: Walter Johnson, *River of Dark Dreams: Slavery and Empire in the Cotton Kingdom* (Cambridge, Mass.: Belknap/ Harvard University Press, 2013), 10.

334   "We have lived long, but this": Curtis M. Geer, *The Louisiana Purchase and the Westward Movement* (Philadelphia: G. Barrie, 1904), 197.

335   "Your Memorialists beg to leave": Memorial to Congress by Permanent Committee of the Natchez District, Oct. 23, 1797, in *The Territorial Papers of the United States*, vol. 5, *The Territory of Mississippi, 1798–1817*, ed. Clarence Edwin Carter (Washington, D.C.: GPO, 1937), 10.

335   the fulfillment of Jefferson's idea: Johnson, *River of Dark Dreams*, 6.

336   "The first chapter of this history": Julian P. Boyd et al., eds., *The Papers of Thomas Jefferson* (Princeton, N.J.: Princeton University Press, 1950–), 29:519.

336   "I am happy in the opportunity": John Clement Fitzpatrick et al., eds., *The Writings of GW from the Original Manuscript Sources, 1745–1799* (Washington, D.C.: GPO, 1931–1944), 31:375.

336   a population of 25,000: Albert Thrasher, *On to New Orleans!: Louisiana's Heroic 1811 Slave Revolt* (New Orleans: Cypress Press, 1996), 1.

336   75 percent of the population was enslaved: Daniel Rasmussen, *American Uprising: The Untold Story of America's Largest Slave Revolt* (New York: Harper, 2011), 9.

337   imported to the Lower Mississippi Valley: Ibid., 23.

337   buoyed by the news: Brandon R. Byrd, *The Black Republic: African Americans and the Fate of Haiti* (Philadelphia: University of Pennsylvania Press, 2020), 2.

337   "the Day of Our Political Jubilee": Gary B. Nash, *The Forgotten Fifth: African Americans in the Age of Revolution* (Cambridge, Mass.: Harvard University Press, 2006), 143.

338   "unknown mode of conveying intelligence": Julius Sherrard Scott and Marcus Rediker, *The Common Wind: Afro-American Currents in the Age of the Haitian Revolution* (London: Verso, 2018), xi.

338   "The negroes have a wonderful art": Ibid., 80.

339   roughly thirty Blacks: Vincent Brown, *Tacky's Revolt: The Story of an Atlantic Slave War* (Cambridge, Mass.: Belknap/Harvard University Press, 2020), 104.

339   Juan de Cádiz: Laurent Dubois and Richard Lee Turits, *Freedom Roots: Histories from the Caribbean* (Chapel Hill: University of North Carolina Press, 2019), 108.

339   occurred in Martinique: Scott and Rediker, *The Common Wind*, 78.

339   ban the importation of slaves from Jamaica: Brown, *Tacky's Revolt*, 210.

339   deploy its most powerful naval squadron: Ibid., 181.

340   provided vital cover: Scott and Rediker, *The Common Wind*, 53.

340   "the elevated freedom of the free": Christopher L. Tomlins, *Freedom Bound: Law, Labor, and Civic Identity in Colonizing English America, 1580–1865* (New York: Cambridge University Press, 2010), 409.

340   Those from Saint-Domingue who fought against the British: Michel-Rolph Trouillot, *Silencing the Past: Power and the Production of History* (Boston: Beacon Press, 1995), 38; Scott and Rediker, *The Common Wind*, 57.

340   "in a land where all property is based": Scott and Rediker, *The Common Wind*, xv.

341   came from the region of Angola and Kongo: John K. Thornton, "African Soldiers in the Haitian Revolution," *The Journal of Caribbean History* 25, no. 1 (1991): 60.

341   The common wind that circulated: Scott and Rediker, *The Common Wind*, 6.

341   "will learn that a man's rights": Walter S. Franklin et al., eds., *American State Papers: Documents, Legislative and Executive, of the Congress of the United States, from the First Session of the First to the Second Session of the Twenty-Second Congress; Inclusive Commencing March 3, 1789 and Ending March 3, 1833*, vol. 7, *Post Office Department* (Washington, D.C.: Gales and Seaton, 1834).

341   "What will be the case": "Memoirs of Capt. Paul Cuffee," New York *Freedom's Journal*, April 6, 1827, 1.

341   a place called Pointe Coupée: Rasmussen, *American Uprising*, 89.

342   "no one who does not shudder": Laurent Dubois and Richard Lee Turits, *Freedom Roots: Histories from the Caribbean* (Chapel Hill: University of North Carolina Press, 2019), 111.

342   "a war on brutes": Tomlins, *Freedom Bound*, 507.

343   "Among their number were men named": Johnson, *River of Dark Dreams*, 18.

344   "a lively and fertile milieu": Sudhir Hazareesingh, *Black Spartacus: The Epic Life of Toussaint Louverture* (New York: Farrar, Straus and Giroux, 2020), 11.

344   "the period of the most active": Peter P. Hinks, *To Awaken My Afflicted Brethren: David Walker and the Problem of Antebellum Slave Resistance* (University Park: Pennsylvania State University Press, 1997), xiv.

346   attack the city's armory: Thrasher, *On to New Orleans!*, 57.

346   smoke from their heavy fusillade: Rasmussen, *American Uprising*, 109.

347   the enemy could then be picked off: Thornton, "African Soldiers in the Haitian Revolution," 58–80.

347   "considerable slaughter": Rasmussen, *American Uprising*, 140.

347   "did not denounce anyone": Ibid., 154–55.

348   given a more formal trial: Johnson, *River of Dark Dreams*, 21.

348   "as a terrible example": "Summary of Trial Proceedings of Those Accused

of Participating in the Slave Uprising of January 9, 1811," *Louisiana History: The Journal of the Louisiana Historical Association* 18, no. 4 (1977): 473.

349 "Though the 1811 uprising": Rasmussen, *American Uprising*, 2.

33. THE BLACK JACOBINS

352 "In August 1791, after two years": C. L. R. James, *The Black Jacobins: Toussaint L'Ouverture and the San Domingo Revolution*, 2nd ed. (New York: Vintage, 1989), ix.

353 one-third of all that external trade: William Doyle, *The Oxford History of the French Revolution* (Oxford: Clarendon/Oxford University Press, 1989), 13.

353 the richest colony ever: Julius Sherrard Scott and Marcus Rediker, *The Common Wind: Afro-American Currents in the Age of the Haitian Revolution* (London: Verso, 2018), 6.

354 15 percent of its economic growth: Trevor G. Burnard and John Garrigus, *The Plantation Machine: Atlantic Capitalism in French Saint-Domingue and British Jamaica* (Philadelphia: University of Pennsylvania Press, 2016), 2.

354 No fewer than a million: Laurent Dubois, *Avengers of the New World: The Story of the Haitian Revolution* (Cambridge, Mass.: Belknap/Harvard University Press, 2004), 21.

354 generated as much trade: Adam Hochschild, *Bury the Chains: Prophets and Rebels in the Fight to Free an Empire's Slaves* (Boston: Houghton Mifflin, 2005), 261.

354 "Never, for centuries": James, *The Black Jacobins*, 45.

354 "The fortunes created at Bordeaux": Ibid., 47.

354 "helped lay the foundation": Dubois, *Avengers of the New World*, 18.

354 sugar mills reaching 450: Scott and Rediker, *The Common Wind*, 6.

355 roughly 685,000 slaves: Sudhir Hazareesingh, *Black Spartacus: The Epic Life of Toussaint Louverture* (New York: Farrar, Straus and Giroux, 2020), 24.

355 "Let an intelligent and educated man": James, *The Black Jacobins*, 112.

356 "the most severe wartime challenge": Burnard and Garrigus, *The Plantation Machine*, 122.

356 forge powerful new identities and alliances: James H. Sweet, *Domingos Álvares, African Healing, and the Intellectual History of the Atlantic World* (Chapel Hill: University of North Carolina Press, 2011), 26.

357 mold-derived mycotoxins: Christina Frances Mobley, "The Kongolese Atlantic: Central African Slavery and Culture from Mayombe to Haiti" (Ph.D. diss., Duke University, 2015).

357 Henri Christophe: Scott and Rediker, *The Common Wind*, 53.

357 "pathologically stratified": Dubois, *Avengers of the New World*, 135.

358 "sacred right of property": James, *The Black Jacobins*, 22.

358 "How can we make a lot of sugar": David Geggus, "Les Esclaves de la plaine du nord à la veille de la revolution française," *Revue de la Société Haïtienne d'Histoire et de Géographie* 142 (1984): 24.

358 "All laws, however just": James, *The Black Jacobins*, 22.
359 "[T]he stain of slavery": Dubois, *Avengers of the New World*, 68.
359 "sleeping at the foot of Vesuvius": James, *The Black Jacobins*, 55.
359 a purge of the coloreds: Dubois, *Avengers of the New World*, 90.
359 stop the "contagion of liberty": Ibid.
360 "All that the negroes lack": Ibid., 57.
360 a student of Machiavelli, Montesquieu, and Rousseau: Hazareesingh, *Black Spartacus*, 12.

34. GILDED NEGROES

361 "the most radical declaration": Brandon R. Byrd, *The Black Republic: African Americans and the Fate of Haiti* (Philadelphia: University of Pennsylvania Press, 2020), 1.
362 "Whatever their color, only one distinction": Neil Roberts, *Freedom as Marronage* (Chicago: University of Chicago Press, 2015), 105.
362 "no other leader anywhere": Adam Hochschild, *Bury the Chains: Prophets and Rebels in the Fight to Free an Empire's Slaves* (Boston: Houghton Mifflin, 2005), 290.
362 "The existence of a negro people in arms": David Nicholls, *From Dessalines to Duvalier: Race, Colour, and National Independence in Haiti* (New Brunswick, NJ: Rutgers University Press: 1996), 36.
362 "the wild and pernicious Doctrines": Hochschild, *Bury the Chains*, 268.
363 "Throw away the image of the god": Carolyn E. Fick, *The Making of Haiti: the Saint Domingue Revolution from Below*, (Knoxville: University of Tennessee Press, 1990), 93–4.
363 If them, why not us: Carolyn E. Fick, *The Making of Haiti: The Saint Domingue Revolution from Below* (Knoxville: University of Tennessee Press, 1990), 97, 106–7.
363 In early November, with violence spreading: Hochschild, *Bury the Chains*, 260.
363 "There can be no cultivation": Jean-Philippe Garran-Coulon, *Rapport sur les troubles de Saint-Domingue* (Paris: 1798–1799), 3:141–44.
364 pronouncing himself the leader: Sudhir Hazareesingh, *Black Spartacus: The Epic Life of Toussaint Louverture* (New York: Farrar, Straus and Giroux, 2020), 11.
364 "I want Liberty and Equality": David Patrick Geggus, *Haitian Revolutionary Studies* (Bloomington: Indiana University Press, 2002), 127.
364 "there was no need to be ashamed": C. L. R. James, *The Black Jacobins: Toussaint L'Ouverture and the San Domingo Revolution*, 2nd ed. (New York: Vintage, 1989), 256.
364 "the possibility of achievement": Ibid., 244.
364 "With the exception always of Bonaparte": Ibid., 256.
365 "Here were white men offering": Ibid., 124.

366 coincide with violent thunderstorms: Hazareesingh, *Black Spartacus*, 80; John K. Thornton, "African Soldiers in the Haitian Revolution," *The Journal of Caribbean History* 25, no. 1 (Jan. 1991): 67.

366 treated fevers with mercury: Hochschild, *Bury the Chains*, 271.

366 the largest this nation had ever sent: Ibid., 276.

366 buying slaves straight off of ships: Taylor, *The Internal Enemy*, 117.

367 "like fighting to conquer a cemetery": Hochschild, *Bury the Chains*, 278.

367 "We are fighting that liberty": Ibid.

367 a regimental banner in remembrance: Ibid., 279, 281.

367 Bonaparte quickly set out to restore: Jeremy D. Popkin, *A New World Begins: The History of the French Revolution* (New York: Basic Books, 2019), 538.

368 "an essential link in a vast chain": Julius Sherrard Scott and Marcus Rediker, *The Common Wind: Afro-American Currents in the Age of the Haitian Revolution* (London: Verso, 2018), 54.

368 "because of the difference": The Louverture Project, https://thelouver tureproject.org/index.php?title=Napol%C3%A9on_Bonaparte_Proclama tion_on_Saint-Domingue_(1799).

368 "the sacred principle of the liberty": Dubois, *Avengers of the New World*, 241.

368 "We are free today": Popkin, *A New World Begins*, 538.

369 "it is not a circumstantial liberty": Dubois, *Avengers of the New World*, 242.

369 "included many good things": Hochschild, *Bury the Chains*, 291.

369 "from the first of blacks": Ibid.

369 an expeditionary force to be deployed: Popkin, *A New World Begins*, 539.

369 "a crusade of civilized people": Dubois, *Avengers of the New World*, 256.

370 "Rid us of these gilded negroes": Hochschild, *Bury the Chains*, 291.

370 "to renew in a philosopher": James Stephen, *The Crisis of the Sugar Colonies: Or, An Enquiry into the Objects and Probable Effects of the French Expedition to the West Indies, and Their Connection with the Colonial Interests of the British Empire, to Which Are Subjoined Sketches of a Plan for Settling the Vacant Lands of Trinidada. In Four Letters to the Right Hon. Henry Addington* (1802; repr., New York: Negro Universities Press, 1969), 75–76.

370 "We must perish": François-Joseph-Pamphile de Lacroix, *Mémoires pour servir à l'Histoire de la Révolution de Saint-Domingue* vol. 2 (Paris: 1819), 63 (author's translation).

370 "I took up arms for the freedom of my color": James, *The Black Jacobins*, 281.

370 "Victors everywhere": Dubois, *Avengers of the New World*, 268.

371 "In overthrowing me": James, *The Black Jacobins*, 334.

371 Jean Baptiste Sans Souci: Michel-Rolph Trouillot, *Silencing the Past: Power and the Production of History* (Boston: Beacon Press, 1995), 67.

371 "Do not think of establishing slavery": James, *The Black Jacobins*, 341.

371 "There will be an earthquake!": Ibid.

372 Charles-Maurice Talleyrand: Dubois, *Avengers of the New World*, 260.

372 "I am for the whites": Popkin, *A New World Begins*, 538.

372   doing nothing to liberate: Taylor, *The Internal Enemy*, 114.

373   "war of extermination": Dubois, *Avengers of the New World*, 291–92.

373   "Send 12,000 replacements": Hochschild, *Bury the Chains*, 293.

373   "expert in atrocity": Dubois, *Avengers of the New World*, 293.

373   "It is not enough to have expelled the barbarians": Laurent Dubois and John D. Garrigus, eds., *Slave Revolution in the Caribbean, 1789–1804: A Brief History with Documents* (New York: Bedford/St. Martin's, 2006).

374   "Napoleon suffered more casualties": Hochschild, *Bury the Chains*, 294.

35. BLUES AND THE AMERICAN TRUTH

376   "Think of it!": Edwidge Danticat, "The Long Legacy of Occupation in Haiti," *The New Yorker*, July 28, 2015.

378   Keith Richards and Mick Jagger had bonded: Ted Gioia, *Delta Blues: The Life and Times of the Mississippi Masters Who Revolutionized American Music* (New York: W. W. Norton, 2008), 205.

378   "flash of the spirit": Robert Farris Thompson, *Flash of the Spirit: African and Afro-American Art and Philosophy* (New York: Vintage, 1984), xiii.

379   "Blues is the parent of all legitimate jazz": Amiri Baraka, *Blues People: Negro Music in White America* (New York: Quill/William Morrow, 1999), 17.

379   "It was Britain's success": David Cannadine, *Victorious Century: The United Kingdom, 1800–1906* (London: Allen Lane, 2017), 45.

380   a remotely comparable leap in economic growth: Sven Beckert, *Empire of Cotton: A Global History* (New York: Alfred A. Knopf, 2014), 63.

380   "anointing chrism": W. E. B. Du Bois, *Black Reconstruction in America: An Essay Toward a History of the Part Which Black Folk Played in the Attempt to Reconstruct Democracy in America, 1860–1880* (New York: Oxford University Press, 2007), 10.

380   "The influence of the Delta": Gioia, *Delta Blues*, 2.

380   As a child he had picked cotton: Ibid., 202.

381   "and especially by conducting oneself": Giles Oakley, *The Devil's Music: A History of the Blues*, 2nd ed. (New York: Da Capo Press, 1997), 197.

381   "I wouldn't say I was supporting myself": Ibid., 221.

381   "a device for making the best": Albert Murray, *The Hero and the Blues* (New York: Vintage, 1995), 36–37.

382   "simply renders him unfit for the work": Nicholas Lemann, *The Promised Land: The Great Black Migration and How It Changed America* (New York: Alfred A. Knopf, 1991), 47.

382   a Chicago-based industrial real estate firm: "Robert L. Stovall: 1932–2009," *Chicago Tribune*, Aug. 6, 2009.

382   "The Europeans made the county": Françoise N. Hamlin, *Crossroads at Clarksdale: The Black Freedom Struggle in the Mississippi Delta After World War II* (Chapel Hill: University of North Carolina Press, 2012), xiv.

383 cotton was the most valuable product: Walter Johnson, *River of Dark Dreams: Slavery and Empire in the Cotton Kingdom* (Cambridge, Mass.: Belknap/Harvard University Press, 2013), 3.

383 one in six British workers: Beckert, *Empire of Cotton*, 73.

383 "there will never be quietness": Jeffrey Ostler, *Surviving Genocide: Native Nations and United States from the American Revolution to Bleeding Kansas.* (New Haven: Yale University Press, 2019), 191.

384 "settle on our [*sic*] lands beyond the Mississippi": Ibid.

384 "Our property may be plundered": Beckert, *Empire of Cotton*, 108.

384 "He believed they were destined": *The Memoirs of John Quincy Adams, Comprising Portions of His Diary from 1795-1848*, ed. Charles Francis Adams (Philadelphia: 1875), 7:90.

384 "Notoriously, during the Nazi conquest": Claudio Saunt, *Unworthy Republic: The Dispossession of Native Americans and the Road to Indian Territory* (New York: W. W. Norton, 2020), xvi. See also Mahmood Mamdani, *Neither Settler nor Native: The Making and Unmaking of Permanent Minorities* (Cambridge, Mass.: Belknap/Harvard University Press, 2020), 98.

36. THE GIFTS OF BLACK FOLK

386 "the cheapest and most available labor in the world": *American Cotton Planter*, April 23, 1853, 152.

386 three elements were considered essential: Walter Johnson, *River of Dark Dreams: Slavery and Empire in the Cotton Kingdom* (Cambridge, Mass.: Belknap/Harvard University Press, 2013), 193.

387 "To sell cotton in order to buy negroes": Joshua D. Rothman, "The Contours of Cotton Capitalism: Speculation, Slavery, and Economic Panic in Mississippi, 1832–1841," in *Slavery's Capitalism: A New History of American Economic Development*, ed. Sven Beckert and Seth Rockman (Philadelphia: University of Pennsylvania Press, 2016), 129.

387 white families in the county possessed: Sven Beckert, *Empire of Cotton: A Global History* (New York: Alfred A. Knopf, 2014), 113.

388 nearly 100,000 slaves left Virginia and Maryland: Alan Taylor, *The Internal Enemy: Slavery and War in Virginia, 1772–1832* (New York: W. W. Norton, 2013), 48.

388 Mississippi alone imported 130,000 slaves: Rothman, "The Contours of Cotton Capitalism," 130.

388 bigger, too, than the emigration of Jews: Edward Ball, "Retracing Slavery's Trail of Tears," *Smithsonian Magazine*, November 2015, https://www.smithsonianmag.com/history/slavery-trail-of-tears-180956968/.

388 "As it became clear": Johnson, *River of Dark Dreams*, 41.

388 regular auctions came to be held: James Oakes, *Slavery and Freedom: An Interpretation of the Old South* (New York: Alfred A. Knopf, 1990), 23.

389 "FOR SALE": Anne C. Bailey, *The Weeping Time: Memory and the Largest Slave Auction in American History* (New York: Cambridge University Press, 2017), 9.

389 "The buyers paraded them": Ibid., 11.

389 produced a torrent of wealth: Johnson, *River of Dark Dreams*, 5.

390 36.5 million pounds: Beckert, *Empire of Cotton*, 104; Edward E. Baptist, *The Half Has Never Been Told: Slavery and the Making of American Capitalism* (New York: Basic Books, 2016), 113.

390 cotton became to the nineteenth-century United States: Beckert, *Empire of Cotton*, 113.

390 two-thirds of American exports: Johnson, *River of Dark Dreams*, 11.

390 "sell their cotton in Liverpool": Oakes, *Slavery and Freedom*, 98.

390 numbered 124 at the time of his death: Mary V. Thompson, *"The Only Unavoidable Subject of Regret": George Washington, Slavery, and the Enslaved Community at Mount Vernon* (Charlottesville: University of Virginia Press, 2019), 244–45.

391 America's "ascriptive hierarchies": Rogers M. Smith, *Civic Ideals: Conflicting Visions of Citizenship in U.S. History* (New Haven: Yale University Press, 1997), 17–18.

391 "Nothing highlighted freedom": Toni Morrison, *Playing in the Dark: Whiteness and the Literary Imagination* (New York: Vintage, 1993), 38.

392 the value of slaves in antebellum America: Thomas Piketty and Gabriel Zucman, "Capital Is Back: Wealth-Income Ratios in Rich Countries 1700–2010," *The Quarterly Journal of Economics* 129, no. 3 (2014): 33.

392 "it was ordinary southerners": Bonnie Martin, "Neighbor-to-Neighbor Capitalism: Local Credit Networks and the Mortgaging of Slaves," in Beckert and Rockman, *Slavery's Capitalism*, 108.

392 20 percent to 175 percent: Ibid.

393 "the North's equivalent of the southern planters": Claudio Saunt, *Unworthy Republic: The Dispossession of Native Americans and the Road to Indian Territory* (New York: W. W. Norton, 2020), 187.

393 "It was black labor that established": W. E. B. Du Bois, *The Gift of Black Folk: The Negroes in the Making of America* (New York: Oxford University Press, 2014), 42.

394 "became the foundation stone": W. E. B. Du Bois, *Black Reconstruction in America: An Essay Toward a History of the Part Which Black Folk Played in the Attempt to Reconstruct Democracy in America, 1860–1880* (New York: Oxford University Press, 2007), 5.

394 "wonderland in which all familiar scenes": Ibid., xxxi.

394 "The cotton trade": Christopher L. Tomlins, *Freedom Bound: Law, Labor, and Civic Identity in Colonizing English America, 1580–1865* (New York: Cambridge University Press, 2010), 413.

37. HOW THE WEST WAS MADE AND "WON"

396 a 1956 book: Constance McLaughlin Green, *Eli Whitney and the Birth of American Technology* (Boston: Little, Brown, 1956).

397 tripled in value: Sven Beckert, *Empire of Cotton: A Global History* (New York: Alfred A. Knopf, 2014), 102.

397 400 percent: Edward E. Baptist, *The Half Has Never Been Told: Slavery and the Making of American Capitalism* (New York: Basic Books, 2016), 128.

397 "In 1801, 28 pounds per day": Ibid., 126.

399 "could become a center": Robert I. Paquette, "Revolutionary Saint Domingue in the Making of Territorial Louisiana," in *A Turbulent Time: The French Revolution and the Greater Caribbean*, ed. David Barry Gaspar and David Patrick Geggus (Bloomington: Indiana University Press, 1997), 207.

399 "drive France's other American possessions": Ibid., 206.

399 "Damn sugar, damn coffee, damn colonies": Ibid., 209.

399 psychologically freeing the British: Michael Taylor, *The Interest: How the British Establishment Resisted the Abolition of Slavery* (Vintage Digital, 2020), 23.

400 "One would expect such 'facts' ": Michel-Rolph Trouillot, *Silencing the Past: Power and the Production of History* (Boston: Beacon Press, 1995), 100.

400 the half million Blacks: Christopher L. Tomlins, *Freedom Bound: Law, Labor, and Civic Identity in Colonizing English America, 1580–1865* (New York: Cambridge University Press, 2010), 411.

400 Indian resistance and Black revolt: Robert G. Parkinson, *The Common Cause: Creating Race and Nation in the American Revolution* (Chapel Hill: University of North Carolina Press, 2016), 24.

400 France's general *lycée* curriculum. British education does little better: Lauren Collins, "The Haitian Revolution and the Hole in French High School History," *The New Yorker*, Dec. 3, 2020; Maya Jassanof, "Misremembering the British Empire," *The New Yorker*, Nov. 2, 2020.

401 "[t]he colonists knew exactly": Annette Gordon-Reed, *The Hemingses of Monticello: An American Family* (New York: W. W. Norton, 2008), 54.

401 "constantly haunts the imagination": Alexis de Tocqueville, *Democracy in America: And Two Essays on America*, trans. Gerald E. Bevan (London: Penguin, 2003), 420.

401 "[T]o the courage and obstinate resistance": Alexander Hamilton, "Purchase of Louisiana," *New York Evening Post*. July 5, 1803.

401 a mere "cannibal": Sudhir Hazareesingh, *Black Spartacus: The Epic Life of Toussaint Louverture* (New York: Farrar, Straus and Giroux, 2020), 3.

401 "Never was so deep a tragedy": Thomas Jefferson, *The Papers of Thomas Jefferson*, vol. 26, ed. John Catanzariti (Princeton, N.J.: Princeton University Press, 1995), 503.

401 diversification away from that crop: Edmund S. Morgan, *American Slavery,*

American Freedom: The Ordeal of Colonial Virginia (New York: W. W. Norton, 1975), 135.

401 cut back on tobacco farming: Philip D. Morgan, "'To Get Quit of Negroes': George Washington and Slavery," *Journal of American Studies* 39, no. 3 (2005): 413.

402 between 34 and 44 percent: Gordon-Reed, *The Hemingses of Monticello*, 50.

402 "By the 1760s, Virginia's leaders": Alan Taylor, *The Internal Enemy: Slavery and War in Virginia, 1772–1832* (New York: W. W. Norton, 2013), 20.

402 strung together in "coffles": Claudio Saunt, *Unworthy Republic: The Dispossession of Native Americans and the Road to Indian Territory* (New York: W. W. Norton, 2020), 43.

403 Maspero's Exchange: Edward Ball, "Retracing Slavery's Trail of Tears," *Smithsonian Magazine*, November 2015, https://www.smithsonianmag.com/history/slavery-trail-of-tears-180956968/.

403 the single year of 1857: Ibid.

403 "Instead, poor whites": Gordon-Reed, *The Hemingses of Monticello*, 53.

404 the second illusion of truth: Here I especially have drawn on arguments of Michel-Rolph Trouillot in *Silencing the Past: Power and the Production of History* (Boston: Beacon Press, 1995), 107.

404 pro-slavery sentiment: Gary B. Nash, *The Forgotten Fifth: African Americans in the Age of Revolution* (Cambridge, Mass.: Harvard University Press, 2006), 72–74.

404 "In addition to the danger": Taylor, *The Internal Enemy*, 113.

405 armed five hundred slaves: Ibid., 323.

405 "Our country will be peopled": William Writ Henry, *Patrick Henry: Life, Correspondence and Speeches* (New York: Charles Scribner's Sons, 1891),1:116.

405 "Deep rooted prejudices": Thomas Jefferson, *Notes on the State of Virginia*, ed. Frank Shuffleton (New York: Penguin Books, 1999), 200.

406 "one could scarcely be found capable": Ibid., 201.

406 never freed any slaves: Gordon-Reed, *The Hemingses of Monticello*, 115.

406 "removed beyond the reach of mixture": Jefferson, *Notes on the State of Virginia*, 143.

406 "dismissed the suffering that losing children": Taylor, *The Internal Enemy*, 403.

406 all but five of his slaves were sold: Nash, *The Forgotten Fifth*, 108.

407 "[T]here is an unwillingness": "Address on Colonization to a Deputation of Negroes," August 14, 1862, in *The Collected Works of Abraham Lincoln*, ed. Roy P. Basler (New Brunswick, N.J: Rutgers University Press, 1953), 5:372.

407 "there was no future for an interracial democracy": Martha S. Jones, *Birthright Citizens: A History of Race and Rights in Antebellum America* (Cambridge: Cambridge University Press, 2018), 37.

407 the objective shifted to Haiti: Sara Fanning, *Caribbean Crossing: African Americans and the Haitian Emigration Movement* (New York: New York University Press, 2014).

407   Lincoln signed a contract: Eric Foner, *Reconstruction: America's Unfinished Revolution: 1863–1877*, rev. ed. (New York: HarperPerennial, 2014), 6.

408   "special subordinate, more bestial caste": Peter P. Hinks, *To Awaken My Afflicted Brethren: David Walker and the Problem of Antebellum Slave Resistance* (University Park: Pennsylvania State University Press, 1997), 205.

408   David Walker, whose urgent 1829 publication: Ibid., xiv.

409   Battle of Horseshoe Bend: Saunt, *Unworthy Republic*, 48.

409   Jackson called for the "voluntary" departure: Ibid., 49.

409   hire a full-time clerk: Walter Johnson, *River of Dark Dreams: Slavery and Empire in the Cotton Kingdom* (Cambridge, Mass.: Belknap/Harvard University Press, 2013), 34, 36.

409   This commodification of the land: Taylor, *The Internal Enemy*, 402.

410   radically increased slave productivity: Johnson, *River of Dark Dreams*, 256.

410   "sought to determine how much labor": Caitlin Rosenthal, *Accounting for Slavery: Masters and Management* (Cambridge, Mass.: Harvard University Press, 2018), 2.

410   "No matter how fatigued": Solomon Northup, *Twelve Years a Slave* (Chapel Hill: University of North Carolina Press, 2011), 117.

38. TOWARD A NEW VISION OF OUR ORIGINS

411   America's biggest city: Jonathan Daniel Wells, *The Kidnapping Club: Wall Street, Slavery, and Resistance on the Eve of the Civil War* (New York: Bold Type Books, 2020), 5.

411   the moral story of the American: Alan Taylor, *The Internal Enemy: Slavery and War in Virginia, 1772–1832* (New York: W. W. Norton, 2013), xvii.

412   "The South was fighting to take slavery": W. E. B. Du Bois, *Black Reconstruction in America: An Essay Toward a History of the Part Which Black Folk Played in the Attempt to Reconstruct Democracy in America, 1860–1880* (New York: Oxford University Press, 2007), 49.

412   "If there be those who would not save": "Abraham Lincoln's Letter to Horace Greeley," August 22, 1862, Abraham Lincoln Online, http://www .abrahamlincolnonline.org/lincoln/speeches/greeley.htm,_accessed December 21, 2020.

412   many escaped slaves arrived in Union camps: Ira Berlin, *The Long Emancipation: The Demise of Slavery in the United States* (Cambridge, Mass.: Harvard University Press, 2015), 160.

412   180,000 Blacks: Eric Foner, *Reconstruction: America's Unfinished Revolution: 1863–1877*, rev. ed. (New York: HarperPerennial, 2014), 6.

412   "[n]othing more clearly marked": Berlin, *The Long Emancipation*, 170.

413   "the largest civil insurrection": Foner, *Reconstruction*, 32.

413   "The problem is solved": Du Bois, *Black Reconstruction in America*, 89.

413   an idea that originated with runaway slaves: Manisha Sinha, *The Slave's Cause: A History of Abolition* (New Haven: Yale University Press, 2016), 48.

413   the "rude bridge" in Concord: Robert G. Parkinson, *The Common Cause:*

Creating Race and Nation in the American Revolution (Chapel Hill: University of North Carolina Press, 2016), 25.

413   **150 Blacks fought in the Battle of Bunker Hill:** Gary B. Nash, *The Forgotten Fifth: African Americans in the Age of Revolution* (Cambridge, Mass.: Harvard University Press, 2006), 8.

414   **King George's statue:** Sinha, *The Slave's Cause*, 49.

414   **"desperation at Valley Forge":** Ibid.

414   **binding together white colonists:** David Brion Davis, *Inhuman Bondage: The Rise and Fall of Slavery in the New World* (New York: Oxford University Press, 2006), 35.

414   **"were not eligible for any of the benefits":** Robert G. Parkinson, *The Common Cause: Creating Race and Nation in the American Revolution* (Chapel Hill: University of North Carolina Press, 2016), 22.

414   **"For African Americans, a revolution":** Nash, *The Forgotten Fifth*, 39.

416   **industrialization as the greatest event:** E. J. Hobsbawm, *The Age of Revolution, 1789–1848* (New York: New American Library, 1980), 44.

416   **twice the size of Britain's economy:** G. John Ikenberry, *A World Safe for Democracy: Liberal Internationalism and the Crises of Global Order* (New Haven: Yale University Press, 2020), 83.

416   **Their willingness to sacrifice entire fleets:** Lawrence James, *Empires in the Sun: The Struggle for the Mastery of Africa, 1830–1990* (London: Weidenfeld & Nicolson, 2016), 40.

416   **"the great question now before our people":** Sven Beckert, *Empire of Cotton: A Global History* (New York: Alfred A. Knopf, 2014), 281.

417   **The rise of the sharecropper system:** Foner, *Reconstruction*, 10.

417   **the mechanical cotton picker:** Nicholas Lemann, *The Promised Land: The Great Black Migration and How It Changed America* (New York: Alfred A. Knopf, 1991), 1, 5.

417   **"Mississippi could easily rank with South Africa":** Simeon Booker, *Black Man's America* (Englewood Cliffs, N.J.: Prentice-Hall, 1964), 161.

418   **called a senior official:** Taylor Branch, *Parting the Waters: America in the King Years, 1954–63* (New York: Simon & Schuster, 1988), 423.

418   **including "malicious mischief":** Foner, *Reconstruction*, 200.

419   **"the usual and common wages":** Ibid., 94.

419   **"The whole South":** Eric Foner and Joshua Brown, *Forever Free: The Story of Emancipation and Reconstruction* (New York: Alfred A. Knopf, 2005), 199.

419   **"We are not Africans now":** Foner, *Reconstruction*, 599–600.

420   **Fielding L. Wright:** Françoise N. Hamlin, *Crossroads at Clarksdale: The Black Freedom Struggle in the Mississippi Delta After World War II* (Chapel Hill: University of North Carolina Press, 2012), 13.

420   **pierced the isolation of the Delta:** Isabel Wilkerson, *The Warmth of Other Suns: The Epic Story of America's Great Migration* (New York: Vintage, 2011), 534.

420   "Many black parents": Ibid., 535.
420   "Chicago was close enough": Lemann, *The Promised Land*, 49.
420   The number of Blacks in Chicago grew: Ibid., 16.

AFTERWORD

424   The story of Jefferson and Hemings: Annette Gordon-Reed, *Thomas Jefferson and Sally Hemings: An American Controversy* (Charlottesville: University Press of Virginia, 1997).

425   the common quest of all African American families: Nicholas Guyatt, *Bind Us Apart: How Enlightened Americans Invented Racial Segregation* (New York: Basic Books, 2016), 70.

INDEX

Note: Page numbers in *italics* indicate illustrations.

ABOUT THE AUTHOR

HOWARD W. FRENCH has been a professor at the Columbia University Graduate School of Journalism since 2008. After teaching at the University of Abidjan, in Côte d'Ivoire, in the early 1980s, he began a career in journalism writing about Africa for *The Washington Post*, *Africa News*, *The Economist* and other publications. Later, after joining *The New York Times*, where he became a foreign correspondent and senior writer, he reported from Central America, the Caribbean, West and Central Africa, Japan, and China and wrote a global affairs column for the *International Herald Tribune*. French is the author of several books on both Africa and East Asia, including, most recently, *Everything Under the Heavens: How the Past Helps Shape China's Push for Global Power*. In addition to his native English, he speaks Chinese, French, Japanese, and Spanish. French was born in Washington, D.C., and now lives in New York with his wife, Avouka.

BORN IN BLACKNESS

Howard W. French

BORN IN BLACKNESS
Howard W. French

DISCUSSION QUESTIONS

1. How does *Born in Blackness* by Howard W. French complicate and challenge traditional narratives of the beginnings of the Age of Discovery?

2. In *Born in Blackness*, French describes a "centuries-long process of diminishment, trivialization, and erasure of Africans and of people of African descent from the story of the modern world" (p. 3). How has the overarching narrative of African inferiority been used as a tool to reinforce white supremacy? In the United States? In Europe?

3. How might the author's experience as a journalist and foreign correspondent inform his work?

4. *Born in Blackness* not only gives due respect to the complexity of African states and cultural institutions but refers to Jesuit "superstitions" (p. 171) and maritime actions by "tribes of whites" (p. 192). To what effect are these terms used?

5. French recounts an "intense struggle" over Elmina, in modern-day Ghana, "that played a crucial, if largely overlooked part not just in the economic fortunes of Portugal and Spain, but in the very destinies of Catholic monarchs" (p. 80). How did Portugal's establishment of a lucrative trade in gold at Elmina influence Spain's decision to finance the voyages of Christopher Columbus?

6. What role did the island of Sâo Tomé play in the birth of plantation agriculture and chattel slavery for the purpose of producing sugar?

7. In Part II, "The Essential Pivot," French writes, "The slave plantation innovations that came together in their final form in Sâo Tomé, terribly inhuman though they were, would be of far greater economic consequence over the long run than even the much more famous expansionary pursuits of Spain in the same era" (p. 122). Do you agree or disagree with the author's assertion?

8. Why did Africans replace Indigenous peoples as plantation agriculture took hold in Portugal's Brazilian colony?

9. Why was sugar such an important economic product in the early modern age? How did the mass consumption of sugar produced by enslaved Africans in the Americas change English society, in particular?

10. What role did Haiti play in the Enlightenment?

11. In Part III, "The Scramble for Africans," French describes Haiti as a "former plantation colony that—after the only successful large slave revolt in world history—became the second republic in the Americas" (p. 224). How did the victory of enslaved Africans in Haiti change the course of the history of the Americas, and, in particular, of the United States?

12. In the twentieth century, what caused the mass migration of African Americans out of the Deep South to such places as Chicago, Los Angeles, and the mid-Atlantic states?

13. *Born in Blackness* tells a six-century story that terminates in the mid-1940s. How might this history be stitched together with that of world history post-1950?

14. With *Born in Blackness*, French reintroduces a number of major African historical figures, from the unimaginably rich medieval emperors who traded with the Near East to the Kongo sovereigns who heroically battled seventeenth-century European powers and the ex-slaves who liberated Haitians from bondage. Who are among the most memorable characters in *Born in Blackness*?

15. What are the most significant ways in which *Born in Blackness* disrupts Eurocentric teaching? How might this book be incorporated into the classrooms of the future?